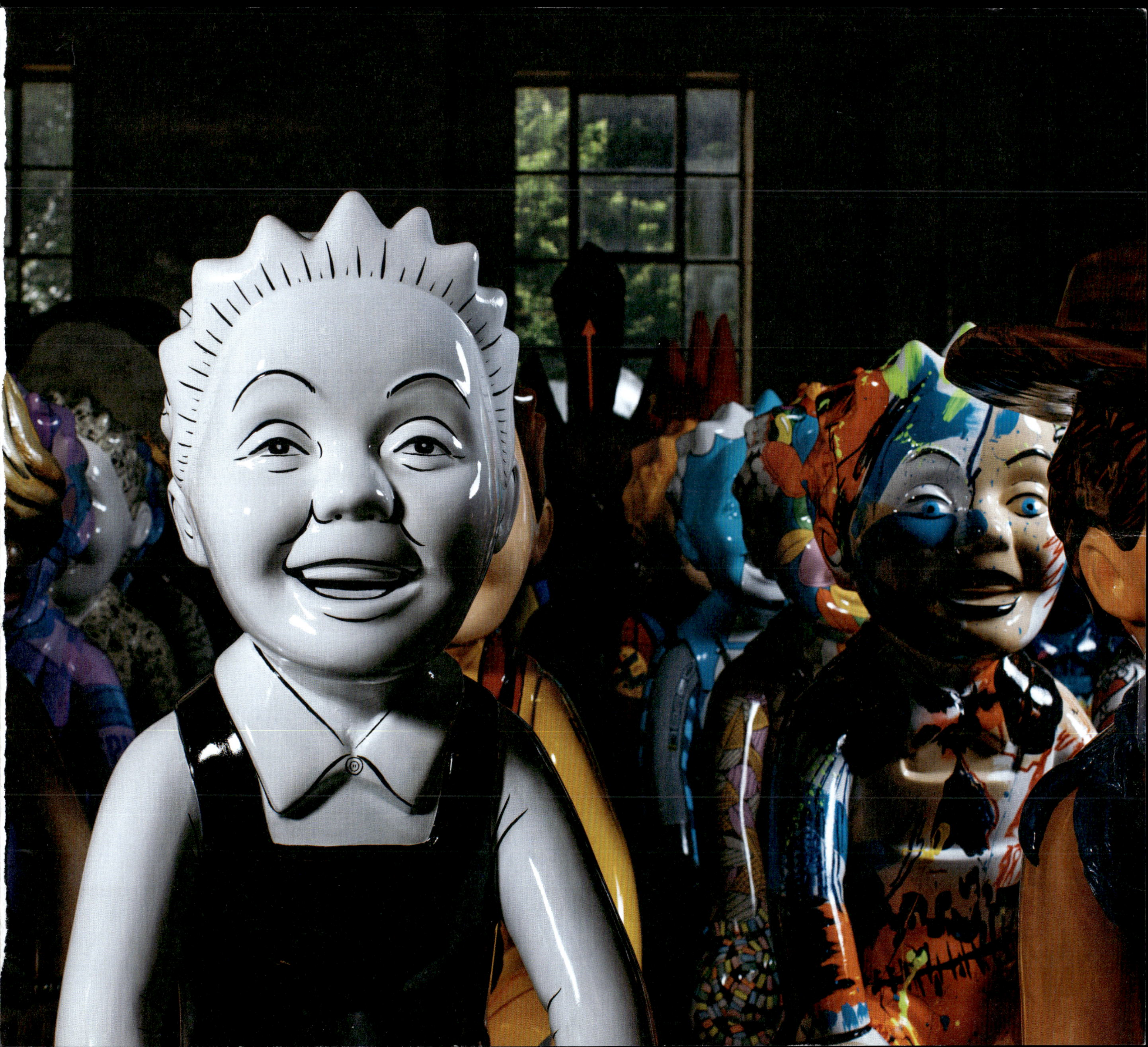

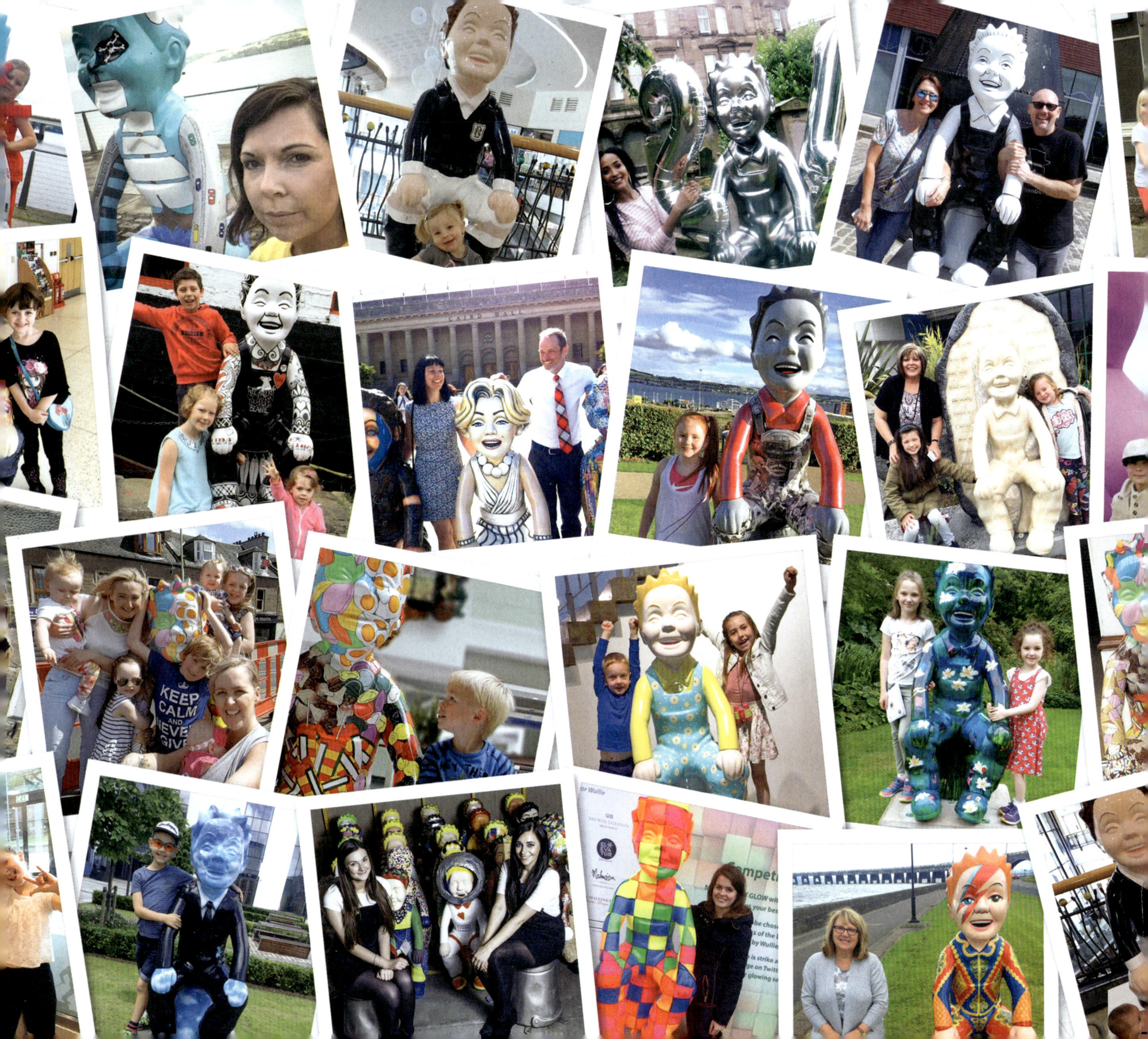
KEEP
CALM
AND

Published in the United Kingdom in 2017
by DC Thomson and Co. Ltd.,
Albert Square, Dundee, DD1 9QJ.

Initiated, developed and written by
Susan Elizabeth McMullan
in aid of The ARCHIE Foundation's
Tayside Children's Hospital Appeal.

Designed by John Hunter Barrie
and produced by DC Thomson and Co. Ltd.

Main photography by Viktoria Begg and Chris Scott.

ISBN 978-1-84535-672-9

DC Thomson

All information regarding the sculptures, artists, winning bidders, purchase amounts and current location of sculptures were correct at the time of writing.

FOREWORD

DC Thomson was extremely proud to play a part in the staggeringly successful Oor Wullie's Bucket Trail in Dundee in the summer of 2016.

The Bucket Trail brought to life the streets of Dundee (and beyond) with 70 giant Oor Wullie sculptures to celebrate his 80th anniversary – as part of the Year of Innovation, Architecture and Design.

It was a memorable auction night at Dundee Rep as community groups, businesses, organisations and individuals came together to bid for the much-loved sculptures to support a great cause – raising an eye-watering £883,000 for the ARCHIE Foundation to help create a new twin operating suite at Tayside Children's Hospital.

What could be better than Scotland's favourite son helping all the sick children in Tayside? As Wullie would say, "Michty me – that Bucket Trail was rare fun but sure had me blawin' having to be in 70 places at the same time!"

Andrew Thomson
Chairman,
DC Thomson & Co. Ltd

Ellis Watson
Executive Chairman,
DC Thomson Media

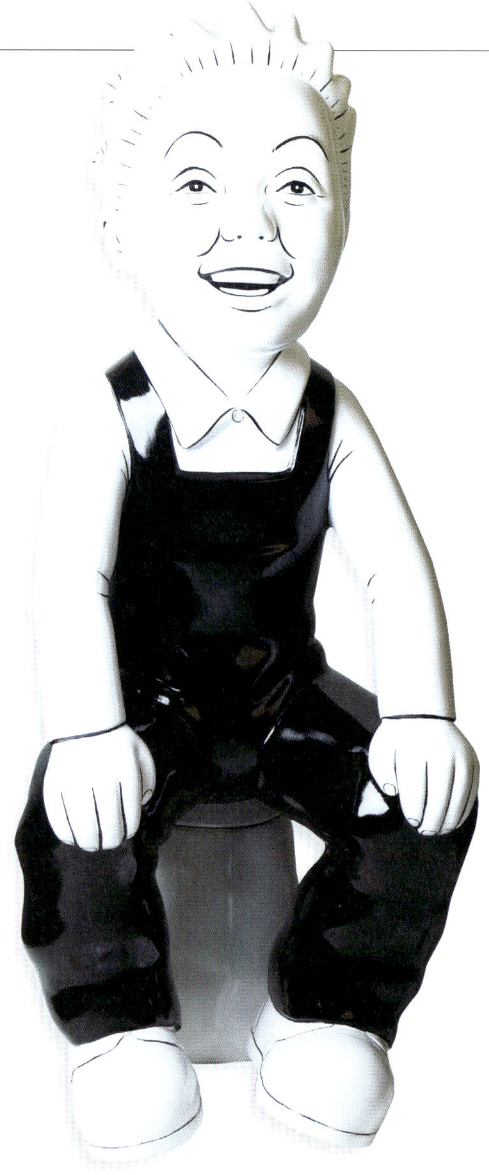

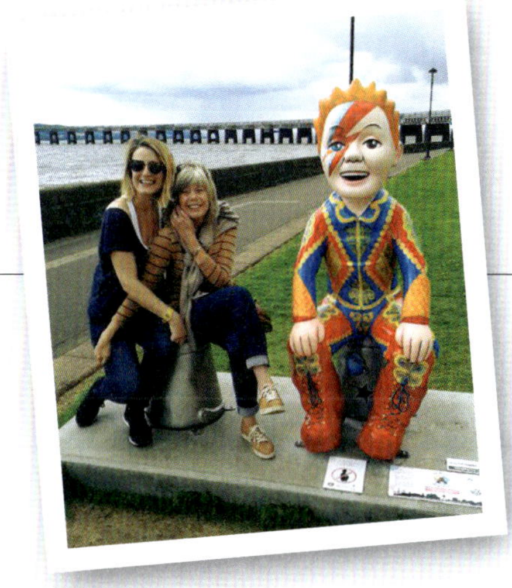

A BRAW TIME FOR ALL!

On behalf of the ARCHIE Foundation, thank you for helping to make Oor Wullie's Bucket Trail such a phenomenal success! I so enjoyed seeing people's reactions and genuine love for the Oor Wullie sculptures. It was particularly touching to see the thousands of 'Oor Selfies' and to be part of the amazing story-telling from people exploring Dundee and making memories with their families and friends. It was also a real pleasure to be able to meet and talk to the adoring Oor Wullie fans who visited the Bucket Trail HQ which was run by the wonderful team of ARCHIE volunteers.

I felt a real sense of reward in seeing a project that was planned for over a year come to life in such a remarkable way. Working in partnership with DC Thomson and Wild in Art was hugely fulfilling and it is important for me to highlight that the success of the Trail would not have been possible without our generous sponsors, talented artists, project team and volunteers – all of whom helped create an unforgettable event. My heartfelt thanks go to Suzanne Scott for coordinating the artistic talent and to Neil Cooney for helping to secure the funds needed for the project to happen. There are so many people who supported the Trail in so many different ways and I'd like to extend my thanks to each and every one of you for your own special contributions. Without you all, the Bucket Trail simply would not have been possible.

Importantly, I'd like to thank Dr Grant Rodney and the paediatric team at Tayside Children's Hospital for their passion and inspiration and for being the main motivator for myself and the ARCHIE Bucket Trail team.

Finally, special thanks from everyone at the ARCHIE Foundation go to the people of Dundee for embracing Scotland's tousle-haired wee laddie with such generosity. The legacy that you have created will mean that children across Tayside in need of surgery will be treated in child-friendly operating theatre suites - making a genuine difference to the lives of thousands of children for generations to come.

Cassie Thompson:
Director of Fundraising, The ARCHIE Foundation.

CONTENTS

PAGE 7..........A WORD FRAE WULLIE

PAGE 8 ....WHAT WAS OOR WULLIE'S BUCKET TRAIL?

PAGE 10 ....MAP OF OOR WULLIE'S BUCKET TRAIL

PAGE 12 ....FROM DREAM TO REALITY:
THE STORY BEHIND OOR WULLIE'S BUCKET TRAIL

PAGE 14 ....OOR WULLIE'S BUCKET TRAIL SUCCESS!

PAGE 16..........WHAT IS THE ARCHIE FOUNDATION?

PAGE 17..........WULLIE'S WILD...IN ART!

PAGE 18..........BUCKETLOADS OF SUPPORT FOR
TAYSIDE CHILDREN'S HOSPITAL

PAGE 20..........OOR WULLIE'S BUCKET TRAIL SCULPTURES

PAGE 132..........OOR WULLIE'S ON TOUR!

PAGE 142..........OOR WULLIE'S BUCKET TRAIL EDUCATION PROGRAMME

PAGE 143..........CHEERIO WULLIE!

PAGE 144..........OOR WULLIE'S BUCKET TRAIL CHARITY AUCTION

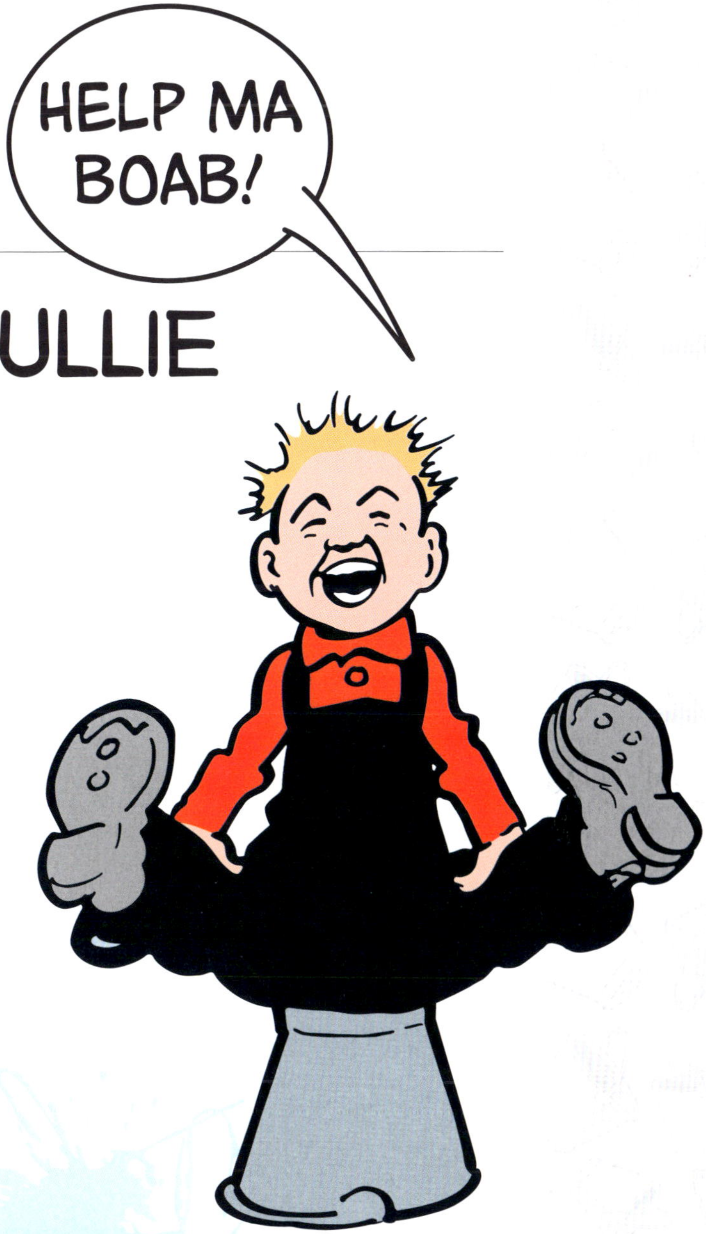

A WORD FRAE WULLIE

The summer o' 2016 really was somethin' special in Dundee. Whit an honour it was for me tae be the face o' the ARCHIE Foundation's Bucket Trail. It fair brought a' the folk o' Dundee together and people frae all o'er the country came tae see whit a' the fuss was aboot.

Even mah moaning auld neighbour Grumpy Green joined in.

Abody took selfies as they walked the Trail and smiles and laughter spread far and wide as word got oot that mah sculptures were the bees knees. Folk frae all o'er the world kent aboot it and I made lots o' new fans. Mibbe mah good looks had somethin' to do wi' it!

It was braw fun tae be dressed up in a' sorts o' outfits by some rare talent. I even got tae tour roond the country showin' aff the smashin' designs. Just as weel I had a bucket tae sit on – it was an awfy tiring job!

Most importantly though, I was michty pleased to support local kids an' help the ARCHIE Foundation an' their tremendous work for Tayside Children's Hospital at Ninewells. Thank you for supporting such a wonderful cause by buying mah luvly book. With your help, we can improve the lives o' sick bairns in Tayside and get them back oot playin' and up tae mischief!

Noo, grab yersel' a cup o' tea an' a jeely piece and enjoy re-living mah Bucket Trail in a' its glory.

Yer pal, Wullie.

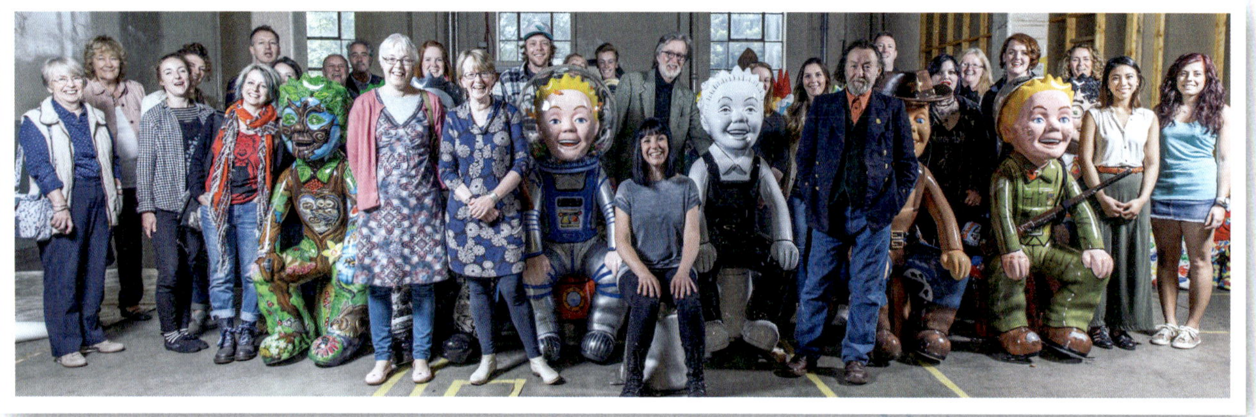

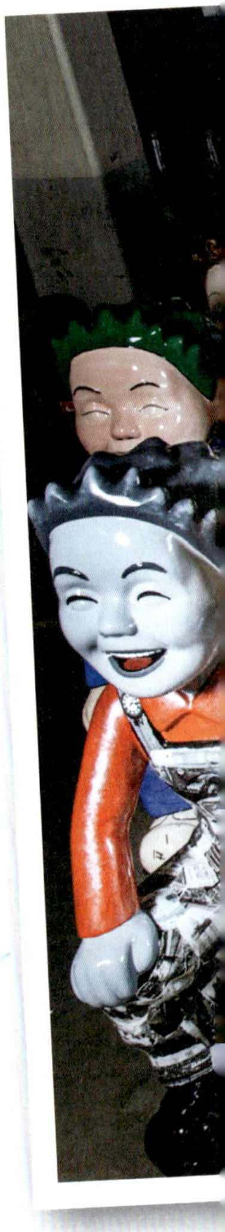

WHAT WAS OOR WULLIE'S BUCKET TRAIL?

Oor Wullie's Bucket Trail was the biggest mass participation public art event of its kind ever to have taken place across Scotland.

Set in and around Dundee, the Bucket Trail ran from 27 June to 27 August 2016. It focused on kindness and compassion through fun, joy and laughter and its purpose was to raise money for the ARCHIE Foundation's appeal for a brand-new twin theatre children's surgical suite at Tayside Children's Hospital. While helping to make a real difference to the lives of sick children and their families across the area, Oor Wullie's Bucket Trail also inspired people to enjoy public art and celebrated the creativity of Scotland during the Year of Innovation, Architecture and Design.

The Trail consisted of 55 incredible sculptures, that were each 5 feet tall, of the loveable character Oor Wullie on his trusty tin bucket – all located at different locations around Dundee for the public to find and admire. There were also two community sculptures: Oor Wullie Snowglobe, who brought smiles and laughter to the patients at Tayside Children's Hospital, and Oor Pirate who was created by the Bucket Trail's artist co-ordinator Suzanne Scott, as her wee adventure buddy. When Oor Pirate wasn't at the Bucket Trail HQ in the Overgate shopping centre, he was out with Suzanne visiting the Hospital and local nurseries and attending events - helping to bring the Bucket Trail to those who weren't able to take part themselves. Most of the sculptures were sponsored and they were painted and decorated by artists and designers, showcasing the wealth of creative talent in the area. One sculpture, Little Hands, was even decorated by patients at Tayside Children's Hospital. Trail maps and a digital app were created to help people find all the sculptures and tick them off their 'bucket' lists.

Celebrating Oor Wullie's 80th birthday, the initiative was brought to the streets of Dundee by the ARCHIE Foundation, the official charity of child health in the north of Scotland; Wild in Art, one of the UK's leading creative producers of mass-appeal public art events and education projects, and DC Thomson, one of the UK's leading media companies who generously lent the Trail the character of the cheeky wee rascal that is Oor Wullie.

While the 55-sculpture Trail was underway in the city, 13 further unique Oor Wullies set off on an eight-week tour of

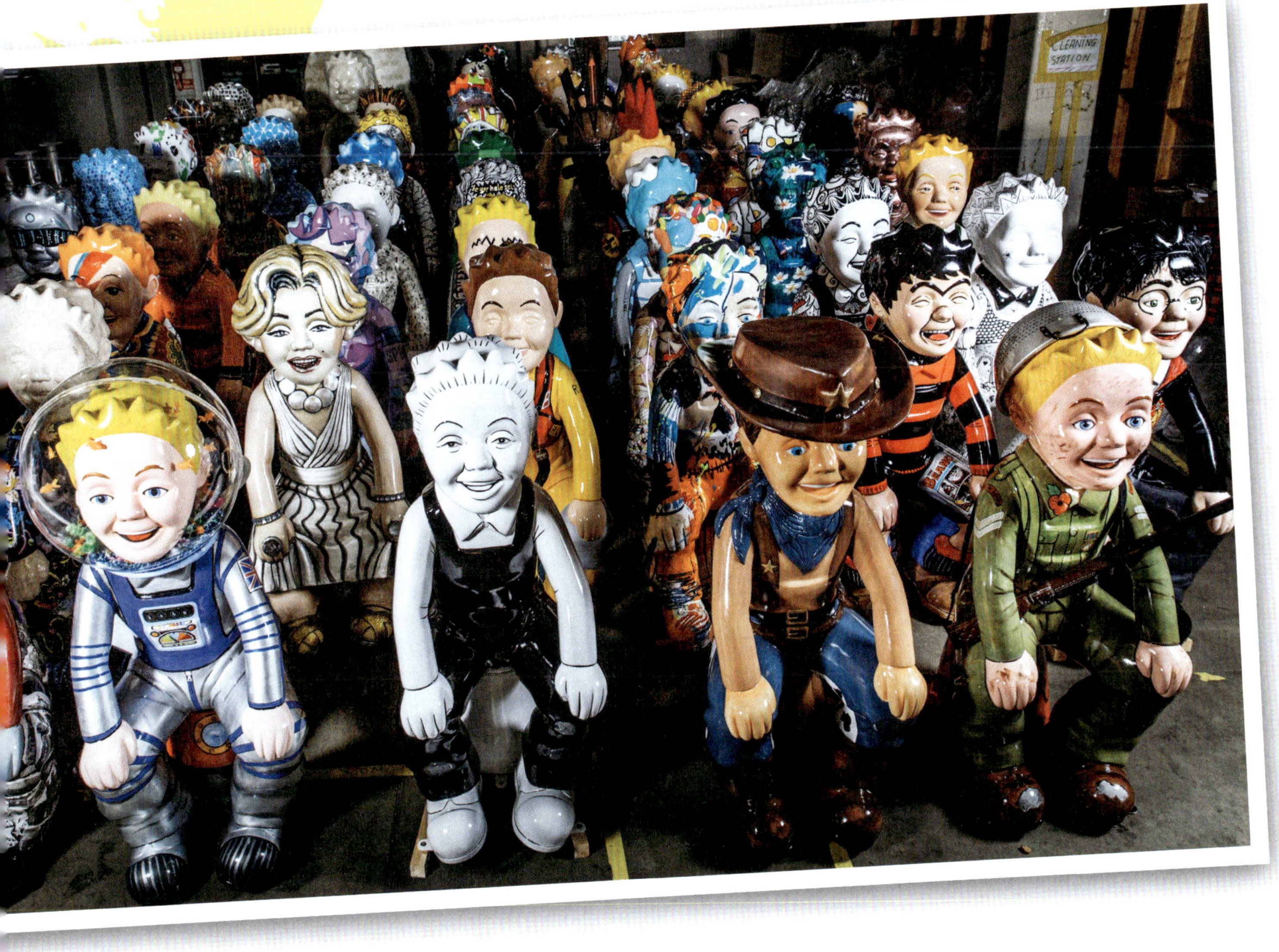

Scotland. There was also a mini trail of 29 wee sculptures which were designed by children from across Dundee as part of Oor Wullie's Bucket Trail Education Programme. At the end of the ten weeks for which the Bucket Trail ran, all the sculptures took part in a celebratory farewell party. Shortly afterwards, the Bucket Trail sculptures and touring Wullies were auctioned off in aid of the ARCHIE Foundation's Tayside Children's Hospital Appeal.

The popularity of Oor Wullie's Bucket Trail exceeded all expectations. The people of Dundee embraced the Trail with unparalleled enthusiasm and affection and as a result, the sculptures even developed into characters in their local communities. Visitors from all over Scotland and the world came to see the one-of-a-kind sculptures and thousands of selfies were taken and shared as people grabbed the chance to be part of the buzz of the Bucket Trail…and of history in the making.

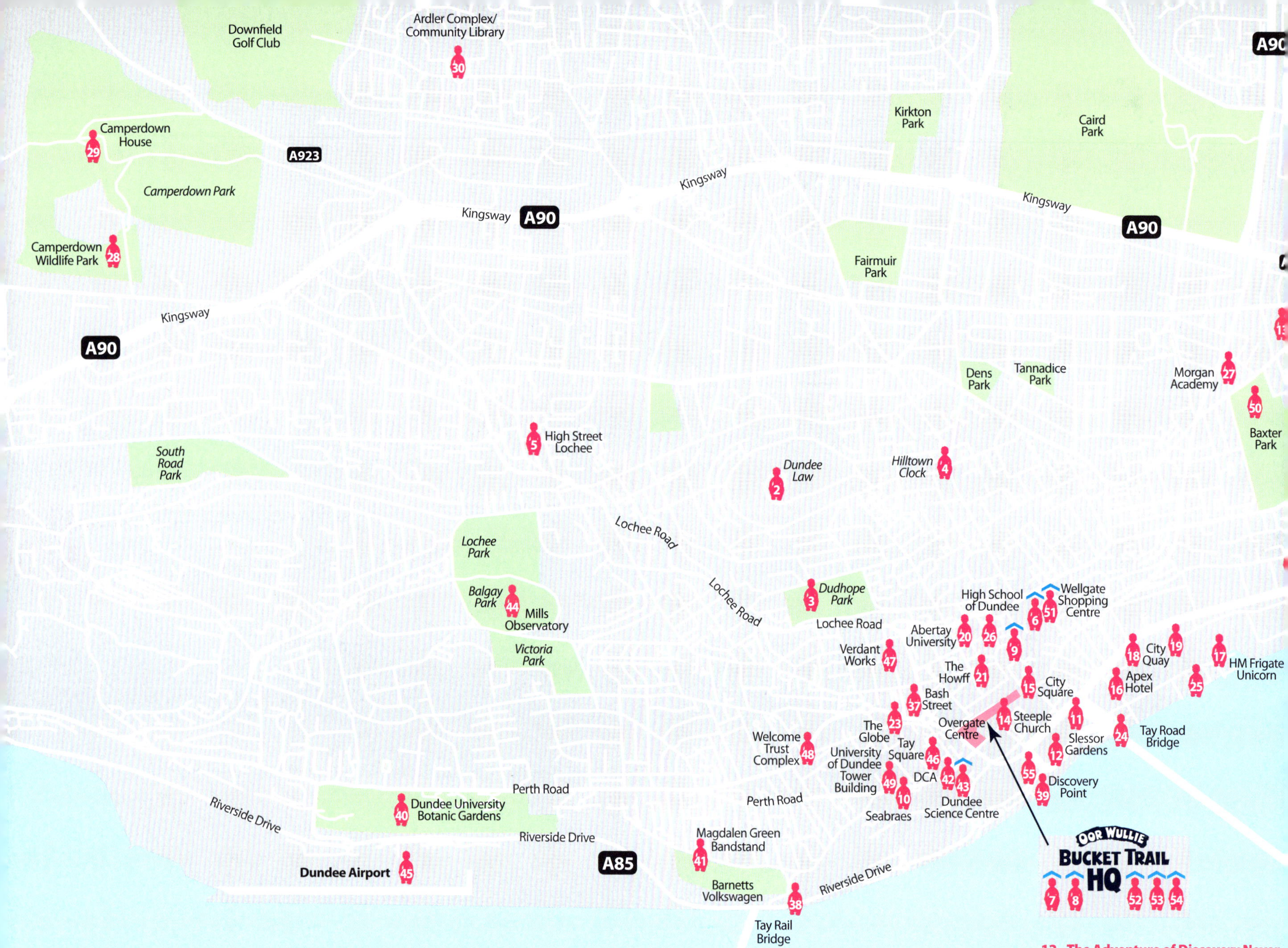

1 Oor Golfer
Location: Carnoustie Golf Links

2 Dun Deagh and 5 Glens
Location: Dundee Law

3 Whars Wullie?
Location: Dudhope Park

4 Sweet Shop
Location: The Hilltown Clock

5 Women of the World
Location: The Dundee Weaver Lochee High Street

6 Tangerine Terror
Location: Wellgate Shopping Centre

7 Oor Bobby
Location: Overgate Shopping Centre

8 Wullie's Cheeky Tales
Location: Overgate Shopping Centre

9 Biscuit Break
Location: The McManus: Art Gallery and Museum

10 Dundee Past & Present
Location: Seabraes

11 Amor Lucis
Location: Slessor Gardens

12 The Adventure of Discovery Never Ends
Location: Slessor Gardens

13 Iron Boy
Location: Stobsmuir "Swannie" Ponds

14 Oor Mechanic
Location: City Churches

15 Oor Ideas
Location: City Square

MAP OF OOR WULLIE'S BUCKET TRAIL

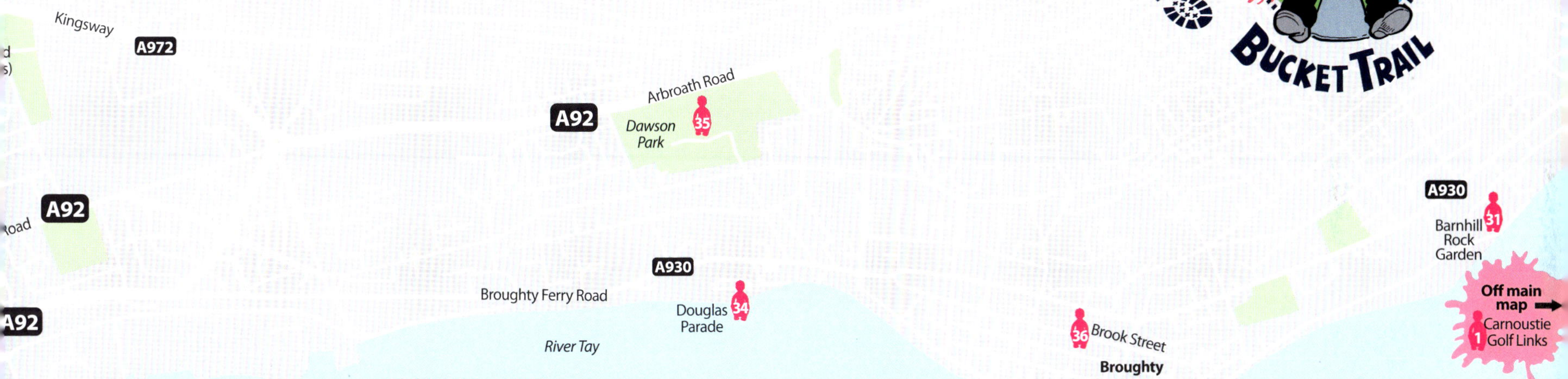

16 Oor Jolomo
Location: Apex Hotel 'Duck Hill'

17 'Oor Rabbie' The Bard and The Bucket
Location: HM Frigate Unicorn

18 Oor Original
Location: City Quay Diving Bell

19 Glow
Location: City Quay D&ACC

20 Oor Lemming
Location: Abertay University Library

21 Whar Ji Cum Fi?
Location: The Howff

22 Oor Wheelie
Location: Dundee Museum of Transport

23 Thick Cut
Location: West Port, The Globe

24 Oor Ink
Location: Underneath Dundee Road Bridge

25 Discovery Bridge
Location: Marine parade Walk / Chandlers Lane

26 High School Wullie
Location: High School of Dundee

27 You're A Wizard Wullie
Location: Morgan Academy

28 Woodland Wullie
Location: Camperdown Wildlife Park

29 Discovery
Location: Camperdown House

30 Yarnbombed
Location: Ardler Complex / Community Library

31 Dreamland
Location: Barnhill Rock Garden

32 Rain Song
Location: Broughty Castle Museum

33 Oor Lifesaver
Location: Broughty Ferry Slippy

34 Oor Wullie Noo
Location: Douglas Parade, Broughty Ferry

35 Oor Bonnie Land
Location: Dawson Park

36 Wullymorph
Location: Brook St, Broughty Ferry

37 Wullie the Menace
Location: Bash Street

38 Oor Bowie, Your Bowie, Abody's Bowie
Location: Dundee Rail Bridge

39 Oor Wai o' Spikin'
Location: Discovery Point

40 Oor Lilies
Location: Dundee University Botanic Gardens

41 From Oor Roots Up
Location: Magdalen Green Bandstand

42 Fried Eggs For Breakfast
Location: Dundee Contemporary Arts

43 Astro Wullie
Location: Dundee Science Centre

44 Silicon
Location: Mills Observatory

45 Hewn Oot the Rocks O' Dundee
Location: Dundee Airport

46 Oor Artifacts
Location: Tay Square (The Rep)

47 Jute Jam & Journalism
Location: Verdant Works

48 The Dreamer
Location: Welcome Trust Complex

49 When Wullie met Dr Manhattan
Location: University of Dundee, Tower Building

50 Little Hands
Location: Baxter Park

51 A Pocketfu' O' Pieces
Location: Dundee Central Library

52 Disco Wullie
Location: Oor Wullie HQ, Overgate

53 Oor Dreamcatcher
Location: Oor Wullie HQ, Overgate

54 Hallyracket
Location: Oor Wullie HQ, Overgate

55 Tartan Wullie
Location: Dundee Railway Station.

FROM DREAM TO REALITY:

THE STORY BEHIND OOR WULLIE'S BUCKET TRAIL

It all began with a sprinkling of imagination and a healthy dose of the belief that nothing is impossible when there is determination, passion and collaboration. It was this mindset that helped the ARCHIE Foundation, DC Thomson and Wild in Art come together and find the courage to turn their Oor Wullie's Bucket Trail dream into reality.

DC Thomson contacted Wild in Art in early 2015 about a possible event to celebrate the upcoming 80th anniversary of Oor Wullie. Wild in Art already had a full schedule for the following year but the overwhelmingly enthusiastic and compassionate response they received at the mere mention of Oor Wullie's name, convinced them that this was something not to be missed! With a little inspiration and lot of ambition, it wasn't long before the idea of the Bucket Trail was born. Soon afterwards, the ARCHIE Foundation was brought on board to lead and manage the Trail, all in aid of their Tayside Children's Hospital appeal.

This was a historic moment. It was the first time a charity had asked to borrow Oor Wullie on such a grand scale. They wanted to clone him, turn him into huge sculptures, paint him and put him out on the streets of Dundee for ten weeks before auctioning him off for charity! However, the spirit of DC Thomson, the Foundation and Wild in Art aligned from the start – they all believe in creativity and in doing good for the benefit of others, with a great sense of fun and purpose. What's more, they had all worked together on Aberdeen's award-winning 2014 tourism event Wild Dolphins and had an idea of what to expect....or so they thought. Little did they know that Oor Wullie's Bucket Trail would prove such a ground-breaking success.

The first hands-on task of making the dream a reality was to choose which Oor Wullie pose would be used for the sculptures. It was unanimously agreed from the outset that the limited edition 70th anniversary Oor Wullie figurine which the current Oor Wullie and The Broons illustrator Peter Davidson had sculpted back in 2006, was the right choice.

Next, the full-size sculptures were created. This took place in Wales and once complete, the blank sculptures were delivered by Wild in Art to DC Thomson, ready to be painted and decorated.

A call-out was then posted online which invited artists and designers from across the UK to submit their creative and inspiring ideas for the design of the sculptures. Around 250 design submissions were ultimately received – too many to choose from. A committee which consisted of Suzanne Scott, the Bucket Trail's artist co-ordinator, and the partners behind the Trail then decided which designs went forward for selection by recruited sponsors.

A sponsorship selection event was held, featuring 100 potential Oor Wullie sculpture designs. The sponsors were each given a sticker and asked to place it on the design they wished to sponsor. Things got fiercely competitive as sponsors sprinted and scrambled to get to their preferred designs first!

Once the designs had been chosen, the sculptures had to be painted and decorated. For this, DC Thomson provided space at its Kingsway office which soon became known as Oor Wullie's Bucket Trail Art Headquarters. Most of the sculptures were painted in Scotland, and more specifically in Dundee and the Dundee area, but two were painted in Aberdeen and several were painted in England.

The furthest someone travelled to paint a sculpture in the Art Headquarters was 140 miles. 68 large sculptures and 2 smaller ones, Oor Wullie Snowglobe and Oor Pirate, were created by 73 adult artists and designers. 25 children and young people also helped design and paint Oor Dreamcatcher and Little Hands. 18 of the sculpture artists graduated from The University of Dundee, the highest number of people working on one sculpture was 17 and 11 of the sculptures were painted live. Most of the sculptures were painted but some also featured a variety of textiles, including knitting!

Then there was the gigantic logistical challenge of getting the Oor Wullie sculptures to their new Bucket Trail homes on the streets of Dundee. First, the Oor Wullies had to be taken to a central warehouse so they could be prepped to go to their locations. They all had to be bolted to concrete plinths which wasn't easy as the plinths themselves weighed a tonne in weight to make sure the sculptures were secured to the ground.

Delivering the sculptures and their concrete plinths around Dundee took place over the course of only one weekend and mostly late at night so that Dundee woke up to the magic of the new sculptures on its streets. It was a phenomenal achievement and one which could only have happened thanks to the efforts of the wonderful installations team.

Then there was the big wait: what would people think of the sculptures? It wasn't long however before it became clear that Oor Wullie's Bucket Trail was taking on a life of its own. Everybody loved seeing the cheeky chappie around Dundee and he brought an energy and new-found vibrancy to the city. The response to the Trail was truly inspiring as the people of Dundee and Scotland took it to their hearts and made it an astonishing success.

Not all the Oor Wullie sculptures wanted to stay put on their plinths, however! Much to the dismay of PC Murdoch, sometimes Wullie got up to tricks in the night and occasionally he was caught playing with some friends who got him into trouble. Thanks to the good folk of Dundee who alerted the ARCHIE Foundation, he was always quickly brought home, given a telling off, his cuts and bruises plastered up and was sent out to play again. Once or twice he did break a bone or two and ended up at the Oor Wullie hospital, nursed by the braw Spray Factory dream team but he healed in no time.

Sometimes Wullie's clothes didn't quite hold up to the Scottish weather and Suzanne and her team had to chase his dungarees around parks! The team used all manner of tools from drills to sewing kits to keep the sculptures in tip-top condition. Nothing was too much of a challenge!

It was this sense of team work, support and partnership which made Oor Wullie's Bucket Trail a sensation. From designers, editors, filmmakers, artists, schools, local businesses, volunteers, Leisure and Culture and Dundee City Council to the staff at Ninewells Hospital and the dedicated ARCHIE Team, the Trail demonstrated just how much a city can achieve when people are passionate and work together for an important cause.

A whole host of hugely impressive people, organisations and institutions worked day and night for almost a year to bring the city alive with the magic of the Trail, brightening people's days and filling the air with a sense of civic pride and community spirit that had to be experienced to be believed.

Thanks to Oor Wullie's Bucket Trail, people from all generations, cultures, backgrounds, abilities and beliefs came together outside to enjoy creativity and art. The Trail was open to the public 24 hours a day and was free to enjoy, giving people the chance to do something unique and exciting during the summer. It made art accessible to all and encouraged people to explore Dundee and see different parts of the city.

Dundee is often described as a tale of two cities. On one hand, there is the incredible academia and the world-leading science, digital and creative industries, and on the other hand there is a city which is still struggling to recover from the loss of more traditional industries.

Oor Wullie's Bucket Trail made it one city. It brought people together from different walks of life, broke through social, political and economic barriers and provided one big adventure for everyone, ensuring Dundee goes down in history as a city brimming with compassion and generosity.

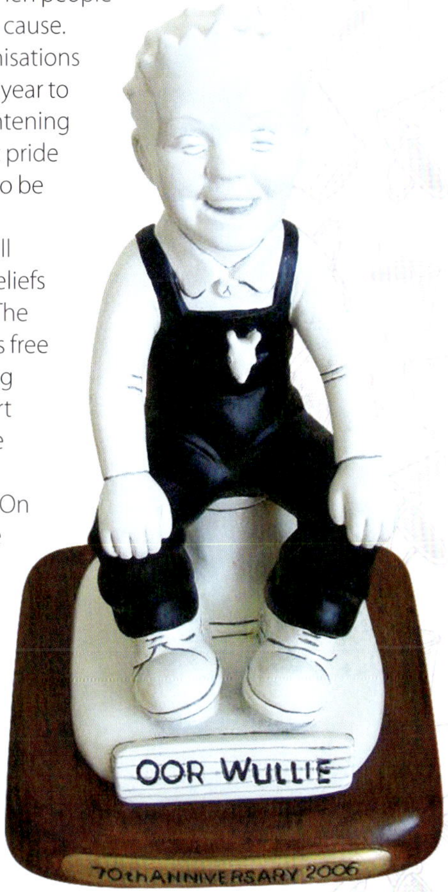

The Oor Wullie 70th anniversary commemorative figurine, created by Peter Davidson.

OOR WULLIE'S BUCKET TRAIL SUCCESS!

Did you know that during Oor Wullie's Bucket Trail, library visits in Dundee went up by 15%? Or that retail sales increased by 40%?

There's no doubt that the Bucket Trail was a resounding success and proved more popular than anyone could have imagined. The results spoke for themselves: over 100,000 locals took part in the Trail and got out and about on the streets of Dundee. Around 137,000 people travelled specifically to the city to take part in the Trail from more than 20 miles away. These 137,000 Bucket Trailers represented a 24% increase in Dundee's visitor numbers for the ten weeks the Trail took place. All of this boosted the local economy, bringing more people to the city to enjoy its restaurants, tourist attractions, shops and leisure facilities.

Jings!

50,000 people saw the 13 touring sculptures, 100,000 Trail maps were handed out to excited Trail Trekkers and 9,500 Trail maps were downloaded. 40,000 maps of the city were snapped up over the ten weeks and 400,000 people visited the Bucket Trail website. 23,000 followers kept up to date with Oor Wullie's Bucket Trail antics on Facebook and a staggering 1.34 million selfies were shared by people enjoying the Trail. By the end of 2016, the Trail's online reach had exceeded 4 million. All of this was on top of the incredible coverage in The Courier, Evening Telegraph and The Sunday Post.

Crivvens!

The Bucket Trail featured on a special episode of the BBC One documentary The Mart, giving fans a chance to re-live the excitement of the Trail and the outstanding auction evening. It was even recognised in the House of Commons and Scotland's First Minister showed her support by featuring Oor Wullie on her official 2016 Christmas card.

Help ma boab!

There was something about Oor Wullie's Bucket Trail that people seemed to think was braw!

But that wasn't all. Because of the Trail, and specifically the mini trail which saw 29 wee sculptures designed by local school pupils and displayed in community libraries across the city, book loans in Dundee increased by 8%. People were borrowing more books because of Oor Wullie's Bucket Trail meaning the effect of the Trail was extending beyond raising money for Tayside Children's Hospital. The Trail benefited entire communities and encouraged people to experience art and learn new things, helping the city of Dundee, the surrounding area and all the people in between.

There are also many wonderful anecdotal stories about the Bucket Trail from people who wanted to share just how much of an impact it had on them and their families. Lots of Trail Trekkers said the experience got them talking to each other more as they exchanged tips for finding the Wullies and waited patiently alongside one another to have their photos taken next to the sculptures. At a time when so many of us only talk online, the Trail brought people together face-to-face and helped them have good old-fashioned conversations.

And it seems that the Trail also helped people overcome difficult times. One particular lady couldn't leave her house. She had been suffering from a phobia of venturing outside but the motivation she experienced to find all the Oor Wullie sculptures was so strong that she was able to summon up the courage to go out every day and enjoy the Trail.

Another man had recently lost his job. He used to enjoy taking photographs but had stopped as he had lost joy in a

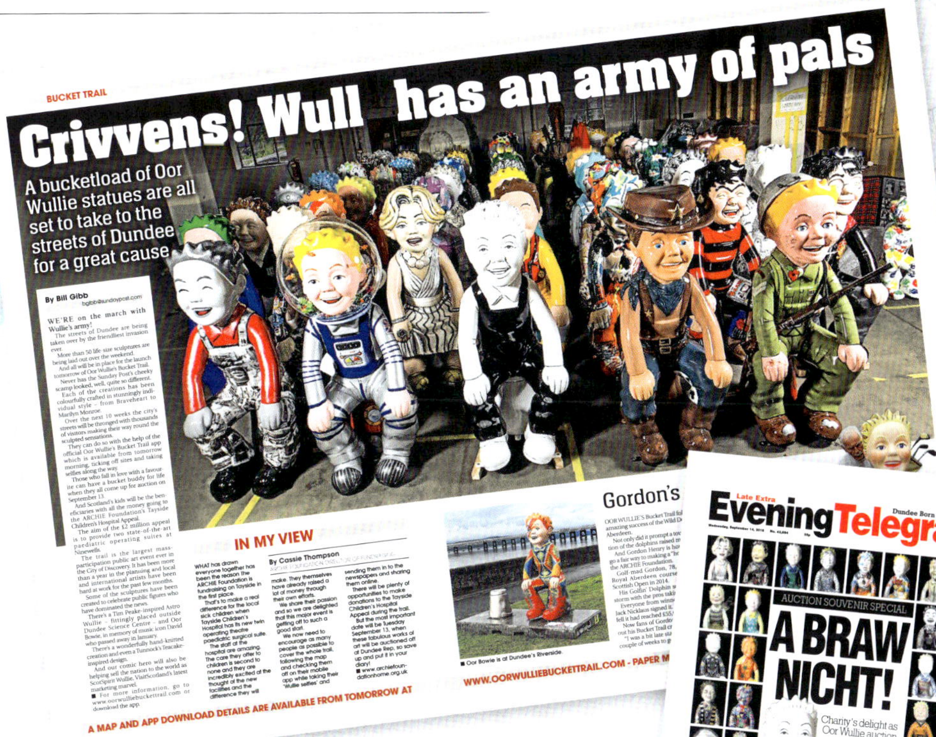
BUCKET TRAIL

Crivvens! Wullie has an army of pals

A bucketload of Oor Wullie statues are all set to take to the streets of Dundee for a great cause

By Bill Gibb

IN MY VIEW

By Cassie Thompson

Gordon's

WWW.OORWULLIEBUCKETTRAIL.COM - PAPER M

A MAP AND APP DOWNLOAD DETAILS ARE AVAILABLE FROM TOMORROW AT

lot of things, including his hobbies. However, the Trail helped him to re-discover his love of photography and find a sense of purpose again.

These are just some of the hundreds of stories that show how Oor Wullie's Bucket Trail touched the hearts and lives of so many people, all while helping to make a huge difference to sick children across Tayside for years to come.

Fundraising for the ARCHIE Foundation's appeal took place throughout the Trail with paint your own figurines and collectables for sale in the ARCHIE Bucket Trail HQ shop in the Overgate Shopping Centre. People loved popping into the shop to buy gifts and to share their experiences of taking part in the Trail.

Much to the amazement of everyone involved though, Oor Wullie's Bucket Trail auction raised an unbelievable £883,000 for the ARCHIE Foundation's appeal for Tayside Children's Hospital. The generosity of the bidders on the evening was overwhelming and the event made worldwide headlines.

Wullie fever continued long after the Trail ended with everything from the Bucket Trail calendar, Fisher & Donaldson biscuits featuring Oor Wullie, and Spree voucher books sold to drive more money towards the worthy cause. There were lots of themed fundraising activities including the incredible Gillies' Christmas window, a New Year raffle, Big Cake Days and even 'Beards for Bairns' which encouraged men to grow beards from Christmas Day to Burns Night! The Trail itself was even awarded the 2017 Evening Telegraph's Community Spirit of the Year Award in recognition of the inspiring efforts of the ARCHIE Foundation and the people of Dundee in raising money for Tayside Children's Hospital. To this day, Oor Wullie related fundraising is still taking place throughout the region!

The aim of this ongoing fundraising is to ultimately raise £2 million for Tayside Children's Hospital. The money will go towards a brand-new twin theatre children's surgical suite which will cost more than £4 million and will be delivered by NHS Tayside. It is hoped that through continued fundraising and support, people will rise to the challenge of reaching - and even exceeding - the £2 million goal.

Abody knew the loveable character Oor Wullie would make the event a phenomenal success but nobody could have imagined just how much of an impact the Trail would have. Oor Wullie brought out the best in Dundee and helped thousands create memories that will last a lifetime, all in support of one of Scotland's most remarkably deserving children's charities. It really is true what they say: Oor Wullie! Your Wullie! Abody's Wullie!"

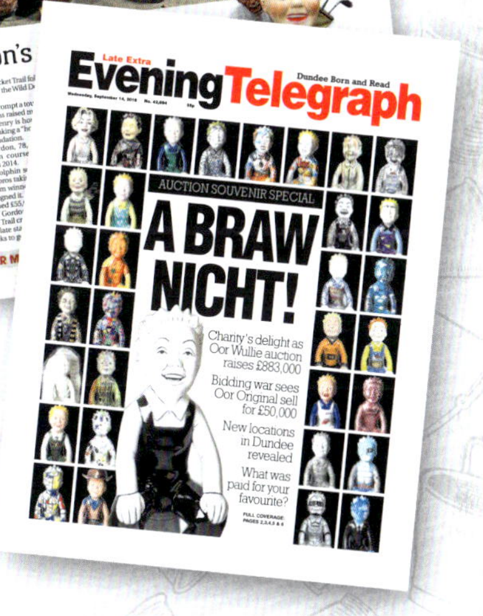
Late Extra

Evening Telegraph

Dundee Born and Read

AUCTION SOUVENIR SPECIAL

A BRAW NICHT!

Charity's delight as Oor Wullie auction raises £883,000

Bidding war sees Oor Original sell for £50,000

New locations in Dundee revealed

What was paid for your favourite?

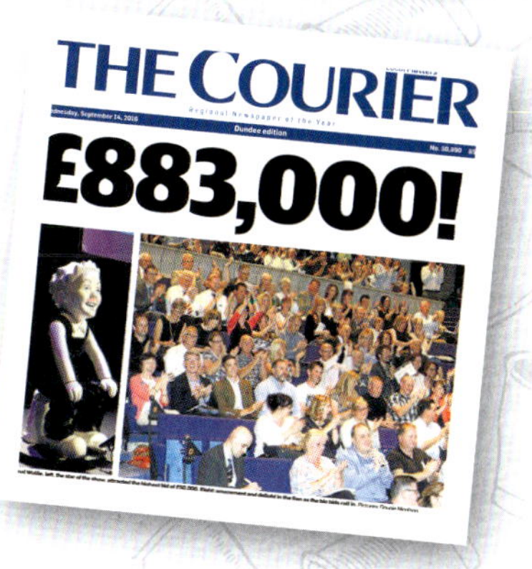
THE COURIER

£883,000!

WHAT IS THE ARCHIE FOUNDATION?

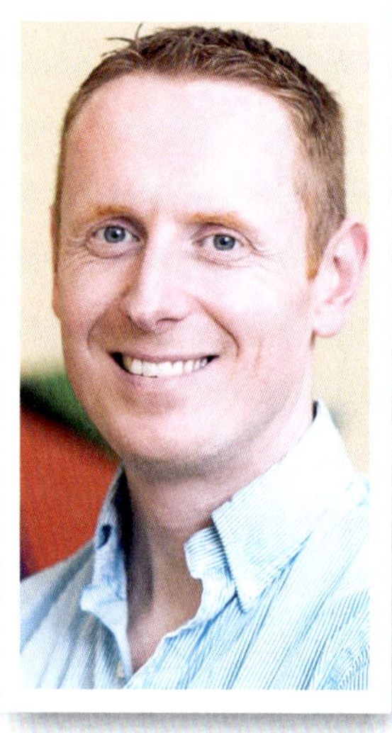

THE ARCHIE FOUNDATION
Making the Difference for Sick Children in the North of Scotland

In the year 2000, the ARCHIE Foundation was formed and albeit in his mum's arms, the character we recognise as Archie today, was first introduced to the public. The ARCHIE Foundation's mission is simple: to make the difference for local children when they are sick, in hospital or require long-term healthcare, providing much-needed extras not already catered for by the NHS.

Thanks to the work of the Foundation, Her Majesty the Queen opened the refurbished Royal Aberdeen Children's Hospital in 2004. Little did the Foundation know at the time that its work was only just beginning. Initially providing support to community children's health and then to the creation of the incredible Highland Children's Unit, the ARCHIE Foundation's reach began to extend across the whole of the north of Scotland, making a huge difference to local sick children and their worried families.

Then at the request of colleagues in Dundee, agreement was reached to support the development of new, world-class facilities at Tayside Children's Hospital. This project will transform the experience of having an operation for hundreds of children every year. When a child is in hospital, having an operation is the one thing that scares them the most. This is where the ARCHIE Foundation comes in. We develop operating theatres that are suitable for children, helping to make patients feel more comfortable and less frightened. This not only makes a difference for scared children and their families but it also has a positive effect on the staff looking after them who are reassured that the children are receiving the best care.

Tayside Children's Hospital is already a great facility in Dundee and provides fantastic care to sick children. With all the mischief that Oor Wullie and his friends get up to, I'm sure they have visited more than once over the years!

However, there is currently just one children's operating theatre in the hospital and this only has capacity for half of all the children who need an operation each year. Those children who aren't lucky enough to access this operating theatre are either operated on in adult facilities or must travel to other cities to have their operations.

Fortunately, NHS Tayside has committed to building a new twin theatre children's surgical suite at Tayside Children's Hospital and thanks to Oor Wullie's Bucket Trail, the ARCHIE Foundation will help to turn the hospital into an amazing child and family centred children's unit – one of the best available in Scotland.

And you are helping too. By purchasing this book, you are directly supporting the ARCHIE Foundation to make a big difference to local sick children across Tayside, now and in the future.

Thank you for your support. I hope you enjoy re-living the fantastic Oor Wullie's Bucket Trail which I'm sure will be talked about and celebrated for many years to come.

David Cunningham:
Chief Executive, The ARCHIE Foundation.

WULLIE'S WILD... IN ART!

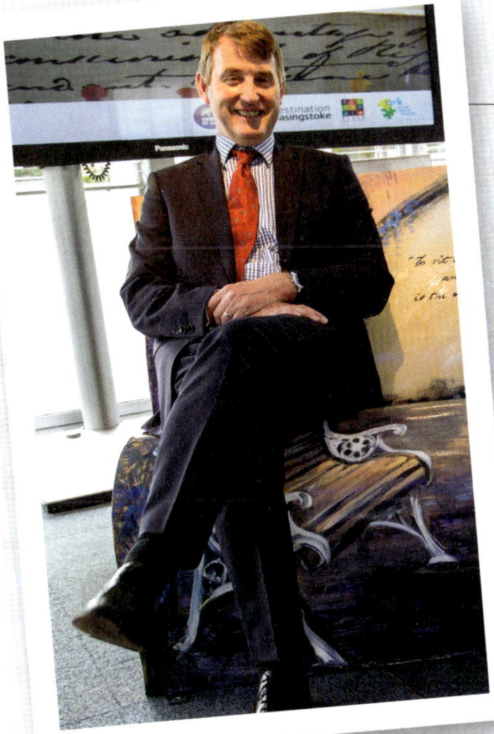

Photo © Markwick, Lovell & Lamb.

Wild in Art produces popular public art events that connect businesses, artists and communities to create a shared experience in which everyone can be involved. Since 2008 we have animated cities across the world including Sydney, Melbourne, Cape Town and São Paulo and have created sculpture trails for the London 2012 Olympics, the 2014 Commonwealth Games in Glasgow, Historic Royal Palaces and Aardman Animations.

Our events have enabled over £10 million to be raised for charitable causes to date and have helped millions of people of all ages to experience art by taking it out of traditional places and putting it into everyday life. In the case of Oor Wullie's Bucket Trail, this meant taking art out onto the streets of Dundee!

When we were asked to organise an 80th anniversary event for DC Thomson's Oor Wullie we just had to get the ARCHIE Foundation involved. Having already made a big splash working with the Foundation on the Wild Dolphins event in Aberdeen in 2014, we were keen to work together again to make even more people aware of the Foundation's work. What's more, we wanted to do it through a fun, family friendly art event that all generations could enjoy and from which the whole city could benefit.

And what better way to celebrate 80 years since the permanently youthful, tin bucket-toting scallywag cartoon character, Oor Wullie first appeared in The Sunday Post newspaper, than by having lots of colourful re-incarnations of him around Dundee to help raise money for a good cause?

Making such a famous character into a blank 3D canvas for artists was a challenge however, the spectacular finished articles spoke for themselves. From designs featuring the city's industrial heritage and iconic landmarks, to famous Scottish faces and sports stars, the sculptures offered something for everyone.

Delivering the blank 3D canvasses to Dundee ready to be painted was also a unique experience! Driving up and down the country's motorways with larger than life sculptures on the back of a pick-up truck attracted some double takes by fellow motorists! With line-ups of cheeky Oor Wullies in transit, we received lots of enthusiastic waving and honking of car horns once we'd crossed north of the border! Even at that stage, there were hints that the Trail was going to be something truly special.

The Bucket Trail really was an unbelievable success for the ARCHIE Foundation's Tayside Children's Hospital appeal and the team at Wild in Art is hugely proud to have been involved. We hope that continued fundraising such as the sale of this book will mean that the Foundation will reach its ultimate target, and more, in no time.

Here's to you, Wullie!

Charlie Langhorne and Sally-Ann Wilkinson:
Directors, Wild in Art.

WILD IN ART

BUCKETLOADS OF SUPPORT FOR TAYSIDE CHILDREN'S HOSPITAL

Way back in 2011, we contacted the ARCHIE Foundation to talk about fundraising options and a possible partnership with NHS Tayside. Lengthy discussions followed and an agreement was eventually reached in 2014 for the ARCHIE Foundation to become the official charity of NHS Tayside's Children's Hospital.

Local fundraising then began in earnest to support the creation of our children's surgical suite with its brand-new twin operating theatres and accompanying ward beds, assessment, procedure and play rooms. Soon after, the Foundation approached us with the idea that some cheeky chappie called Wullie might be able to help us. The rest as they say...is history!

I started working at the Tayside Children's Hospital in 1995 and have led children's anaesthesia and surgical services since around 1998. I've made it my ambition to establish and develop an outstanding children's surgical department that provides top-quality care and facilities for everyone that uses it.

In my job, I see first-hand just how the money raised from the amazing Oor Wullie's Bucket Trail will benefit so many children and their families. While Tayside Children's Hospital currently provides excellent clinical care in all areas, it only has one dedicated children's operating theatre. Only 50% of the nearly 3000 children who need operations each year (including dental operations) can be accommodated in this single theatre. By doubling our theatre capacity, we will be able to care for many more children in an appropriate environment, with state-of-the-art facilities. This is important as it will allow us to focus the appropriate trained staff, specialised equipment and all the play and emotional support necessary for children and families, in a single child-friendly location which will cater for children of all ages, from babies to adolescents.

The ARCHIE Foundation is raising £2 million, to add to the £4 million NHS Tayside contribution, to help make the new surgical suite as attractive and effective as possible for the children and families who will be using it. The contribution from the ARCHIE Foundation will fit with their 'making the difference' commitment to specifically enhance and create truly outstanding children's facilities. The suite will feature adjacent ward bed and trolley spaces so that families can stay with their children while they are in hospital. This makes a huge difference for the children having operations who can sometimes feel very frightened and lonely without their families by their sides.

The suite, which will be developed at the west side of the hospital, beside the existing children's inpatient ward and outpatients' facility, will also include reception spaces, assessment and treatment rooms, play facilities for all ages (including a separate teenager space) and staff and teaching facilities. It's hoped that the unit will also house exciting innovations, such as virtual reality corridors, where children

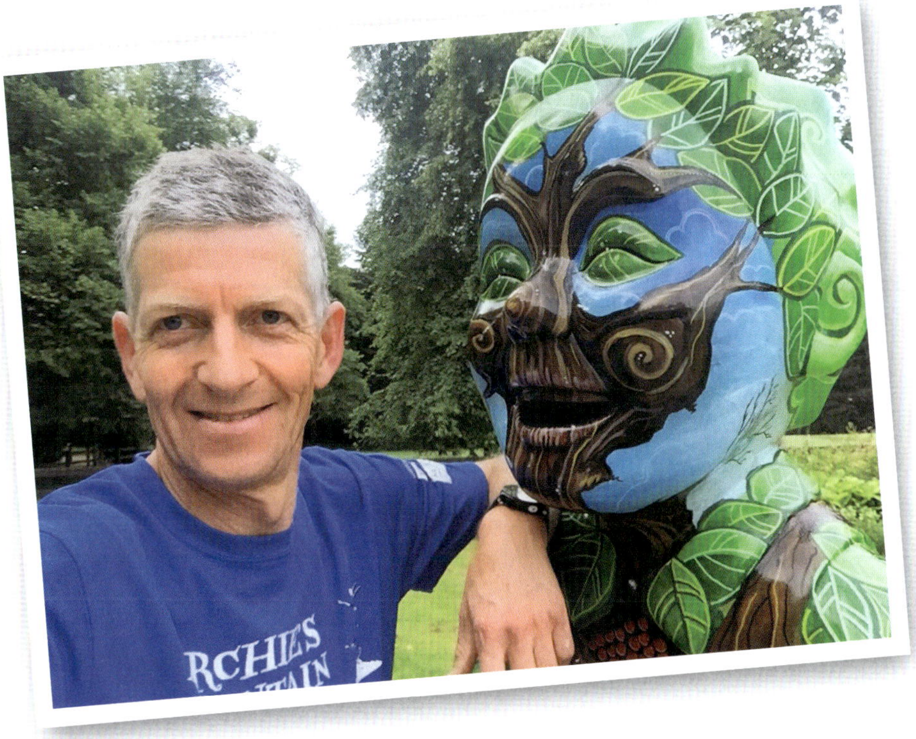

Tayside Children's Hospital Appeal

For a New Children's Theatre Suite

can be surrounded, for example, by virtual sea creatures that swim and play alongside them on their journey to the operating theatres. We'd like to have themed artwork on the walls in admission and waiting areas too. The design element is extremely important and stems directly from the Oor Wullie legacy, with ongoing involvement of local art and design ideas planned. Importantly, the facility will have a relaxed atmosphere to help ease anxieties at what can be a very stressful time for children and parents alike.

The co-location of the new unit and the existing facilities will also enhance sharing and teamwork among medical and surgical staff and will provide a focus that builds on the concept and status of Tayside Children's Hospital.

Our new twin theatre children's surgical suite will be up and running in 2019/2020 and we will soon be able to welcome new patients and provide the top-quality care and facilities that we have dreamt for so long could become a reality.

We hope that this children's surgical suite project will be the first of many joint projects with the ARCHIE Foundation and just the start of a long-term relationship with NHS Tayside Children's Hospital.

Thank you so much for supporting such a wonderful cause, for buying this book and for going out to find Oor Wullie on the streets of Dundee. With your help, we are making an incredible difference to the lives of sick children across Tayside, giving them hope for a brighter tomorrow.

Dr Grant Rodney: *Consultant anaesthetist and lead clinician for children's surgical services, Tayside Children's Hospital.*

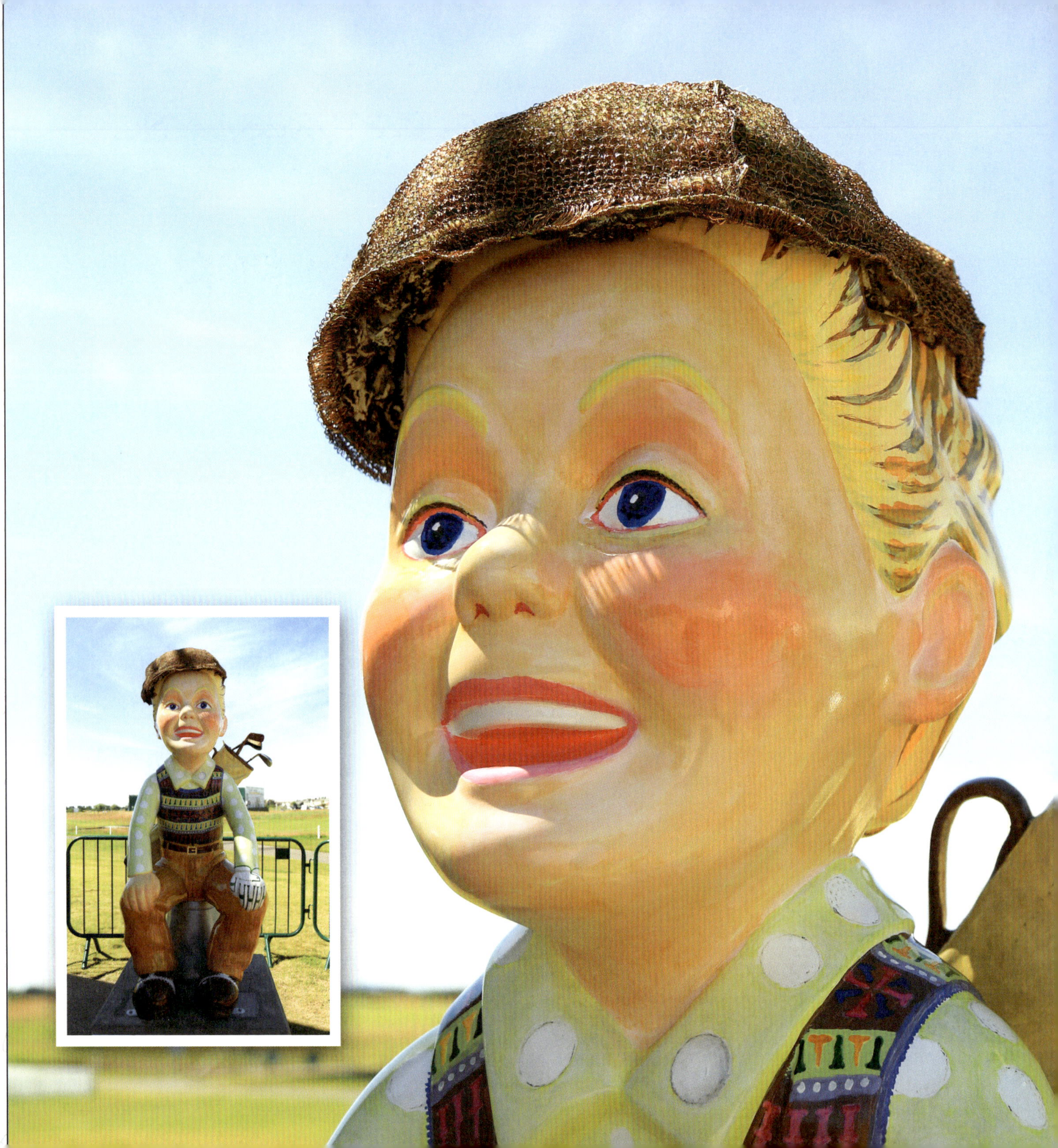

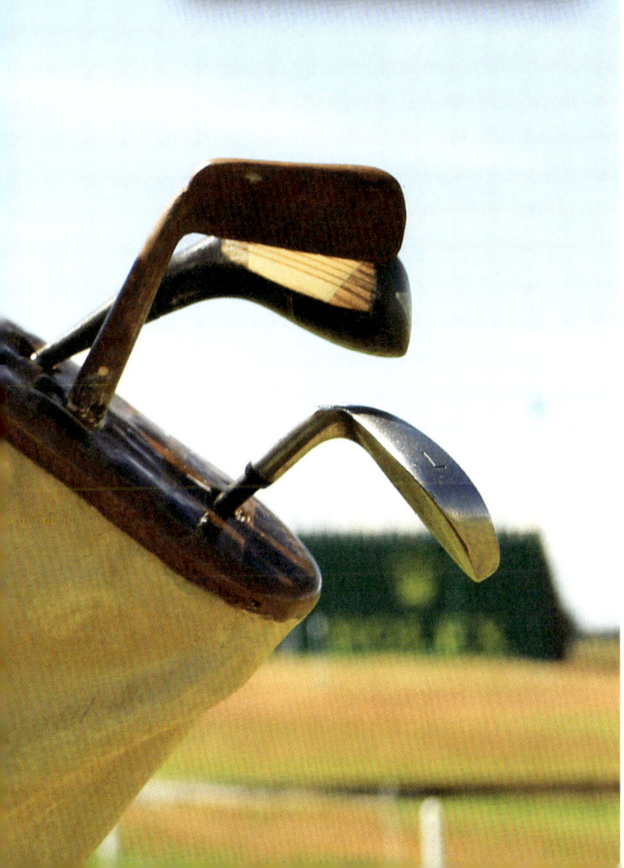

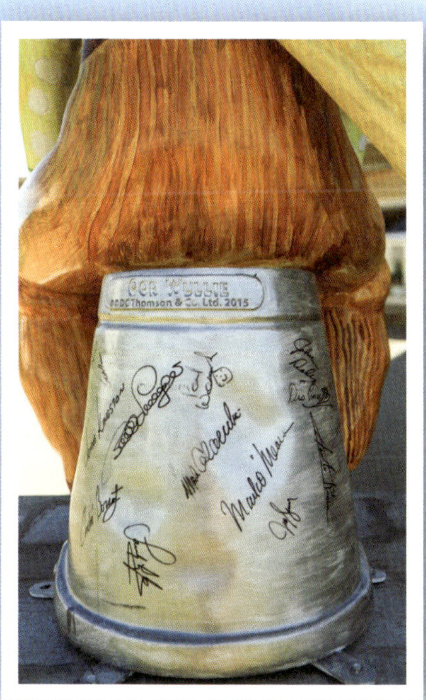

OOR GOLFER

Location on the Bucket Trail:
Carnoustie Golf Links.

Designed by:
Peter Davidson, Gordon Henry, Elena Costella, Roddy Mathieson.

About this sculpture:
Oor Golfer is a collaboration piece and was designed by Peter Davidson, the current Oor Wullie illustrator. It was painted by Gordon Henry, an artist from Aberdeen and Oor Wullie's golf bag was created by sculptor Roddy Mathieson, while his wire hat was knitted by designer Elena Costella. This sculpture celebrates the 2016 Senior Golf open at Carnoustie Golf Links and was signed by many of the famous golfers.

Sponsor: Carnoustie Golf Links.

Winning bid: £20,000.

Winning bidder: Gillian Bayford, local business woman.

Where is he now? Spreading joy and happiness in Carnoustie!

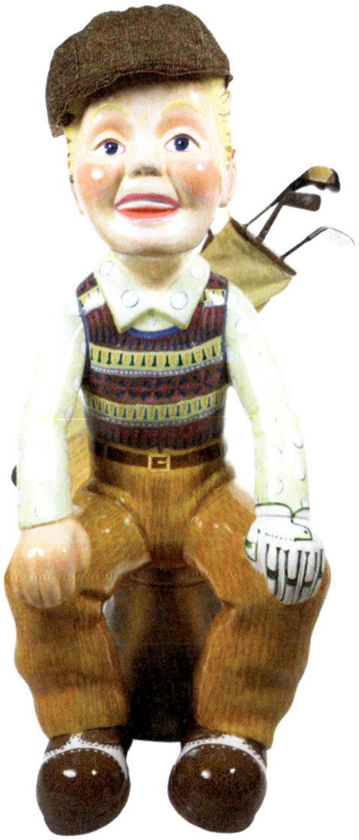

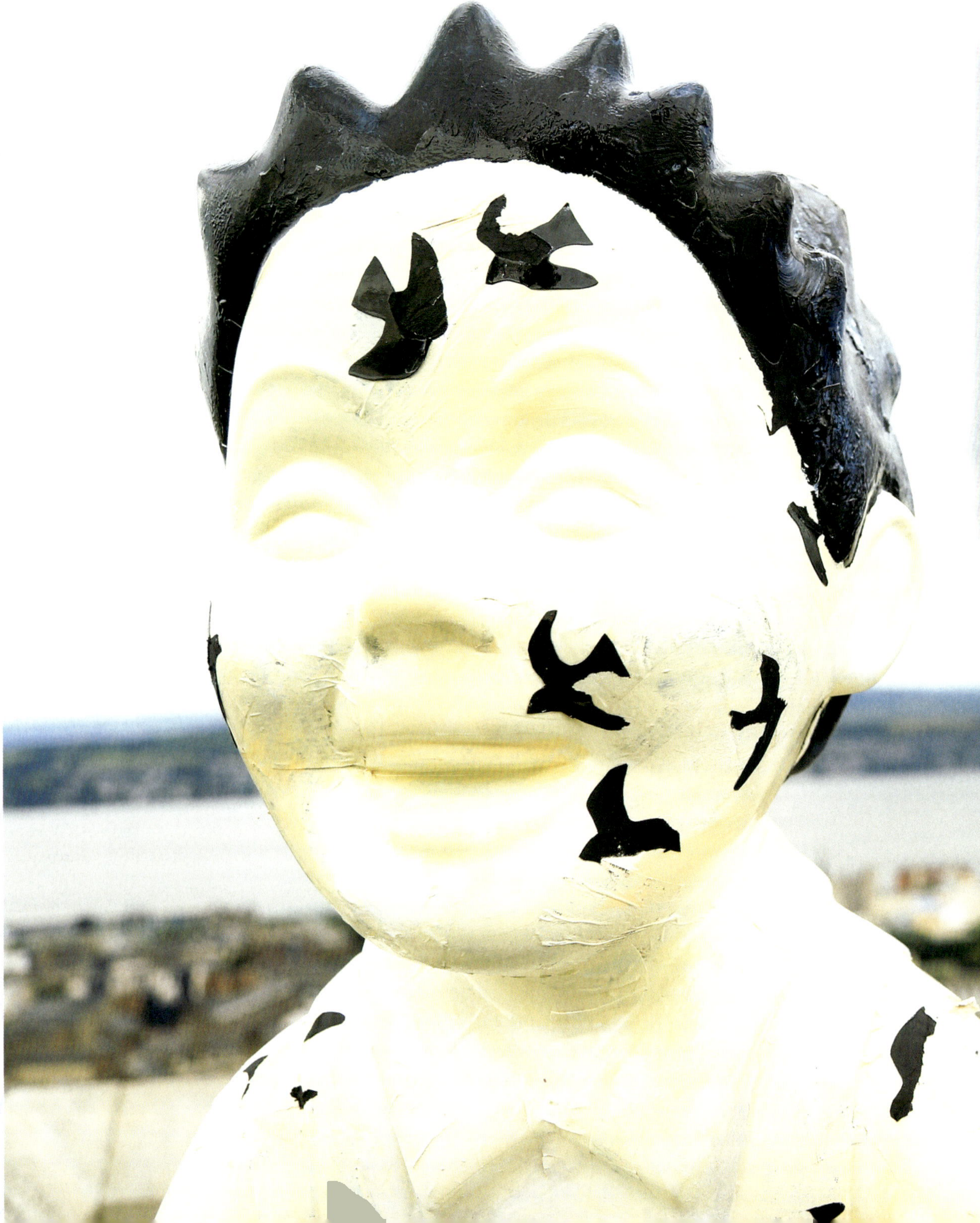

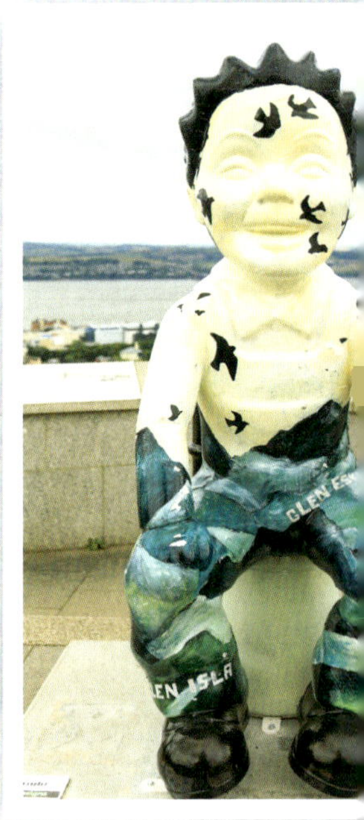

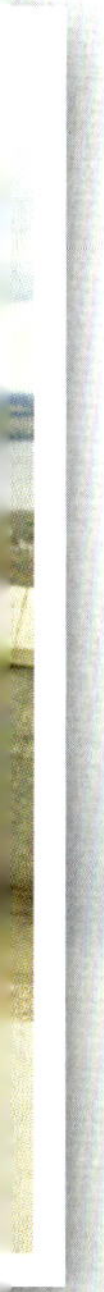

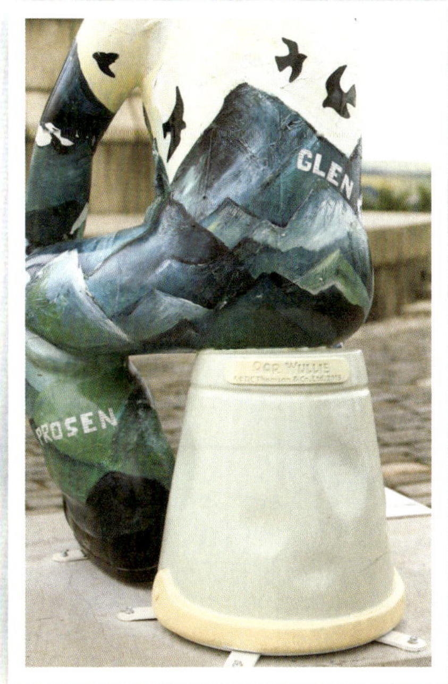

DUN DEAGH & THE 5 GLENS

Location on the Bucket Trail:
Dundee Law.

Designed by:
Catherine Redgate.

About this sculpture:
Dundee sits on the east coast of Scotland and is protected by the Angus Glens. Dun Deagh & The 5 Glens celebrates this rich environment which can be reached easily from the city.

Inspired by the way life comes together, Catherine works in mixed media, playing with images, words, papers, textures and marks. Her current interest in travel, adventure and the outdoors is evident in her work as she explores the interaction and relationship of paint and paper.

Sponsor: Nane but too guid no'tae include!

Winning bid: £6,500.

Winning bidder: Jeanette Gibson.

Where is he now? Learning the tricks of the trade at the Scottish Antique & Arts Centre.

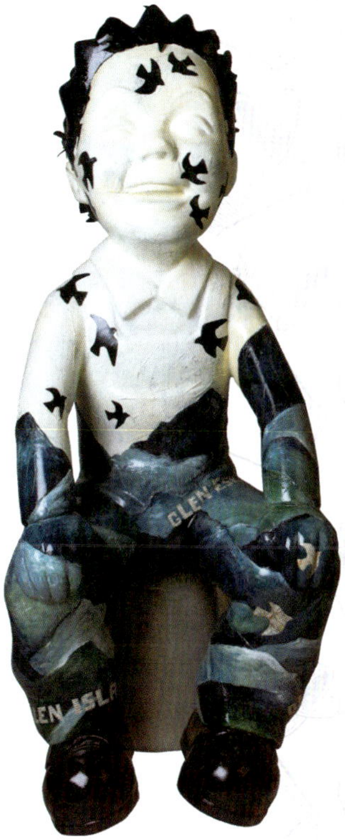

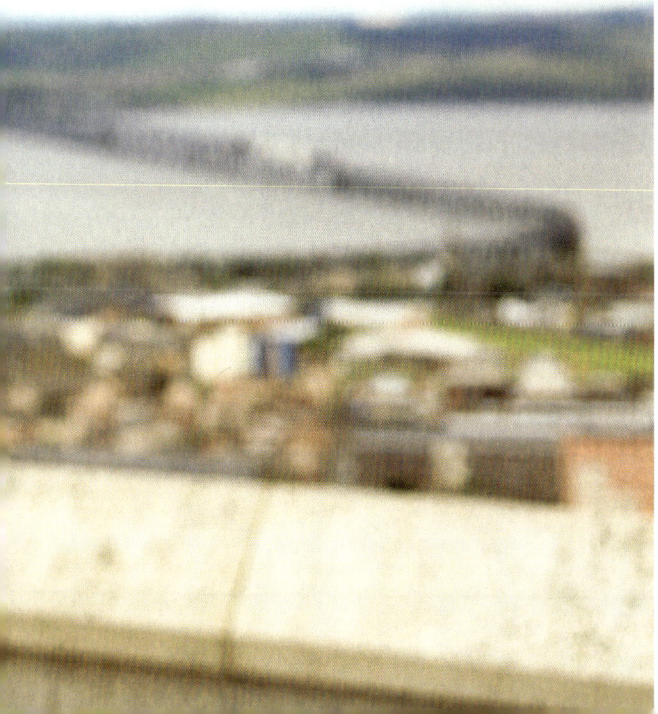

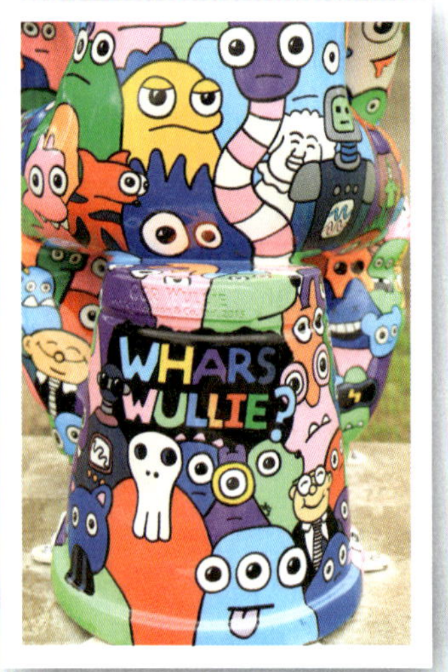
WHARS
WULLIE?

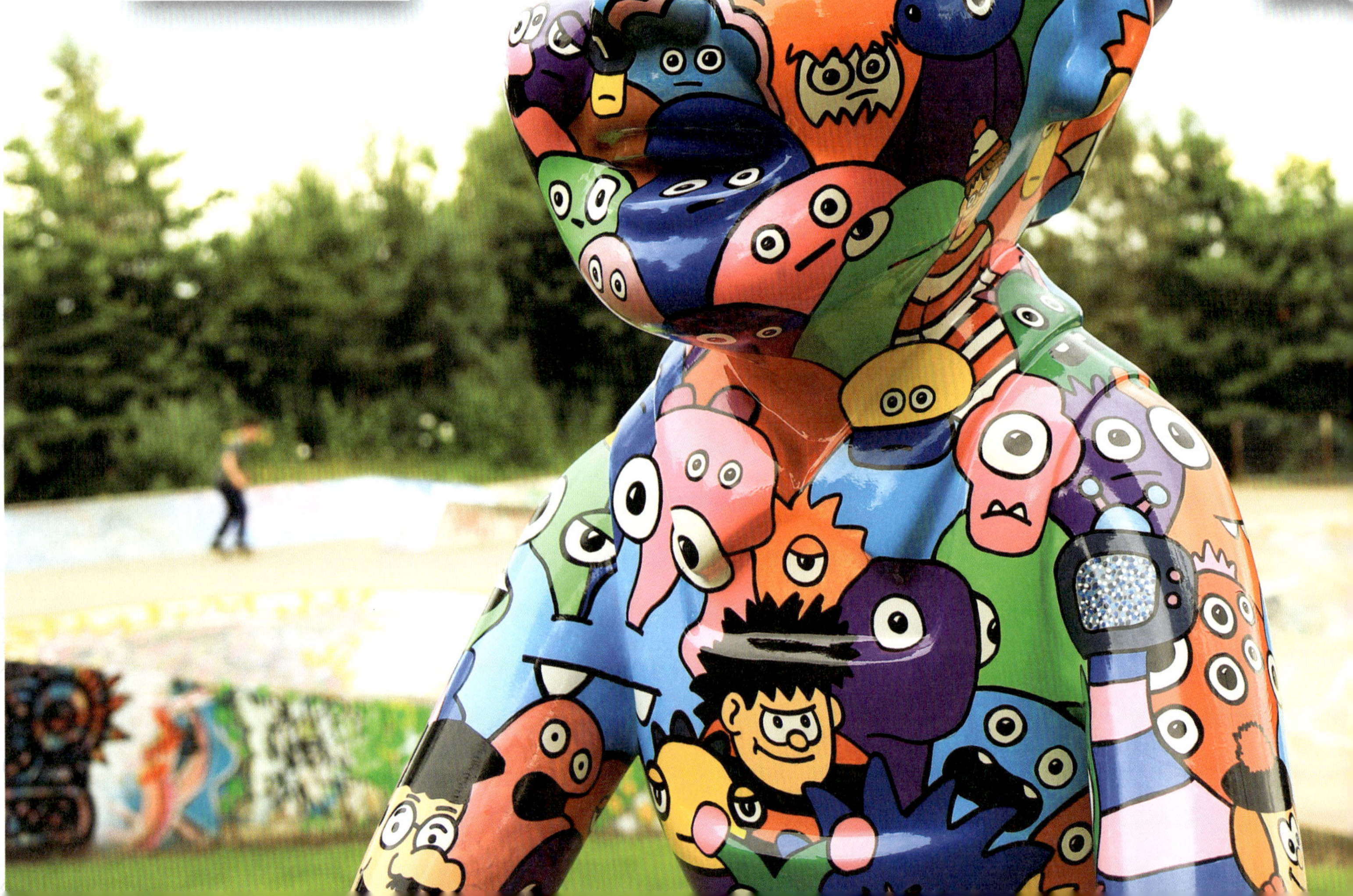

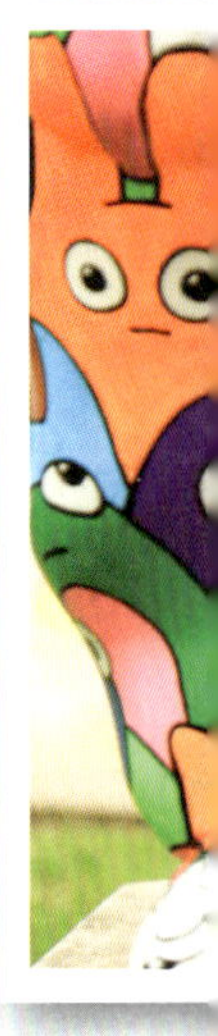

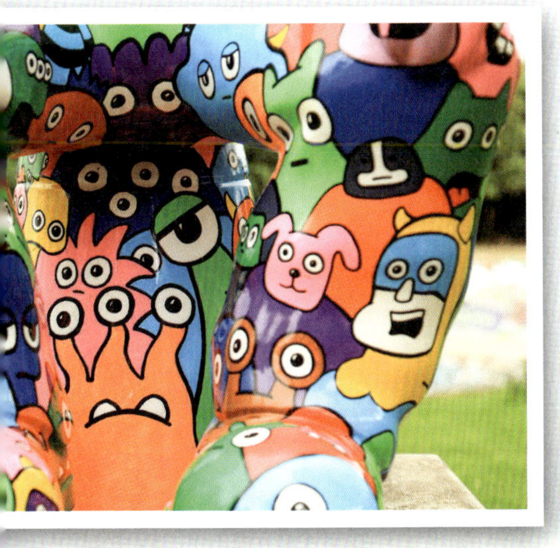

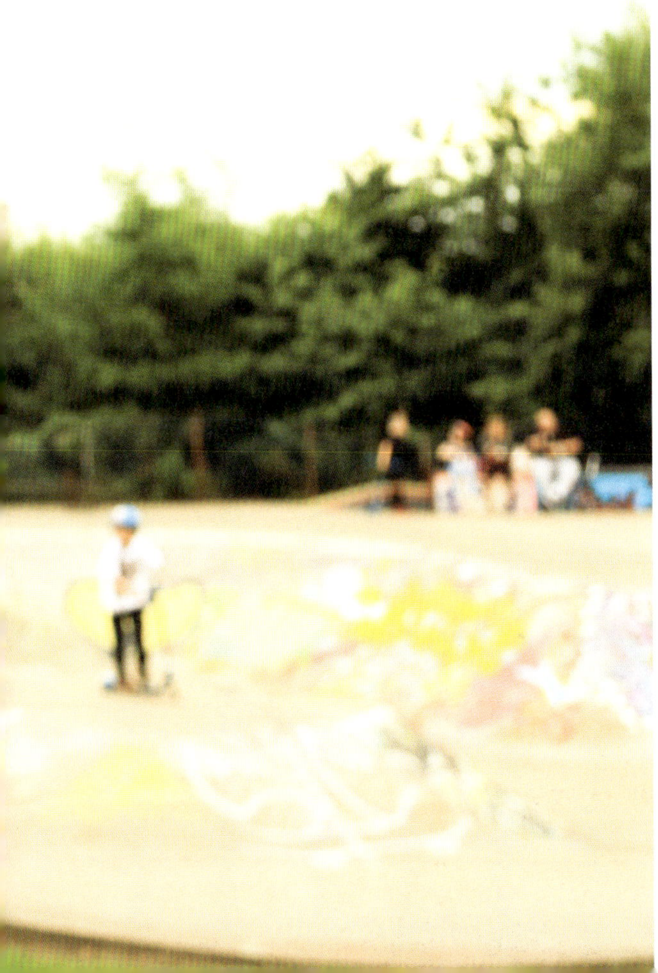

WHARS WULLLIE?

Location on the Bucket Trail:
Dudhope Park.

Designed by: Blair McCafferty
(Creature Emporium).

About this sculpture: The artist of this sculpture wanted to incorporate all of DC Thomson's wonderful characters and infuse them with his own creatures. He likes busy looking art and wanted to create something for children to enjoy. He loved 'Where's Wally' when he was young so he thought the game of finding a character in amongst lots of others would be fun for wains!

Blair is an artist, graphic designer, illustrator, creator and doodle monkey. He is also the master creature creator at Creature Emporium, suppliers of unique arts and gifts.

Sponsor: Inverurie Precast Ltd.

Winning bid: £11,000.

Winning bidder: Birkhill Inn.

Where is he now? Whars Wullie lives at the Birkie but he sometimes goes on his holidays to Redwood Leisure's other properties in Dundee, including the Woodlands Hotel and the Invercarse Hotel.

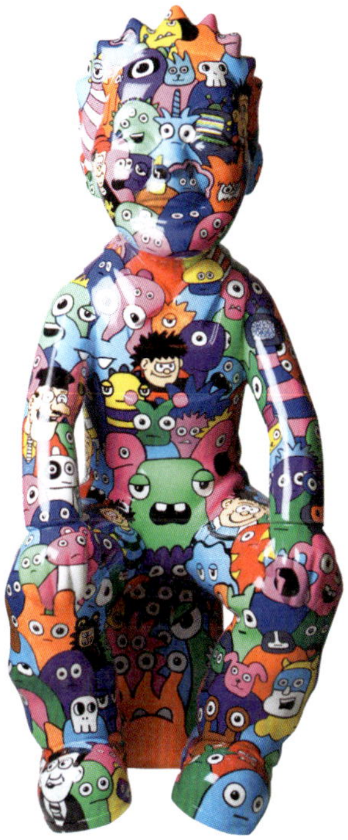

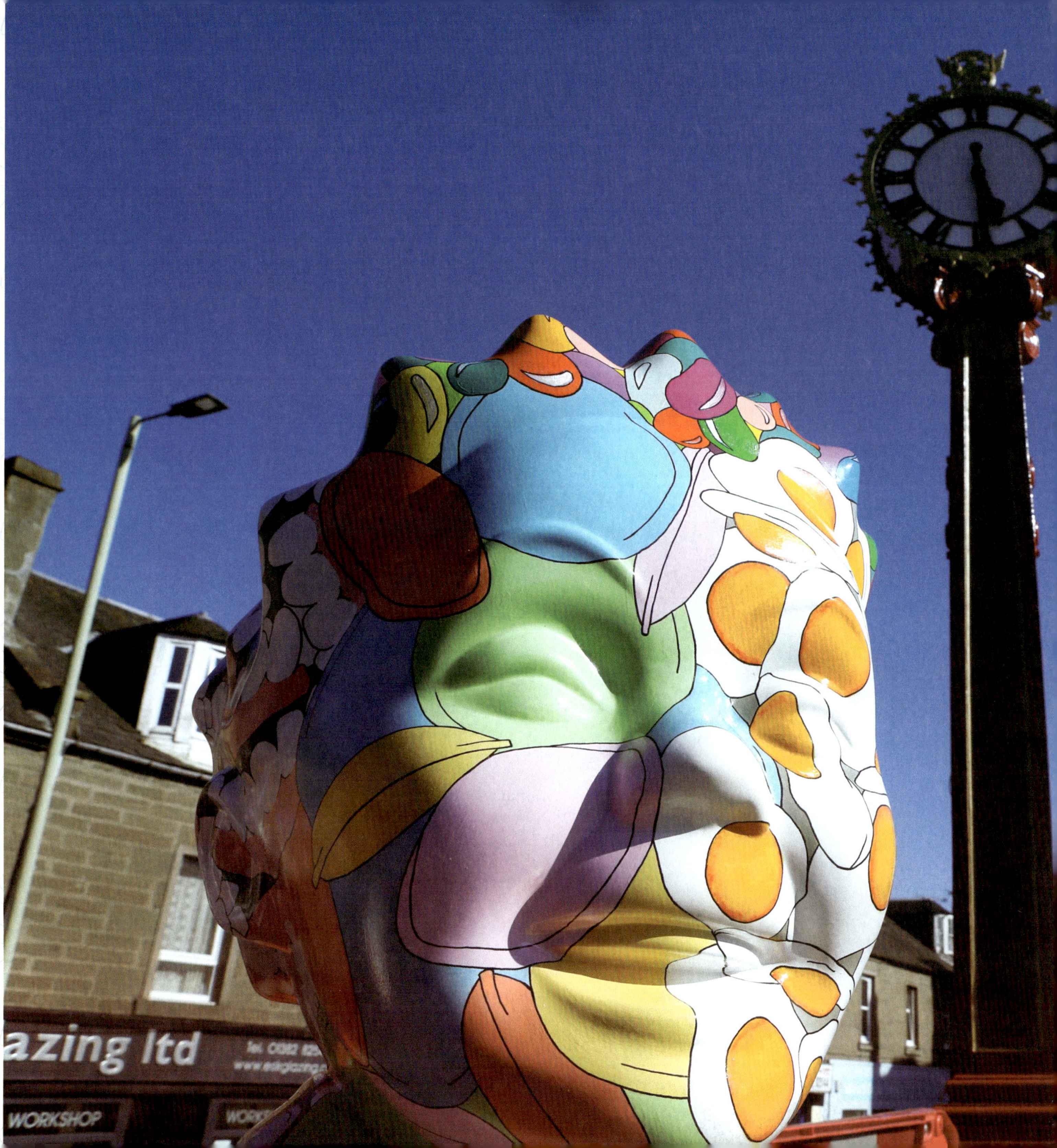
azing ltd
WORKSHOP

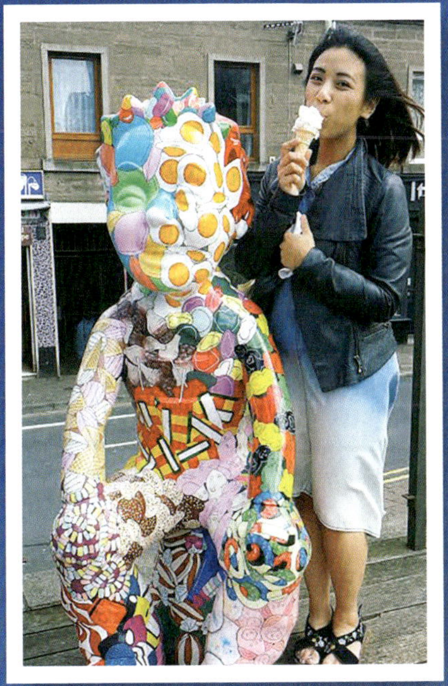

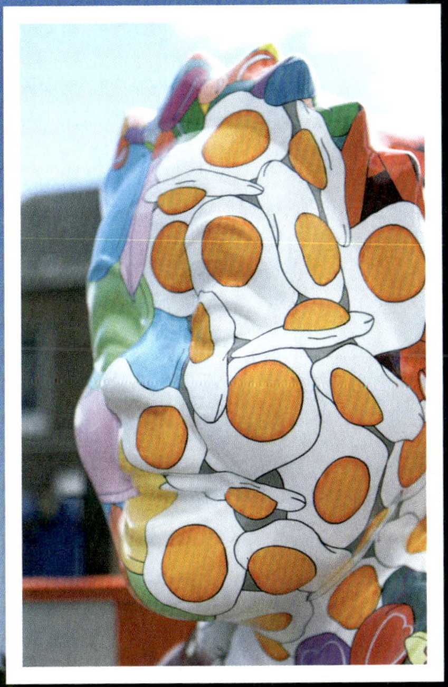

THE SCULPTURES No.4

SWEET SHOP

Location on the Bucket Trail: The Hilltown Clock.

Designed by: Rachelle Wong.

About this sculpture: Over the years, Oor Wullie has sweetened the hearts of many in Scotland and beyond so what better way to celebrate the life of the beloved young menace than by featuring abody's favourite sweets? Eighty years on, Oor Wullie lives strong in our memories just like the confectionery of yesteryear.

Rachelle Wong graduated from Duncan of Jordanstone College of Art and Design in 2015 and is now based in Edinburgh. She recently launched a creative homeware business called Rachelle W Designs and is best known for her love of colour and pattern, inspired by subjects close to her heart. Sweet!

Sponsor: DC Thomson.

Winning bid: £11,000.

Winning bidder: Susan and William Barnett.

Where is he now? Sunning himself in Mijas, Spain!

Why was he bought? Susan and William said: "The Hilltown and the sweet shop there have special memories for us both and it seemed right for us to purchase him."

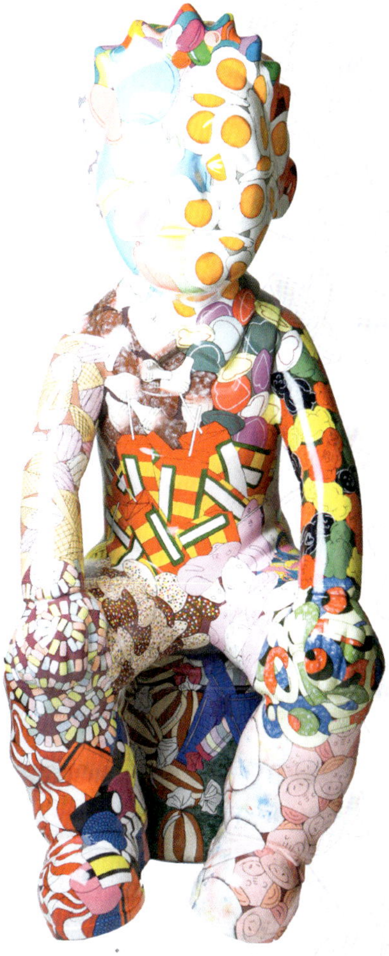

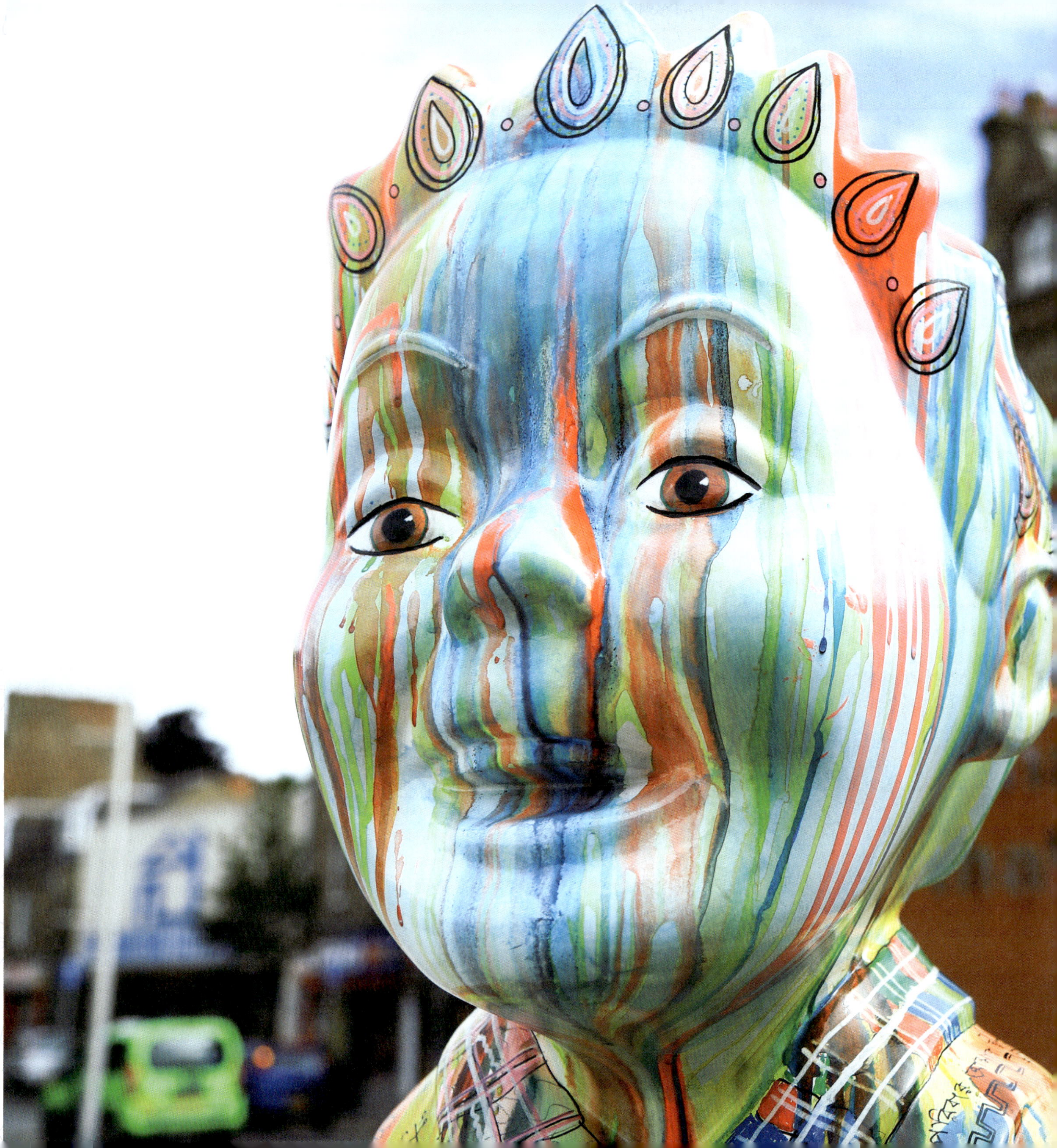

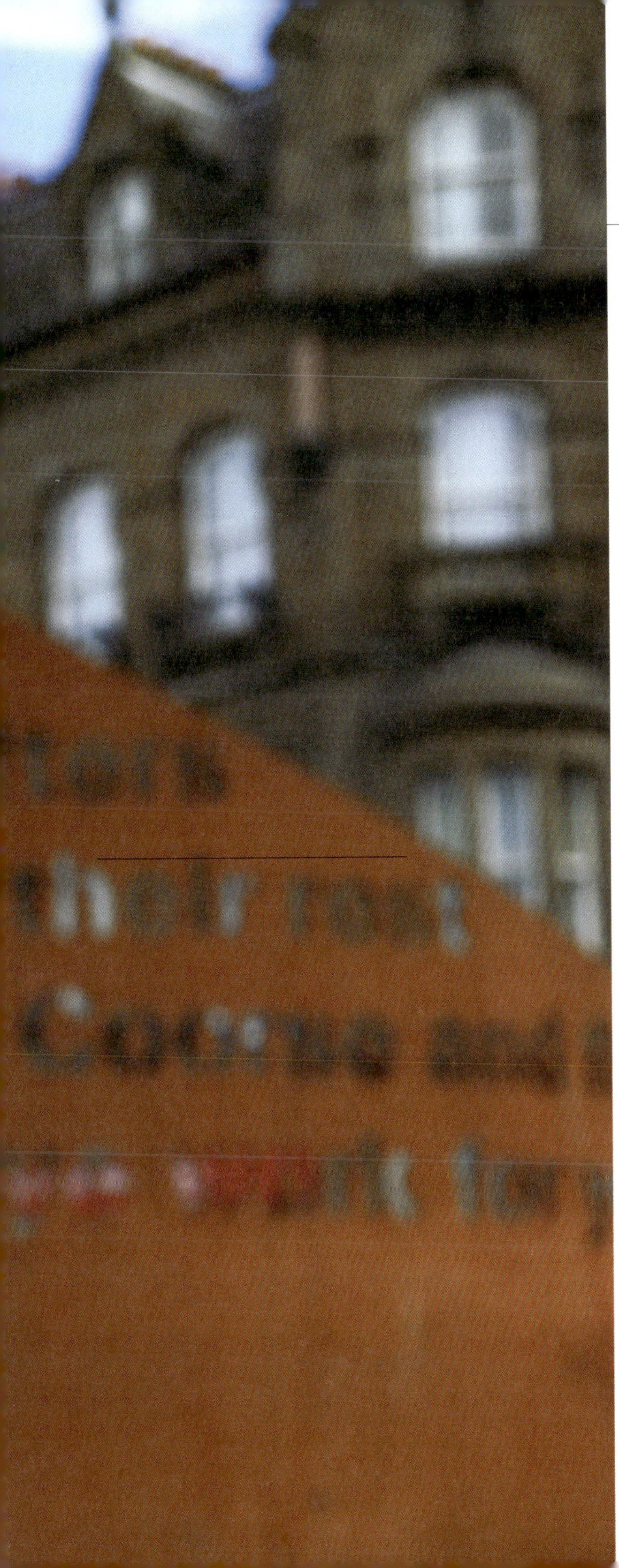

WOMEN OF THE WORLD

Location on the Bucket Trail: The Dundee Weaver, Lochee High Street.

Designed by: Laura Darling and Dundee International Women's Centre (DIWC).

About this sculpture: Painted by women who have migrated to Dundee, Women of the World is a vibrant celebration of multiculturalism. Handwriting, layers of colours and folk art inspire the patterns on this sculpture and they overlap and intertwine to create new visual narratives, incorporating six different languages.

Dundee International Women's Centre exists to address the needs of women with an emphasis on those from black and ethnic minority communities. Since 1969, DIWC has promoted and created opportunities for women's social, political and economic inclusion by establishing an environment where women can become self-empowered and achieve their personal life goals.

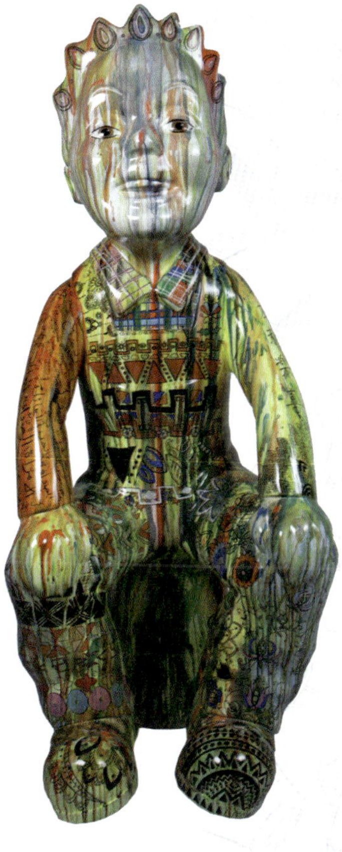

Sponsor: Wellgate Centre.

Winning bid: £8,000.

Winning bidder: Dundee City Council.

Where is he now? Greeting visitors in the reception area of Dundee House!

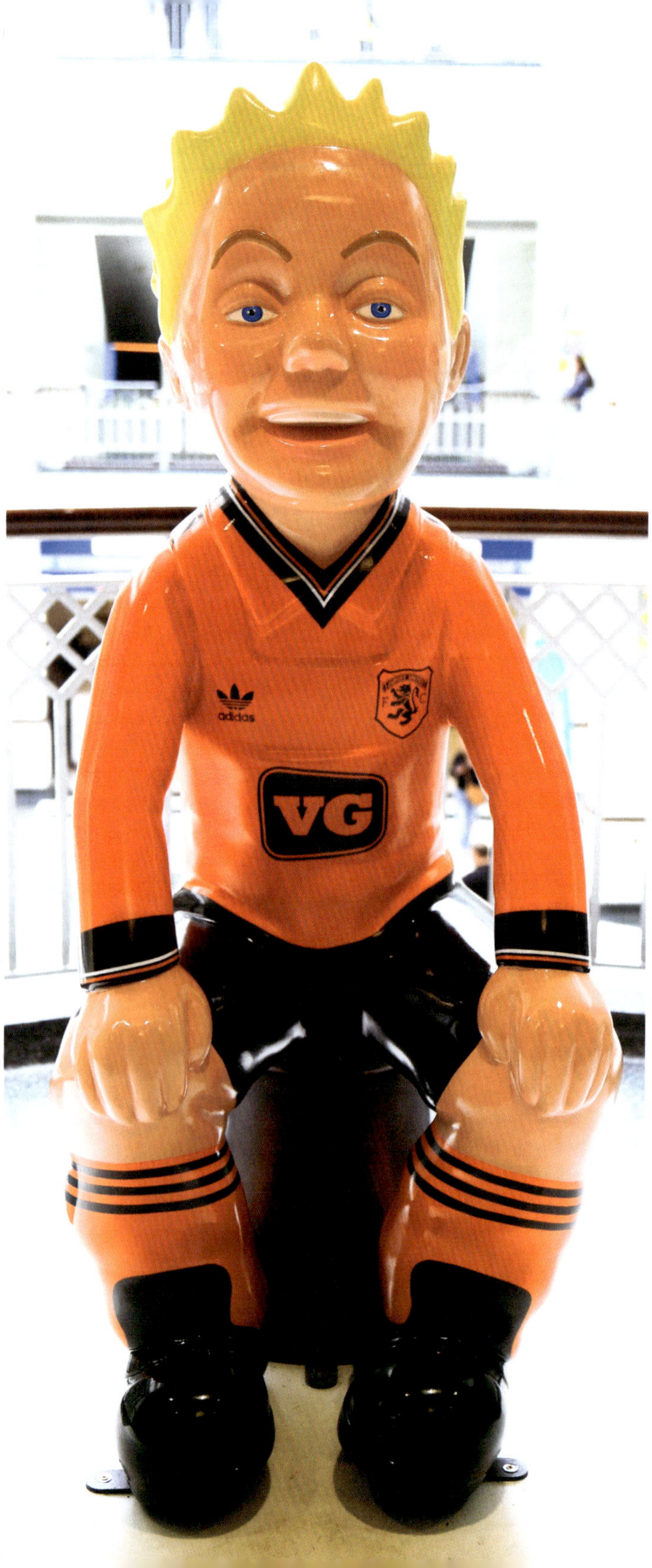
adidas
VG

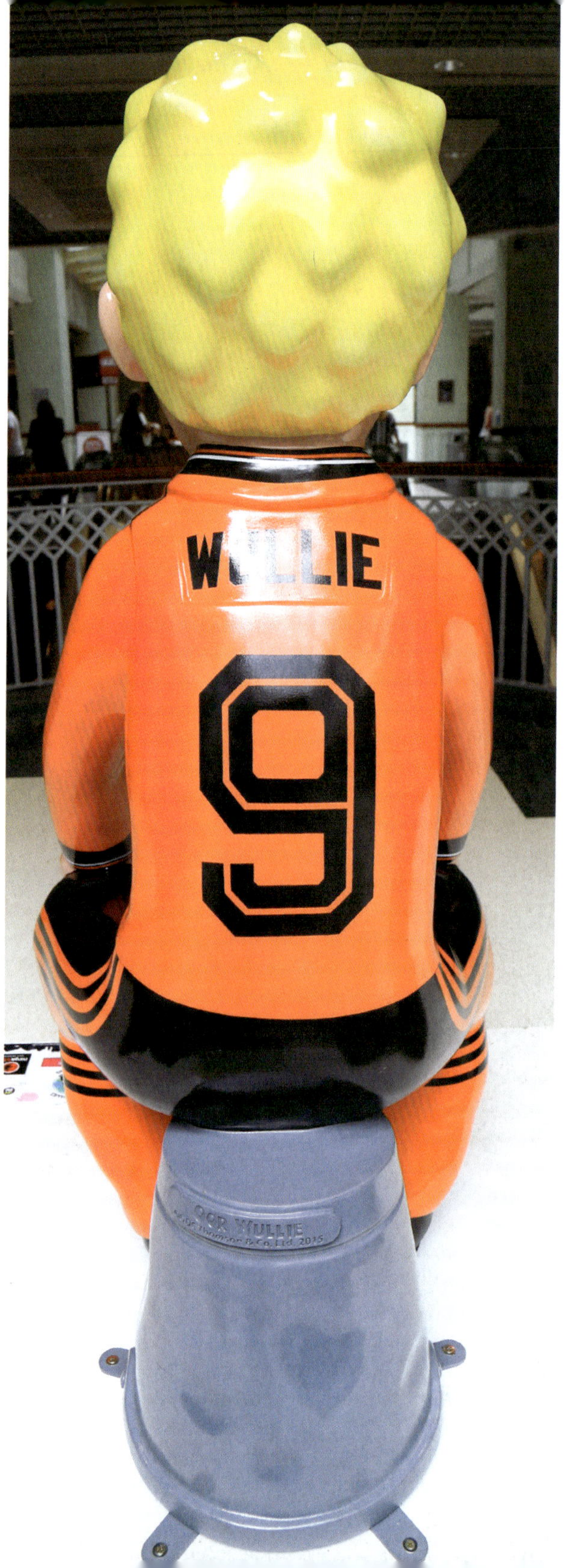
9

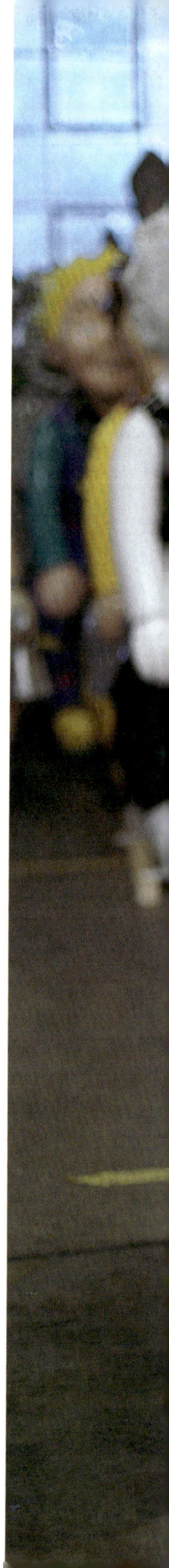

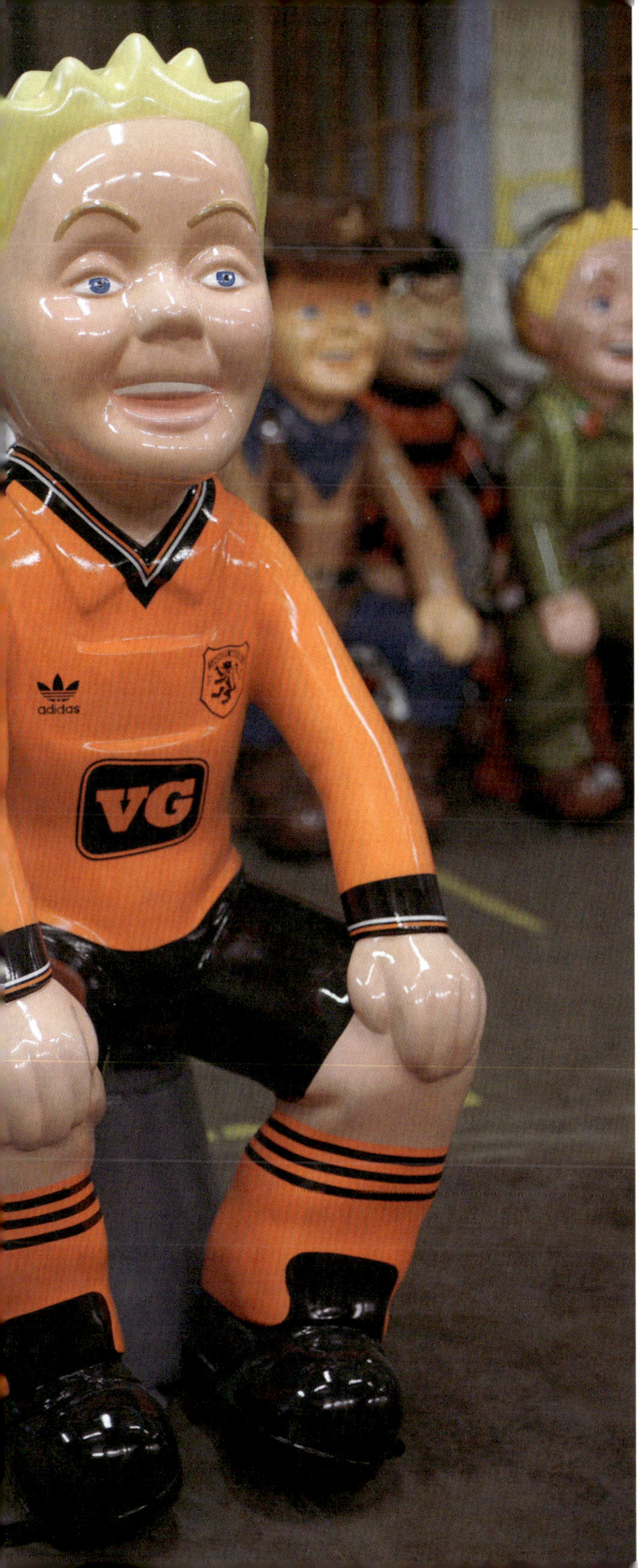

THE SCULPTURES No.6

TANGERINE TERROR

Location on the Bucket Trail: Wellgate Centre.

Designed by: Matthew Low and Lorraine Kelly.

About this sculpture: Tangerine Terror celebrates Dundee United's 1986/7 Barcelona-beating team. This sculpture is based on Dundee United fan, and well-known television presenter, Lorraine Kelly's design and was painted by artist, Matthew Low.

Having studied at Adam Smith College, Matthew currently works as an optical assembly technician but spends his spare hours working on personal projects and commissions. He is interested in urban art forms, illustrations and pop-impressionism. He always feels the need to be creating something and always has paint on his clothes!

Sponsor: Ninja Kiwi.

Winning bid: £16,000.

Winning bidder: Cath Thompson, Honorary President, Dundee United Football Club.

Where is he now? Sitting resplendent in the Club's superstore keeping an eye on the comings and goings and welcoming the Club's supporters as they enter the store!

Why was he bought? Cath Thompson, Honorary President, Dundee United Football Club, said: "I bought the sculpture simply because he is wearing 'oor team colours'. It was right that he was where he belongs at Tannadice Park."

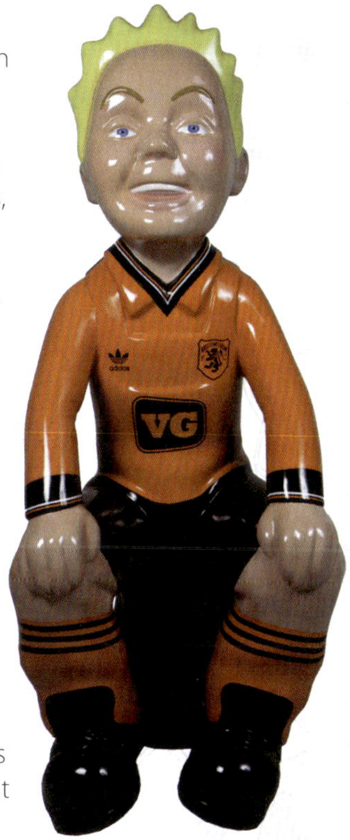

THE SCULPTURES No.7

OOR BOBBY

Location on the Bucket Trail: Overgate Shopping Centre.

Designed by: Nina Garty.

About this sculpture: Oor Bobby was Dundee Football Club's star player of 2016! He is modelled on Bobby Cox, a local boy who was born within earshot of Dens Park and who grew up to become captain of his beloved Dundee FC, leading the team to win the Scottish league for the first and, to date, only time in their history. The stuff of legends!

Nina Garty studied jewellery and silversmithing at Duncan of Jordanstone College of Art and Design in Dundee.

Sponsor: Dundee FC and TPLD, leading creators of games-based learning solutions, software and toolsets.

Winning bid: £12,000.

Winning bidder: Dundee FC Supporters' Society.

Where is he now? Singing along with fans at Dens Park!

Why was he bought? Dundee FC said: "The Club were honoured to launch Oor Bobby in memory of our legendary Championship winning skipper, Bobby Cox, when our customised version for Oor Wullie's Bucket Trail was revealed. The sculpture has Cox 3 on the back and scenes from the 1962 title-winning squad are featured on the bucket.

"The Club teamed up with local games-based learning company TPLD to help support the ARCHIE Foundation and was very grateful to the Garty family, long-time supporters of Dundee FC, for all their efforts. Mike Garty of TPLD helped with the sponsorship, and his daughter Nina both designed and decorated the Official Dundee FC Oor Bobby.

"The Trail was a fantastic event for the whole city and Oor Bobby was a popular figure in the Overgate Shopping Centre and continues to be in the Club shop and at any events which we hold at the stadium."

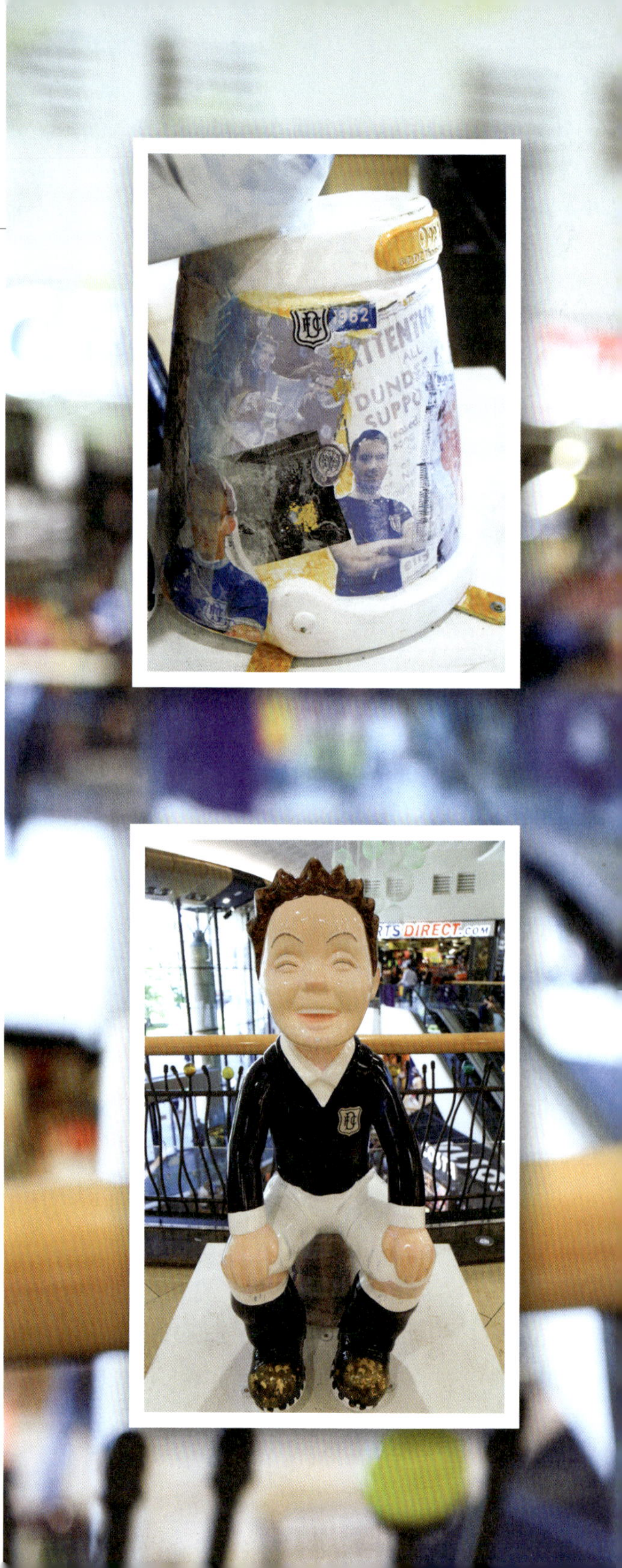

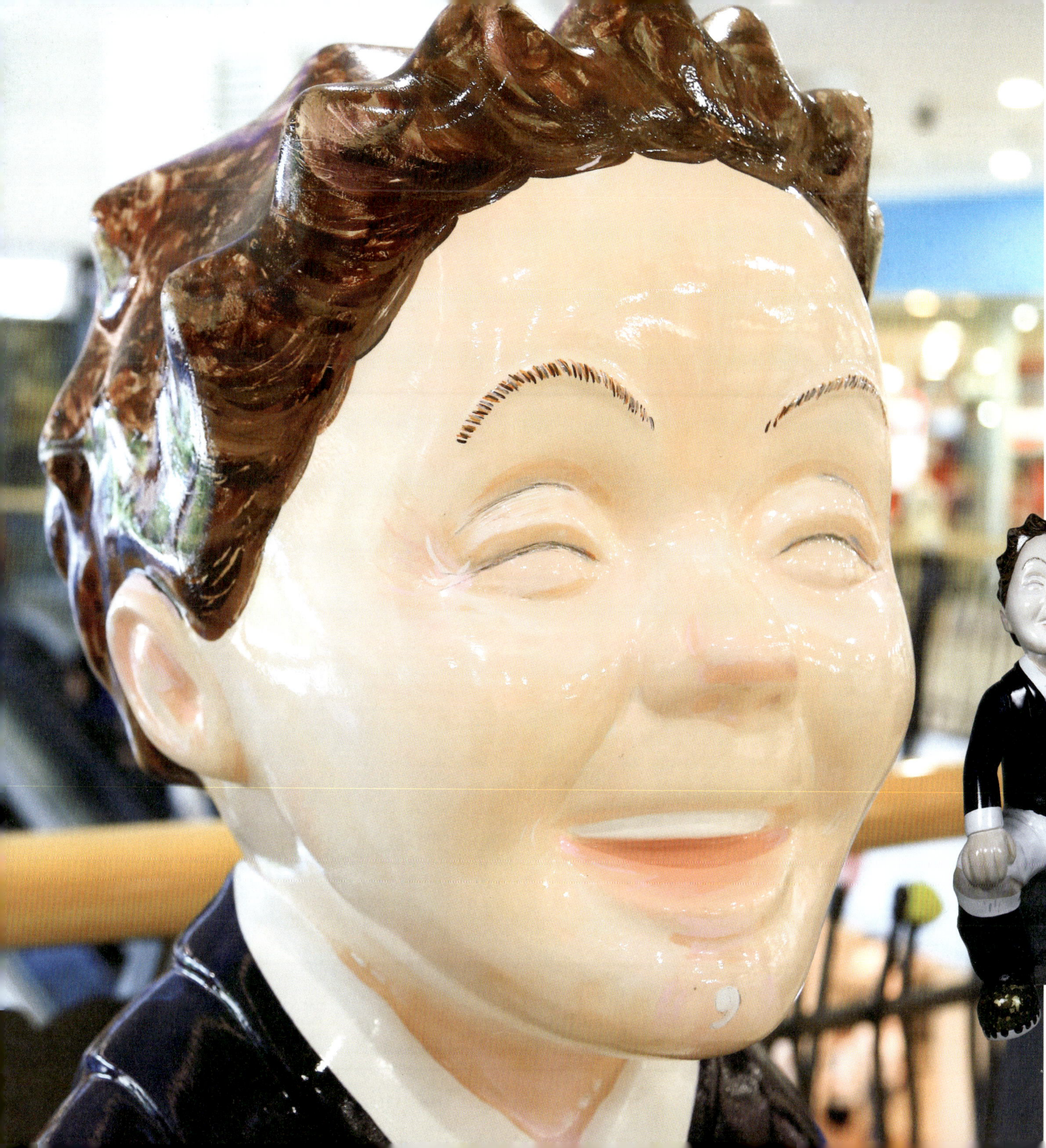

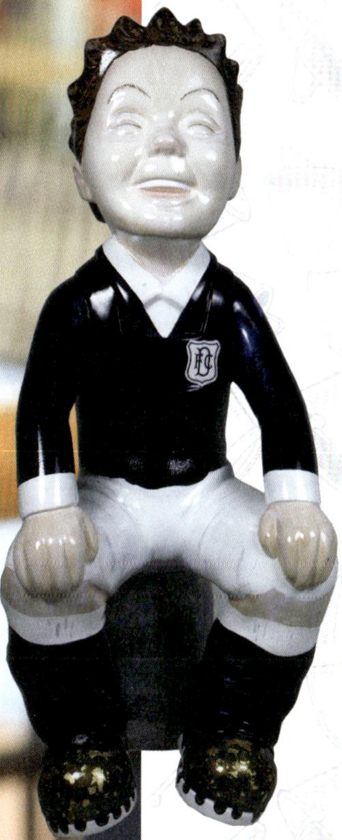

THE SCULPTURES No.8

WULLIE'S CHEEKY TALES

Location on the Bucket Trail: Overgate Shopping Centre.

Designed by: Nicki Bradwell.

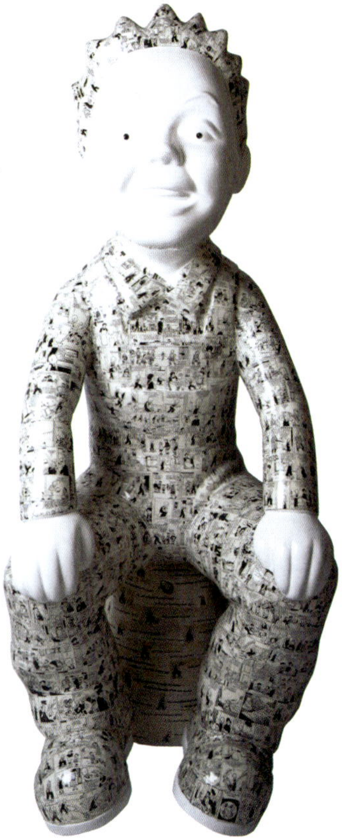

About this sculpture: The ARCHIE Foundation commissioned Nicki to cover an Oor Wullie sculpture in Oor Wullie annual comic strips. The result is a beautiful, busy collage which portrays the cheeky tales of Oor Wullie.

Nicki is based in Fife and graduated in printed textile from Duncan of Jordanstone College of Art and Design in 2005. She splits her time between teaching art and design, being a mum to Jack, and creating her own design work – beautiful, colourful and patterned stationery and gifts, produced from original drawings which are inspired by Scottish wildlife, flora and fauna.

Sponsor: Overgate Shopping Centre.

Winning bid: £13,000.

Winning bidder: We dinae ken!

Where is he now? We dinae ken that either but he disnae like shopping so he'll be playing in his shed!

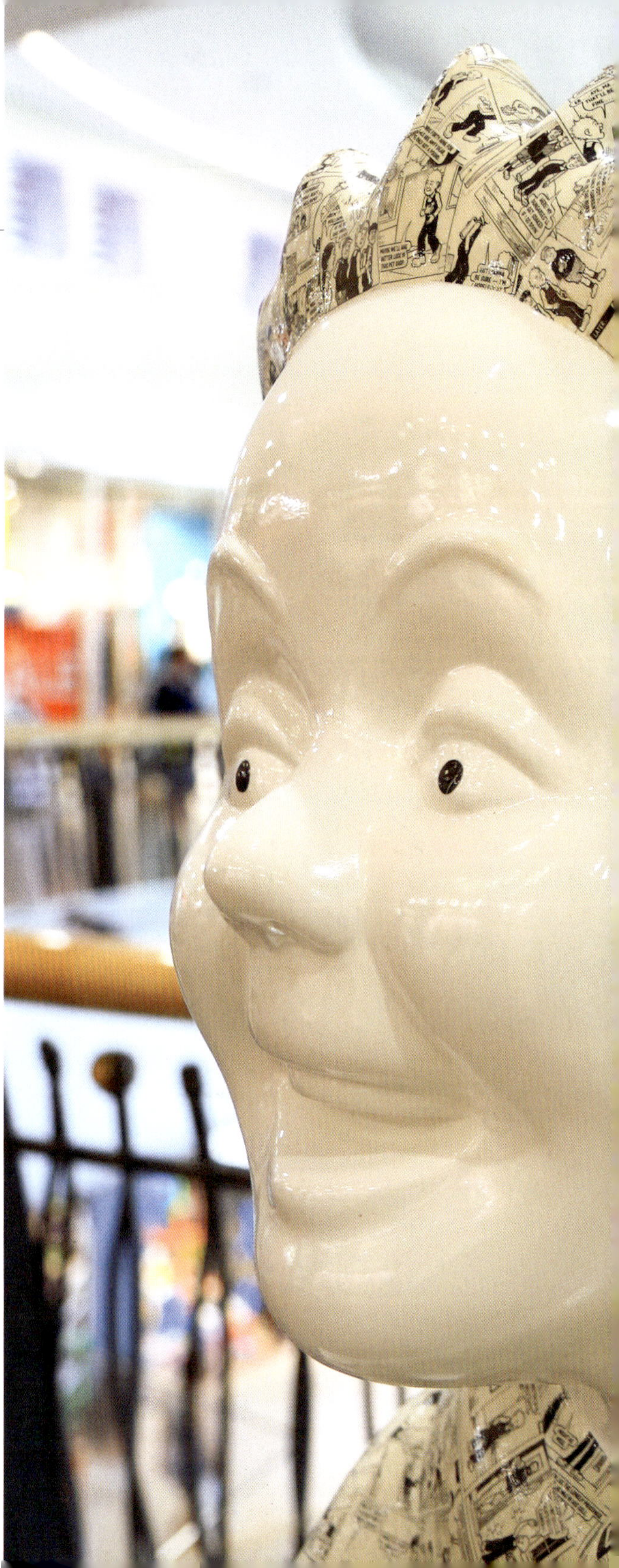

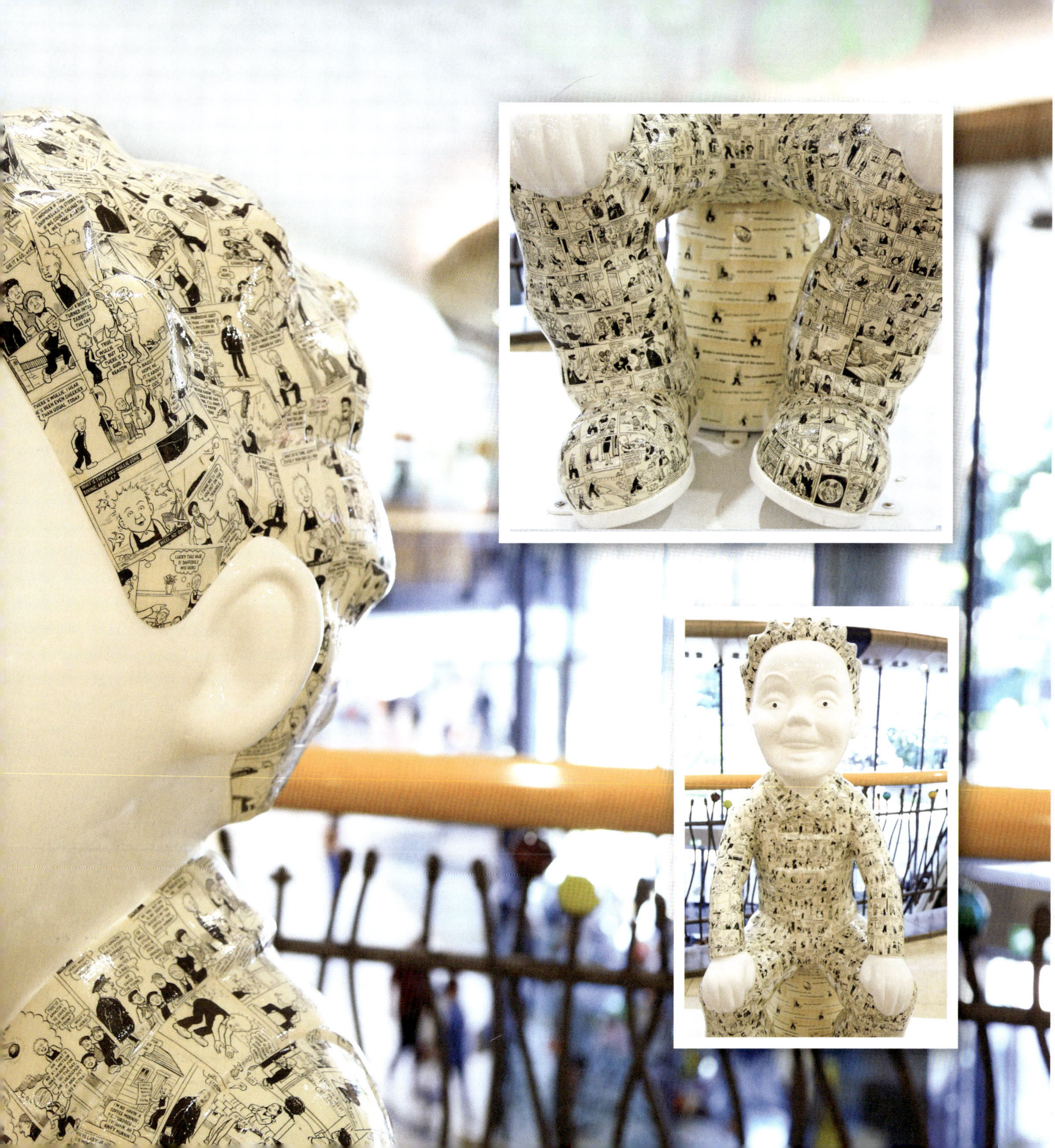

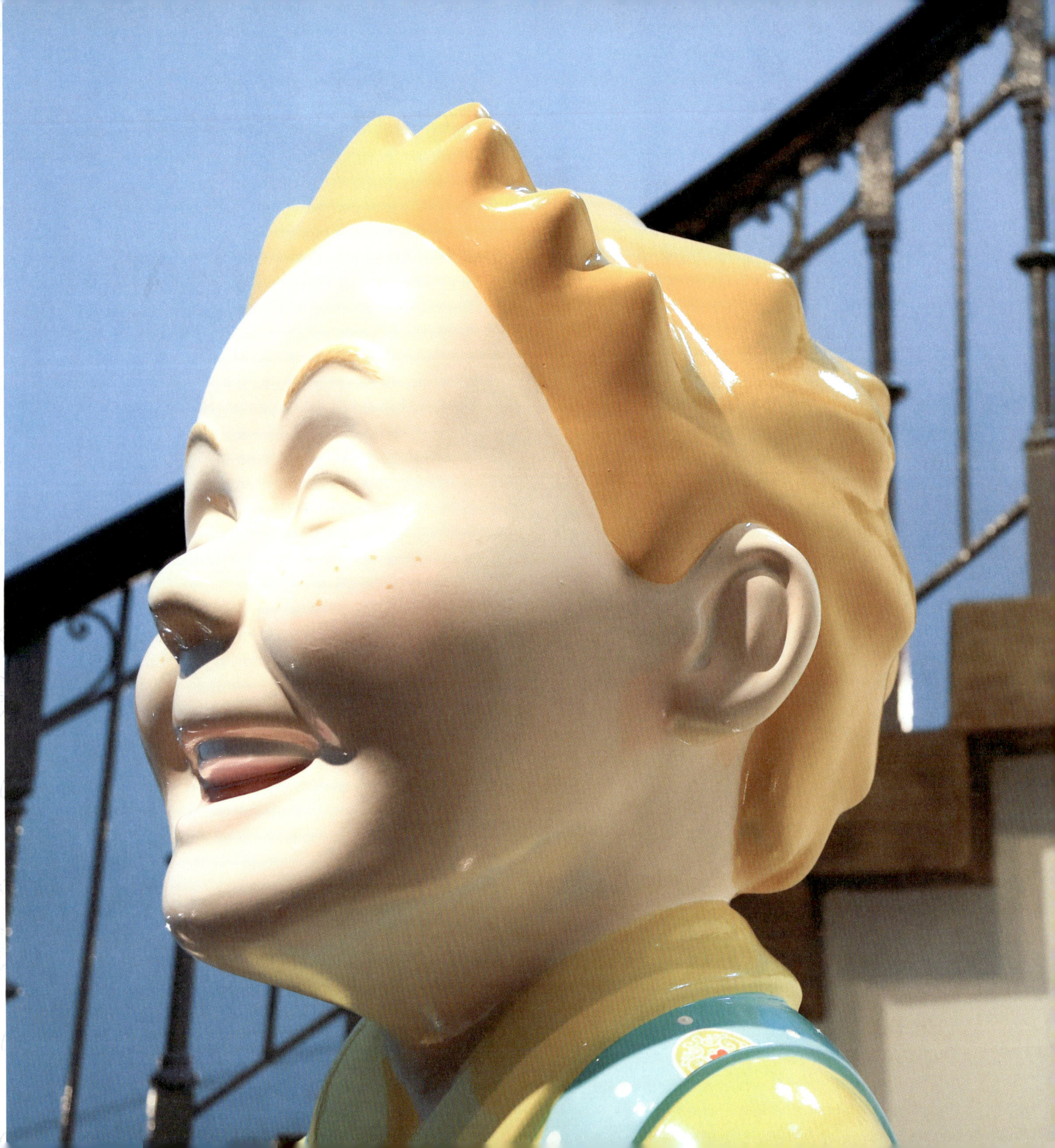

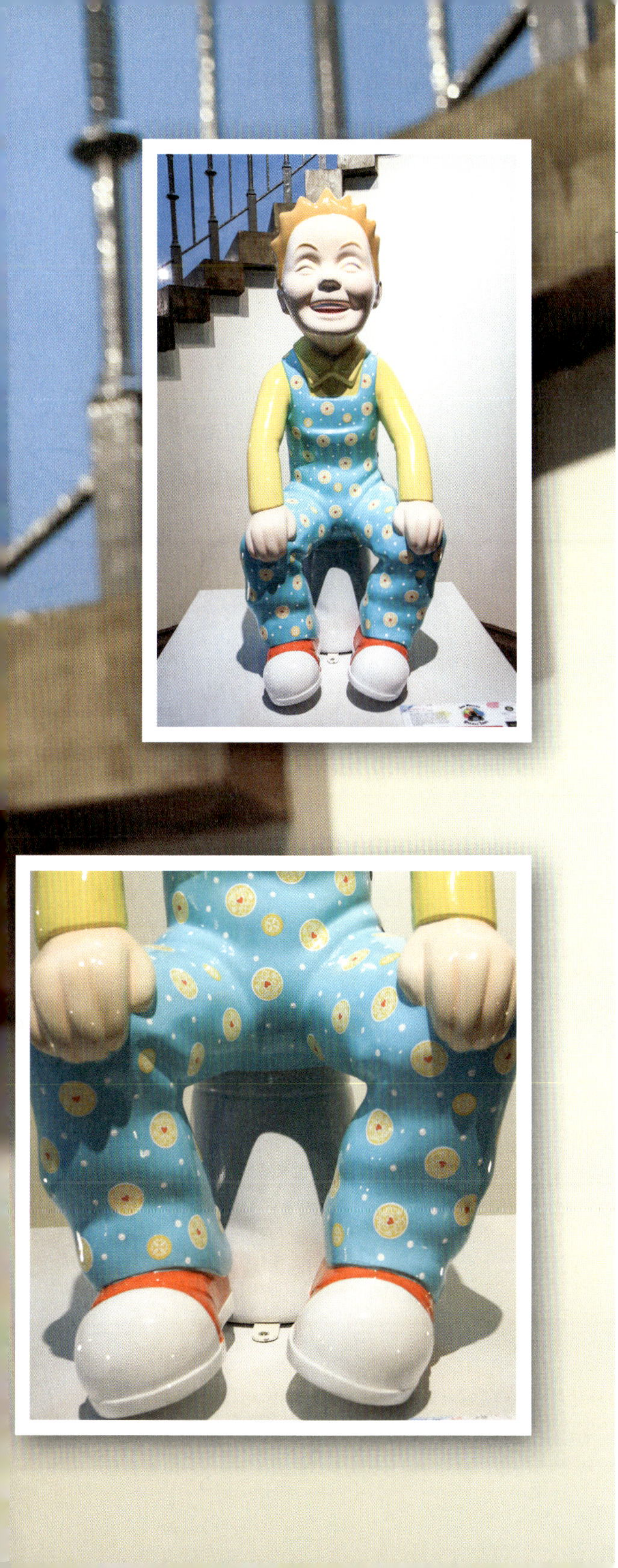

BISCUIT BREAK

Location on the Bucket Trail: The McManus Art Gallery and Museum.

Designed by: Nikki McWilliams.

About this sculpture: Inspired by her love of the ritual of the tea break and of pop culture, Nikki McWilliams designed some bright and playful patterned dungarees for this Oor Wullie – all with a biscuity theme!

Nikki is Creative Director, Founder and Chief Biscuit Taster at Nikki McWilliams Ltd. She studied fine art at Duncan of Jordanstone College of Art and Design before going on to create her own homeware and accessories label in 2009.

Sponsor: Leisure and Culture Dundee.

Winning bid: £9,000.

Winning bidder: Stagecoach.

Where is he now? Taking the wheel at Stagecoach!

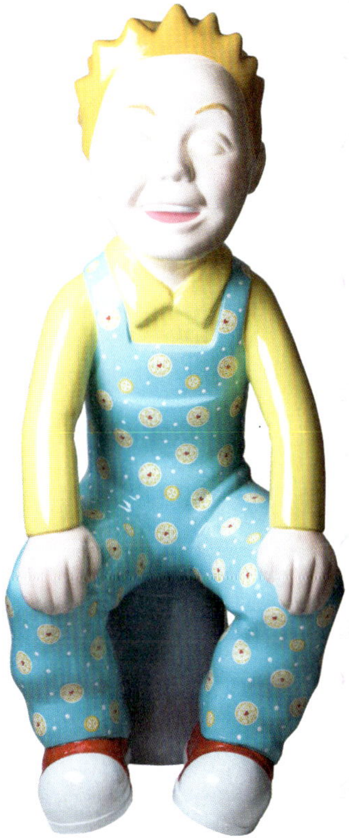

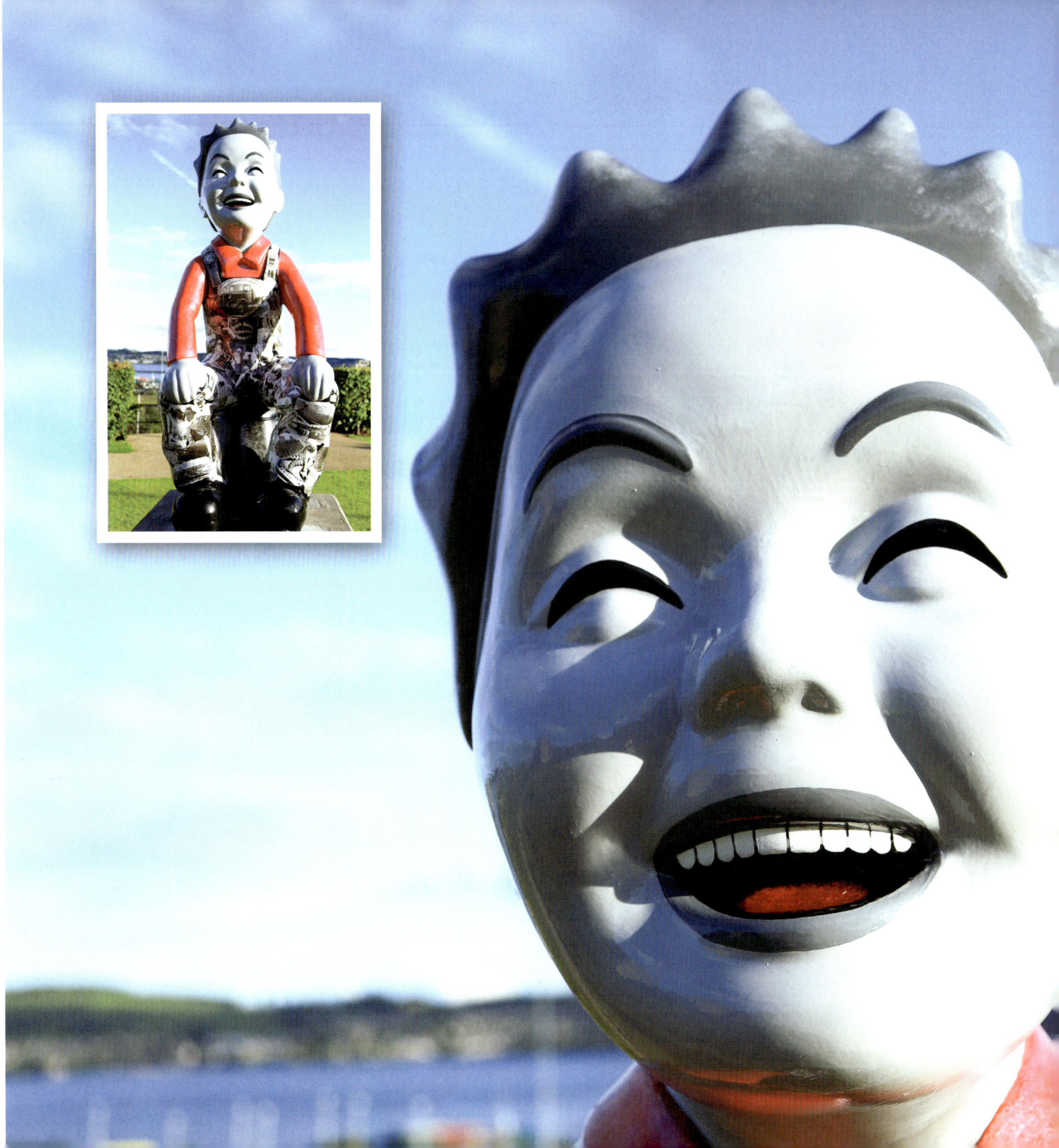

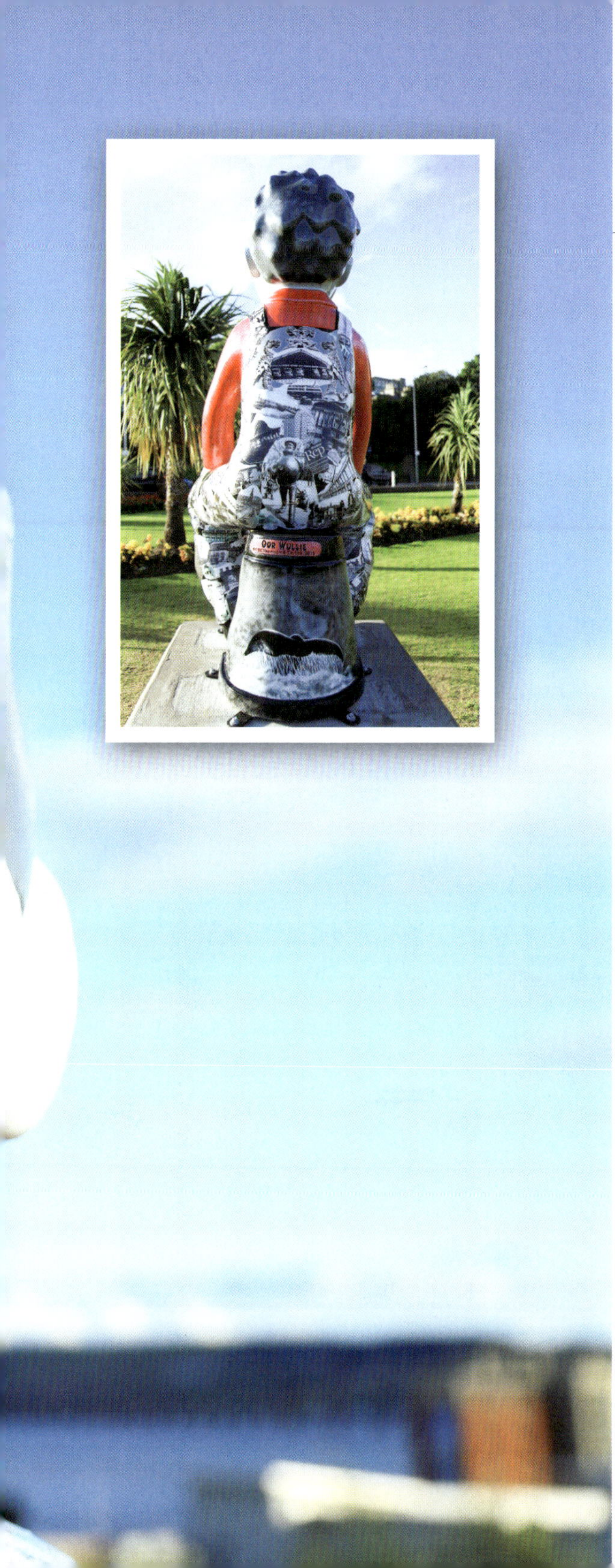

DUNDEE PAST & PRESENT

Location on the Bucket Trail: Seabraes.

Designed by: Nichola Martin.

About this sculpture: Nichola's interpretation of Oor Wullie resulted in a beautiful visual storybook of Dundee's past and present industries, architecture, people and life.

Nichola graduated in fine art from Duncan of Jordanstone College of Art and Design in 2007 and is an award-winning artist, having received two awards from the Royal Scottish Academy. Since graduating, she has exhibited in numerous galleries around the UK and her works feature in private collections across the world.

Sponsor: Kerr's Dairy.

Winning bid: £12,000.

Winning bidder: Kelvin Kerr, Kerr's Dairy.

Where is he now? Sippin' a pint o' milk at the Dairy and going out on trips to school fetes and local businesses to help raise more money for the ARCHIE Foundation!

Why was he bought? Kelvin Kerr, owner of Kerr's Dairy, said: "As a proud Dundonian with a business that has been successfully trading for the last 100 years, we were just delighted to be able to do something special for a local cause."

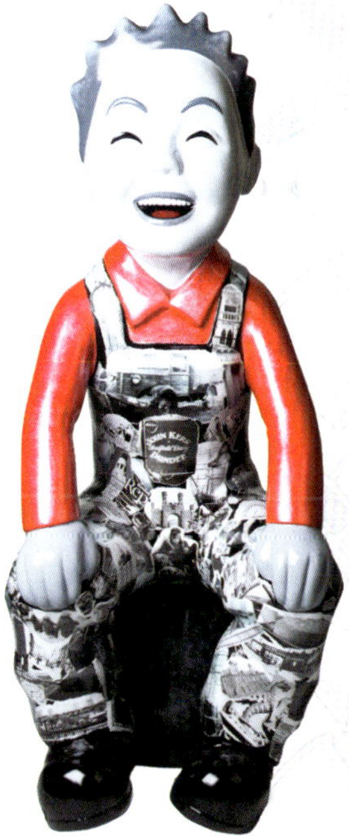

AMOR LUCIS

Location on the Bucket Trail:
Slessor Gardens.

Designed by: Tony Morrow.

About this sculpture: In this sculpture, Tony Morrow wanted to acknowledge the hard work of medical staff that care for sick children beyond daylight hours. His sculpture, painted in a glowing pure bright white, reflects their commitment - while we rest, many children battle illness with the help and support of exceptional medical staff. May the light protect these sick children during the darkness.

Tony is an established artist and sculptor. His work can be found in the National Portrait Gallery, exhibited in London, in every city centre in Scotland and in collections around the world. Tony takes those who view his work on a beautiful journey through life with him.

Sponsor: Avian.

Winning bid: £13,000.

Winning bidder: Alison Wiseman, former chief executive of Dundee & Angus Chamber of Commerce.

Where is he now? Relaxing with his feet up in Tealing Village!

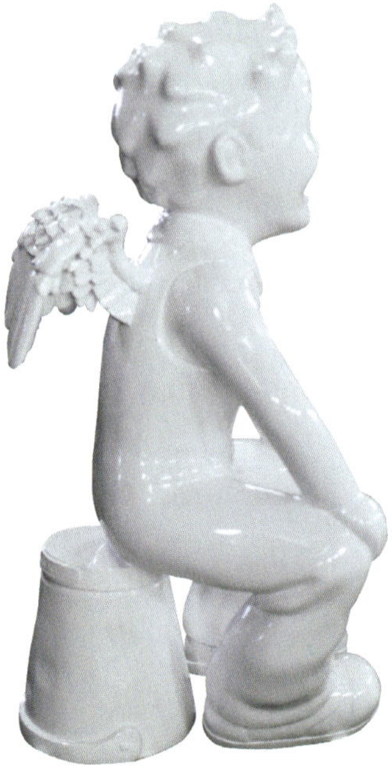

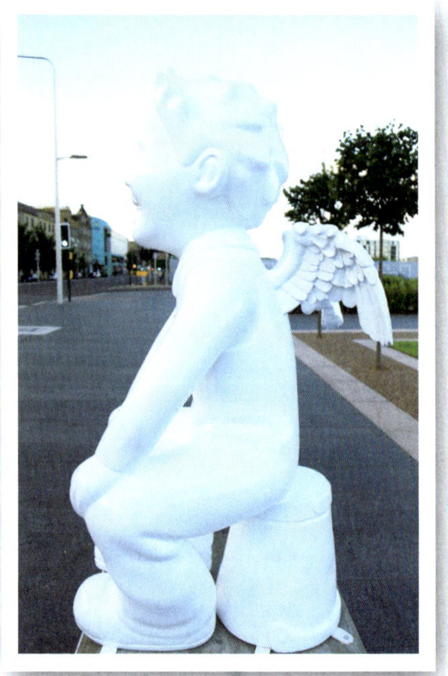

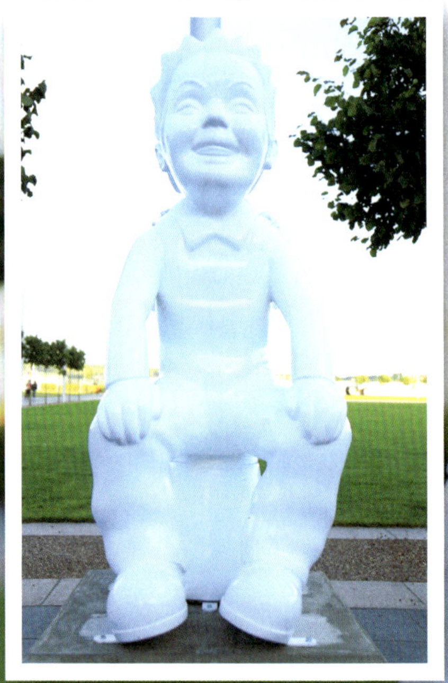

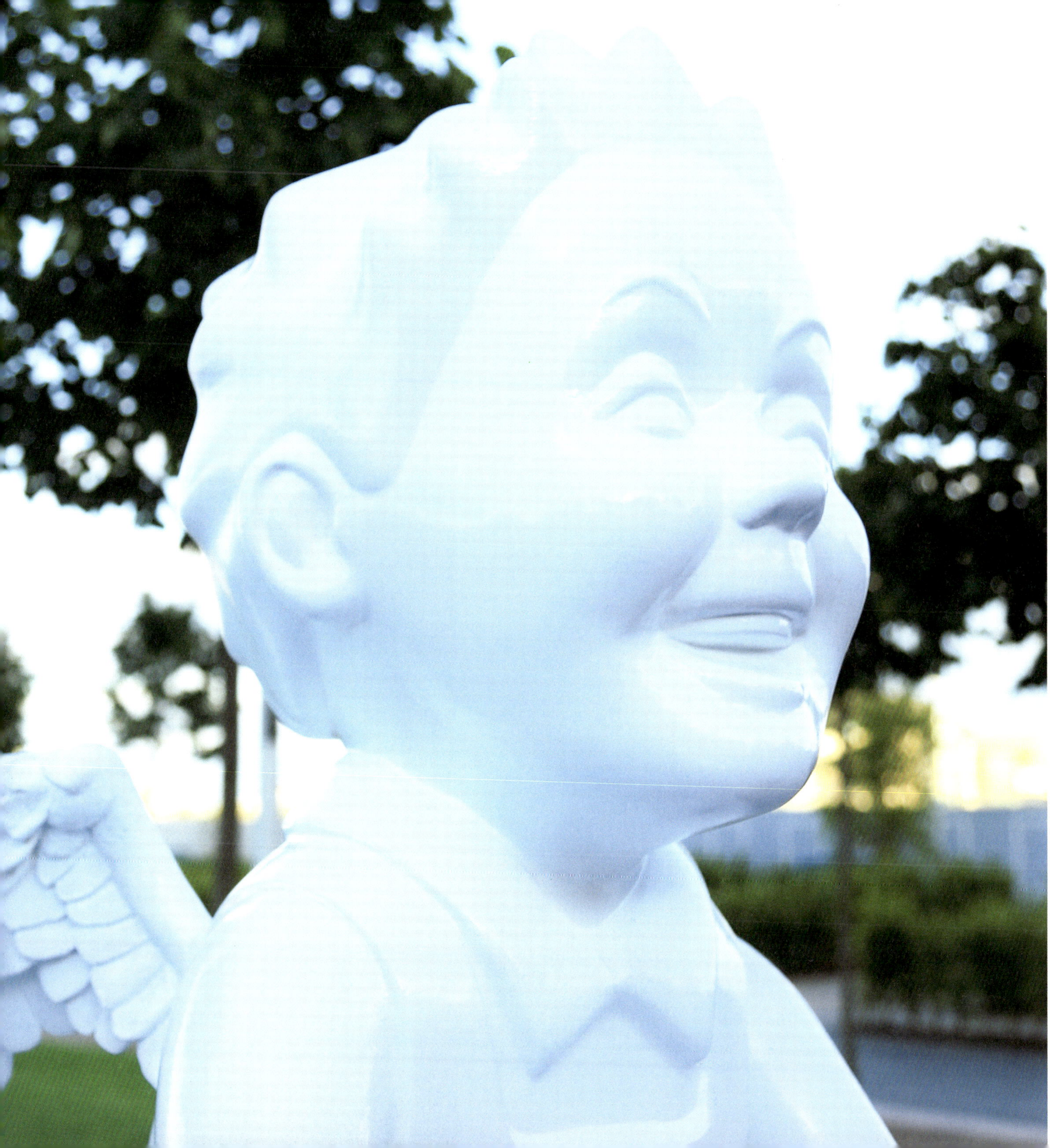

THE ADVENTURE OF DISCOVERY NEVER ENDS

Location on the Bucket Trail: Slessor Gardens.

Designed by: Suzanne Scott (WhimSicAL LusH).

About this sculpture: Inspired by Dundee and its people, the images on this sculpture represent the adventures Oor Wullie has had over the years, exploring Dundee and learning all about its history. Many of the illustrations are based on the designs Suzanne created for Discovery Walk on Dundee's new waterfront.

Suzanne is an artist and illustrator based in Dundee, working under the name WhimSicAL LusH. She loves going on inky adventures and adores the little things in life. Whether she is creating creatures or castles, houses or robots, or turning people's ideas into reality, there is always a story on her drawing board.

Sponsor: DC Thomson, The Courier.

Winning bid: £16,000.

Winning bidder: DC Thomson.

Where is he now? DC Thomson bought four sculptures; each visit the company's offices on rotation.

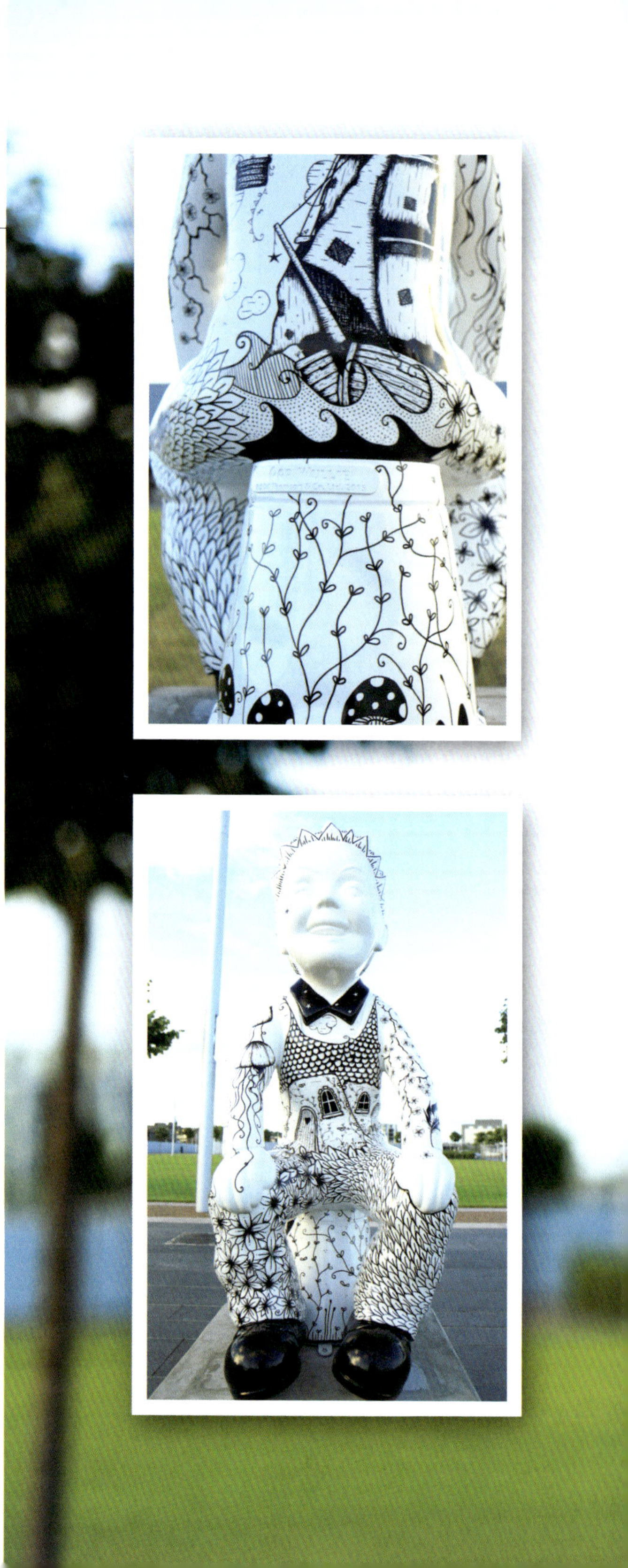

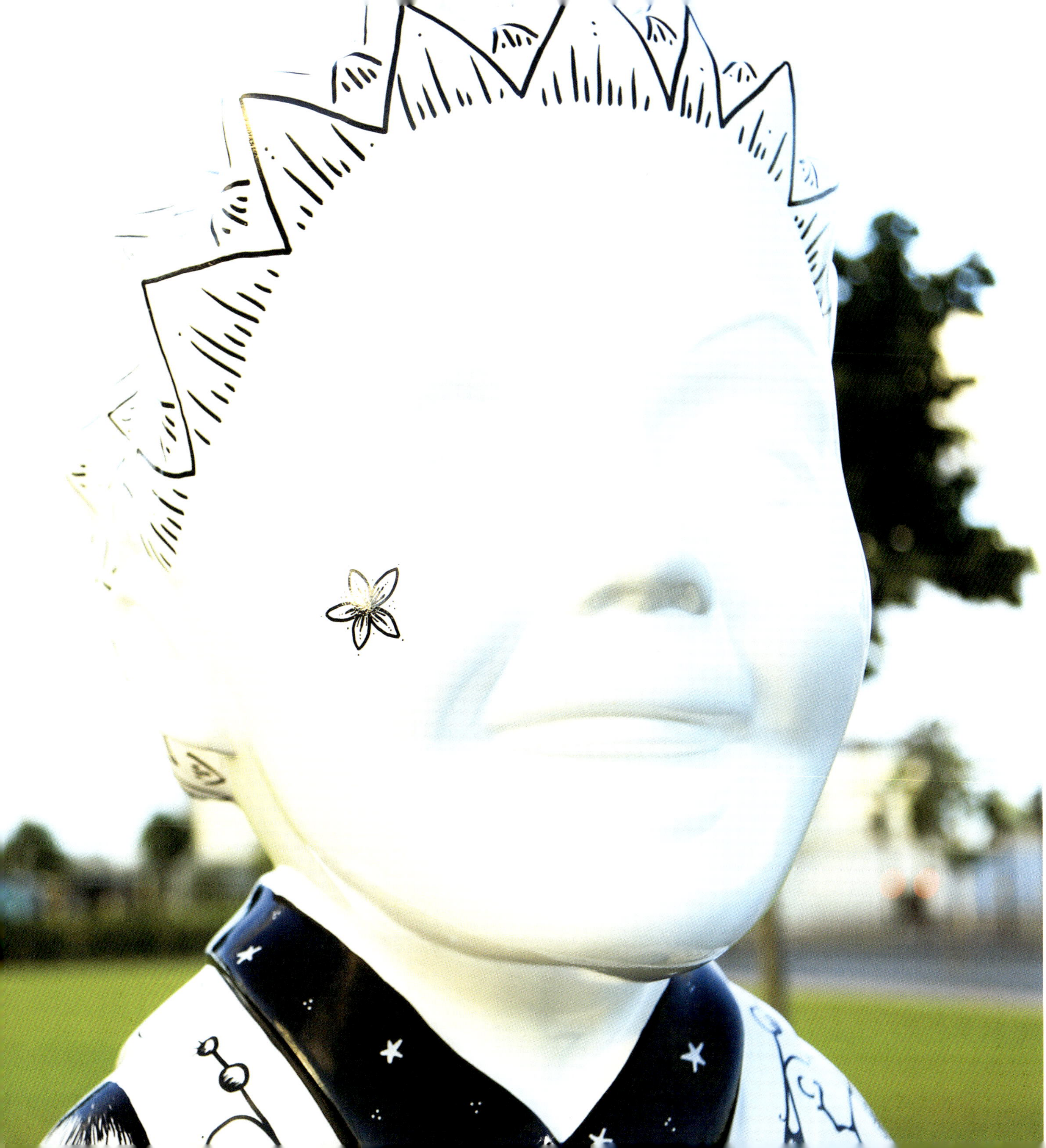

IRON BOY

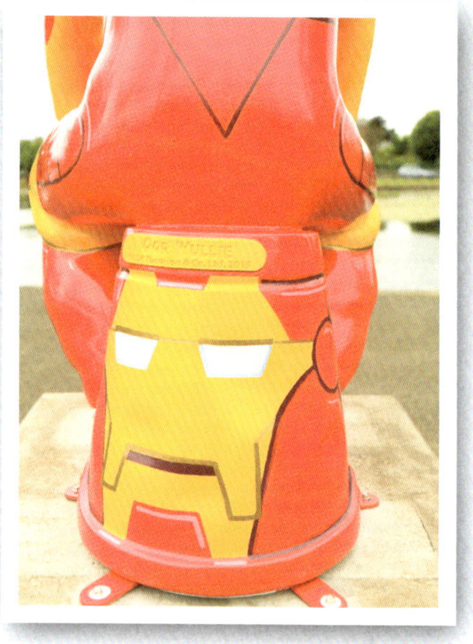

Location on the Bucket Trail: Stobsmuir 'Swannie Ponds'.

Designed by: Sophie Green.

About this sculpture: Every sculpture trail needs a hero but sometimes even heroes need a rest! Inspired by Marvel's Iron Man, this hero's helmet is made from his trusty bucket.

Working from her Liverpool studio, Sophie creates work which is light, bright and full of character. Sophie was recently named 'one to watch' as part of the Independent on Sunday's Rainbow List.

Sponsor: Buildright.

Winning bid: £9,000.

Winning bidder: We dinae ken!

Where is he now? We dinae ken that either but we hope he's living like a hero!

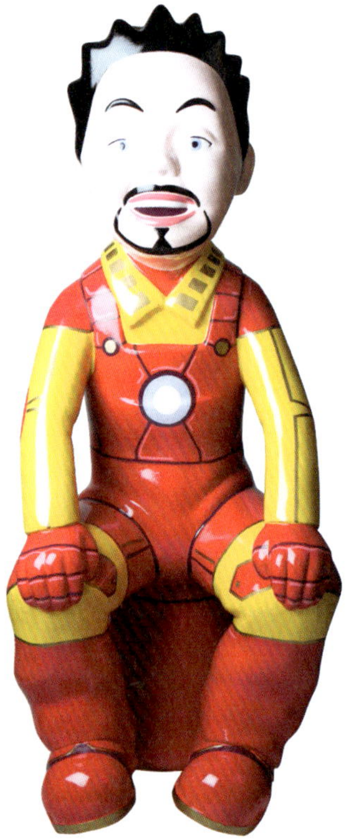

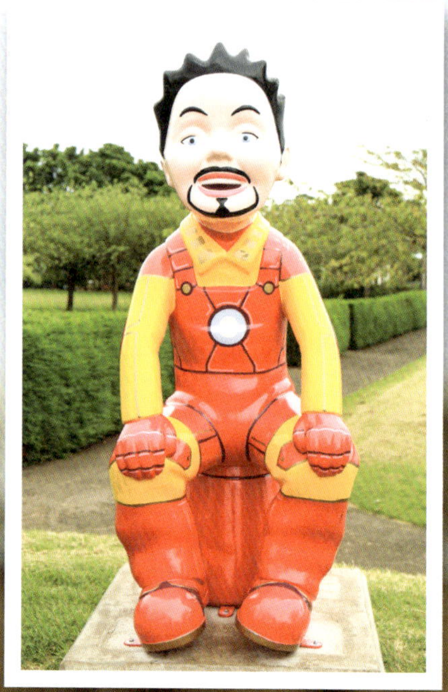

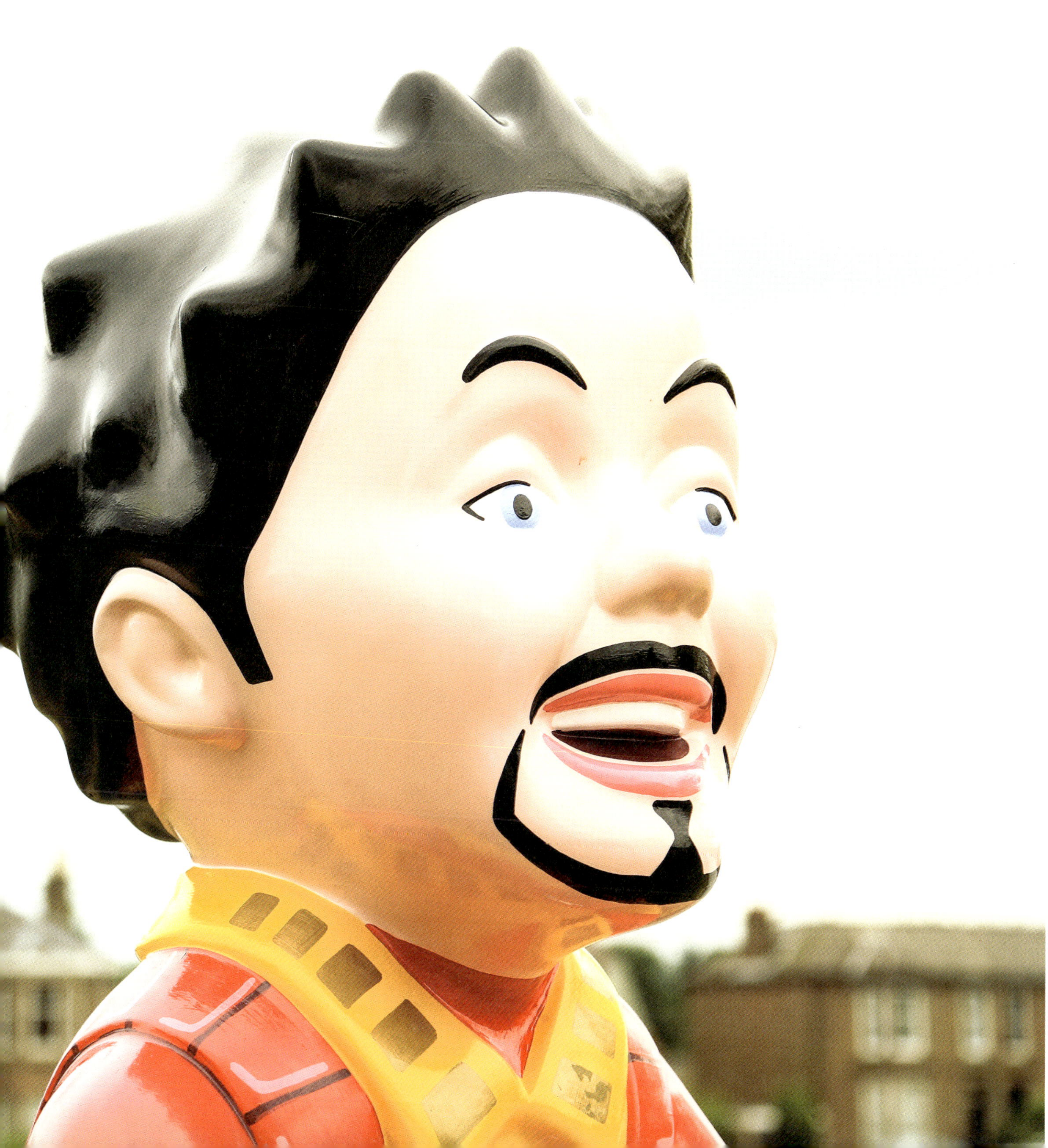

THE SCULPTURES No.14

OOR MECHANIC

Location on the Bucket Trail: City Churches.

Designed by: Emma L Pawley.

About this sculpture: Designed for Michelin, this sculpture pays tribute to the company's automotive industry history and Wullie portrays a mechanic of a past age.
Emma is a Dundee artist. Her creativity is inspired by life's light and dark contrasts.

Sponsor: Michelin.

Winning bid: £9,000.

Winning bidder: Sandemans Cars, Forfar.

Where is he now? Becoming a top-class mechanic at Sandemans Cars and helping to raise money for charity!

Why was he bought? Heather Sandeman said: "Oor Wullie's Bucket Trail really captured everyone's heart. We bought him because the money raised was going to a fantastic cause in our area to benefit local children. He's located at our garage most of the time and brings a smile to everyone's face when they walk through the door. We intend to continue using him to raise money for charity locally. He collects for the ARCHIE Foundation and has also been out on his travels raising money for other local charities including The Guide Dogs, Laura's Fun Day and the local Race for Life team from the Bank of Scotland."

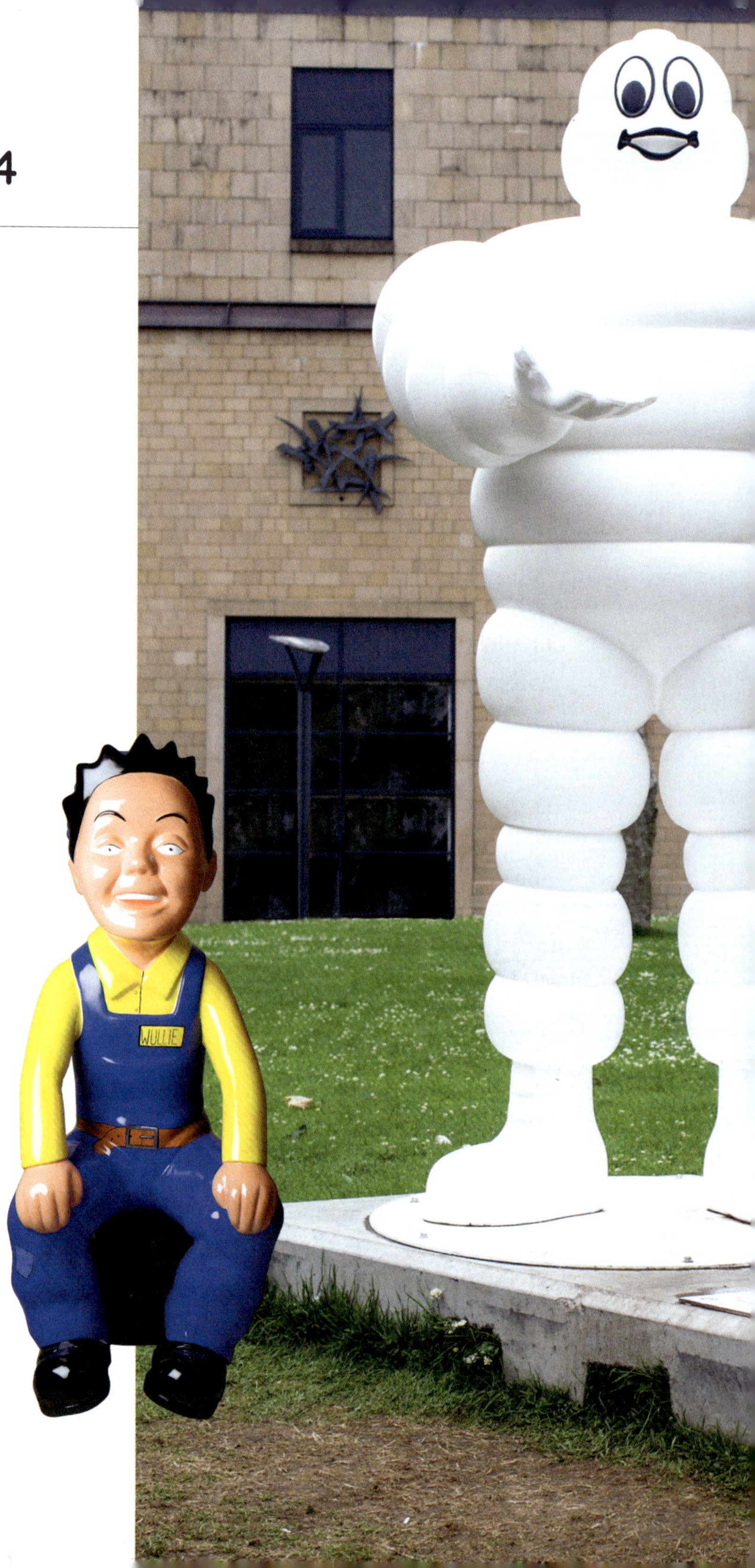

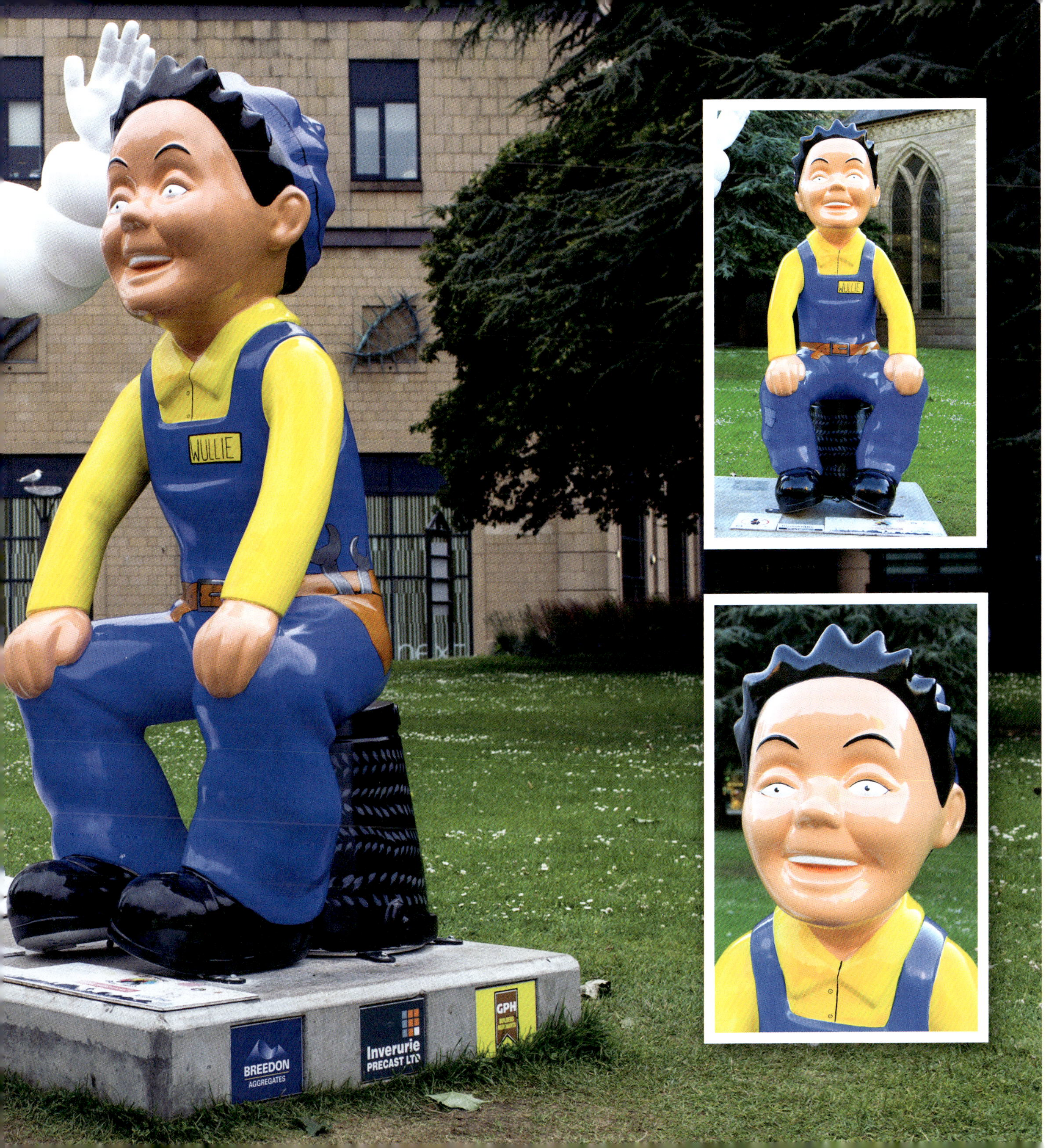
WULLIE
BREEDON
AGGREGATES
Inverurie
PRECAST LTD
GPH
WULLIE

THE SCULPTURES No.15

OOR IDEAS

Location on the Bucket Trail: City Square.

Designed by: Gilly Beech and Danny Wallace.

About this sculpture: Dundee is home to some amazing 'light bulb moments' including the invention of the electric lightbulb and the adhesive postage stamp. Here Wullie's hair and body are covered in twelve different types of adhesive stamp, each one a different colour and each one depicting something invented in, or influenced by, Dundee. This sculpture also came complete with a lightbulb fixed above Wullie's head, representing all of Dundee's bright ideas. The lightbulb didn't feature in the Trail as it would have broken off but it was fixed in place for auction. Oor Ideas was designed by broadcaster Danny Wallace and was brought to life by artist and art tutor, Gilly Beech. Gilly works in a variety of mediums and styles. Her work is influenced by her childhood and love for the outdoors. Working mainly with vulnerable groups, she has a compassion that is shared among many and is explored in her own work.

Sponsor: Dundee City Council.

Winning bid: £9,500.

Winning bidder: Gillies.

Where is he now? Making himself at home at Gillies in Broughty Ferry!

Why was he bought? Gillies said: "After the hugely successful Bucket Trail which attracted vast amounts of public engagement, as well as fantastic profile-raising of the ARCHIE Foundation, Gillies were very keen to extend the lifespan of the Trail within Broughty Ferry by purchasing an Oor Wullie for the firm. On hearing that all the money would be going to the ARCHIE Foundation, the Board of Directors agreed a £10,000 spend allowance for the cause, without specific instructions to which one in particular should be bought. Therefore, it was with great delight that on bid 2 of the evening, ARCHIE benefitted to the sum of £9,500, and Gillies gained a new member of staff: Oor Ideas. He sits proudly at the Brook Street entrance and welcomes customers daily, even managing to fill a collection can every couple of months from kind donations."

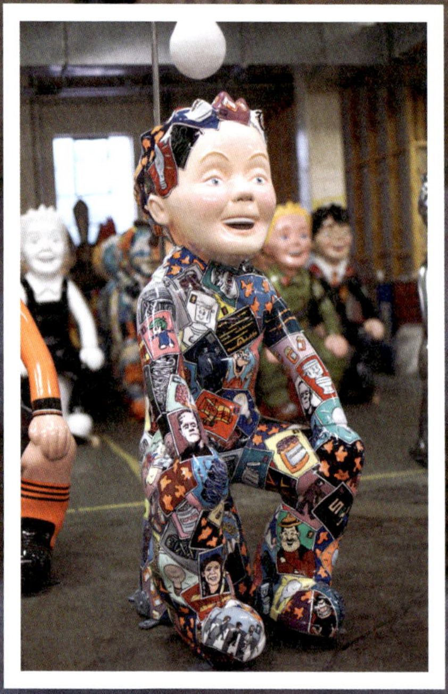

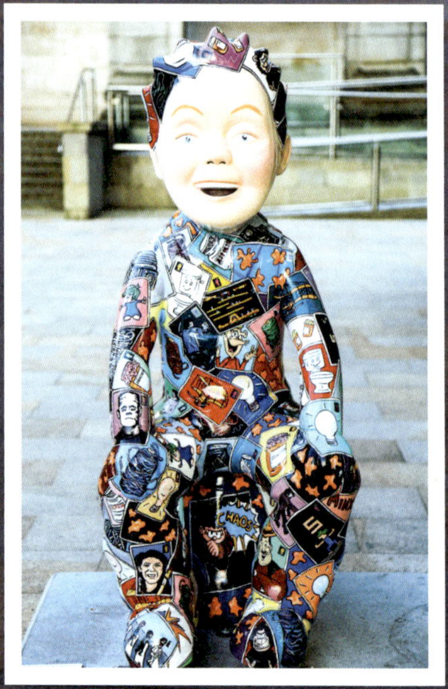

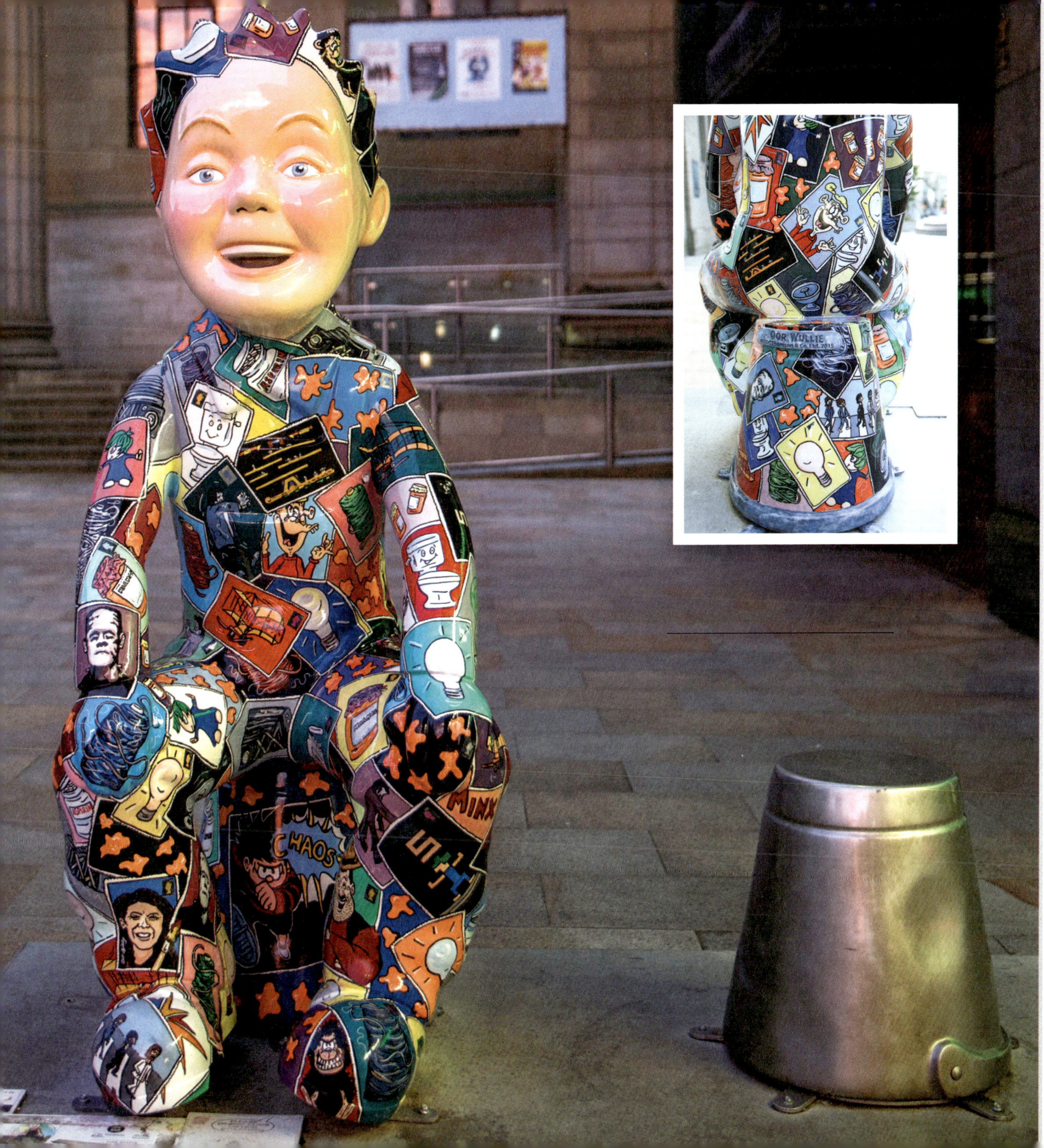
CHAOS
MINX
OOR WULLIE
©DC Thomson & Co. Ltd. 2015

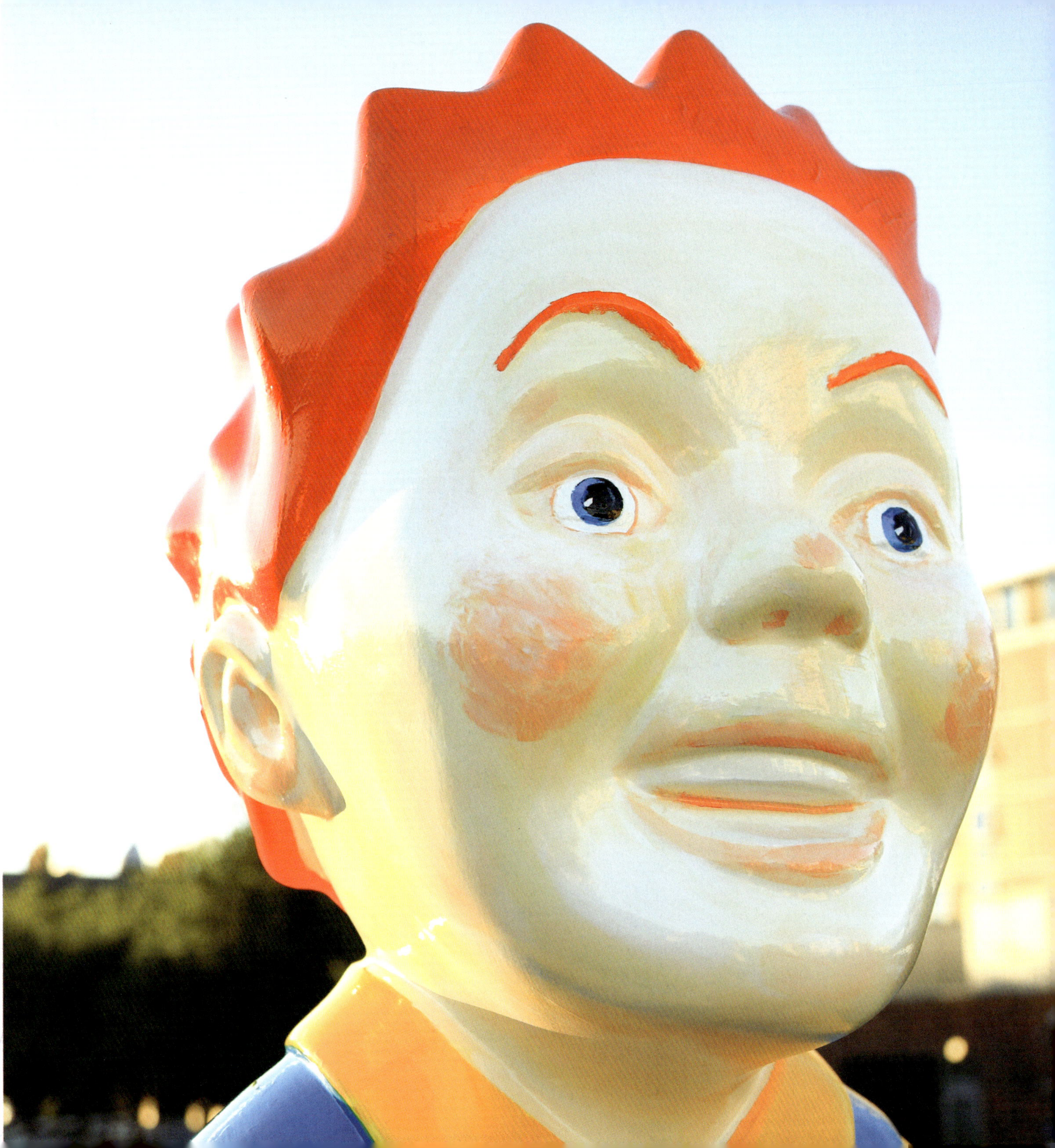

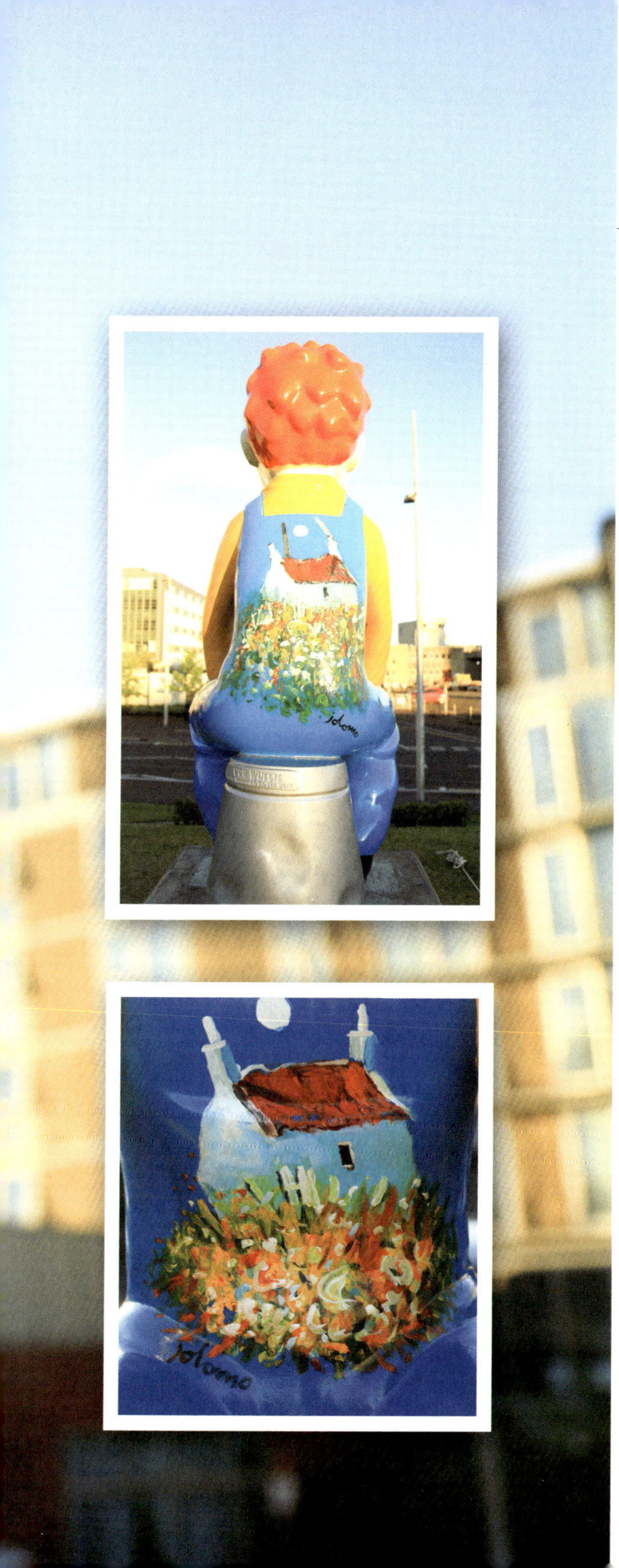

OOR JOLOMO

Location on the Bucket Trail: Apex City Quay Hotel & Spa.

Designed by: JOLOMO (John Lowrie Morrison, OBE).

About this sculpture: This Oor Wullie proudly sports Scottish artist, JOLOMO's well-known red roofed croft on his dungarees - a lovely connection with The Broons' But n' Ben which Oor Wullie loves to visit. Last New Year the Broons had a right big party there; one to be remembered!

JOLOMO is one of Scotland's most successful and best-loved contemporary artists. He has been a painter for over 50 years and his work has covered Argyll and the Hebrides, lighthouses, coastscapes, croftscapes and the people and the light of the Scottish west coast.

Sponsor: John Hunter Barrie (JoHuBa), artist and graphic designer.

Winning bid: £15,000.

Winning bidder: Norman Sutherland, Higher Ground Health & Care Planning.

Where is he now? Visiting lots of different places including Roxburghe House and the Apex City Quay Hotel & Spa!

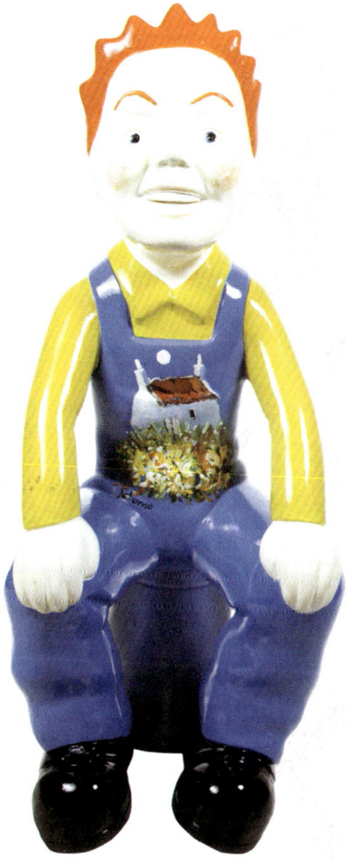

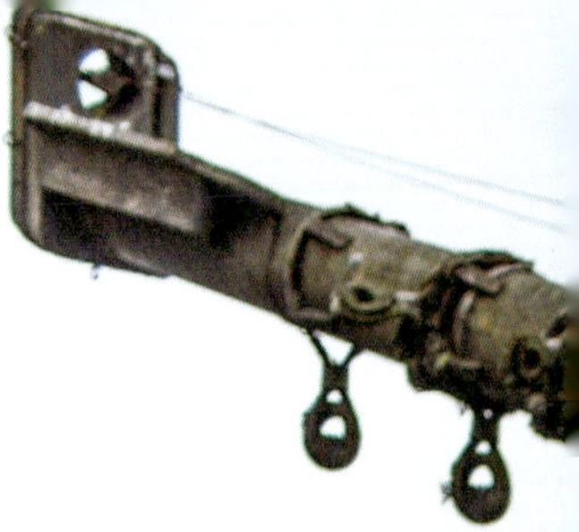

OOR RABBIE' THE BARD & THE BUCKET

Location on the Bucket Trail:
HM Frigate Unicorn.

Designed by: Susan McGill.

About this sculpture: This design brings together two Scottish icons: Oor Wullie and Robert Burns. Both inspirational in their use of the Scots language, together they make the perfect Scotsman with wit, ingenuity, humour, passion, romance, moosies and dungarees!

Susan is a Scottish ceramicist and designer. She trained at Duncan of Jordanstone College of Art and Design and currently works from her studio in Fife. Her ceramics are based on traditional shapes and are decorated with black and white patterns and words, inspired by Scottish songs, poems and sayings.

Sponsor: blue2, web design and development agency.

Winning bid: £22,000.

Winning bidder: Briggs Marine Contractors, Fife.

Where is he now? Greeting visitors in the reception area of Briggs Marine Contractors!

Why was he bought? Briggs Marine Contractors said: "The company donate each year to a number of local charities so it seemed like a great way to purchase and donate. Susan's Oor Wullie really was the top of our list. The ARCHIE Foundation is an incredibly worthwhile cause and so we were really happy to make that donation."

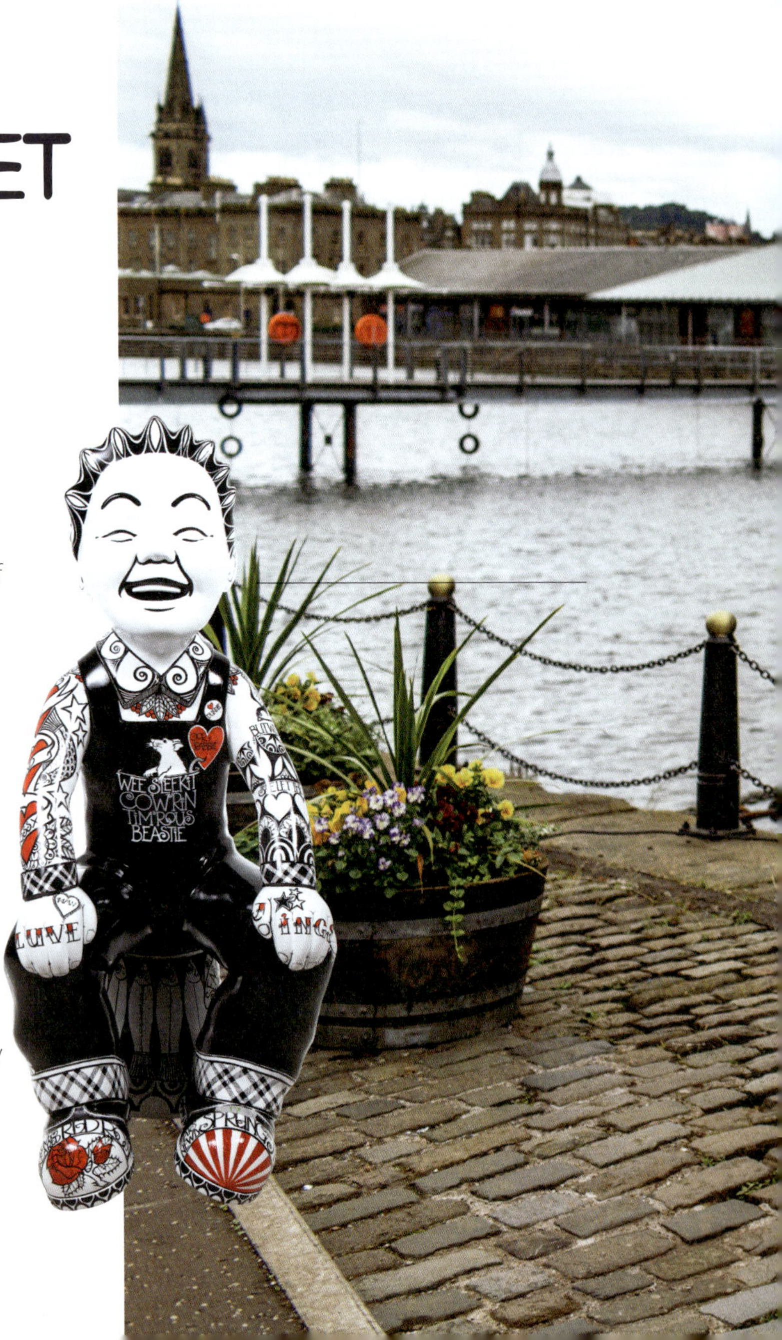

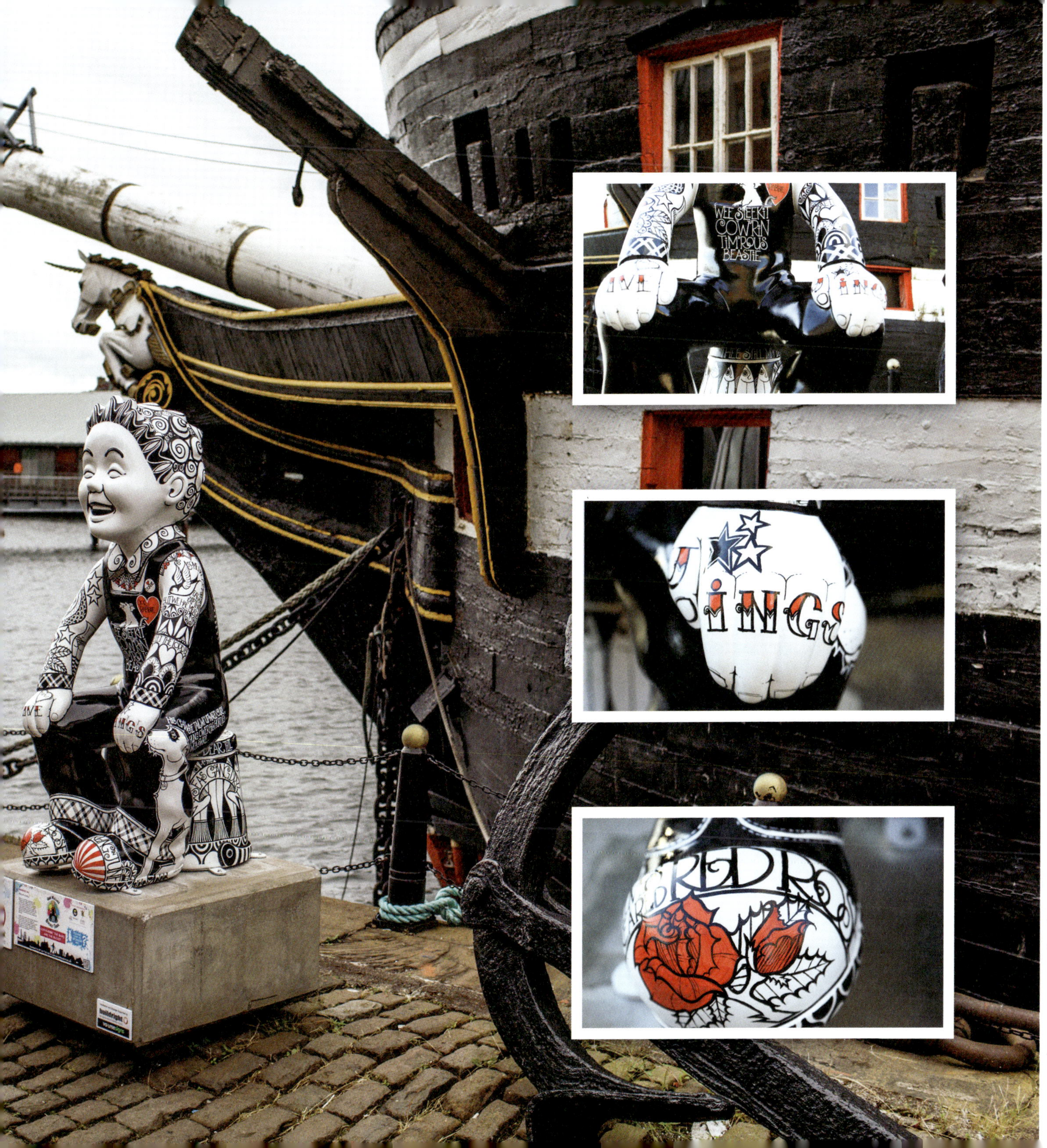
WEE SLEEKIT
COW'RIN
TIM'ROUS
BEASTIE
INGS

THE SCULPTURES No.18

OOR ORIGINAL

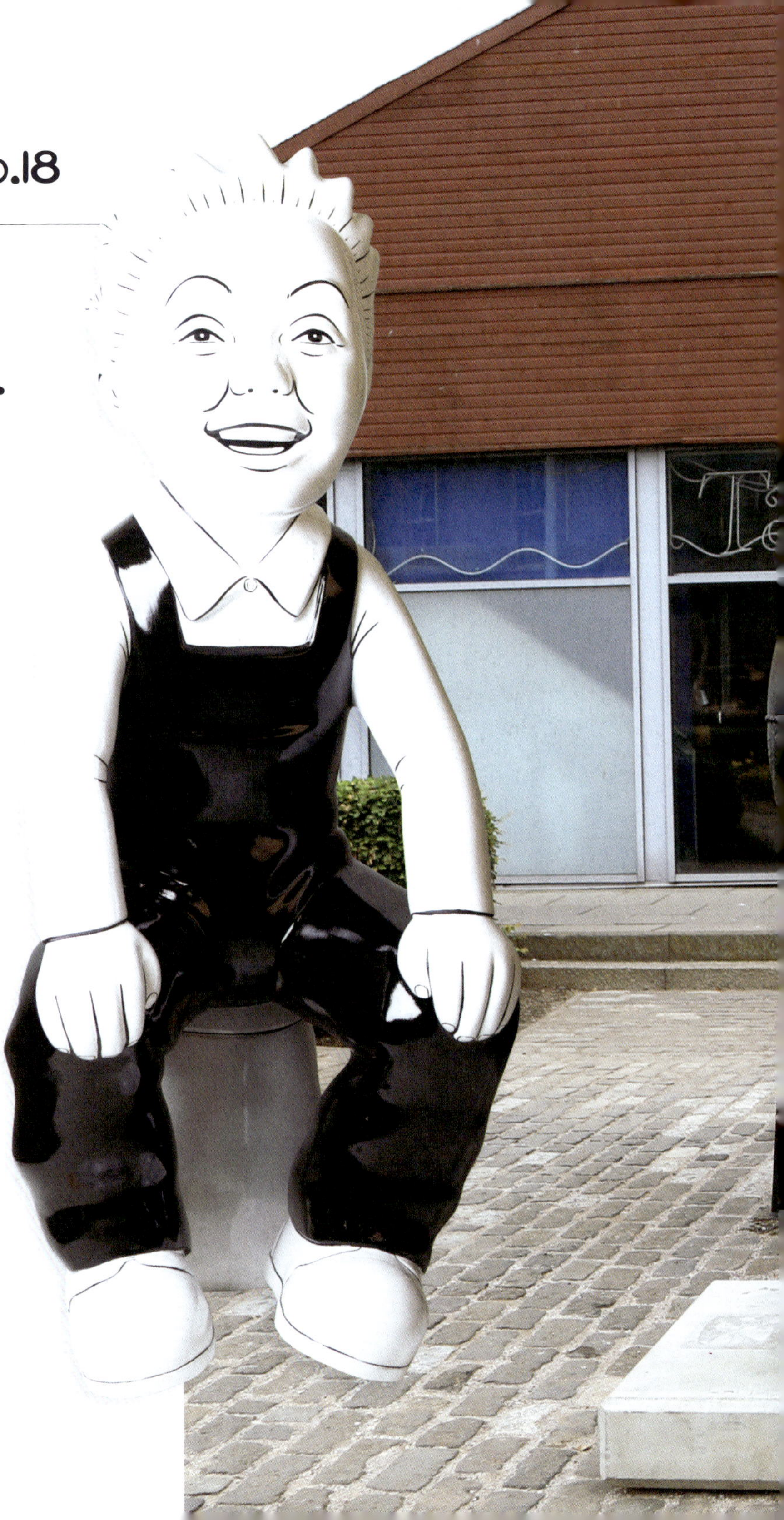

Location on the Bucket Trail:
City Quay Diving Bell.

Designed by: Peter Davidson.

About this sculpture: For this classic Oor Wullie, artist Peter Davidson teamed up with Suzanne Scott from WhimSicAL LusH who painted the sculpture. Peter added the finer details to Wullie's face and clothes to make him look like he just stepped off the page!

Peter has been a commercial artist for almost 40 years. His work has appeared in numerous publications, including national newspapers, sports magazines and books. He is also a painter and is the current illustrator of the iconic Broons and Oor Wullie comic strips for The Sunday Post.

Suzanne is an artist and illustrator based in Dundee, working under the name WhimSicAL LusH. She loves going on inky adventures and adores the little things in life. Whether she is creating creatures or castles, houses or robots, or turning people's ideas into reality, there is always a story on her drawing board.

Sponsor: Tradeprint.

Winning bid: £50,000.

Winning bidder: Sir Ian and Lady Helen Wood.

Where is he now? We dinae ken but we like to think he's still spreading joy and happiness!

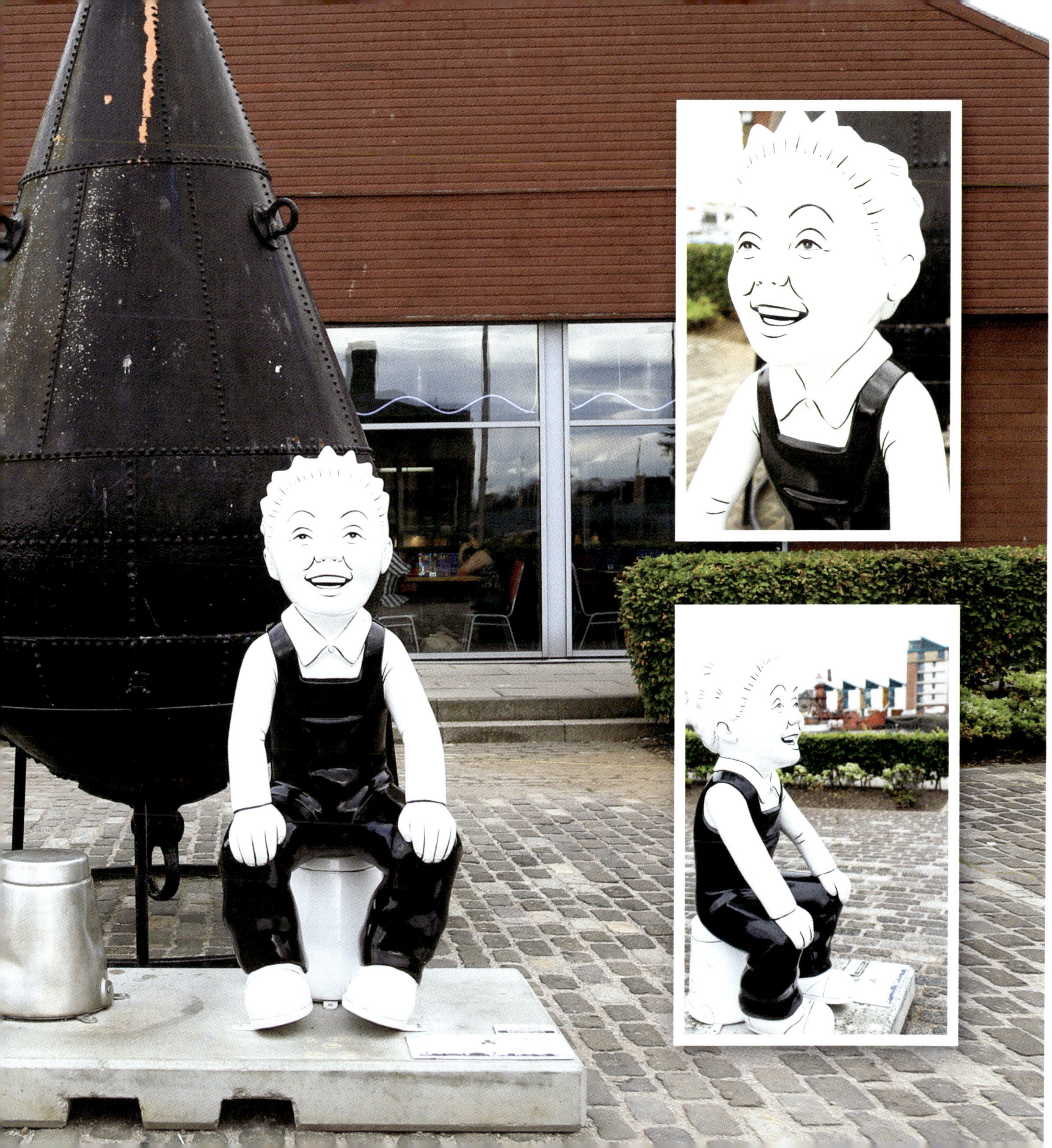

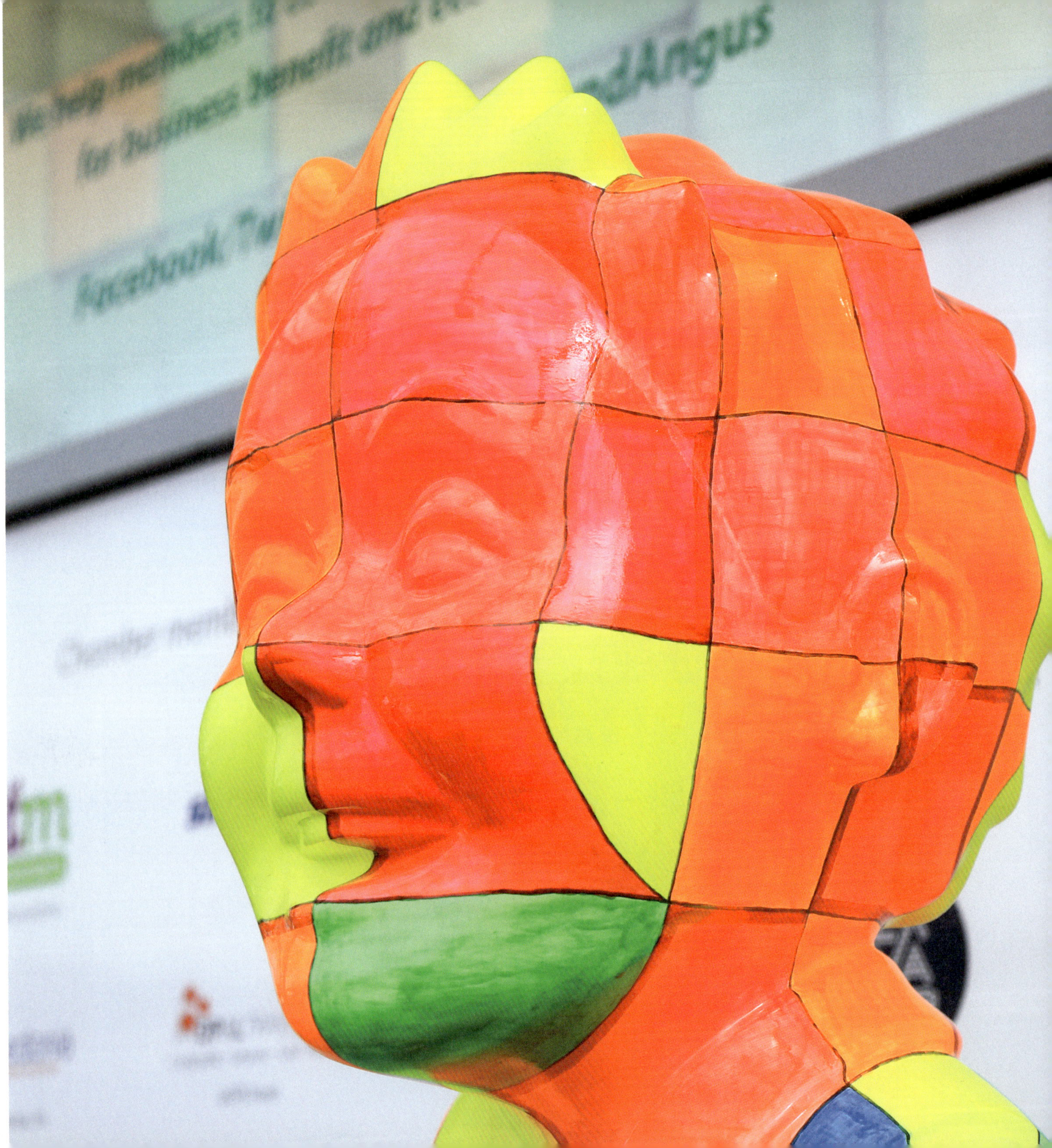

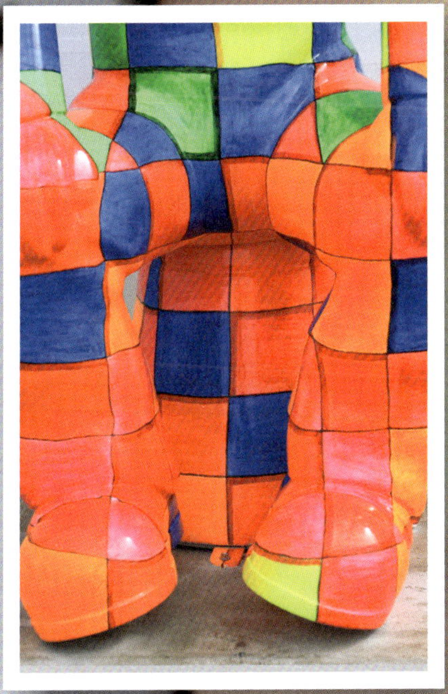

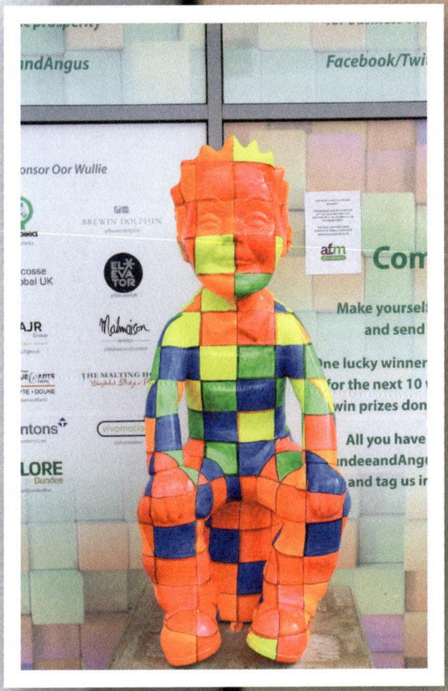

GLOW

Location on the Bucket Trail: City Quay, Dundee & Angus Chamber of Commerce.

Designed by: Tinto Architecture.

About this sculpture: Glow represents the Northern Lights and Dundee's connection with nature. It features glow-in-the-dark paint, allowing Wullie to come alive after dark. The larger than life pixel pattern links to Dundee's creative and media industries.

Tinto is an Aberdeen-based architecture company.

Sponsor: Dundee & Angus Chamber of Commerce.

Winning bid: £12,000.

Winning bidder: We dinae ken!

Where is he now? We dinae ken that either but he's probably glowing in front o' Paw's cosy coal fire!

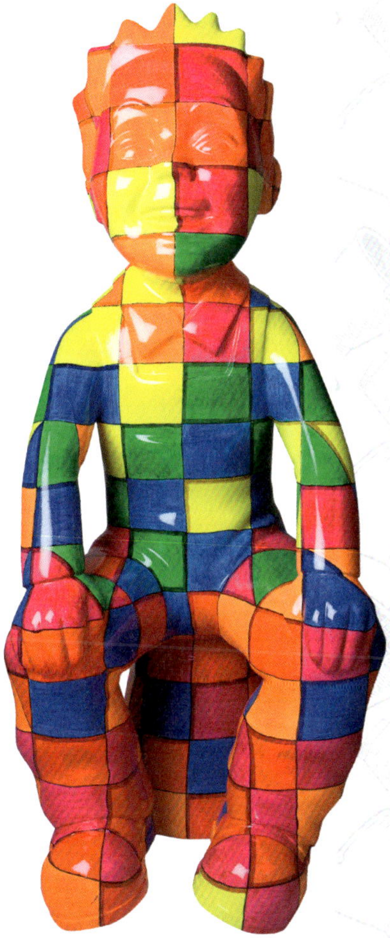

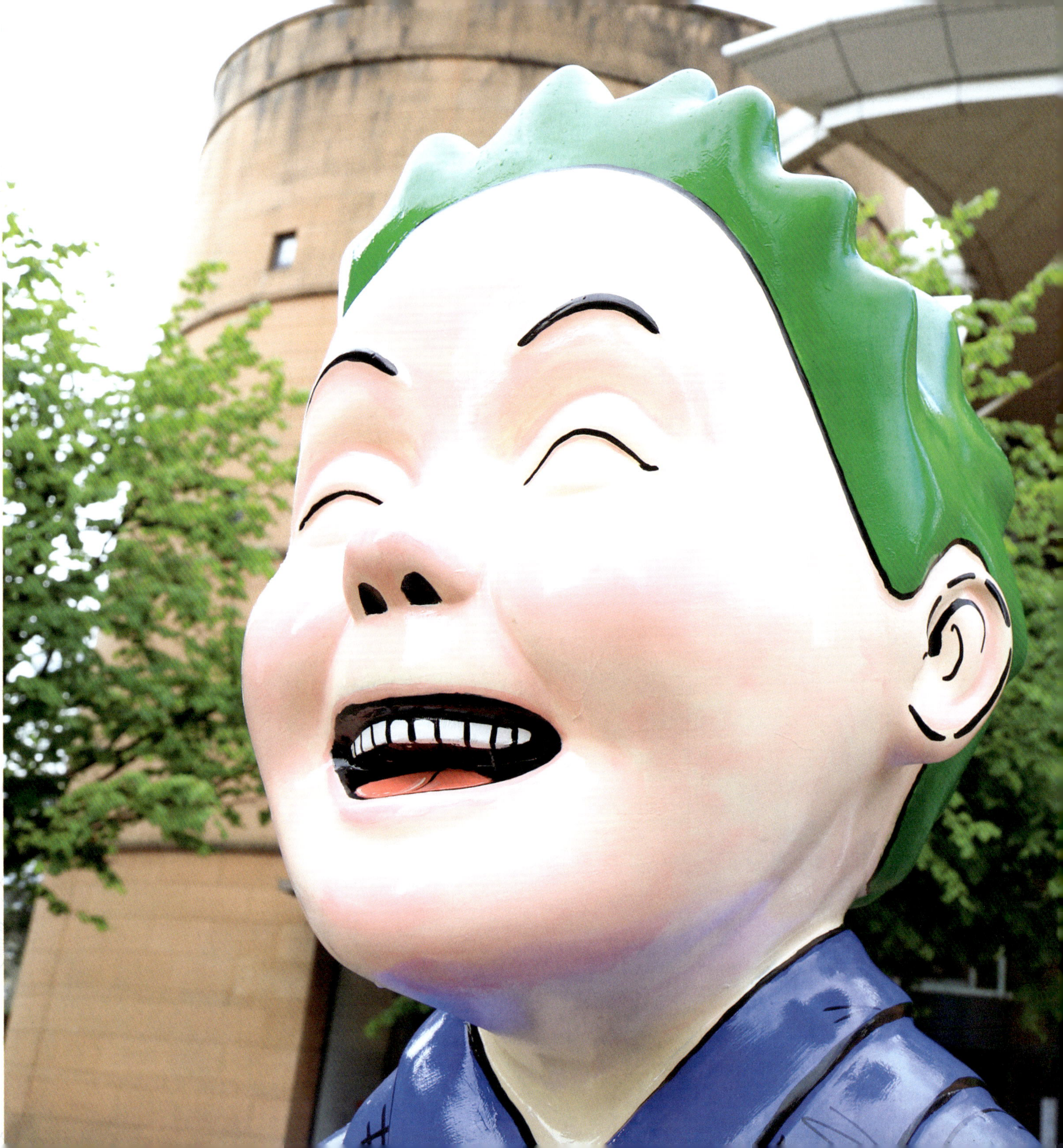

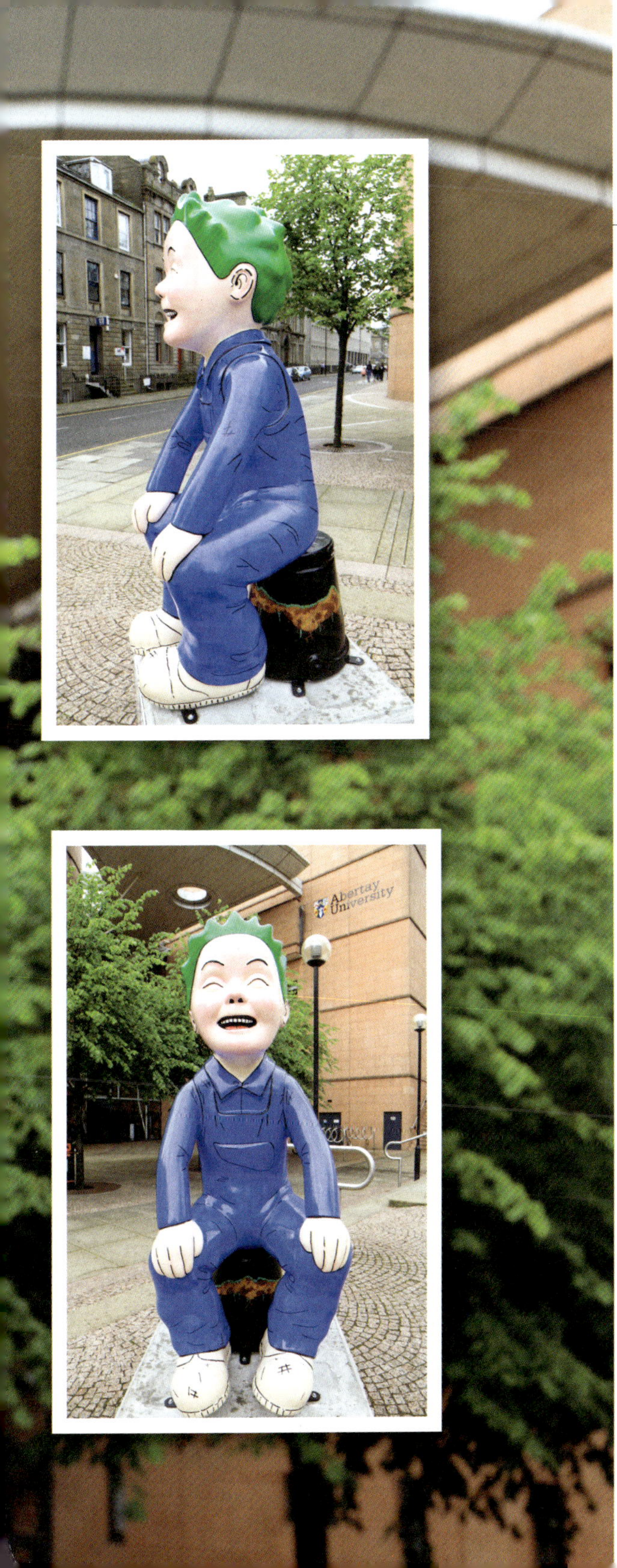

OOR LEMMING

Location on the Bucket Trail: Abertay University Library.

Designed by: Ryan Locke.

About this sculpture: Lemmings are a Dundee icon and are recognised by computer games players around the world. They have come to playfully represent Dundee's legacy and contribution to the computer games industry. With their blue gowns and fuzzy green hair, they remind us of the fun to be found in Dundee. This sculpture sees Wullie dressed up just like a Lemming and has been signed by Dave Jones, the creator of Lemmings and one of the pioneers of Dundee's position as a world-leader in the games industry.

Dave studied at Abertay University before setting up DMA design in 1987. Lemmings computer game was the first major international success for his company and was one of the first multi-million selling video games.

Ryan Locke is an artist and illustrator, currently lecturing in media design at Abertay University. With a self-confessed obsession of computer game art, all things design and collaborative practice, Ryan is always looking for innovative ways to bring creatives together and challenge the way they work.

Sponsor: Abertay University.

Winning bid: £10,000.

Winning bidder: Reagent Games.

Where is he now? We dinae ken but mibbe he's having a go at a computer game!

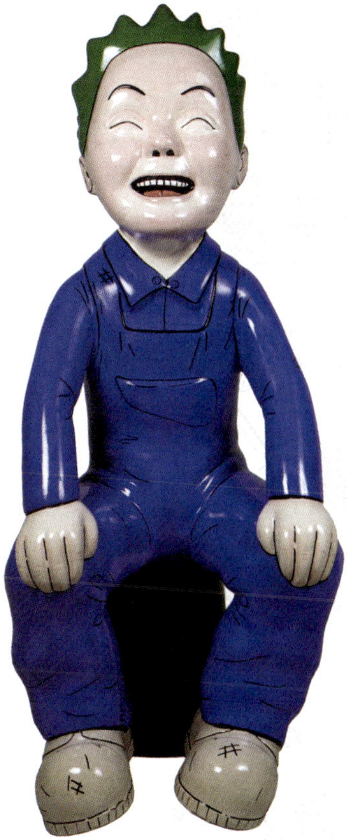

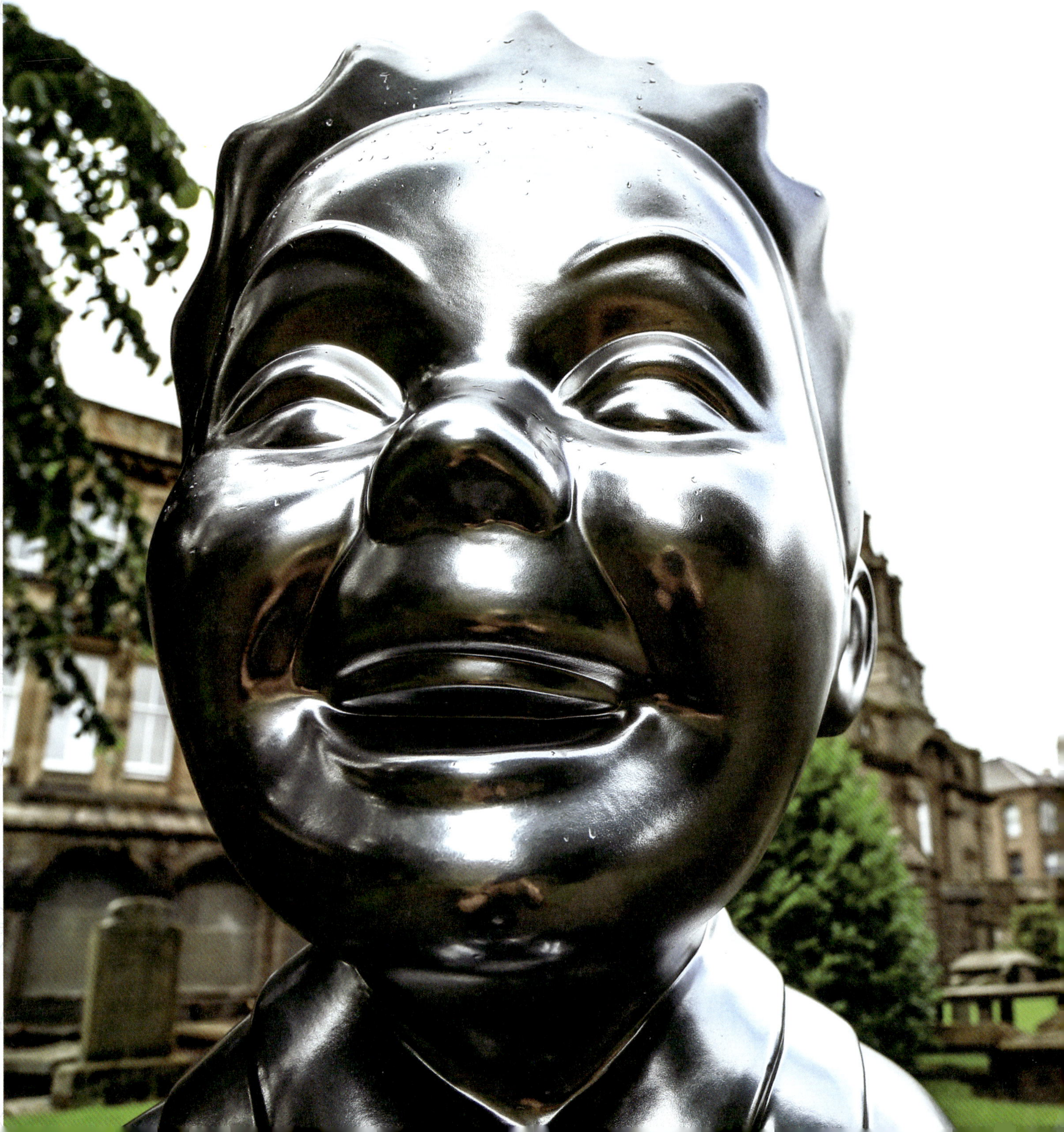

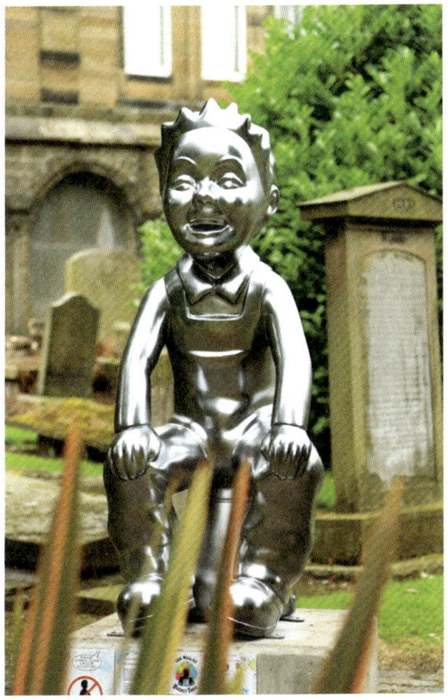

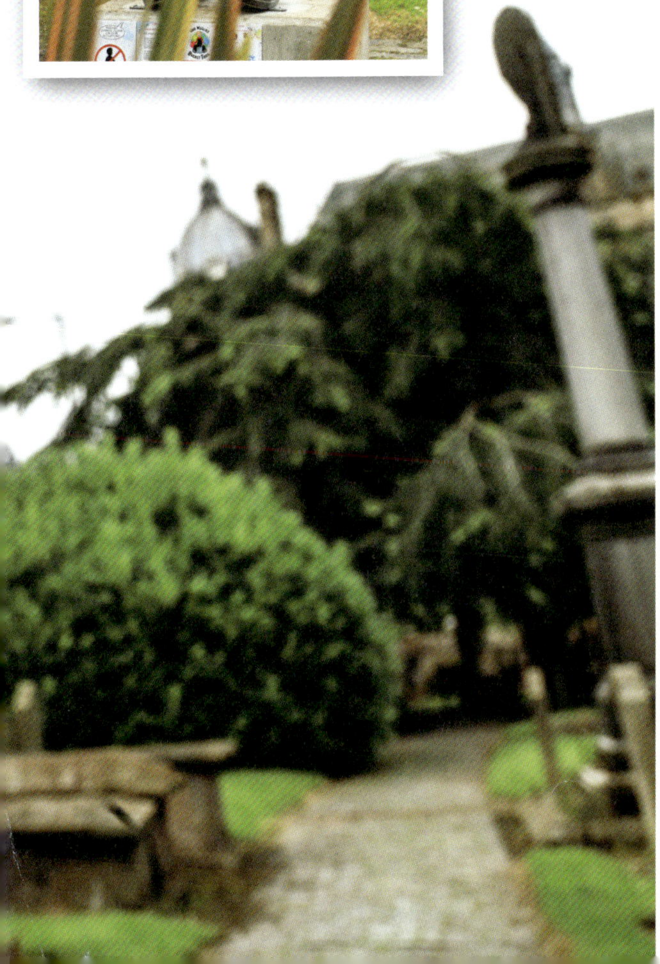

WHAR JI CUM FI?

Location on the Bucket Trail:
The Howff.

Designed by: Belinda Langlands.

About this sculpture: The idea behind this sculpture is to show a reflection of the people of Dundee – as they see themselves in Oor Wullie and as Oor Wullie sees himself in them and his surroundings.

Belinda is a pioneer of digital art education in Dundee and beyond. She has also worked as an artist on many varied projects, from illustration and graphic design to kinetic art and digital illustrations.

Sponsor: Tokheim.

Winning bid: £16,000.

Winning bidder: GA Engineering.

Where is he now? On display in Gordon's garden, putting smiles on the faces of the kids and parents from neighbouring schools!

Why was he bought? Gordon Deuchars, managing director, GA Engineering, said: "Being involved in the Oor Wullie event was a fantastic experience! Being born in the city I love the saying 'whar ji cum fi?" and have it used on many occasions! The sculpture has been used regularly to raise funds for charity and will always be available for future events."

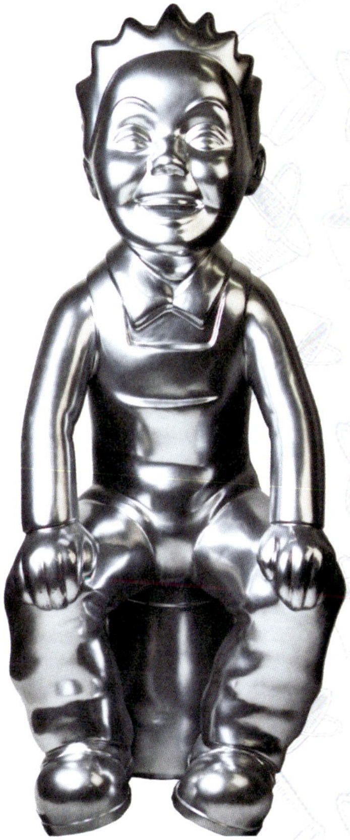

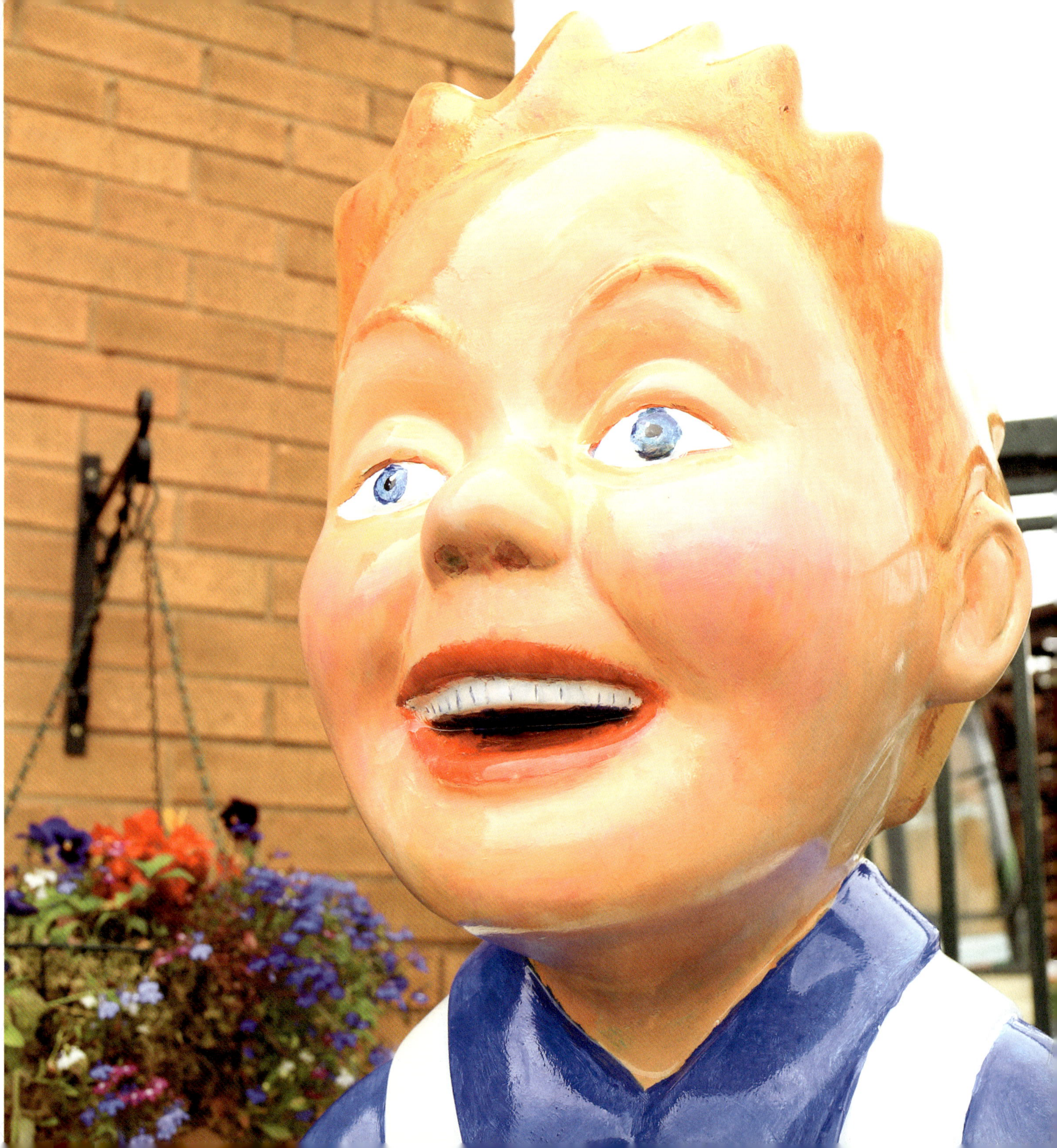

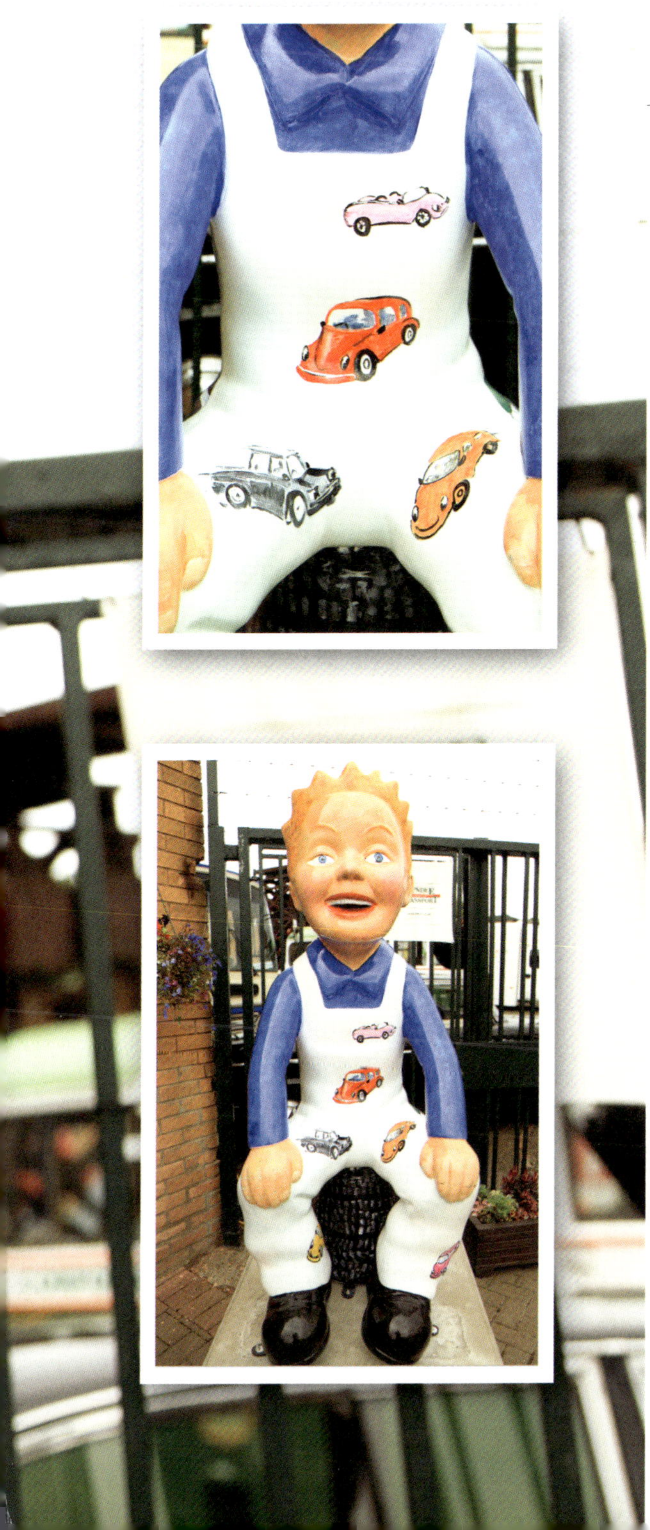

OOR WHEELIE

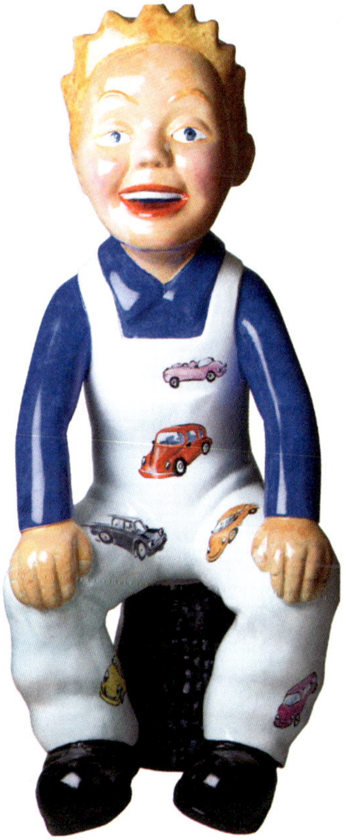

Location on the Bucket Trail: Dundee Museum of Transport.

Designed by: Howard Butterworth.

About this sculpture: The wee rascal's love of cars was the inspiration behind this sculpture! Lots of coloured cars and even Wullie's cartie make up the pattern on his dungarees.

Howard Butterworth is a renowned Scottish artist who is influenced by beautiful Scottish landscapes and whose works hang in many private collections, including those of HM Queen Elizabeth.

Sponsor: John Clark Motor Group.

Winning bid: £14,000.

Winning bidder: Gillian Bayford, local business woman.

Where is he now? We dinae ken but he's mibbe helpin' Paw Broon fix his auld banger o'a car!

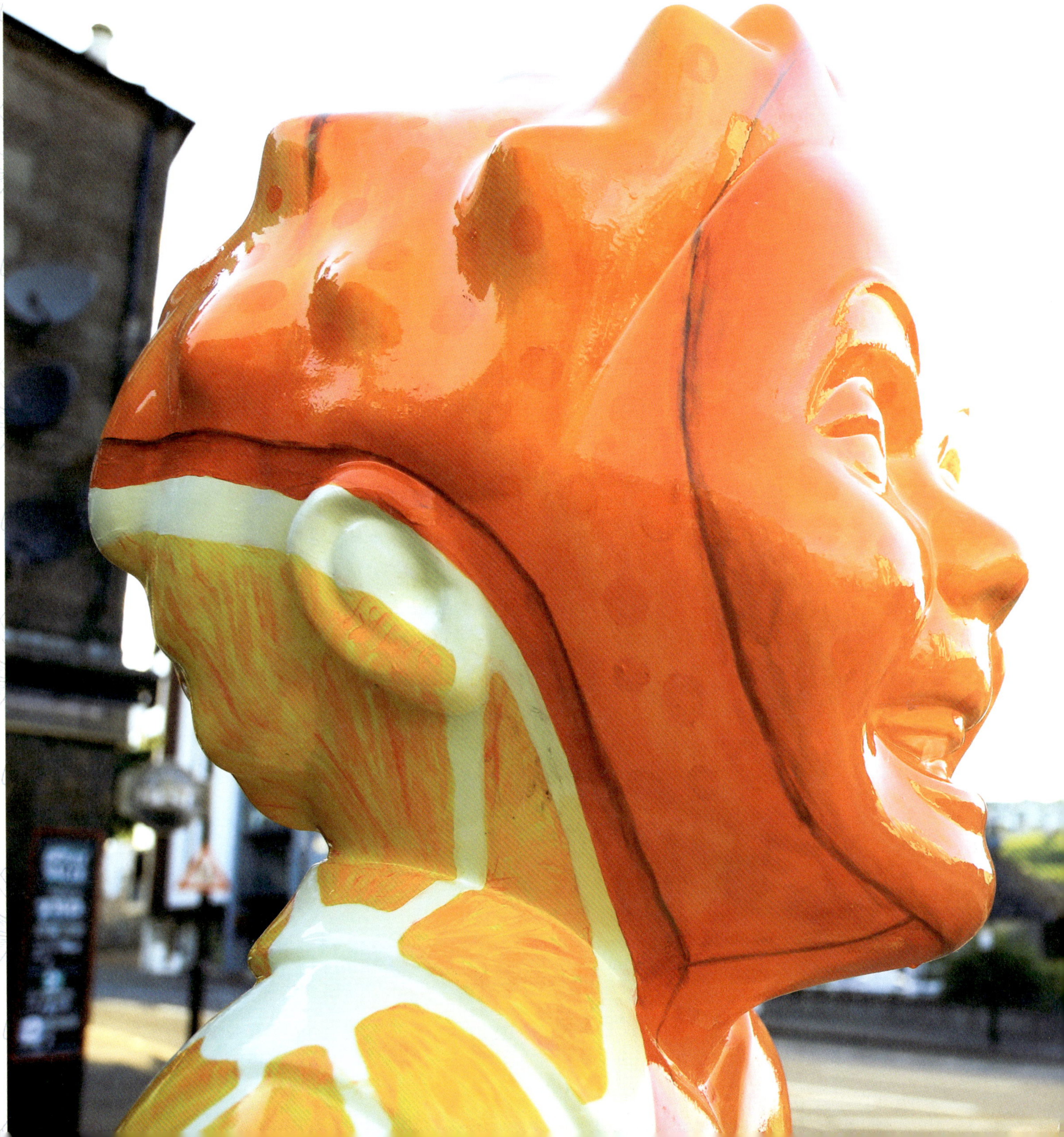

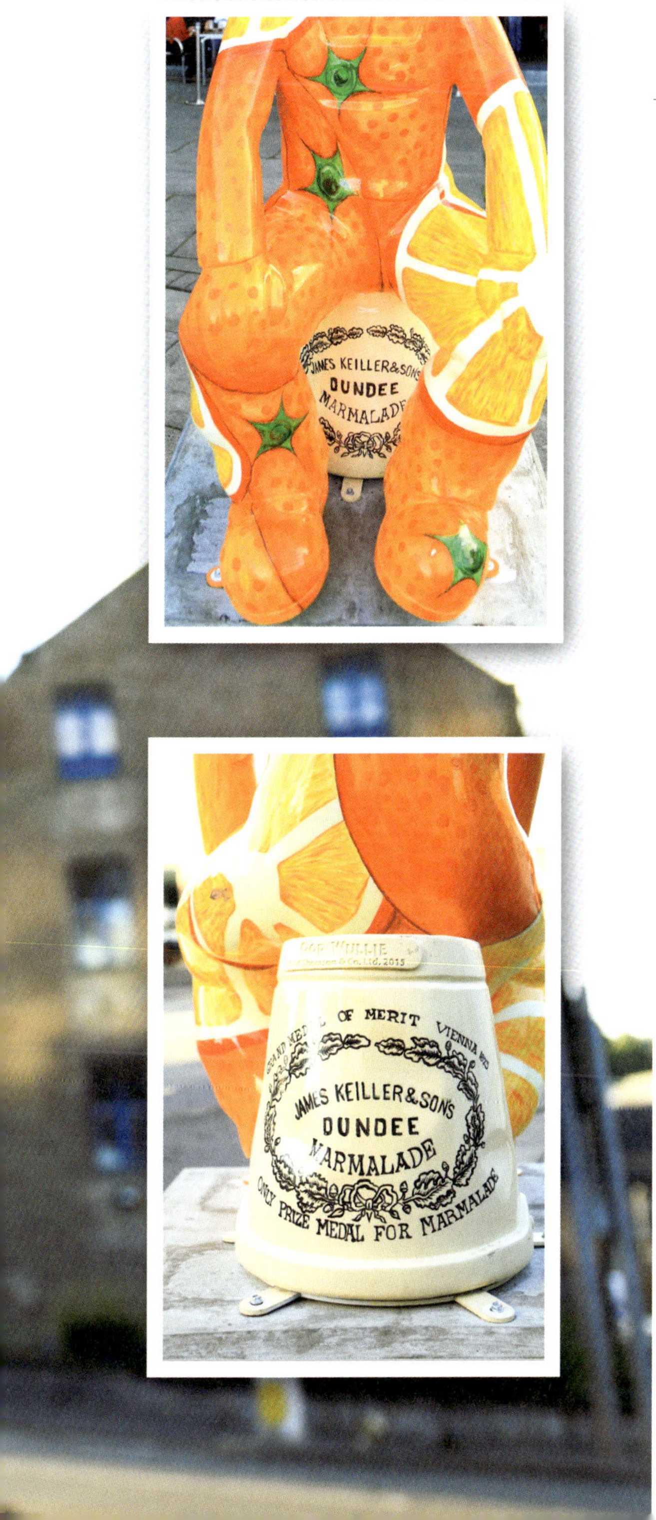

THICK CUT

Location on the Bucket Trail:
West Port, The Globe.

Designed by: Catherine J. Bell.

About this sculpture: Wullie's in a jam! He's covered in oranges waiting to be made into marmalade, preferably with shredded peel and his bucket has been replaced with a big Keiller's ceramic jar! Dundee was home to the first commercial brand of marmalade and today, ceramic jars from the iconic Keiller's brand can still be found all over the country.

Catherine graduated from Glasgow School of Art in 2007 and spent 4 years as a graduate assistant in the ceramics department before completing her Master's degree. She now tutors in ceramics in Hamilton, south Lanarkshire. Catherine's work is influenced by her story and a love of the unusual.

Sponsor: James Keiller Investments / The Greenroom Beauty Salon / Westport Luxury Serviced Apartments.

Winning bid: £14,000.

Winning bidder: Bruce Linton, James Keiller Estates.

Where is he now? Welcoming all the visitors at the Greenroom Beauty Salon!

Why was he bought? Zoe Linton, owner of The Greenroom, said: "Oor Wullie Thick Cut was a welcome addition for The Greenroom. He takes pride of place in our waiting area and enjoys a regular selfie with customers of all ages. He has been a real talking point."

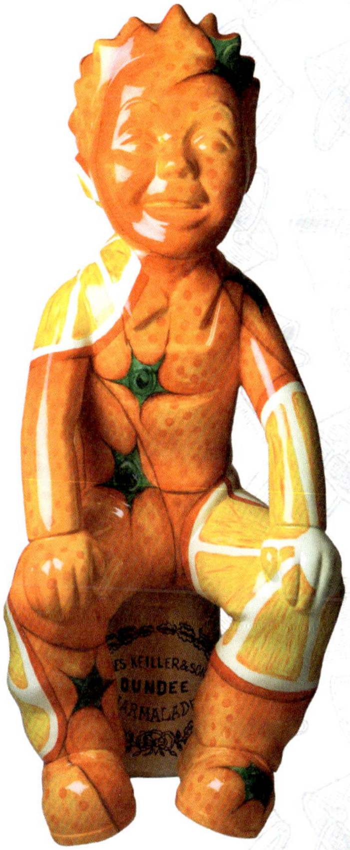

OOR INK

Location on the Bucket Trail:
Underneath the Tay Road Bridge.

Designed by: Abody at Dundee Design Festival.

About this sculpture: Hundreds of people contributed to Oor Ink under the guidance of curator, Kirsty Whitten. In the ink room at DC Thomson's former print works, West Ward Works, employees used to clean excess ink from the machines with rags and then throw the rags in the bin, bouncing them off the adjacent walls. This left ink marks on the walls as the rags dropped down into the bins!

At the first Dundee Design Festival in 2016, young and old were encouraged to pick up a rag or sponge covered in an ink of their choice and create their own marks on this Oor Wullie!

DC Thomson's famous annuals were once printed in West Ward Works. Oor Ink reflects the design heritage of the building, echoing the ink marks and stains that are still visible in the building today – all made by the very people who brought DC Thomson's characters into the homes of millions.

Sponsor: Dundee United Nations Educational, Scientific and Cultural Organisation (UNESCO) City of Design.

Winning bid: £6,500.

Winning bidder: Peter Vardy Car Store, Dundee.

Where is he now? Trying out some new wheels at the Peter Vardy Car Store!

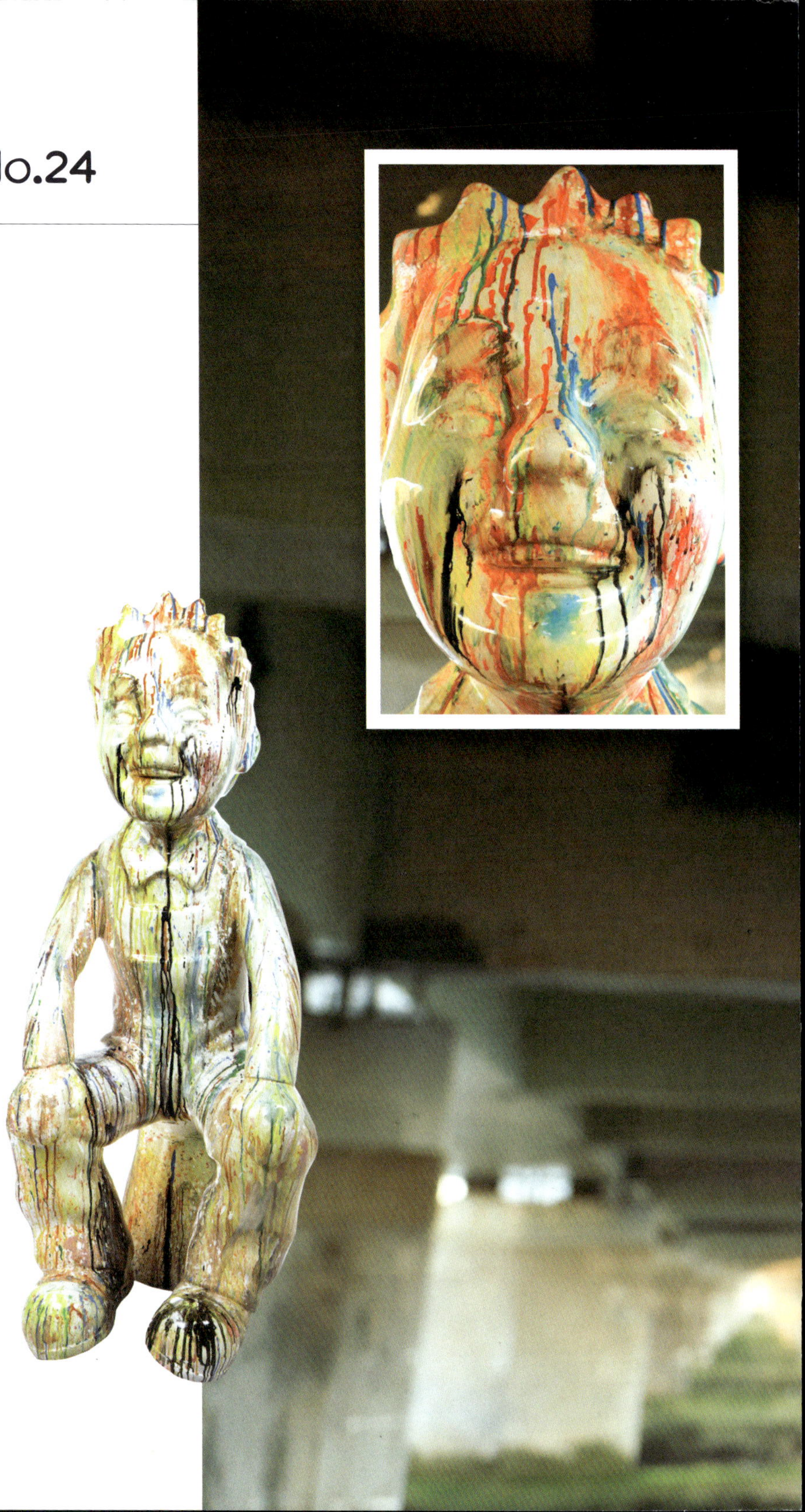

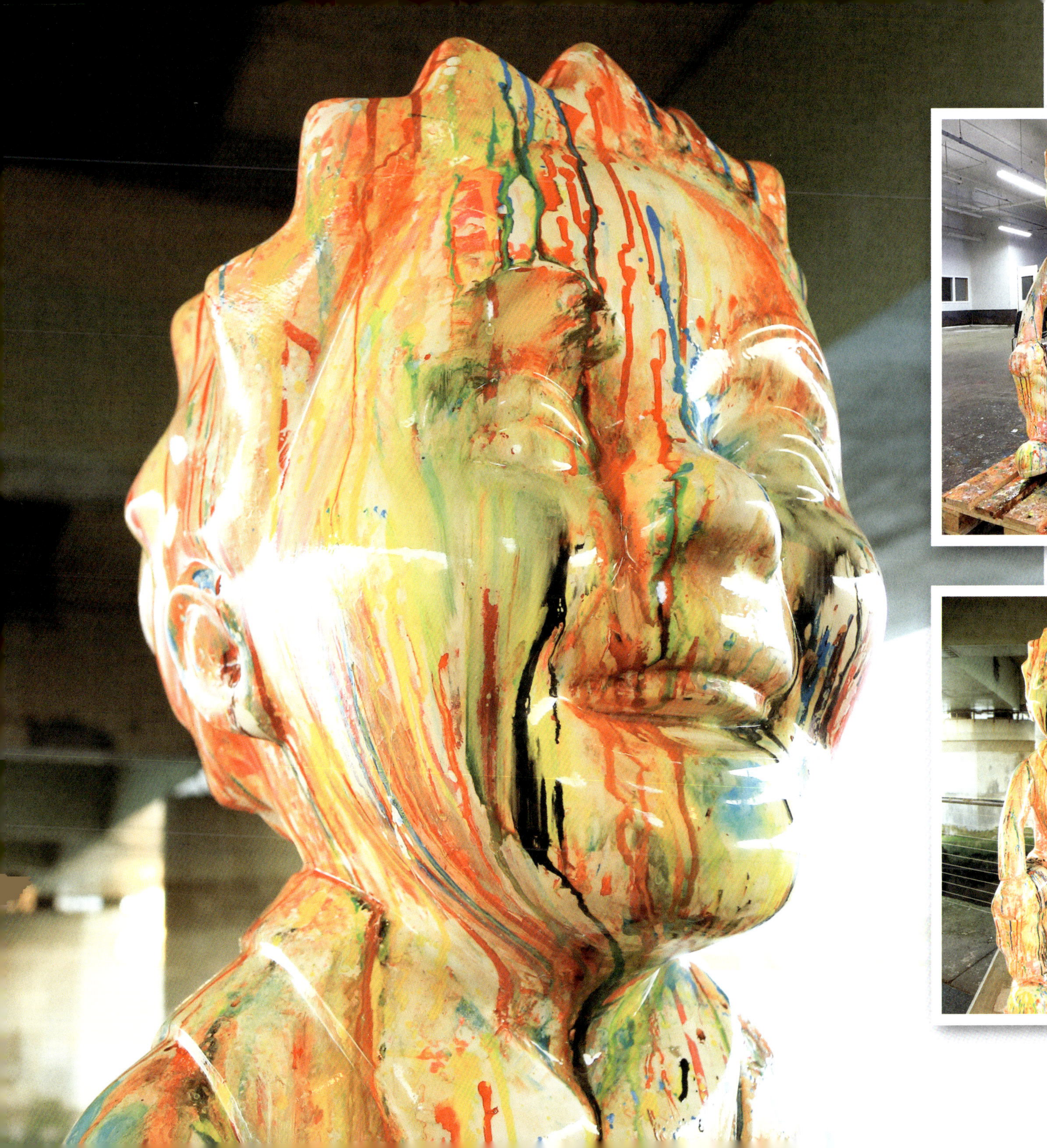
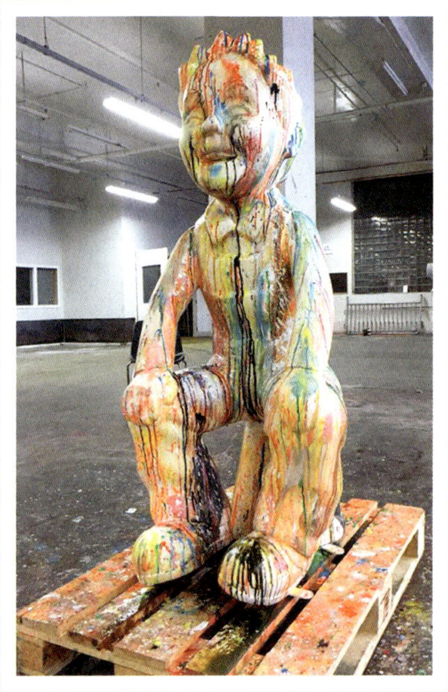
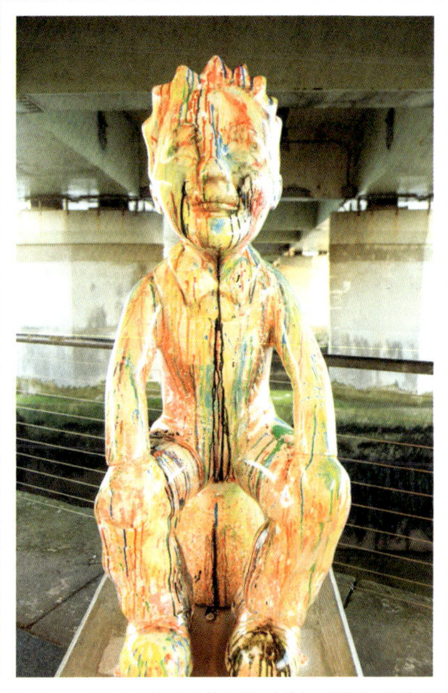

DISCOVERY BRIDGE

Location on the Bucket Trail: Marine Parade Walk / Chandlers Lane.

Designed by: Paul Walker.

About this sculpture: Connecting Dundee to Fife, Dundee's two bridges are an iconic part of the city. In 2016, the year of the Oor Wullie Bucket Trail, the Tay Road Bridge celebrated its 50th anniversary.

Paul was born in Fife but has never been a stranger to Dundee. He completed his degree in computer arts at Abertay University and owns a small business, Wonderful Wooden Wishes, creating handmade wooden wall art.

Sponsor: Al-Maktoum College of Higher Education.

Winning bid: £8,000.

Winning bidder: NCR, world-leader in consumer transaction technologies.

Where is he now? Keeping everyone right at the NCR premises, Dundee!

Why was he bought? Adam Crighton, VP and general manager, NCR said: "Our Research and Development Centre in Dundee is called the 'Discovery Building', so named because discovery in the context of research and development is all about learning, exploring and ultimately innovating to create new solutions that add value for our customers. Clearly our choice was also strongly influenced by our long-standing presence and relationship with the 'City of Discovery' - something we are extremely proud of as an organisation.

"The statue is proudly on display in our reception area and always creates a talking point with our customers."

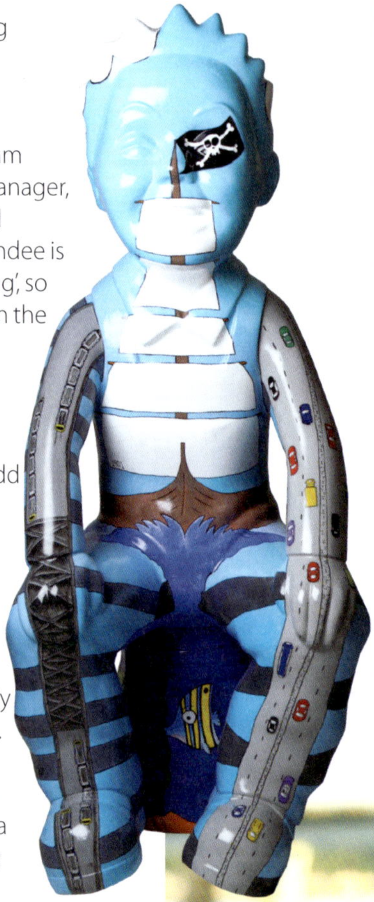

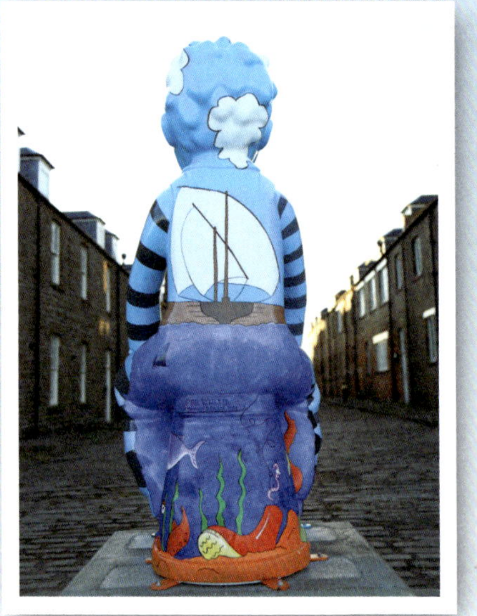

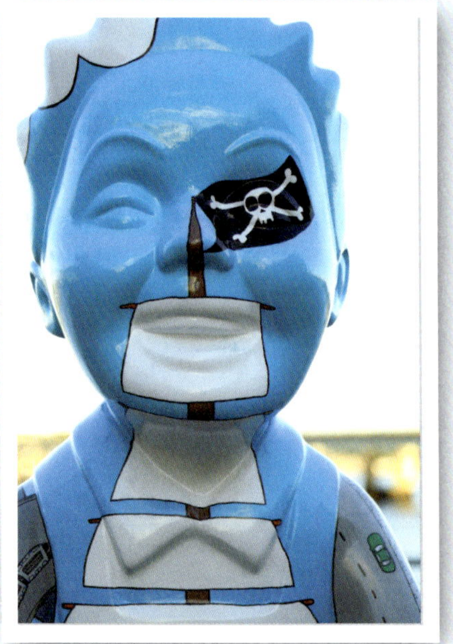

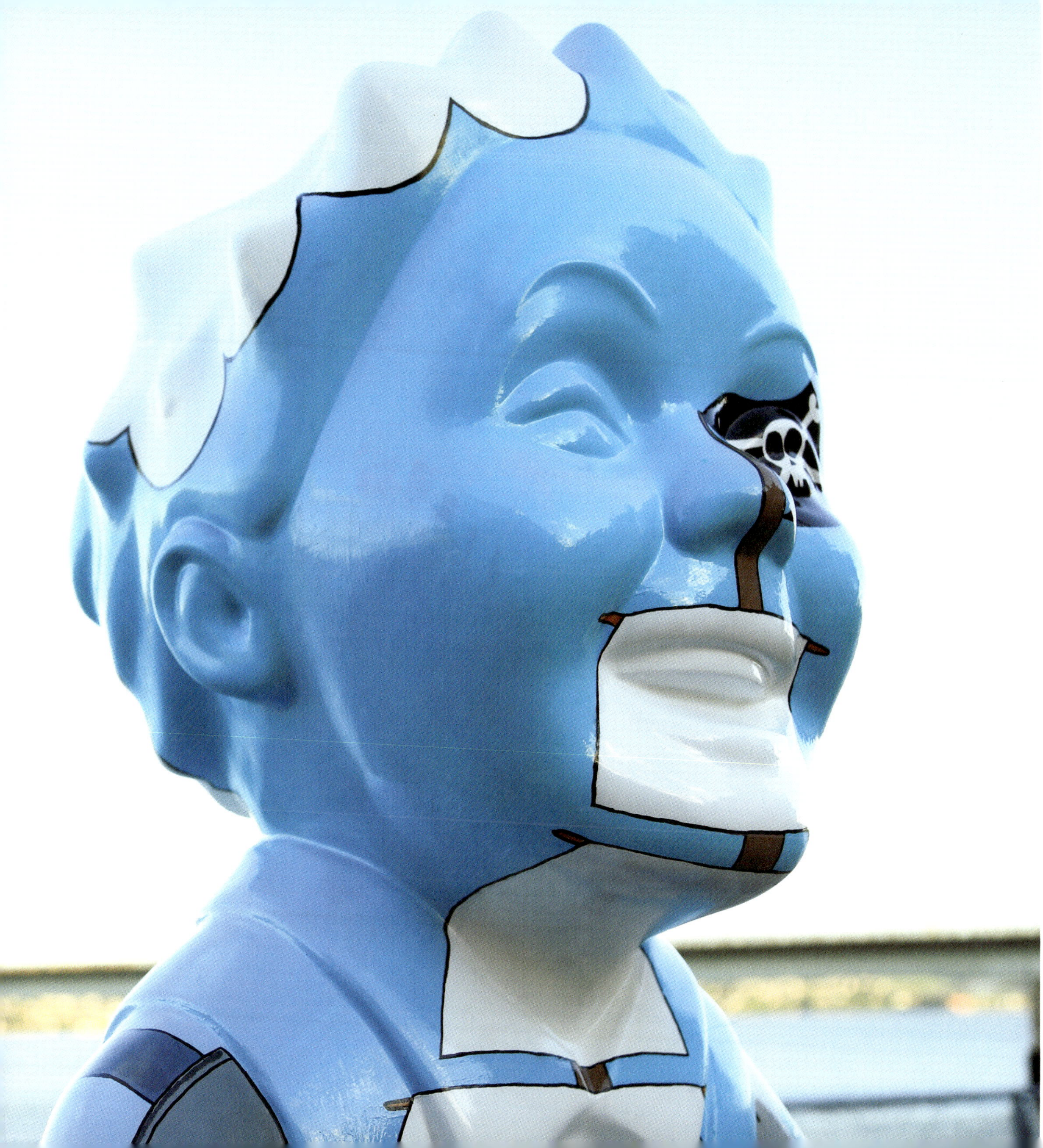

HIGH SCHOOL WULLIE

Location on the Bucket Trail: High School of Dundee.

Designed by: High School of Dundee pupils.

About this sculpture: Here's Wullie dressed up as a cheeky wee schoolboy who enjoyed creating some wonderful artwork at Dundee High School. He had such a great time that he didn't even notice all the paint flying around. His maw wisnae best pleased when she saw his clothes, mind you!

A group of pupils from Dundee High School designed and painted this arty Oor Wullie.

Sponsor: High School of Dundee.

Winning bid: £11,000.

Winning bidder: We dinae ken but the winning bidder kindly donated the sculpture back to the High School of Dundee!

Where is he now? Studying hard to become head boy at the High School of Dundee!

Whey was he bought? Dr John D Halliday, Rector, said: "We were thrilled to support the ARCHIE Foundation to raise money for Tayside Children's Hospital appeal. We commissioned and sponsored High School Wullie, which we hoped to bid for at the auction. Our pupils competed to produce a design. Alas we lost out to an unknown telephone bidder. The whole school community was down in the dumps at the disappearance of High School Wullie! But our sadness turned to joy when the successful bidder – a former pupil - decided to give it to the school on long-term loan!

"So, after a triumphant 'return to school' High School Wullie now occupies pride of place in and around the High School as a permanent reminder of such a wonderful experience".

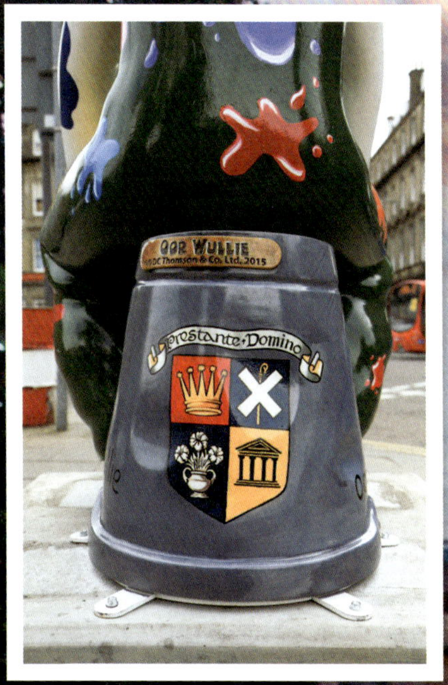

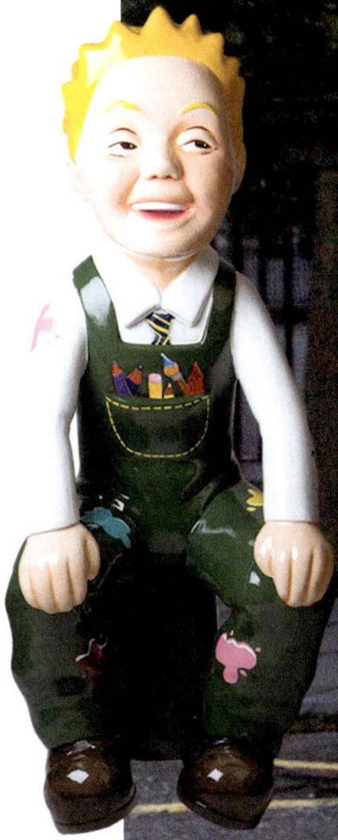

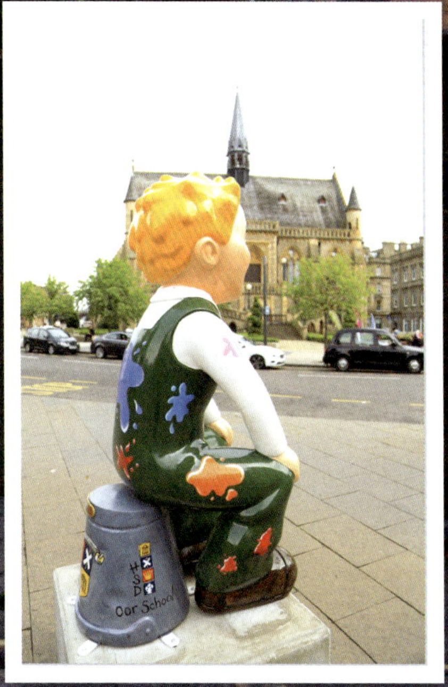

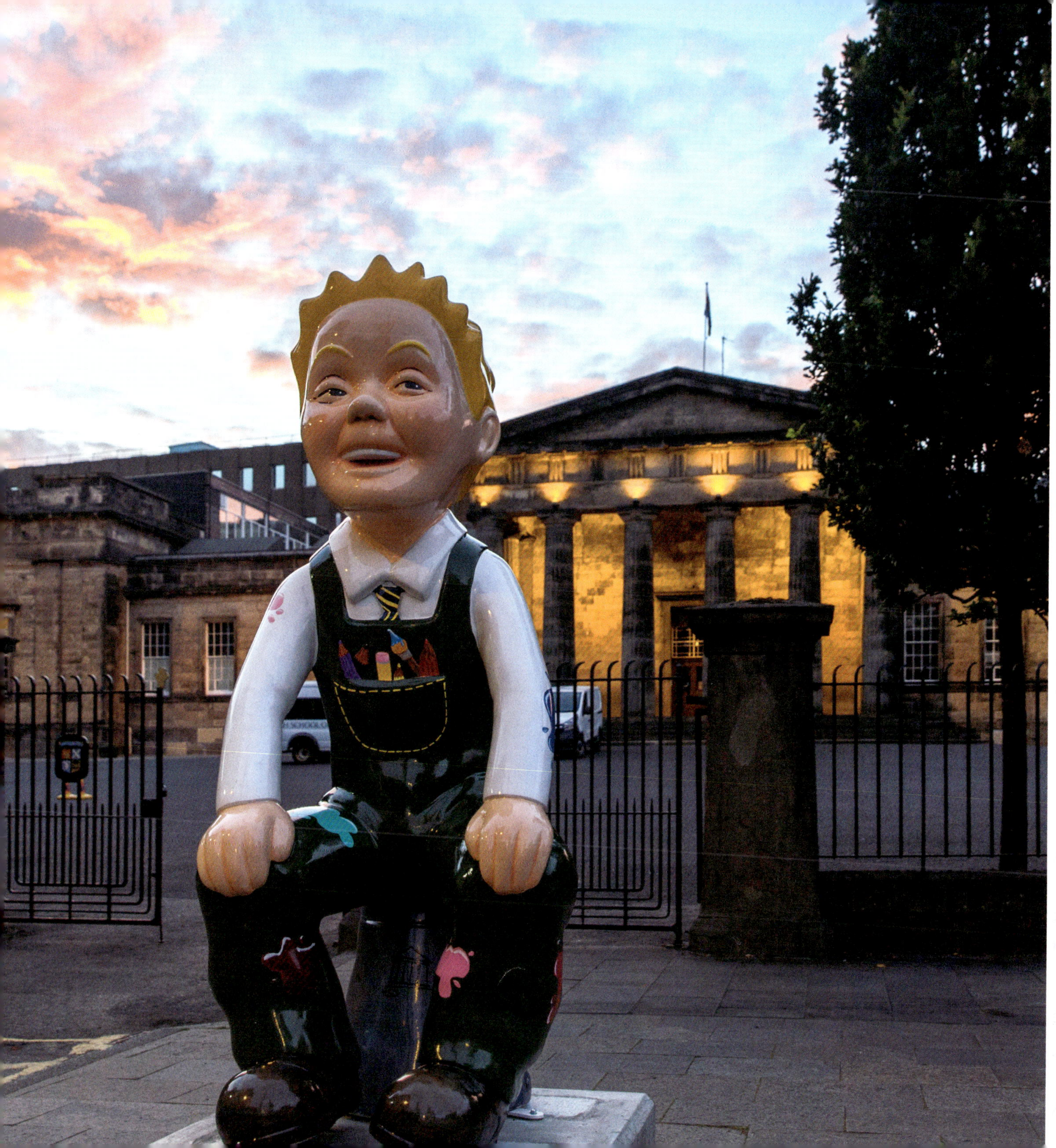

THE SCULPTURES No.27

YOU'RE A WIZARD WULLIE

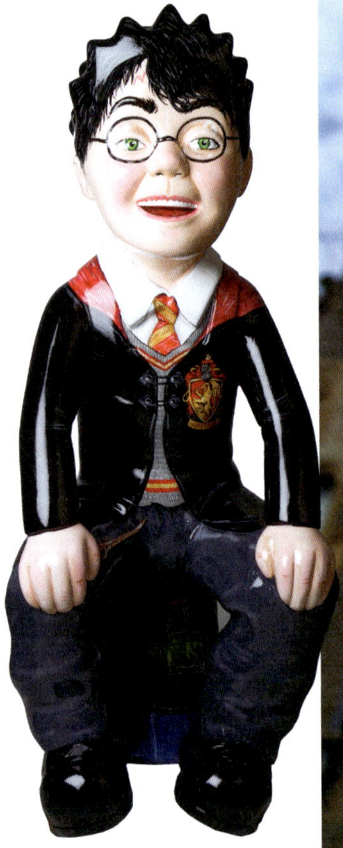

Location on the Bucket Trail: Morgan Academy.

Designed by: Lee O'Brien.

About this sculpture: This Harry Potter inspired Oor Wullie made a magical contribution to the Bucket Trail. Designer Lee O'Brien is a big fan of the Harry Potter books and films and has always wanted to recreate the boy wizard in art form.

Lee is a Liverpool-based art teacher and illustrator. When he's not marking books, he enjoys creating humorous artwork, largely inspired by his home city and the interesting characters who live there.

Sponsor: The ARCHIE Foundation.

Winning bid: £22,000.

Winning bidder: Lynda and Phil Mulholland.

Where is he now: We dinae ken but we hope he's still spreading joy and happiness!

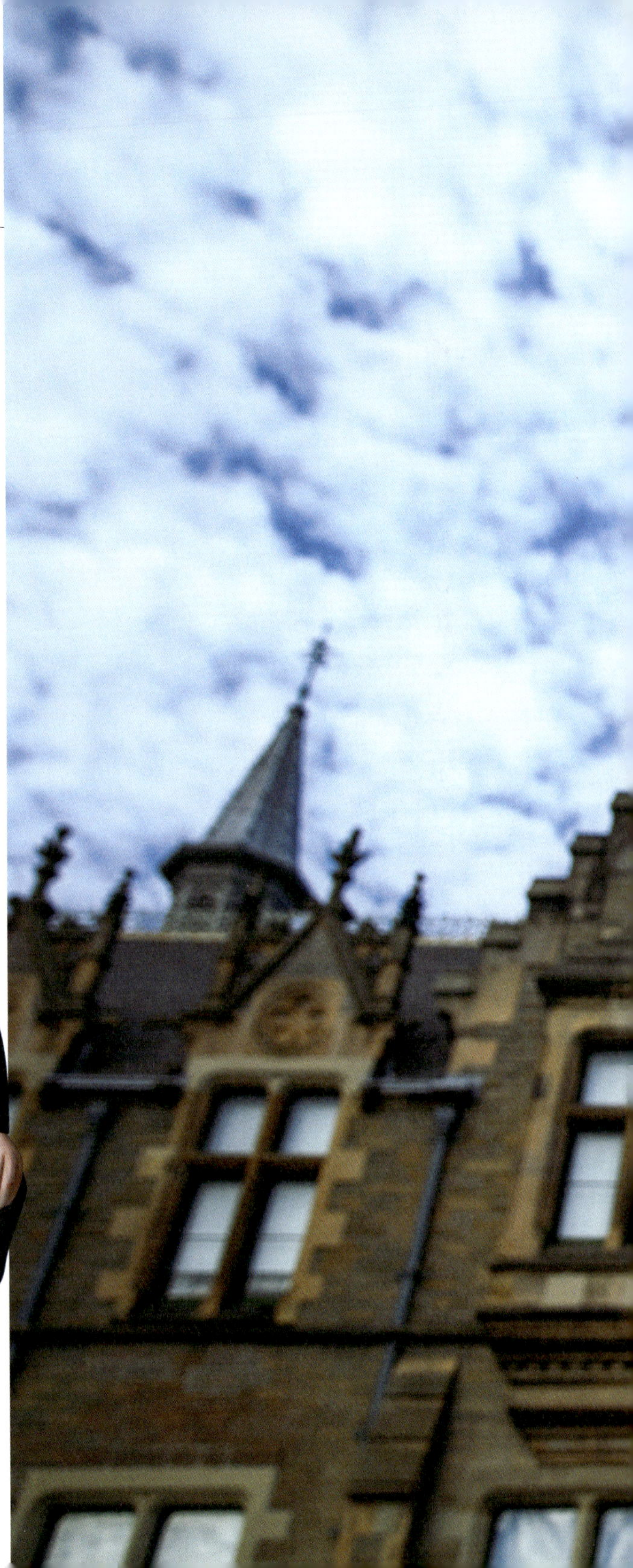

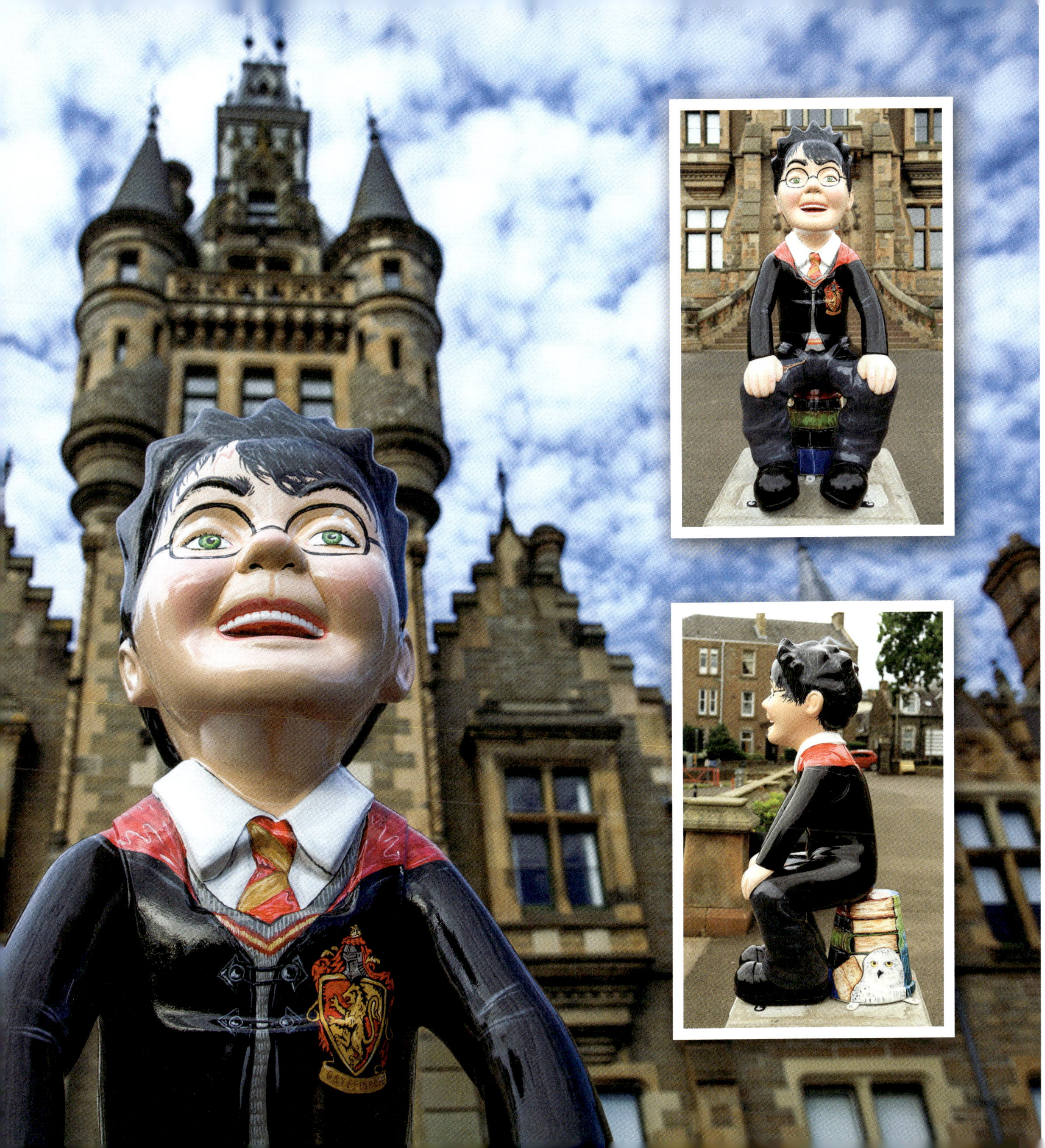

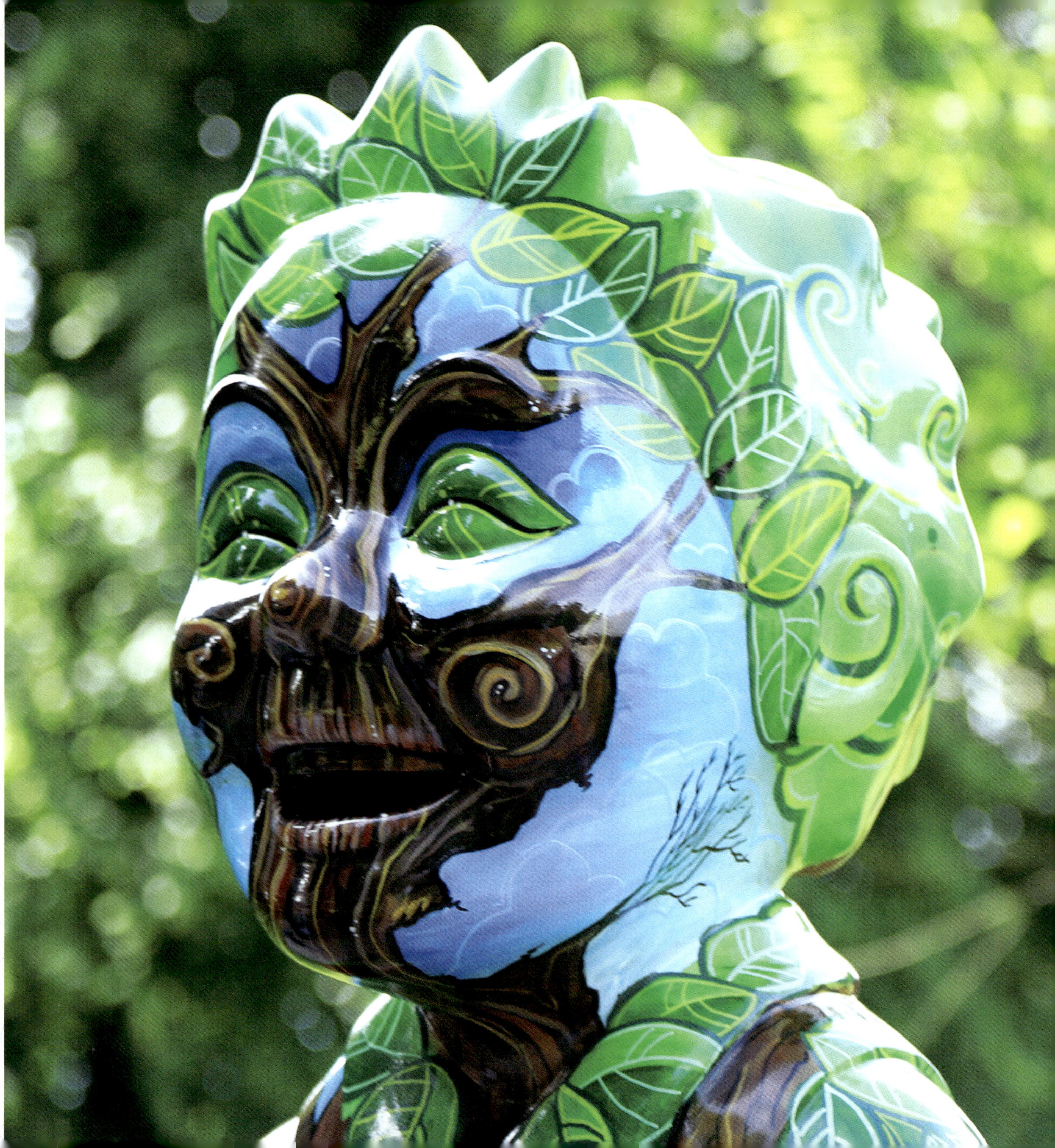

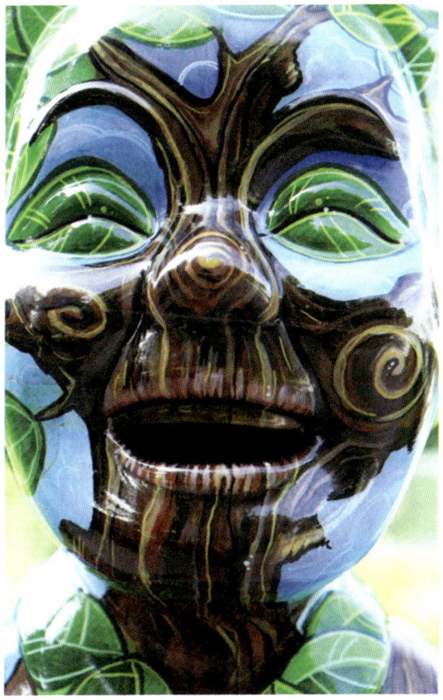

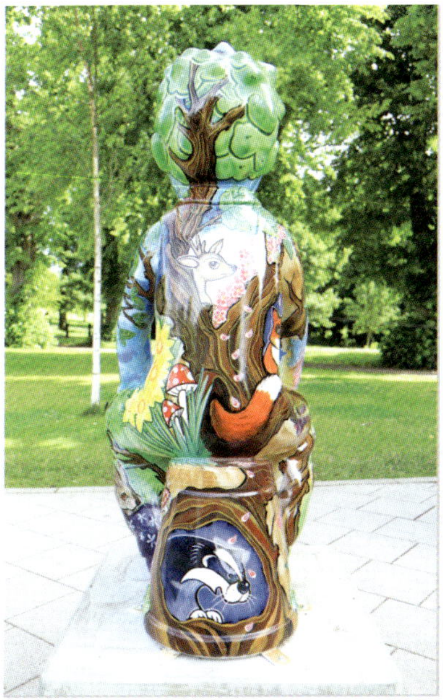

WOODLAND WULLIE

Location on the Bucket Trail: Camperdown Wildlife Park.

Designed by: Judi Milne.

About this sculpture: Designer Judi Milne has been a fan of Oor Wullie since she was wee and has always been entertained by his adventures (sometimes mis-adventures). She wanted Woodland Wullie to bring a bit of the countryside to the city – imagining Wullie hiding in the woods to escape the wrath of PC Murdoch!

Judi started her career as a graphic designer and then moved into freelance cartooning, landing the role of first female cartoonist at DC Thomson and working on The Dandy. Fifteen years ago, after completing an apprenticeship in tattooing, Judi set-up her now multi-award winning tattoo studio, Ink Minx in Montrose.

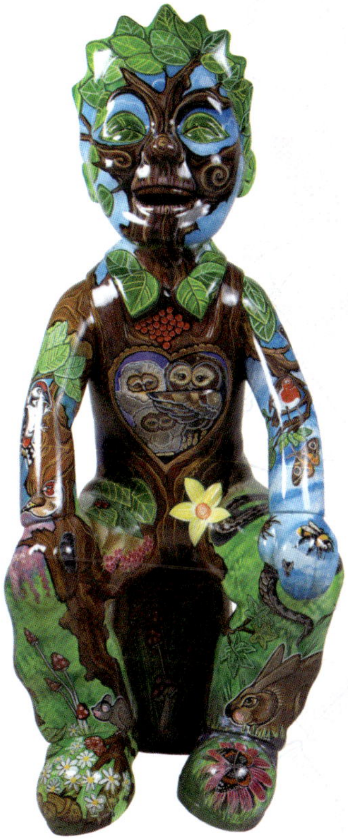

Sponsor: ARR Craib / Jarvie Plant Hire / Harry Lawson.

Winning bid: £16,000.

Winning bidder: Gillian Bayford, local businesswoman.

Where is he now? Spreading joy and happiness in Carnoustie!

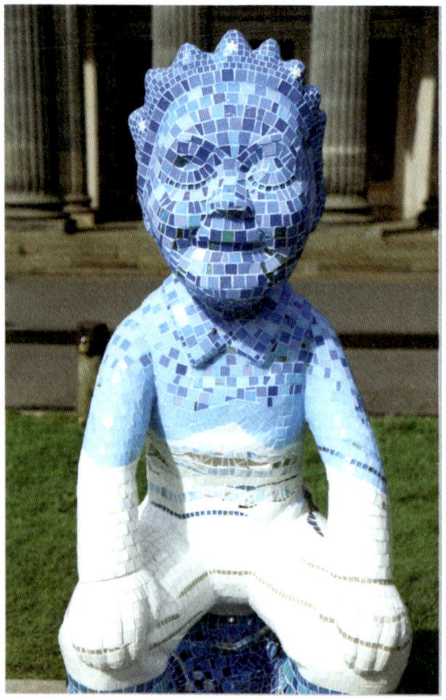

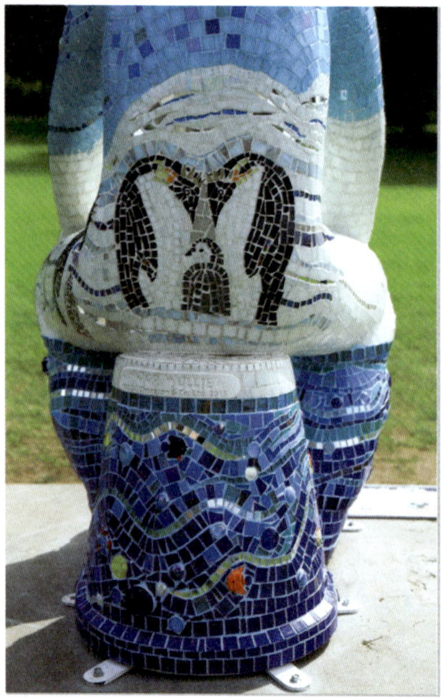

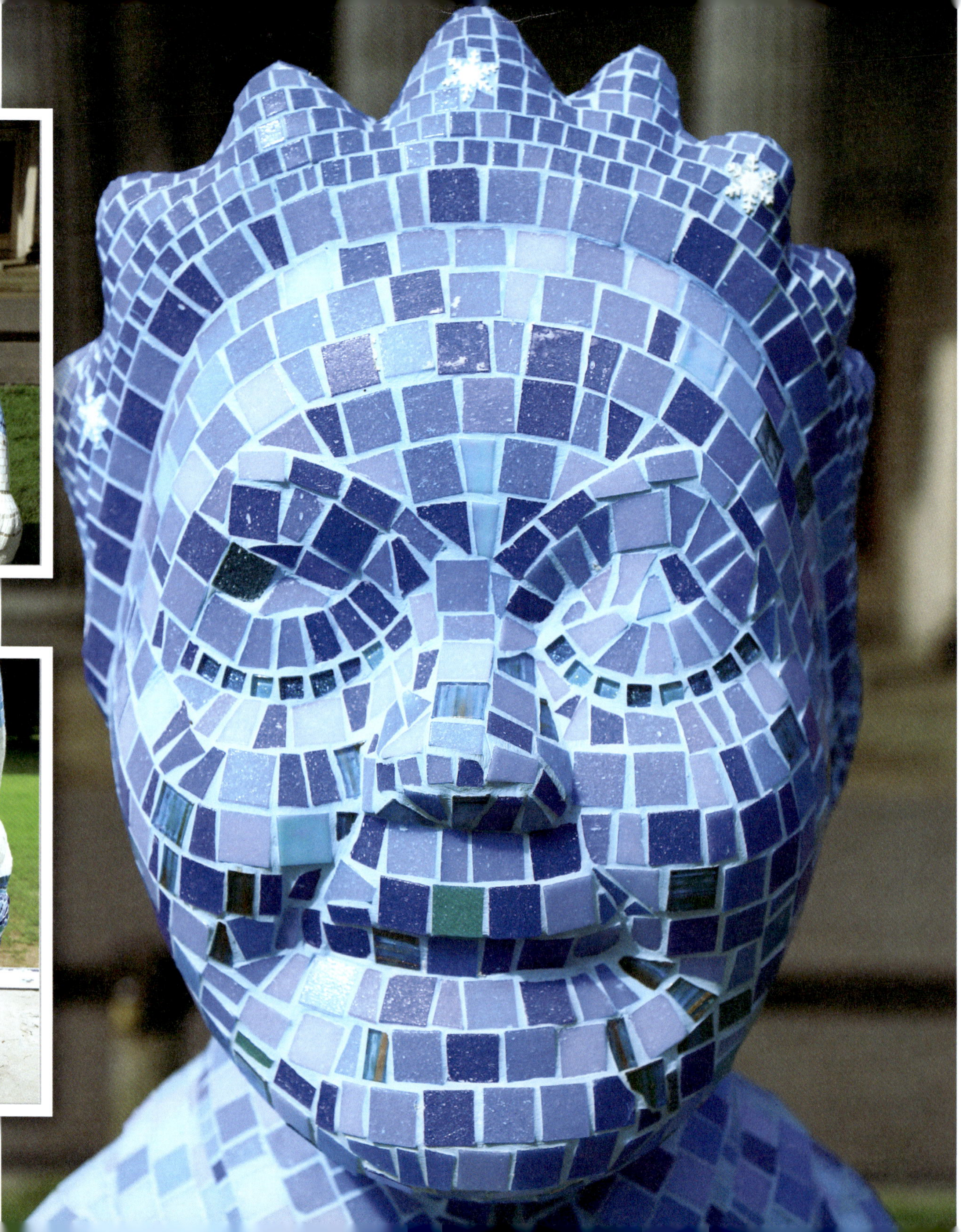

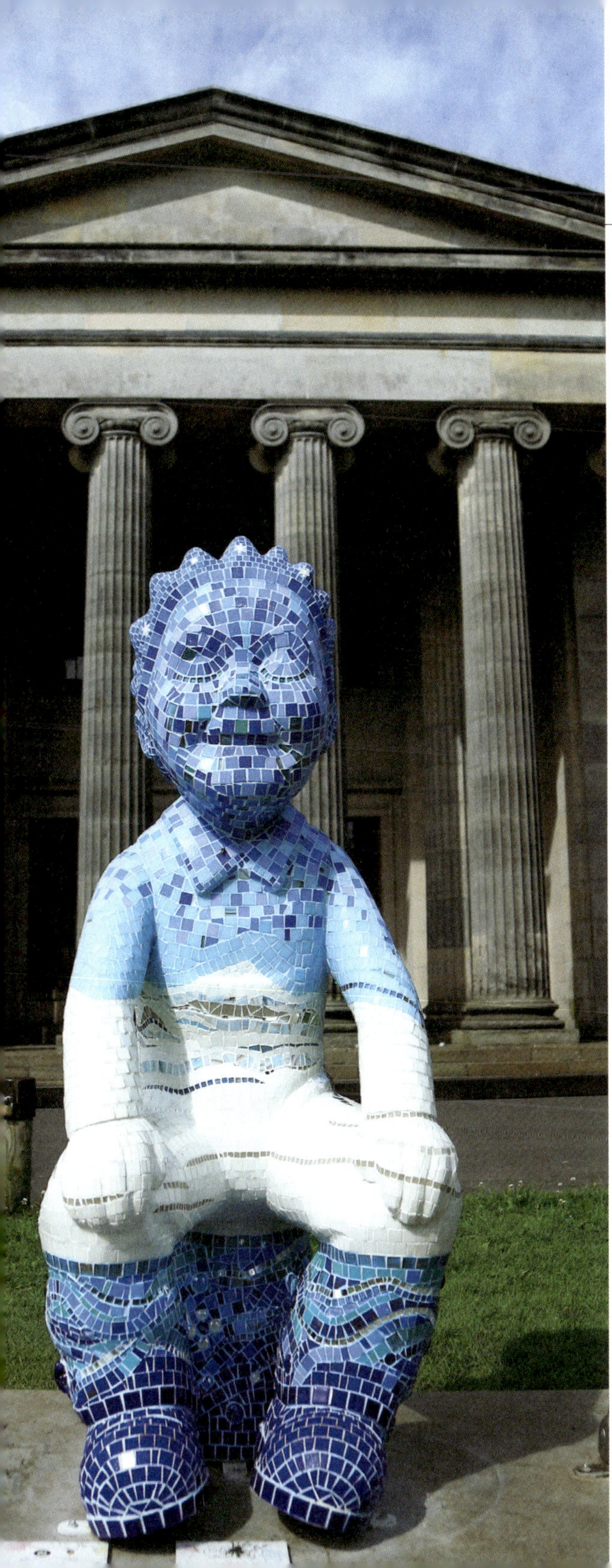

DISCOVERY

Location on the Bucket Trail:
Camperdown House.

Designed by: Debbie Ryan.

About this sculpture: Discovery pays tribute to Dundee's very own RRS Discovery. Built in Dundee and designed for Antarctic research, the Discovery's first mission was the British National Antarctic Expedition that carried Robert Falcon Scott and Ernest Shackleton on their first, successful journey to the Antarctic. This was known as the Discovery Expedition.

Debbie is a visual artist who specialises in making contemporary mosaics and is based in her studio in Glasgow. She likes to create work that explores and celebrates the variety of the natural world. Debbie has created large mosaic sculptures which have been shown in places such as Shanghai, Auckland and her home town of Liverpool. Most recently she created a large beach mosaic sculpture / shelter with the community of Inverbervie, on the east coast of Scotland.

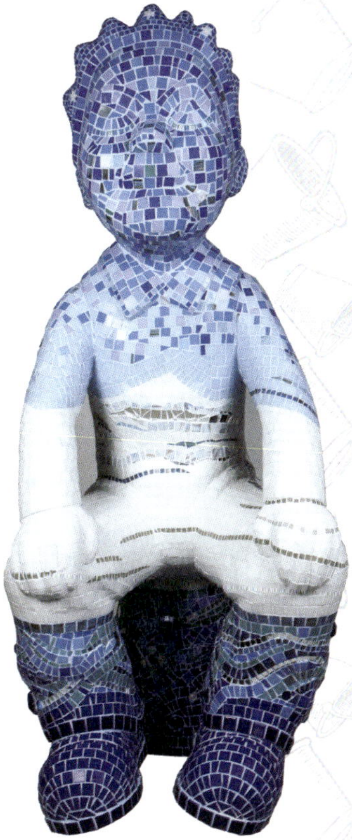

Sponsor: King Foods.

Winning bid: £11,000.

Winning bidder: We dinae ken!

Where is he now? We dinae ken that either but his dinner's on the table and Maw isnae happy!

YARNBOMBED

Location on the Bucket Trail:
Ardler Complex / Community Library.

Designed by: Pam Kelly.

About this sculpture: 'Yarn-bombing', or secretly decorating street furniture and sculptures by covering them with knitting or crocheting, is fun and colourful. Rather than yarn-bomb Oor Wullie with wool, which is temporary and unofficial, the designer of this sculpture thought a more permanent, painted version would be an exciting and vibrant addition to the Bucket Trail.

Pam attended Dundee and Angus College to study art as a mature student. Before this she had an office-based career but always maintained an interest in various arts and crafts, including knitting and painting, and enjoyed developing her artistic skills through classes. Pam enjoyed painting Yarnbombed in the reception space at Dundee and Angus College.

Sponsor: DC Thomson.

Winning bid: £9,000.

Winning bidder: We dinae ken!

Where is he now? We dinae ken that either but we like to think he's still spreading joy and happiness!

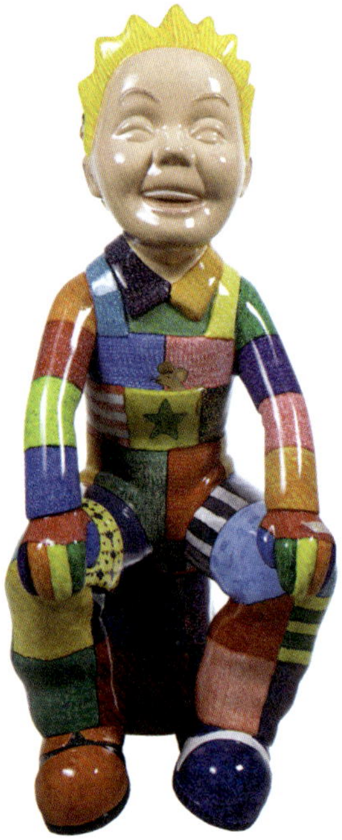

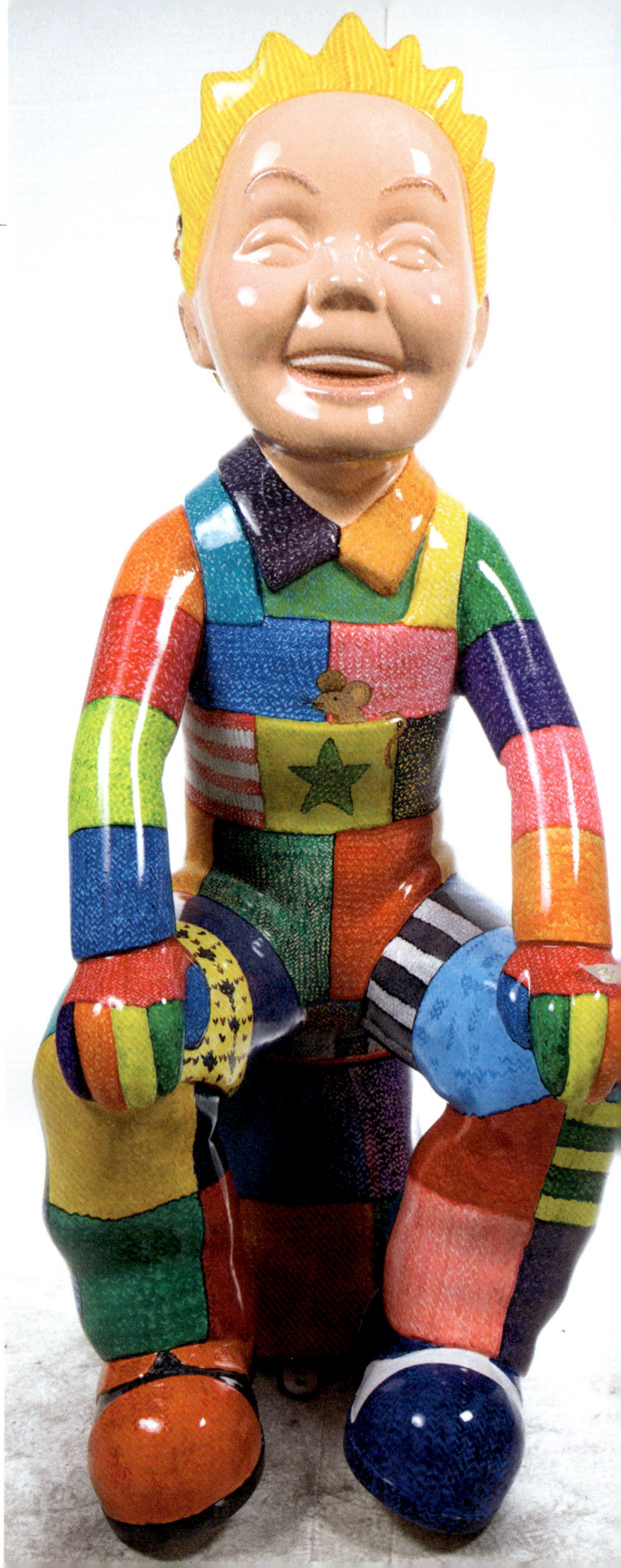

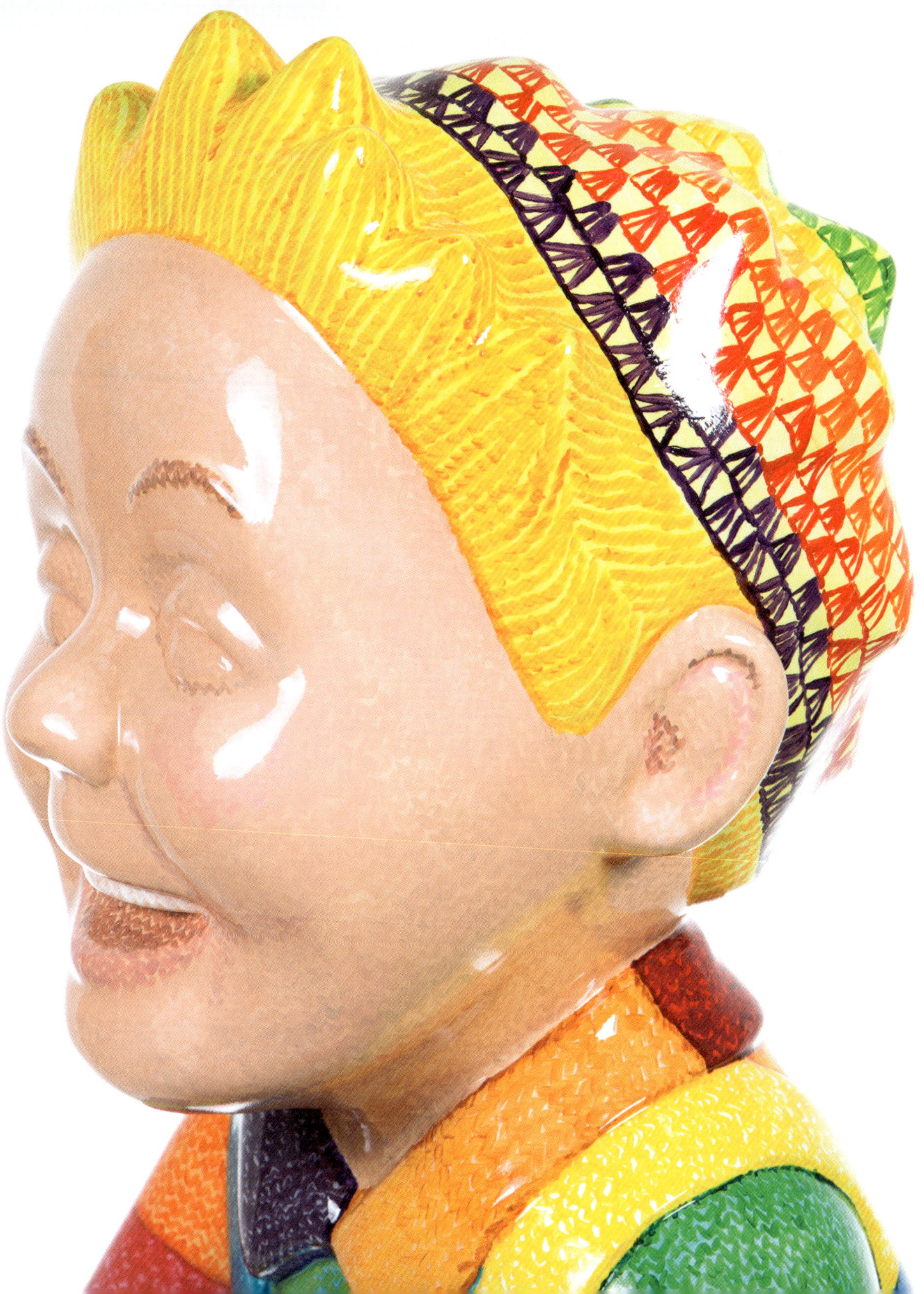

DREAMLAND

Location on the Bucket Trail:
Barnhill Rock Garden.

Designed by: Ruby Coyne.

About this sculpture: This Oor Wullie design was inspired by the artist's love of colour and 1980s print. The concept was created to showcase the vivid colour, horizon of opportunities and unique individuals that make Dundee such a wonderful city.

Ruby is a Dundee girl who studied fashion and textiles at Gray's School of Art. She also completed fashion design internships in London and Paris and created Dreamland – a clothing label celebrating colour and nostalgia. Ruby and her label Dreamland were recently selected as one of ten graduates in the country to showcase at Graduate ASOS Marketplace 2016.

Sponsor: Vision Sound & Light.

Winning bid: £8,000.

Winning bidder: Nicoll's Bar and Restaurant.

Where is he now? Enjoying a jeely piece at Nicoll's Bar and Restaurant!

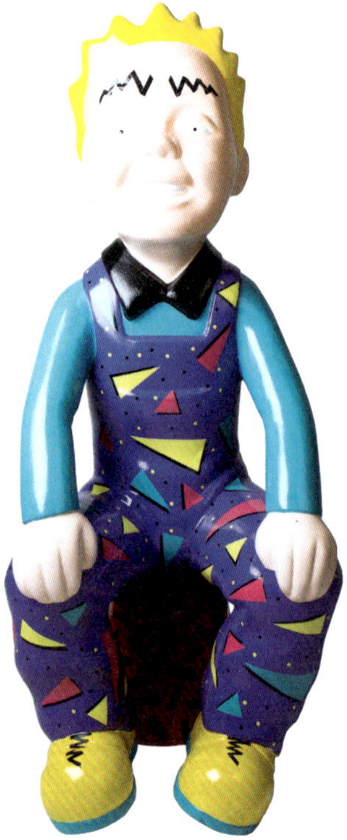

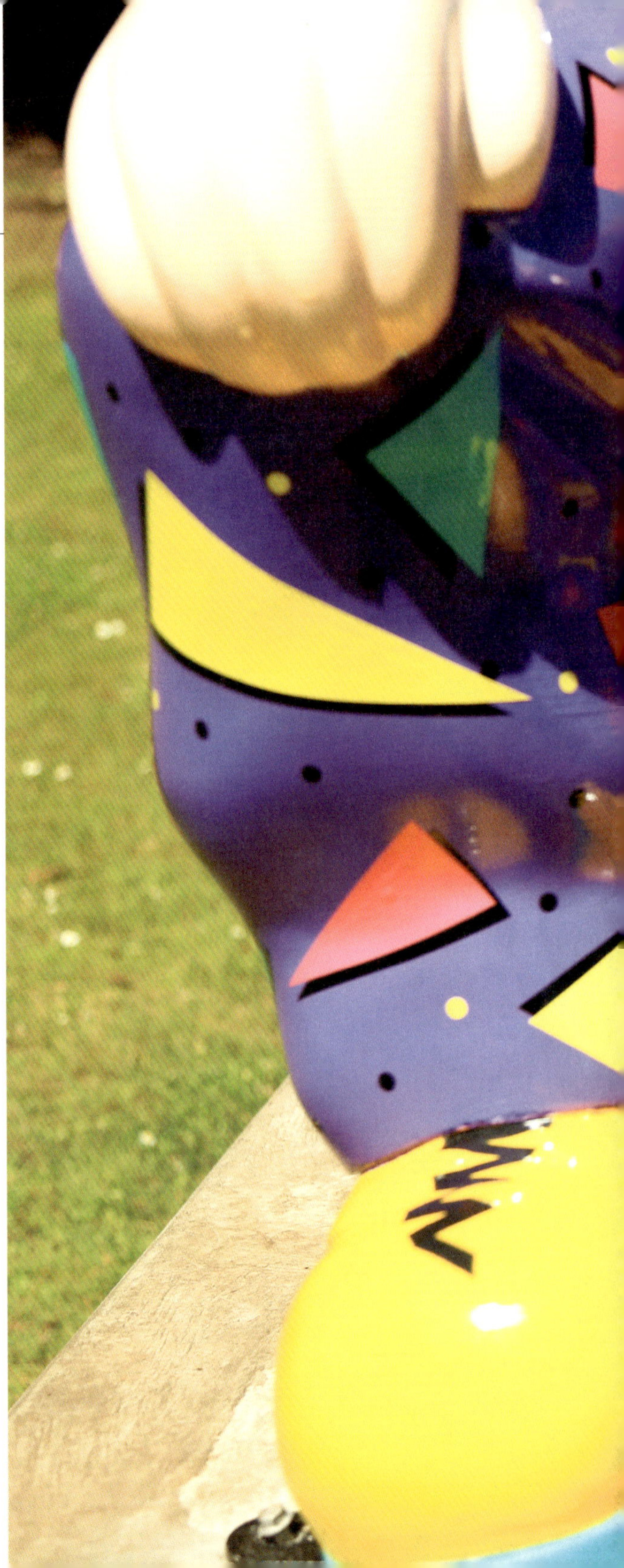

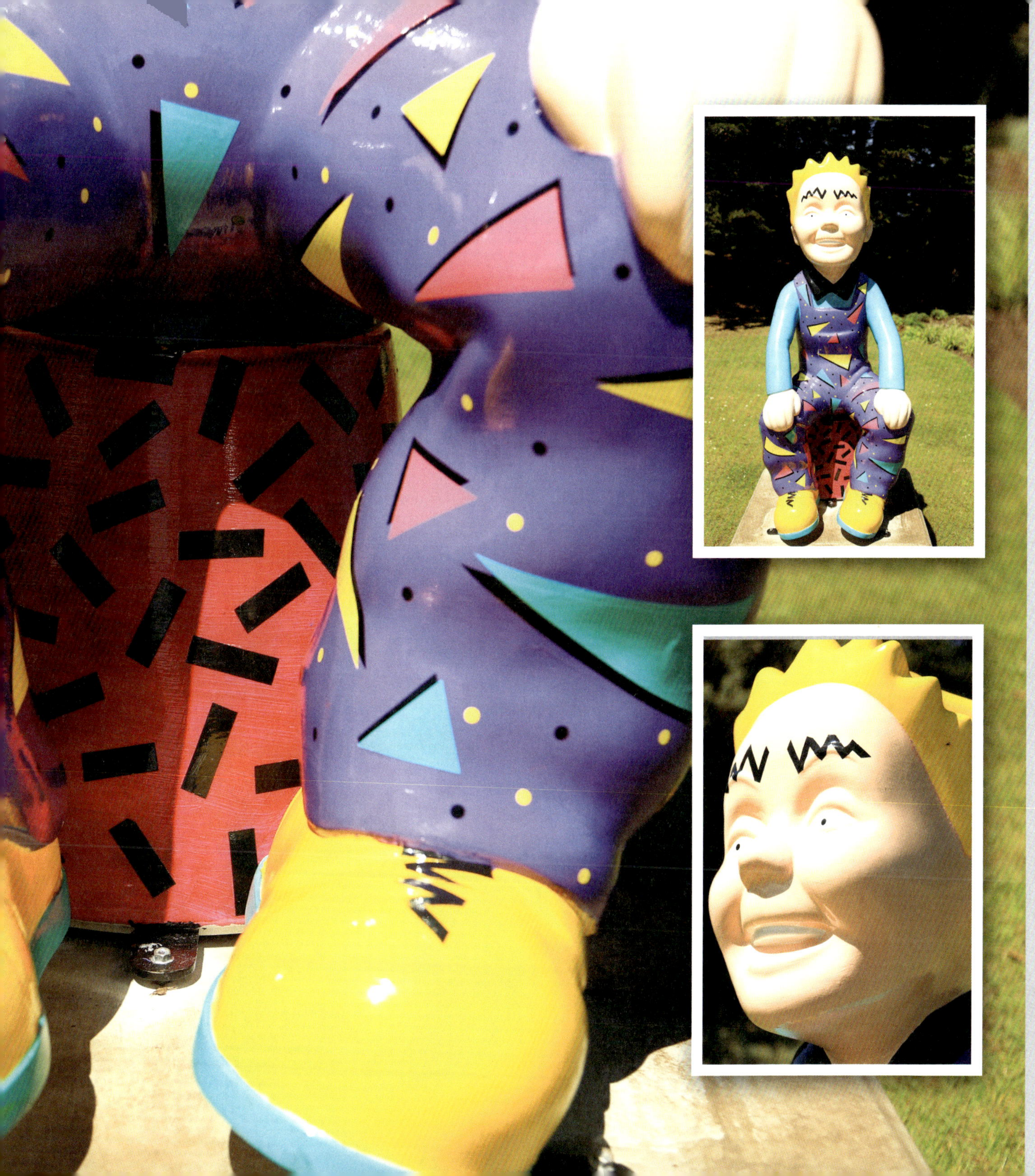

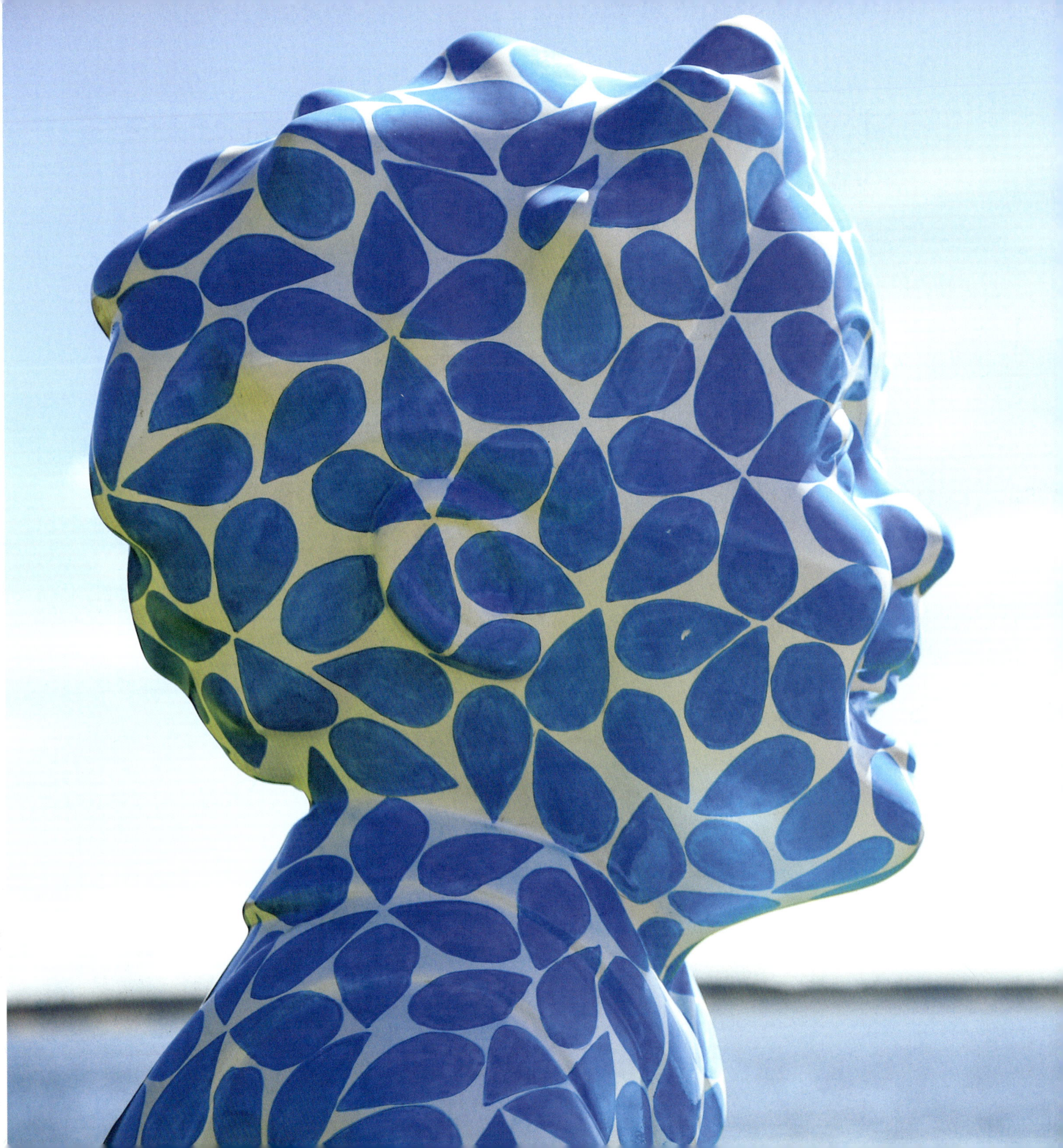

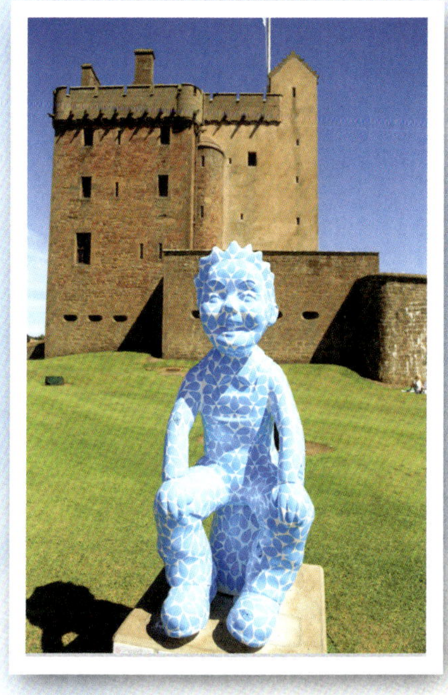

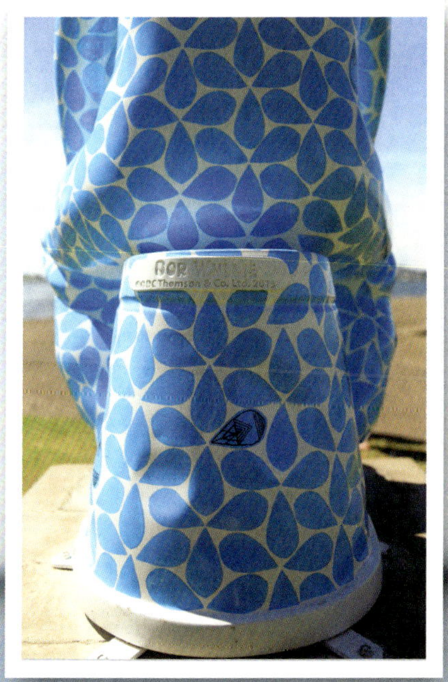

RAIN SONG

Location on the Bucket Trail: Broughty Castle Museum.

Designed by: Lynne Strachan.

About this sculpture: Rain Song represents the relationship we have with natural elements and the spaces that surround us every day. The raindrops on this sculpture contain linear maps that represent the silent thoughts, feelings and journeys of people as they walk by, while the sounds and forms of raindrops themselves create a beautiful rhythm as they fall and tumble from the sky, bringing a musical serenity in the chaos of our lives.

Lynne lives and works in a small town in the north-east of Scotland. As a visual artist, her work explores the interaction between science and art, through presenting the forgotten and invisible as visible.

Sponsor: Chris Scott Photography.

Winning bid: £12,000.

Winning bidder: F J Esposito Ltd.

Where is he now? In the foyer area at Ninewells Hospital, cheering up all the visitors!

Why was he bought? Frank Esposito, owner of F J Esposito Ltd, and the cafe at Ninewells, said: "I wanted to give something back to the hospital. People see it when they come in and it just adds to the whole concourse. I feel it's important to do what I can to try to keep the momentum of the appeal going - this is my way."

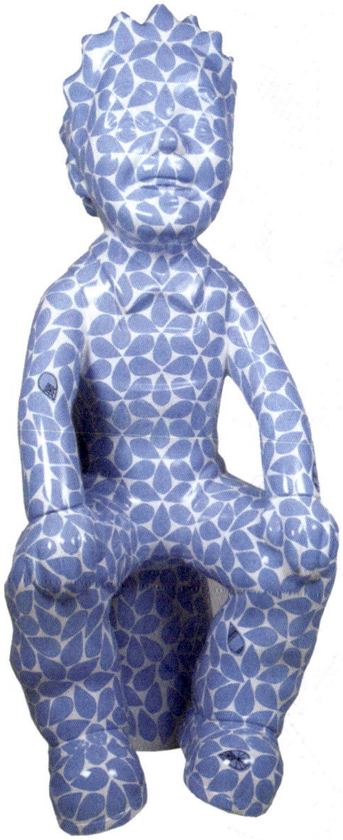

OOR LIFESAVER

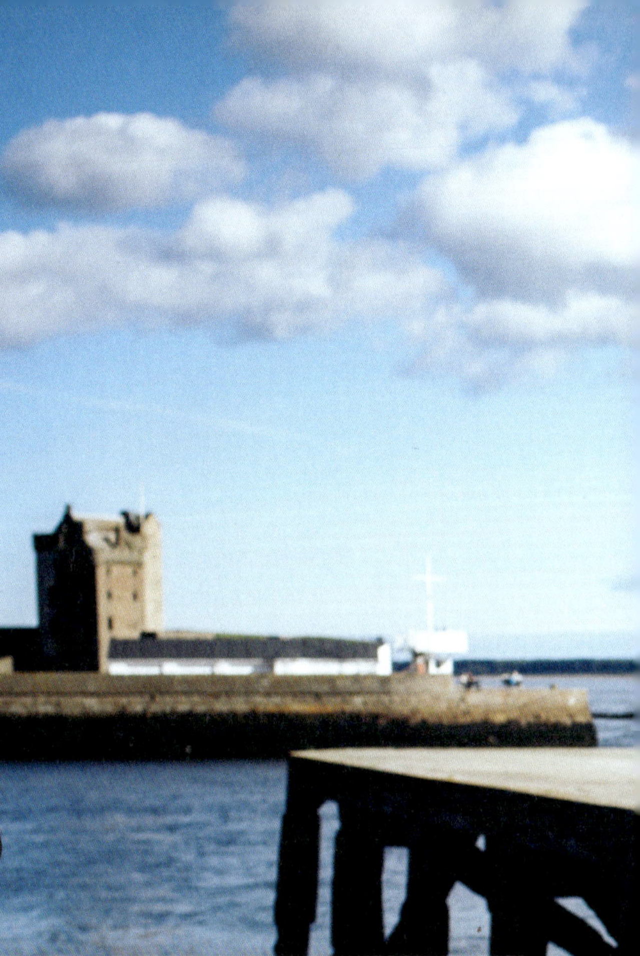

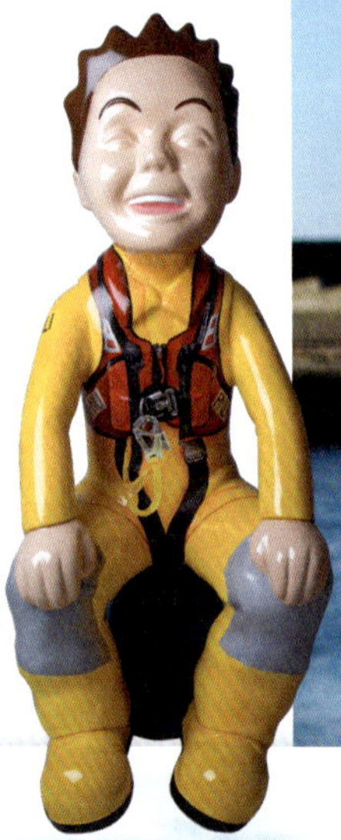

Location on the Bucket Trail: Broughty Ferry Slippy.

Designed by: Fiona Hay.

About this sculpture: Having lived in Broughty Ferry all her life, designer Fiona Hay has always been aware of the Royal National Lifeboat Institution (RNLI). Fiona works at the Fisherman's Tavern which has a close relationship with the Broughty Ferry Lifeboat volunteers and regularly raises money and awareness for the RNLI. She wanted her Oor Wullie to relate to the Ferry and in raising money for the ARCHIE Foundation, she is also raising awareness for another very worthy cause, the RNLI.

Fiona graduated in fine art from Duncan of Jordanstone College of Art and Design in 2015. Whilst there, she specialised in time-lapse photography and paper-craft. She now also paints commissions and is working on her own body of work which is inspired by animals and nature.

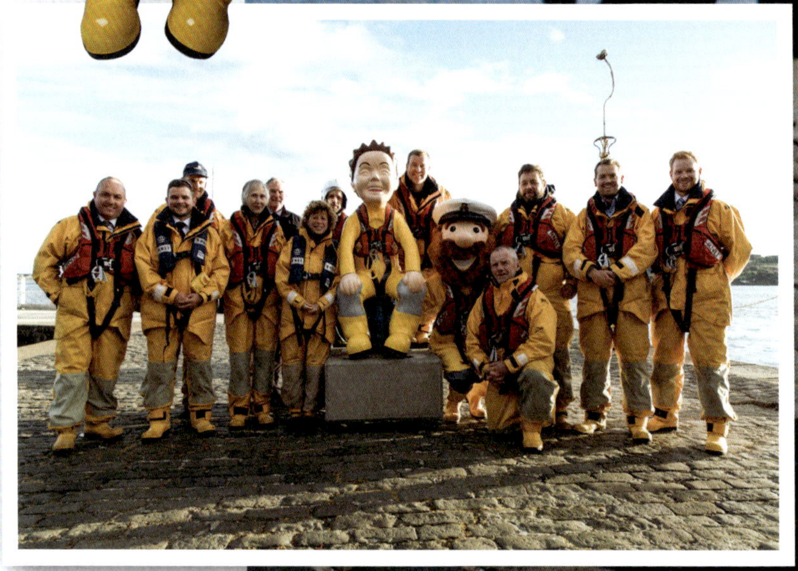

Sponsor: Broughty Ferry Traders' Association.

Winning bid: £10,000.

Winning bidder: Crowdfunded.

Where is he now? Helping the wonderful crew at Broughty Ferry lifeboat station!

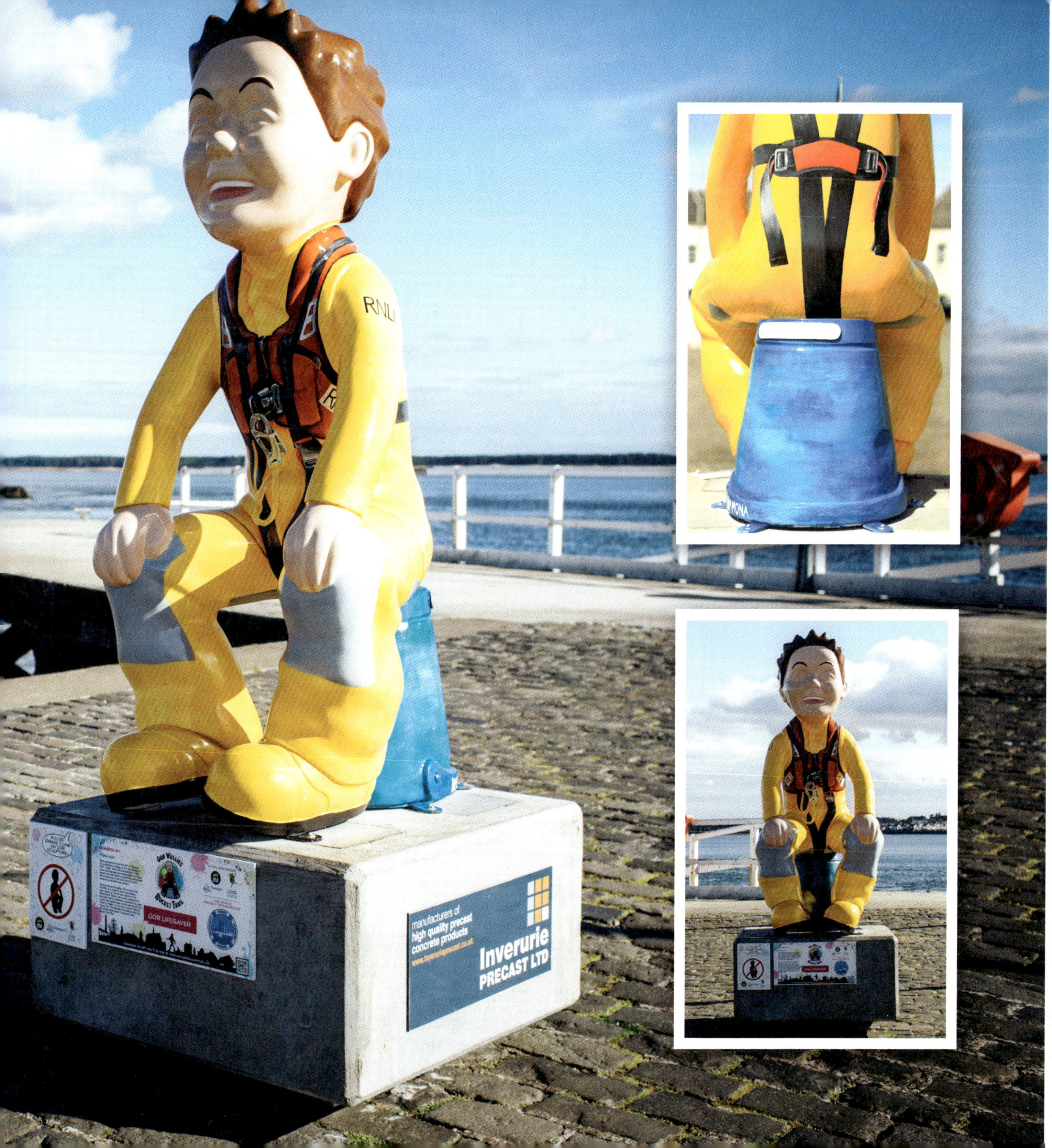
RNLI
OOR LIFESAVER
manufacturers of
high quality precast
concrete products
www.inverurieprecast.co.uk
Inverurie
PRECAST LTD

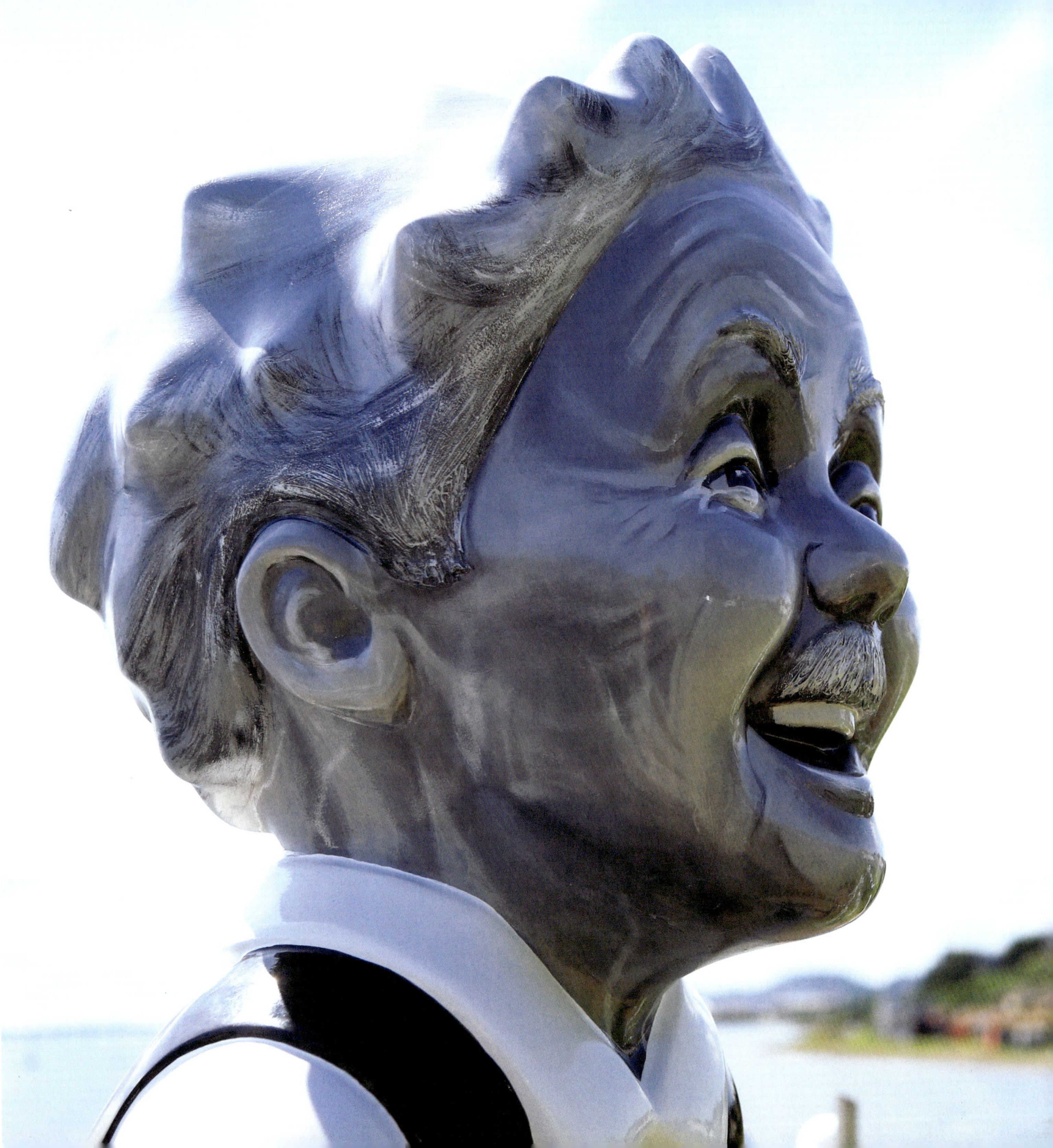

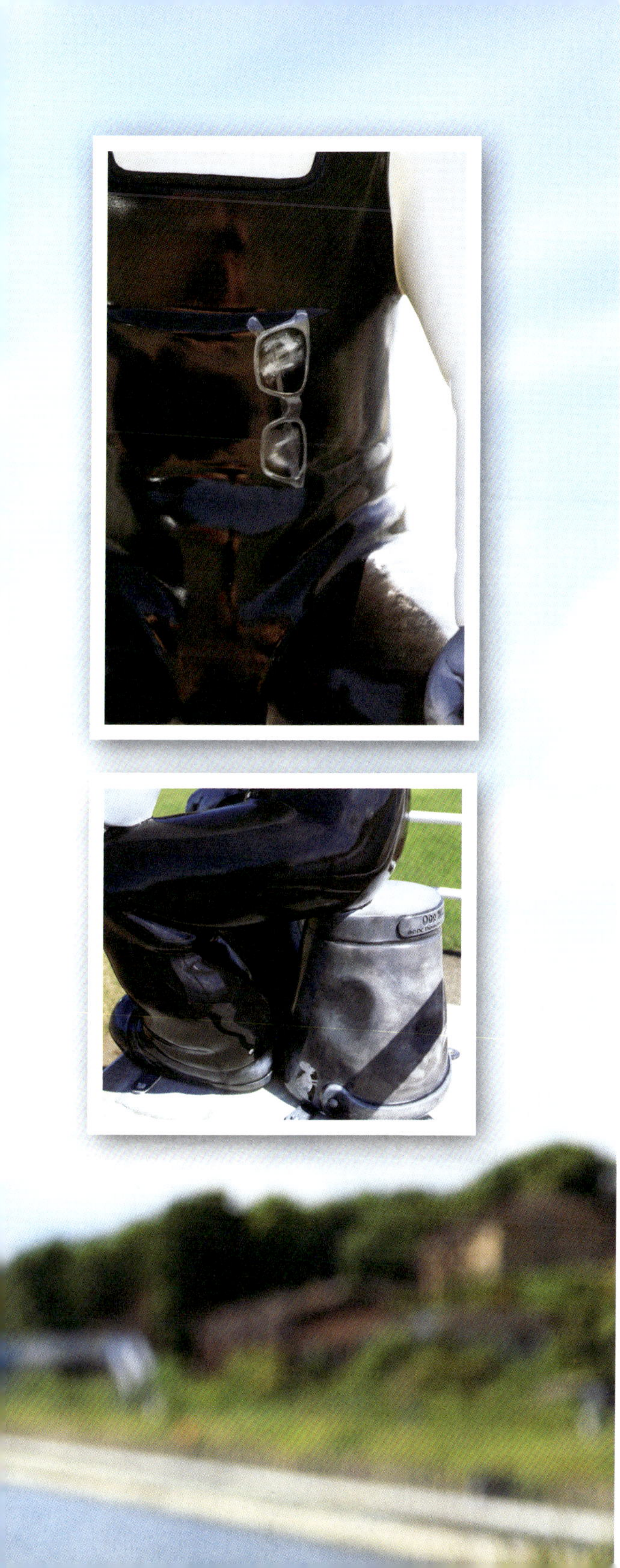

OOR WULLIE NOO

Location on the Bucket Trail: Douglas Parade, Broughty Ferry.

Designed by: Alison Price.

About this sculpture: Like many others, Alison grew up with Oor Wullie in The Sunday Post and regularly received the Oor Wullie Christmas annuals from Santa. All Oor Wullie's fans have aged over the years and this sculpture depicts what Wullie might have looked like in 2016 at 80 years old.

Alison is a graduate of Duncan Of Jordanstone College of Art and Design and uses acrylics and oils to produce paintings of her local surroundings in Perthshire. Inspired by the light and space of landscapes, her work also translates into ceramic pieces which reflect the imagery and textures of landscapes themselves.

Sponsor: Balhousie Care Group.

Winning bid: £18,000.

Winning bidder: Tony Banks, Chairman and Founder of Balhousie Care Group.

Where is he now? Visiting all 24 of the Balhousie Care Homes to help put a smile on the residents' faces!

Why was he bought? Balhousie Care Group said: "Oor Wullie Noo was painted using the facial and hand features of two of our residents, Raymond and Barbara from our St Ronans care home in Dundee.

"During the time that Oor Wullie Noo was being painted, we listened to many stories and fond memories from residents reminiscing about their childhoods growing up with Oor Wullie and the adventures his stories provided.

"It seemed only right that we brought Oor Wullie Noo into Balhousie Care Group where he could continue to encourage special memories for all our residents."

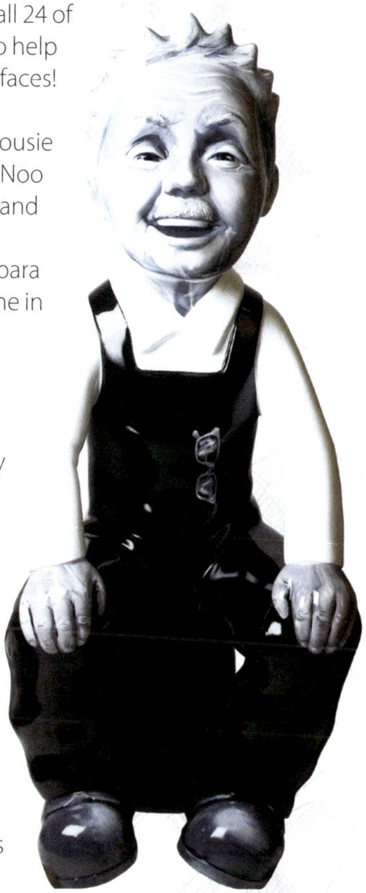

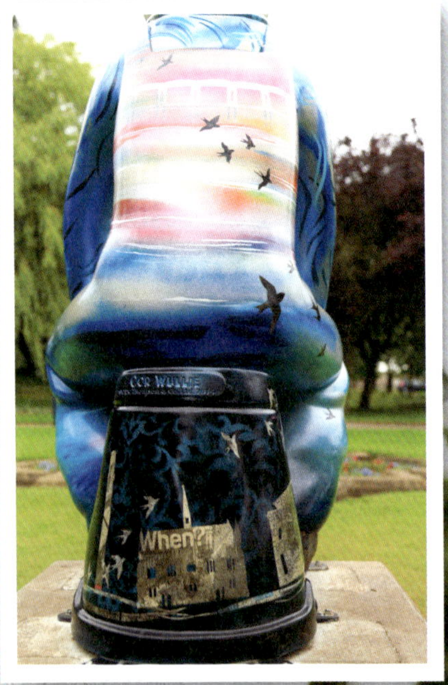
When?

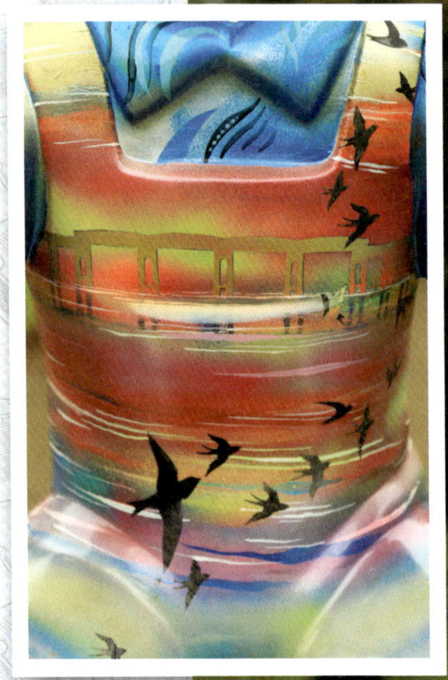

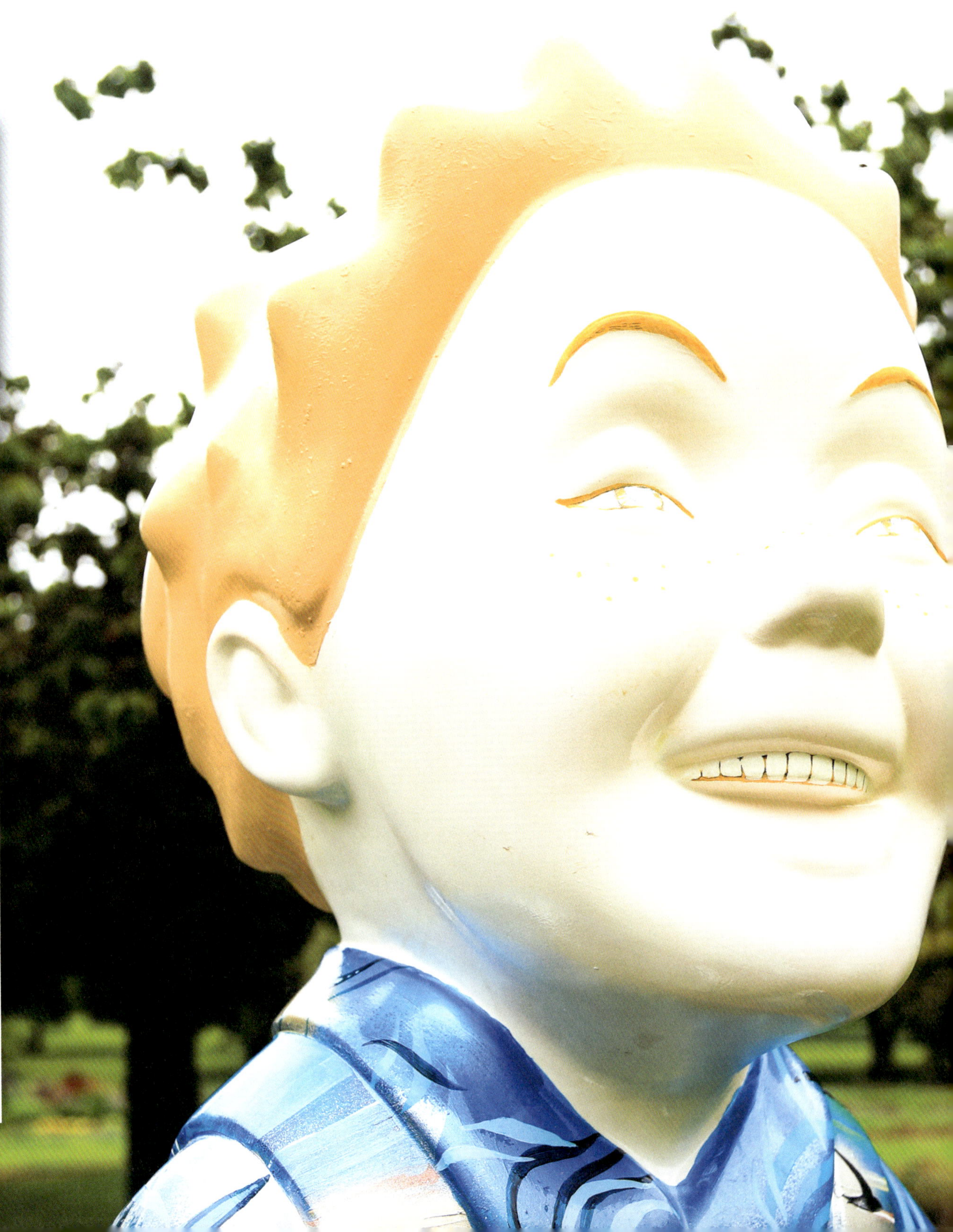

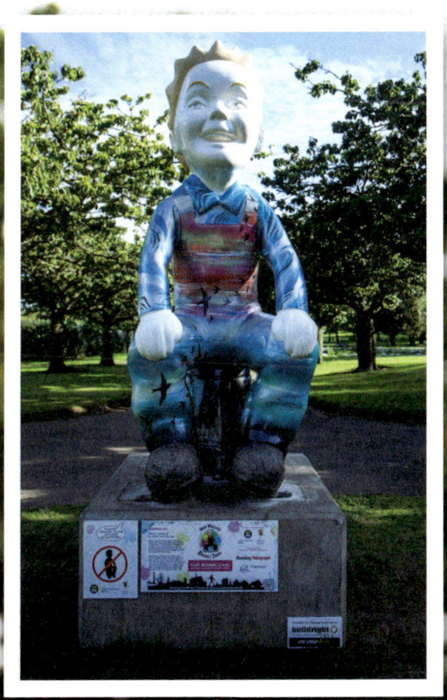

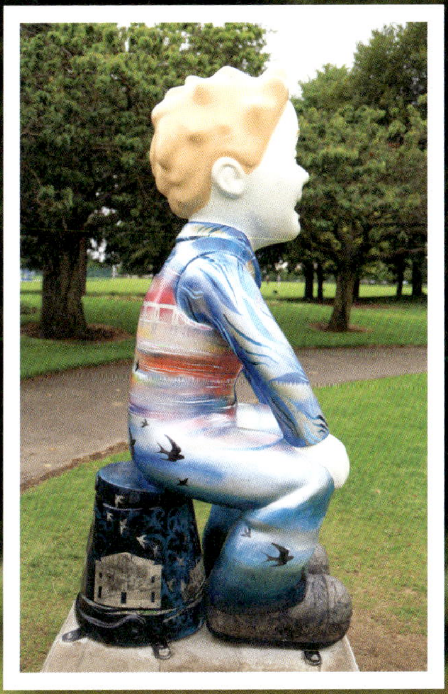

OOR BONNIE LAND

Location on the Bucket Trail: Dawson Park.

Designed by: Fiona Chance and Anna Whitelaw (12 years old).

About this sculpture: Anna won a competition for school pupils, which was run by The Evening Telegraph, for her design to be recreated by artist Fiona Chance on a full-size Oor Wullie sculpture. Anna's concept was to depict some of the many iconic images that stay with you after visiting Dundee and Fiona brought this to life using jute on Wullie's boots, local newspaper for the collage and spray paint to reflect the majestic silvery Tay on Wullie's shirt and dungarees. Fiona added in some of her own flourishes too, including beautiful silhouetted birds and a city skyline, making this piece a wonderful collaboration.

Fiona is a mixed media artist from Dublin and now lives in Aberdeen. She originally studied fine art printmaking at the National College of Art in Dublin. When she's not painting, spraying, sticking and printing, Fiona can be found running creative workshops for adults and children.

Sponsor: DC Thomson, The Evening Telegraph.

Winning bid: £11,000.

Winning bidder: We dinae ken!

Where is he now? We dinae ken that either but we like to think he's still spreading joy and happines!

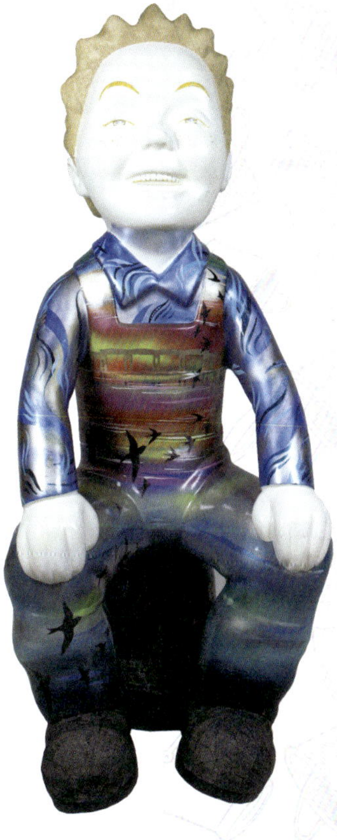

WULLYMORPH

Location on the Bucket Trail: Brook Street, Broughty Ferry.

Designed by: Islay Spalding.

About this sculpture: For this sculpture, Oor Wullie is embellished with a collection of fragmented patterns which were inspired by the idea of viewing our surroundings from different perspectives at the same time. Cellular forms, geological structures, patterns in nature and architectural shapes combine with a distorted slant into a metaphysical landscape of Biomorphs, Oddgons, Angulars and Quarks.

Islay is a jewellery designer / maker who creates unique items of jewellery and bespoke kilt pins. She studied at Duncan of Jordanstone College of Art and Design and now works from her workshop in Dundee. A night time doodler and lover of the black line, her drawings create a basis for her jewellery designs.

Sponsor: Nane but too guid no'tae include!

Winning bid: £6,500.

Winning bidder: Perth decorator firm owner, Martin Pankhurst.

Where is he now? We dinae ken but we like to think he's still spreading joy and happiness!

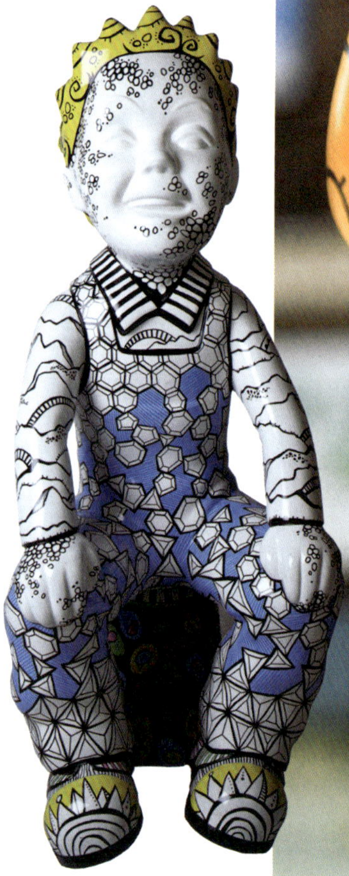

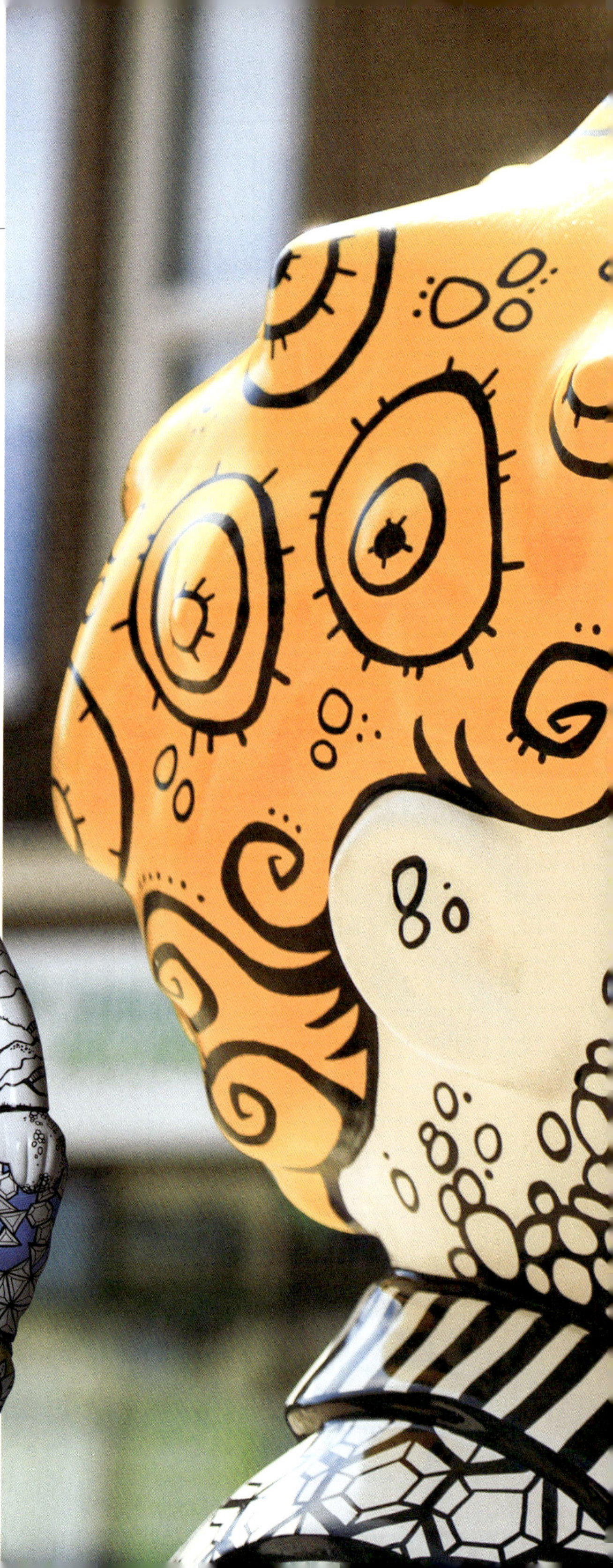

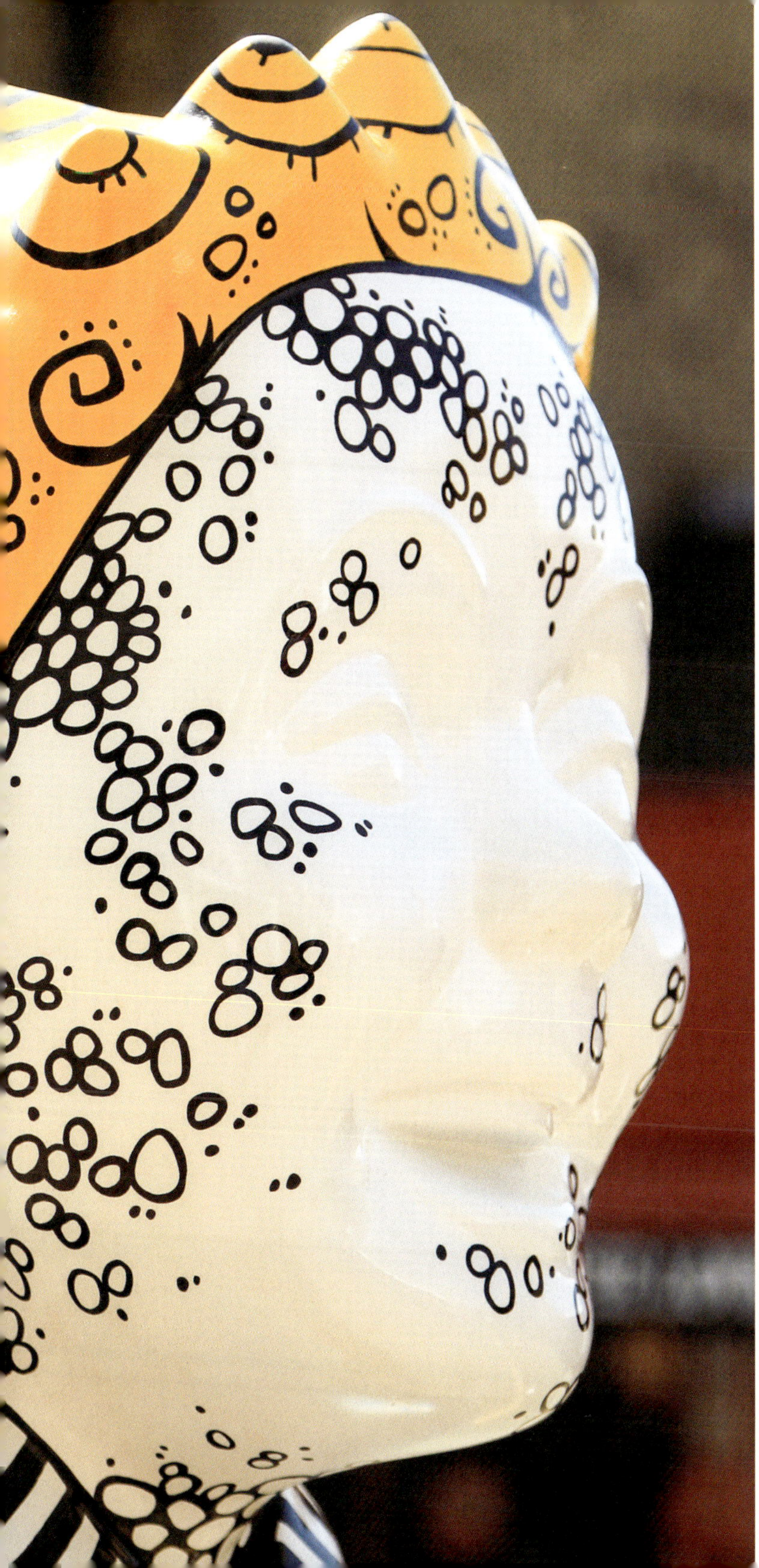

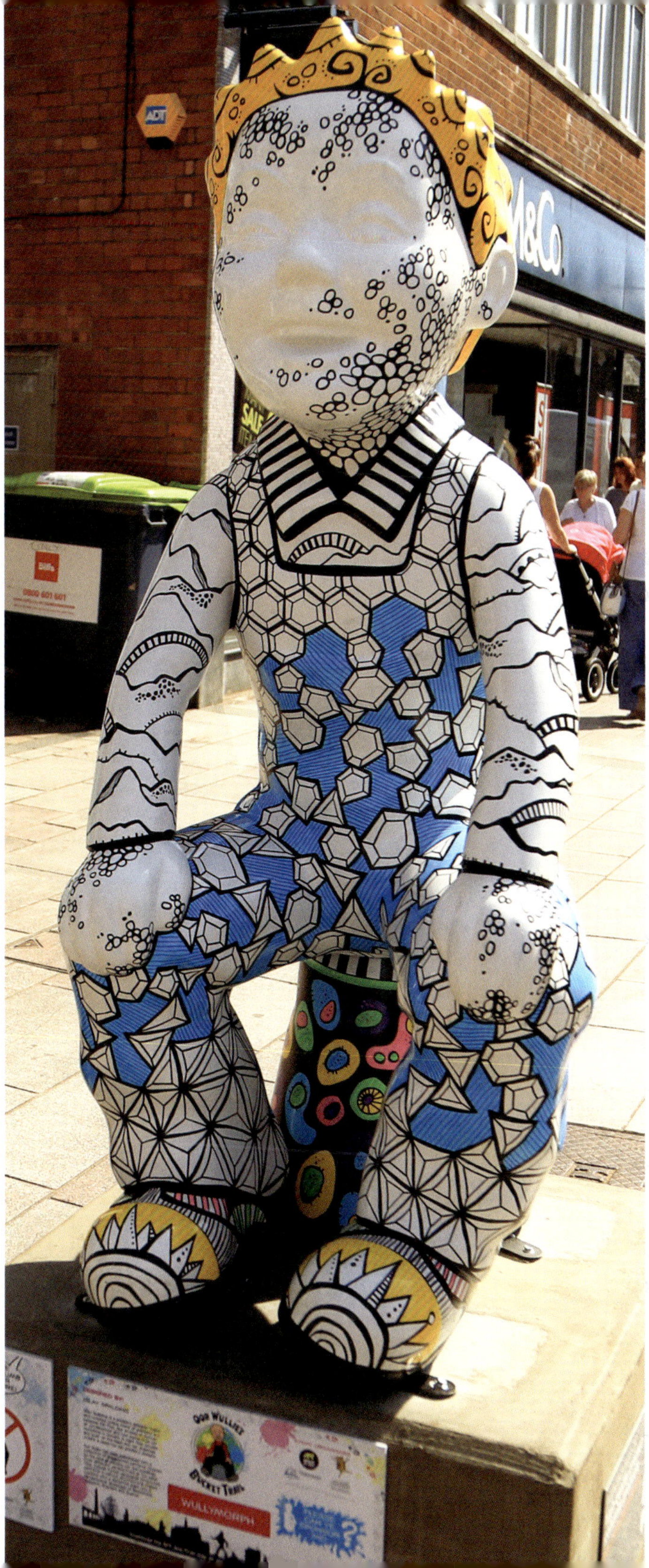
OOR WULLIE'S
BUCKET TRAIL

WULLIE THE MENACE

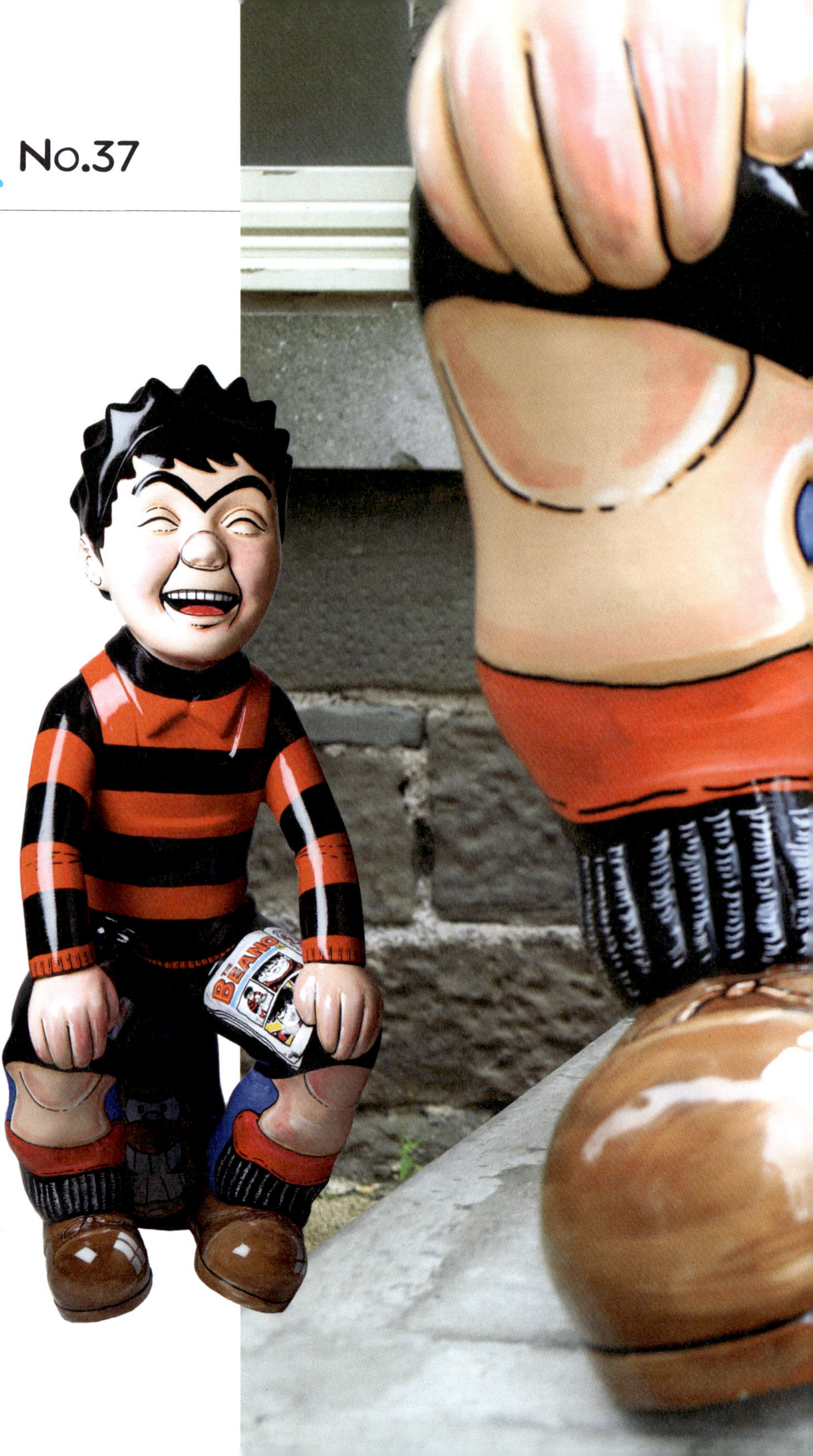

Location on the Bucket Trail: Bash Street.

Designed by: Lee O'Brien.

About this sculpture: This sculpture brings together two naughty characters - both with links to Scotland. The Beano's Dundee roots inspired the artist of this sculpture to merge Dennis the Menace with Oor Wullie. The outfit and slingshot are a perfect reflection of the naughty behaviour for which they are both known.

Lee is a Liverpool-based teacher and illustrator. When he's not marking books, he enjoys creating his own humorous art work, largely inspired by his home city and the interesting characters who live there.

Sponsor: DC Thomson, The Sunday Post.

Winning bid: £14,000.

Winning bidder: DC Thomson.

Where is he now? DC Thomson bought four sculptures; each visit the company's offices on rotation.

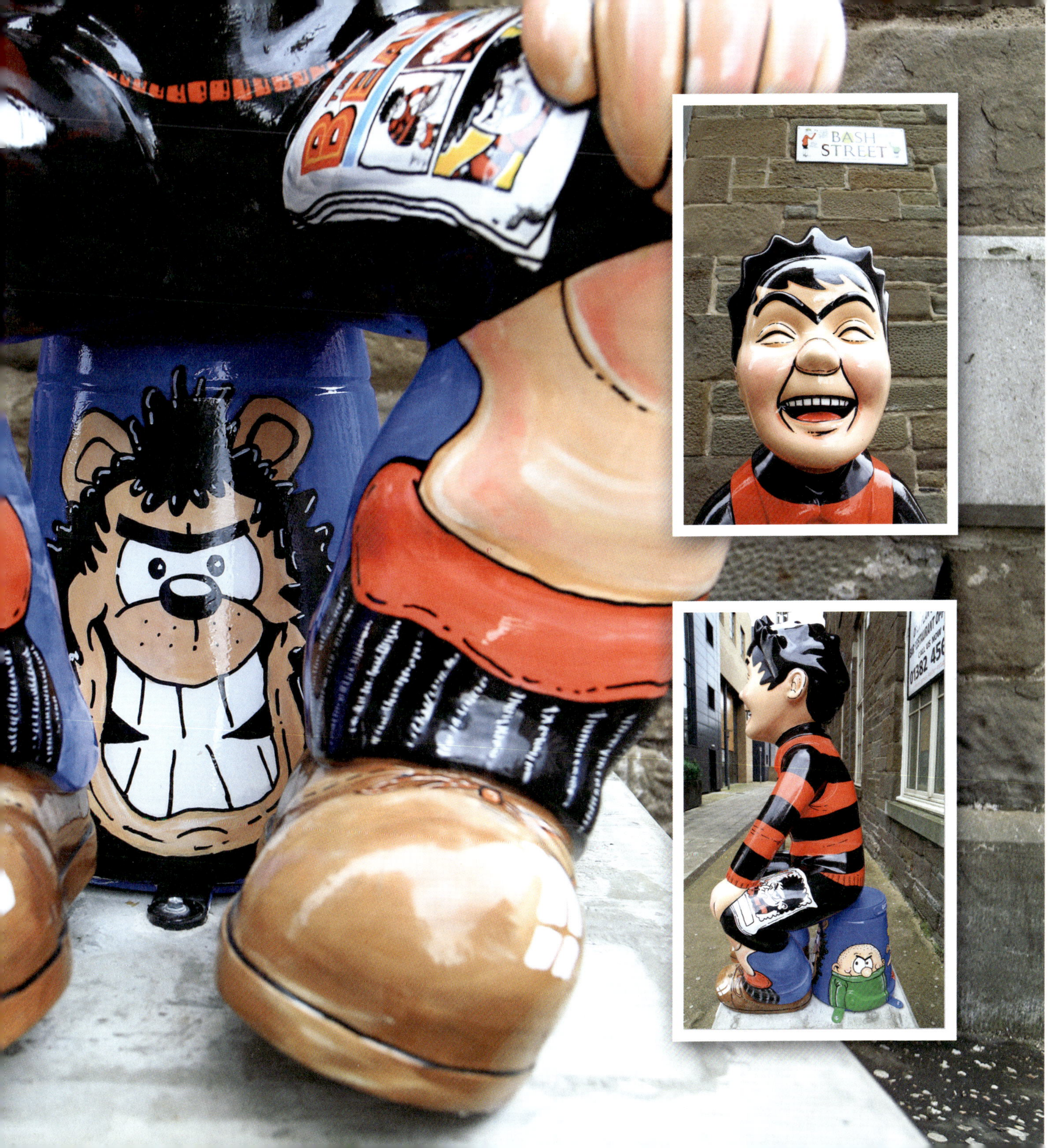
BASH
STREET

OOR BOWIE! YOUR BOWIE! ABODY'S BOWIE!

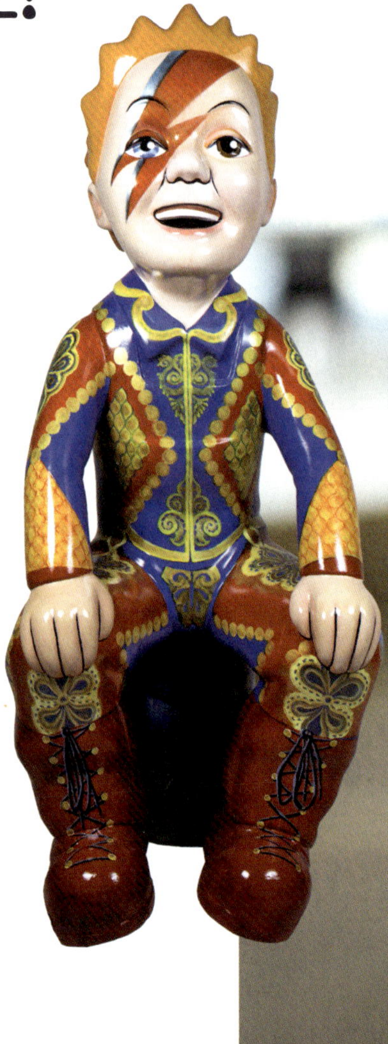

Location on the Bucket Trail: Dundee Rail Bridge.

Designed by: Rhiannon Moore (Kitchimama) Martin Lindsay and John Hunter Barrie (JoHuBa).

About this sculpture: What better way is there to mark the 80th anniversary of Scotland's favourite son than by combining him with a celebration of the life, work and memory of Britain's brightest shining music ' Starman', the late David Bowie?

This sculpture was painted by Rhiannon Moore (Kitchimama) who studied illustration at Brighton University and traditional painting techniques at West Dean College in Sussex. Rhiannon describes her works as magical realism. Martin is the licensing manager at DC Thomson and the man behind the idea of the Bucket Trail, and John Hunter Barrie is a former DC Thomson graphic designer.

Sponsor: Barnetts Volkswagen.

Winning bid: £19,000.

Winning bidder: Gillian Bayford, local businesswoman.

Where is he now? Spreading joy and happiness in Carnoustie!

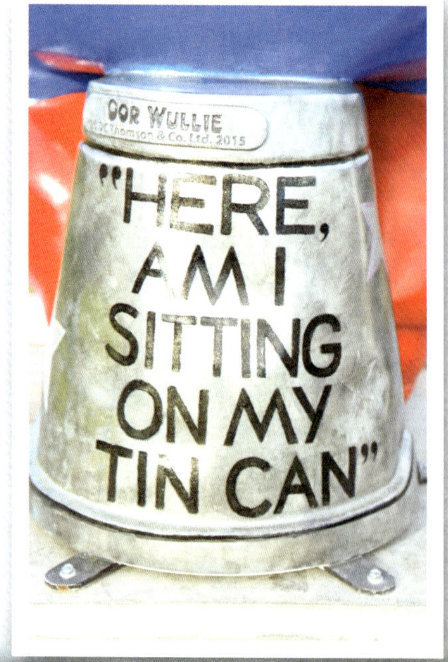

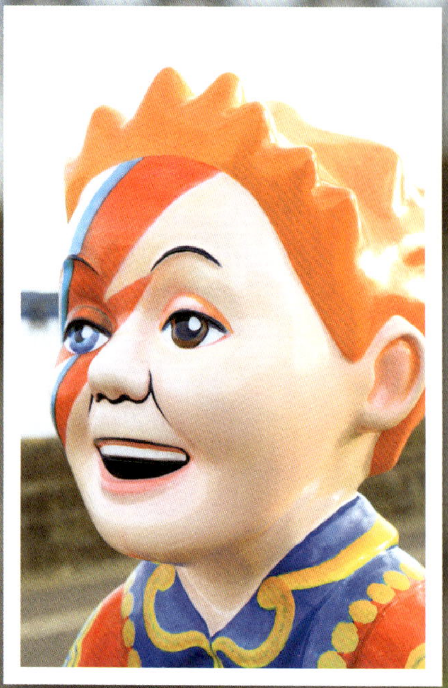

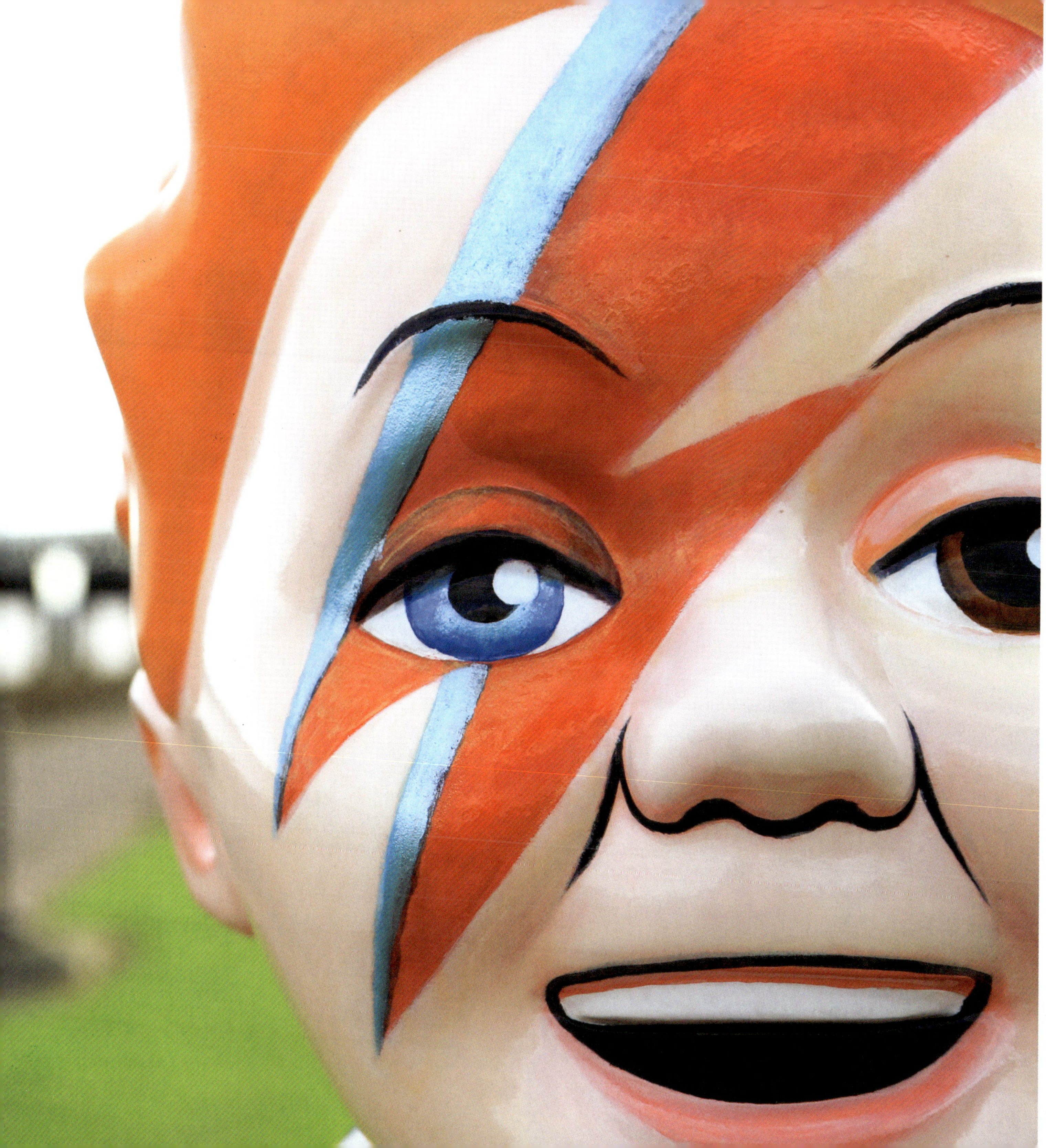

OOR WAI O' SPIKIN'

Location on the Bucket Trail: Discovery Point.

Designed by: Small Stories by Gabrielle Reith.

About this sculpture: Oor wai o'Spikin' is inspired by the words that give Scotland a unique identity. Gabrielle loves exploring Scottish language and dialects in her artistic practice. The words she selected for this sculpture were inspired by the location where it was displayed and the ethics of the sponsor, Insights.

Gabrielle is an artist, illustrator and maker who is based in Scotland. Her work is the magical world of small stories where every piece tells a tale. She makes elaborate pen and ink drawings which evolve into beautiful stories based on her and her children's imaginations, infused with traditional tales. She graduated in drawing and painting from Gray's School of Art in 1998.

Sponsor: Insights.

Winning bid: £8,000.

Winning bidder: Andy Lothian, CEO, Insights.

Where is he now? Learning and developing at Insights!

Why was he bought? Andy Lothian, CEO, Insights, said: "It's an honour to support the city of Dundee and the ARCHIE Foundation in a way that is so significant to our organisation. In many ways, Discovery Point marks the start of Insights' journey and our sculpture, stunningly realised by artist Gabrielle Reith, represents both our journey as a global organisation and our work to enable individual journeys through self-awareness."

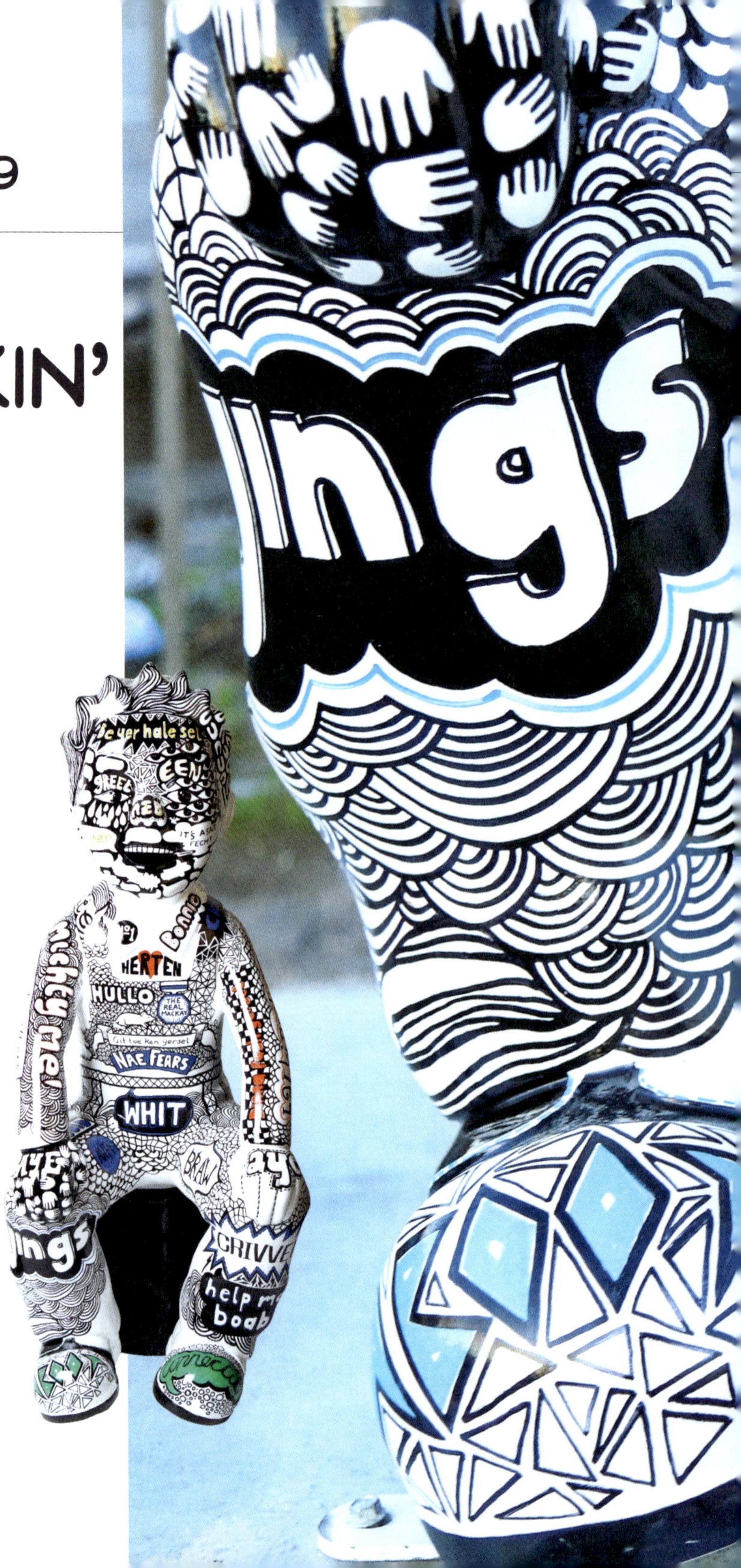

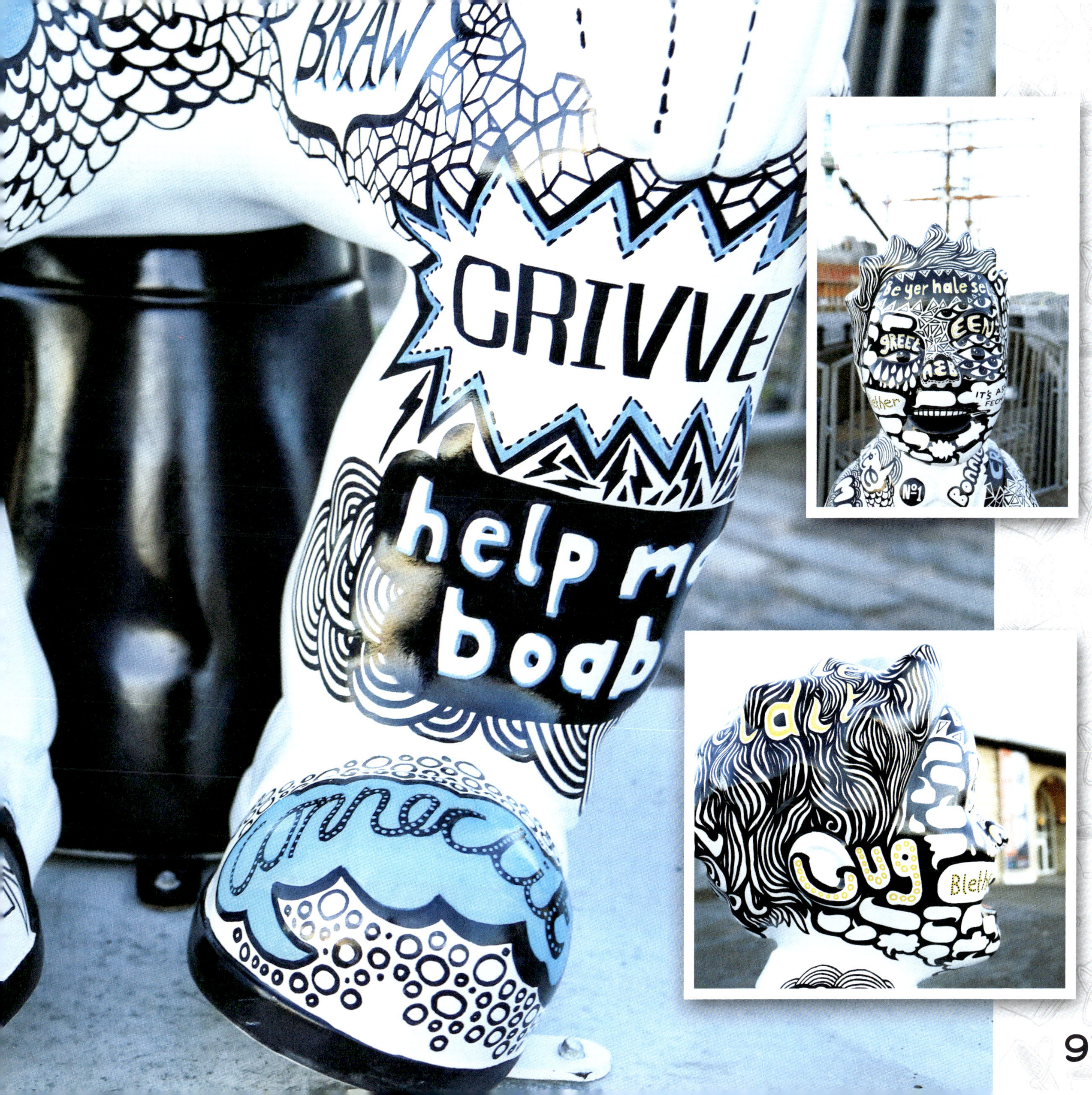
BRAW
CRIVVE
help
boab
Be yer hale
EEN
GREEL
№1

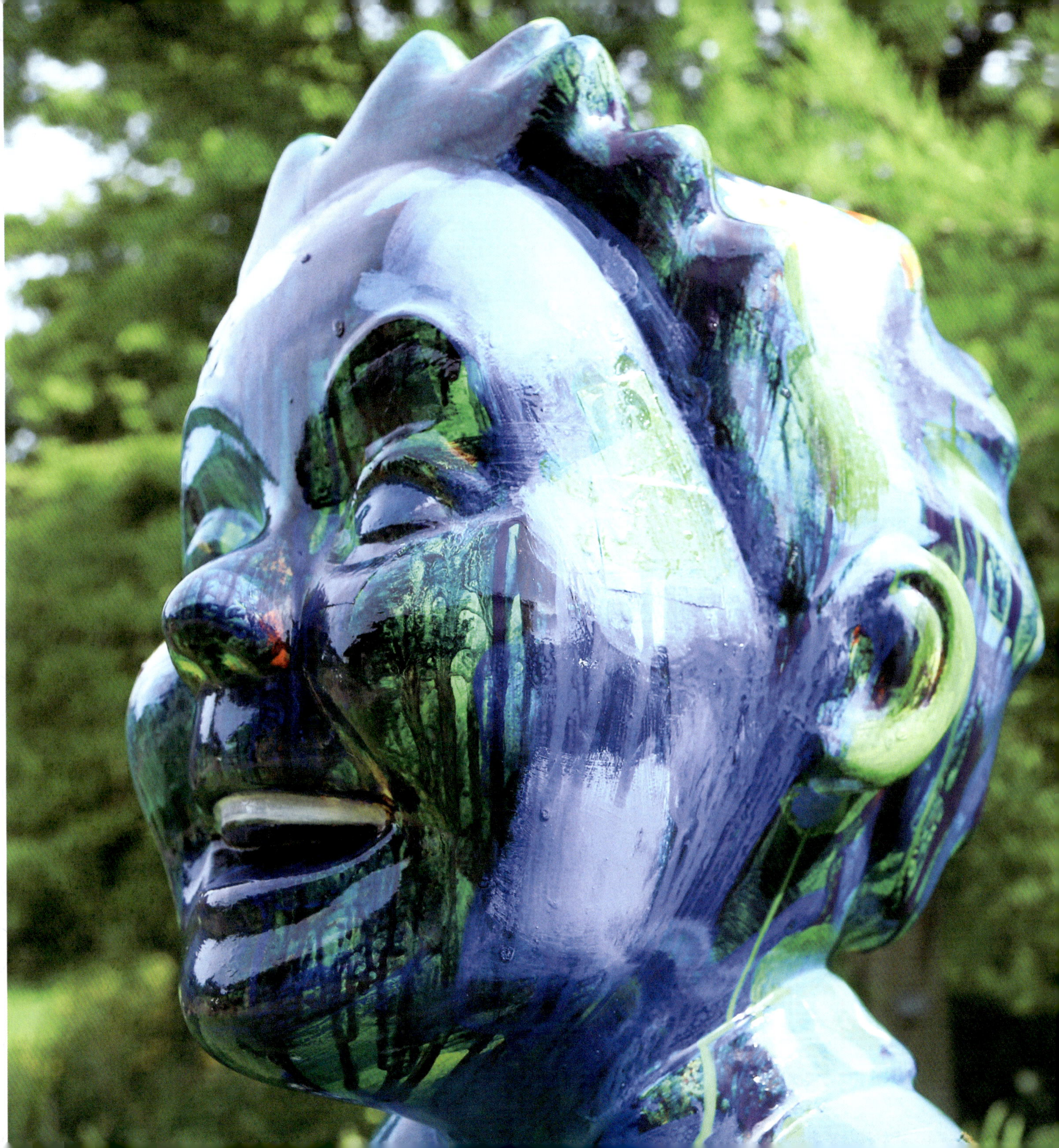

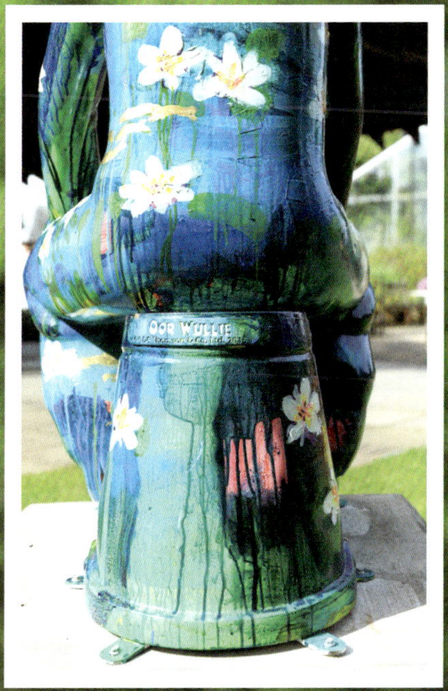

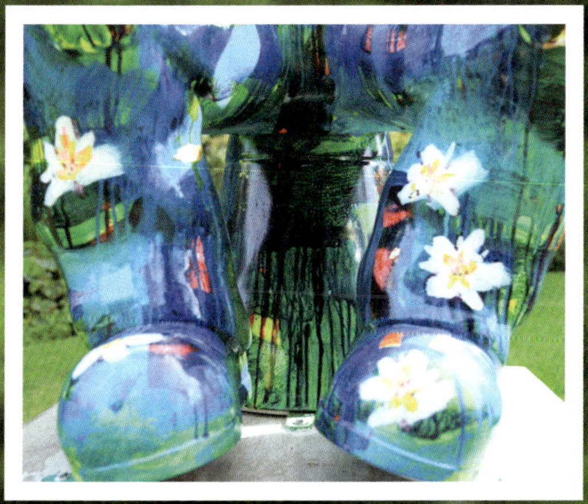

OOR LILIES

Location on the Bucket Trail: University of Dundee Botanic Garden.

Designed by: Francis Boag.

About this sculpture: Inspired by Monet's paintings of water lilies in his garden at Giverny, Francis has often painted the water lilies that grow in his own garden pond. Francis and his wife Teresa are very proud of their lilies and both being from Dundee, refer to them as oor lulies! This simple sound association of Wullie and lily was the spark for the idea behind this sculpture.

In June 2001, after nearly 30 years of teaching art in schools around Scotland, Francis decided to challenge the maxim that 'those who can, do and those who can't, teach'. So, he left behind the security of his post as head of art at Aberdeen Grammar School to achieve a life-long ambition of establishing a career as an artist. Francis is now one of Scotland's most popular and best-selling painters, exhibiting widely at home and abroad, including in New York, Dublin, Belfast, Paris, Munich, Michigan and Seattle.

Sponsor: The Vine.

Winning bid: £11,000.

Winning bidder: Thorntons Property.

Where is he now? Doing a great job as a new trainee at Thorntons!

Why was he bought? Colin Graham, Chairman at Thorntons, said: "We became aware of the ARCHIE Foundation's project at Ninewells very early on and we were keen to support them as much as we could. The Bucket Trail was fantastic with so many great designs but Oor Lilies, with its bright colour and design, was certainly a favourite for the firm. "We regularly take Oor Lilies out to community and client events to help fundraise further for the Foundation. Recent visits also include Roxburghe House, a palliative care unit for cancer patients, Cupar in Bloom - Beechgrove Garden Q&A event, and the Arbroath Relay for Life."

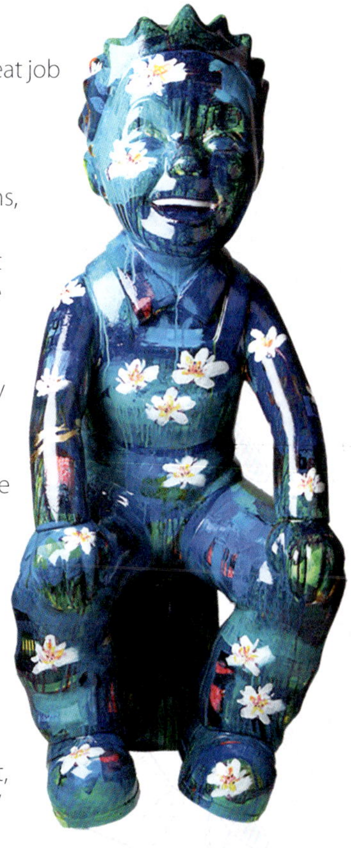

FROM OOR ROOTS UP

Location on the Bucket Trail: The Magdalen Green Bandstand.

Designed by: Joanne MacFadyen.

About this sculpture: From Oor Roots Up is inspired by Dundee's re-development – the new areas that are emerging on the waterfront are blossoming from roots that have been laid by the city's history.

Joanne is a Dundee-based artist and designer and the founder of Tea Green Events. Foremost a jeweller, she specialises in using precious metals and metal clays, enamel and gemstones to create unique and distinctive jewellery. Her work is led by a love of experimenting with materials and by her wide-eyed attitude to the world.

Sponsor: Nane but too guid no' tae include!

Winning bid: £10,000.

Winning bidder: Hillcrest Housing Association.

Where is he now? Ruling the roost at Hillcrest Housing Association!

Why was he bought? Angela Linton, chief executive, The Hillcrest Group of Companies, said: "We are absolutely delighted to be keepers of the fantastic From Oor Roots Up sculpture and a small part of the legacy of Oor Wullie's Bucket Trail.

"Now our most famous recruit, Wullie's main duty is greeting visitors into our HQ in Dundee, but he regularly gets out of the office and visits tenants' open days, care service celebrations and other special events.

"With his sincere smile, bold features and noble background in charity, it's safe to say Wullie has been a winning addition to team Hillcrest!"

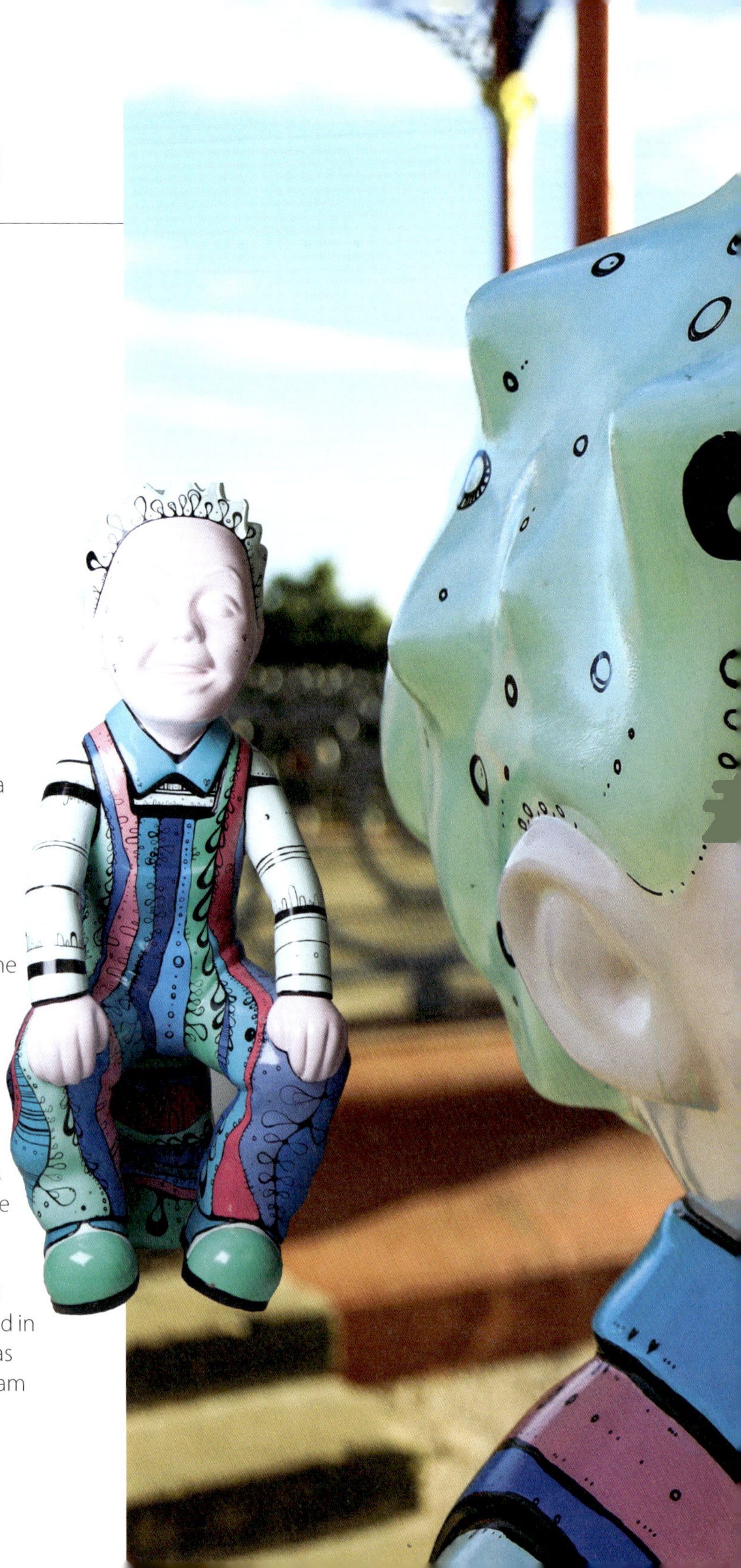

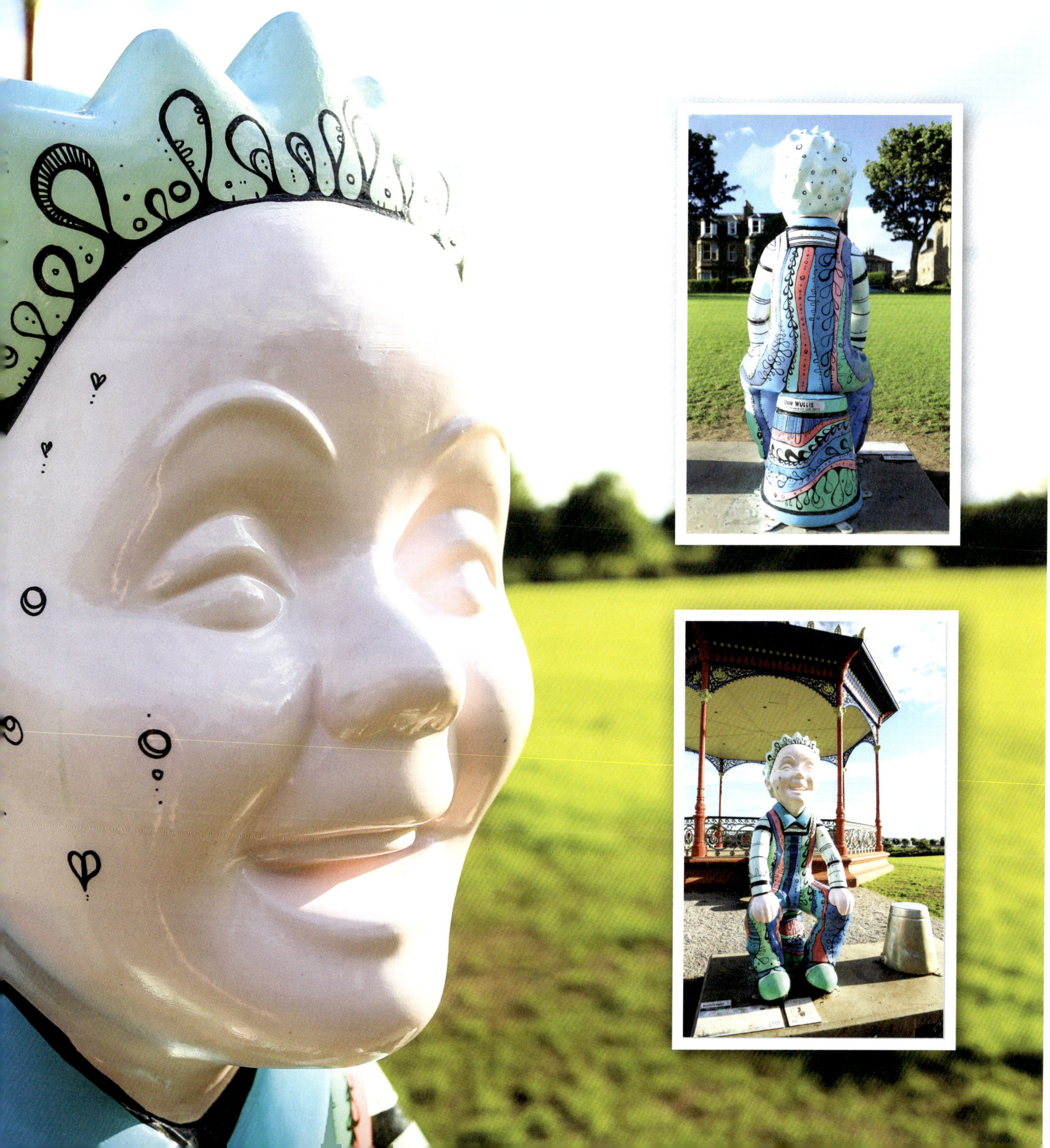
OUR WULLIE

FRIED EGGS FOR BREAKFAST

Location on the Bucket Trail: Dundee Contemporary Arts.

Designed by: Philip Colbert.

About this sculpture: The fried eggs symbolise the power of everyday life and the artist of this sculpture believes that on one level they have abstract aesthetic purity, while on the other they capture the humour of the greasy British fry up. For Colbert, art is about creating a world of fantasy and escapism and Fried Eggs for Breakfast is about bringing a touch of pop fantasy to the Trail.

Philip Colbert is a British artist and fashion designer based in London. He is known for creating the pop art label The Rodnik Band and is often described as the 'godson of Andy Warhol.'

Sponsor: Garreth and Nicola Wood.

Winning bid: £12,000.

Winning bidder: We dinae ken!

Where is he now? We dinae ken that either but he's probably tucking into his porridge if it's breakfast time!

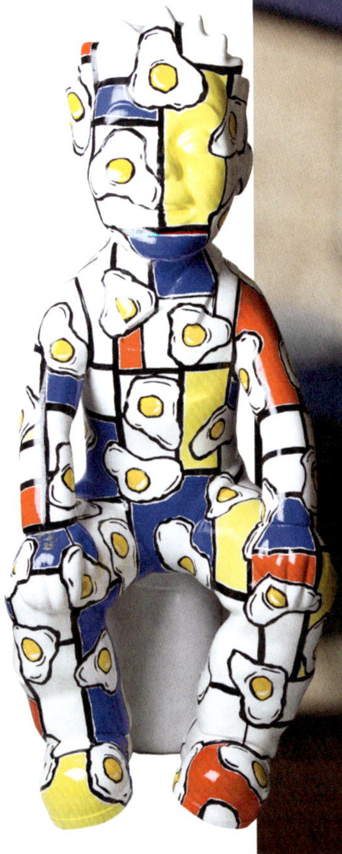

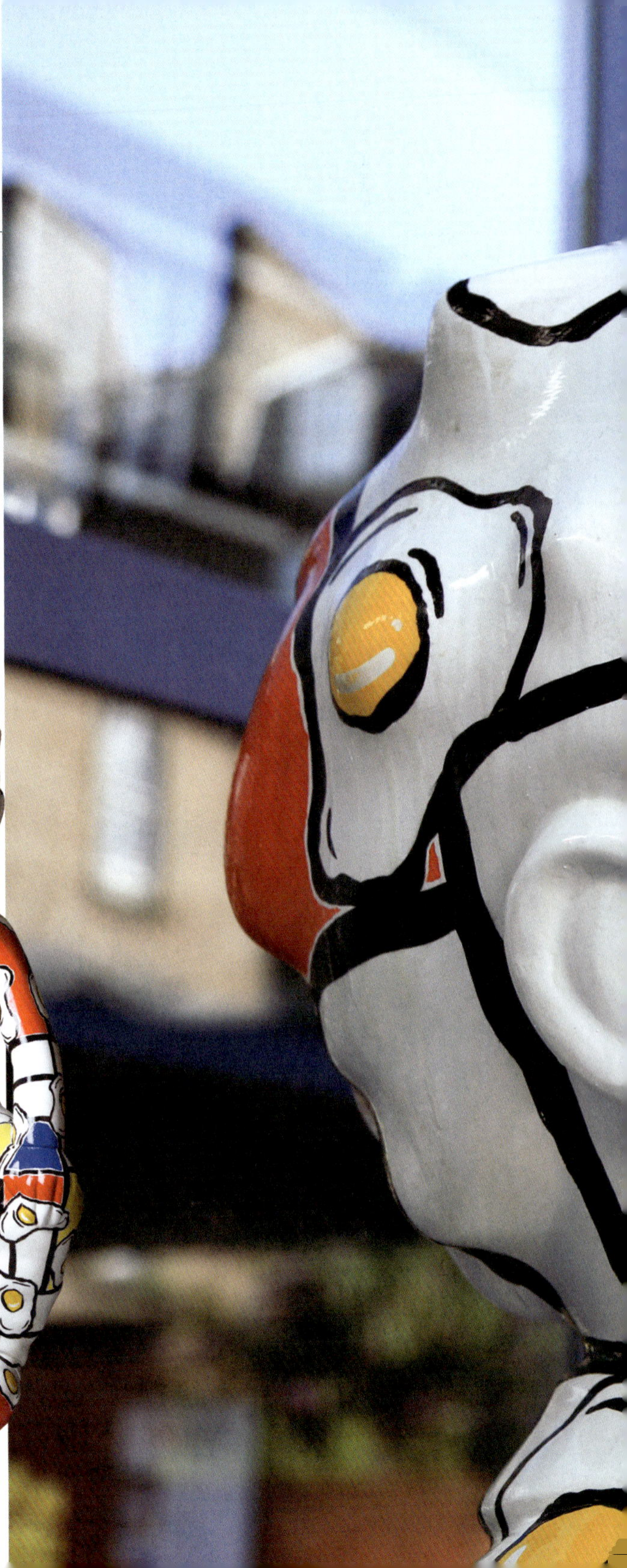

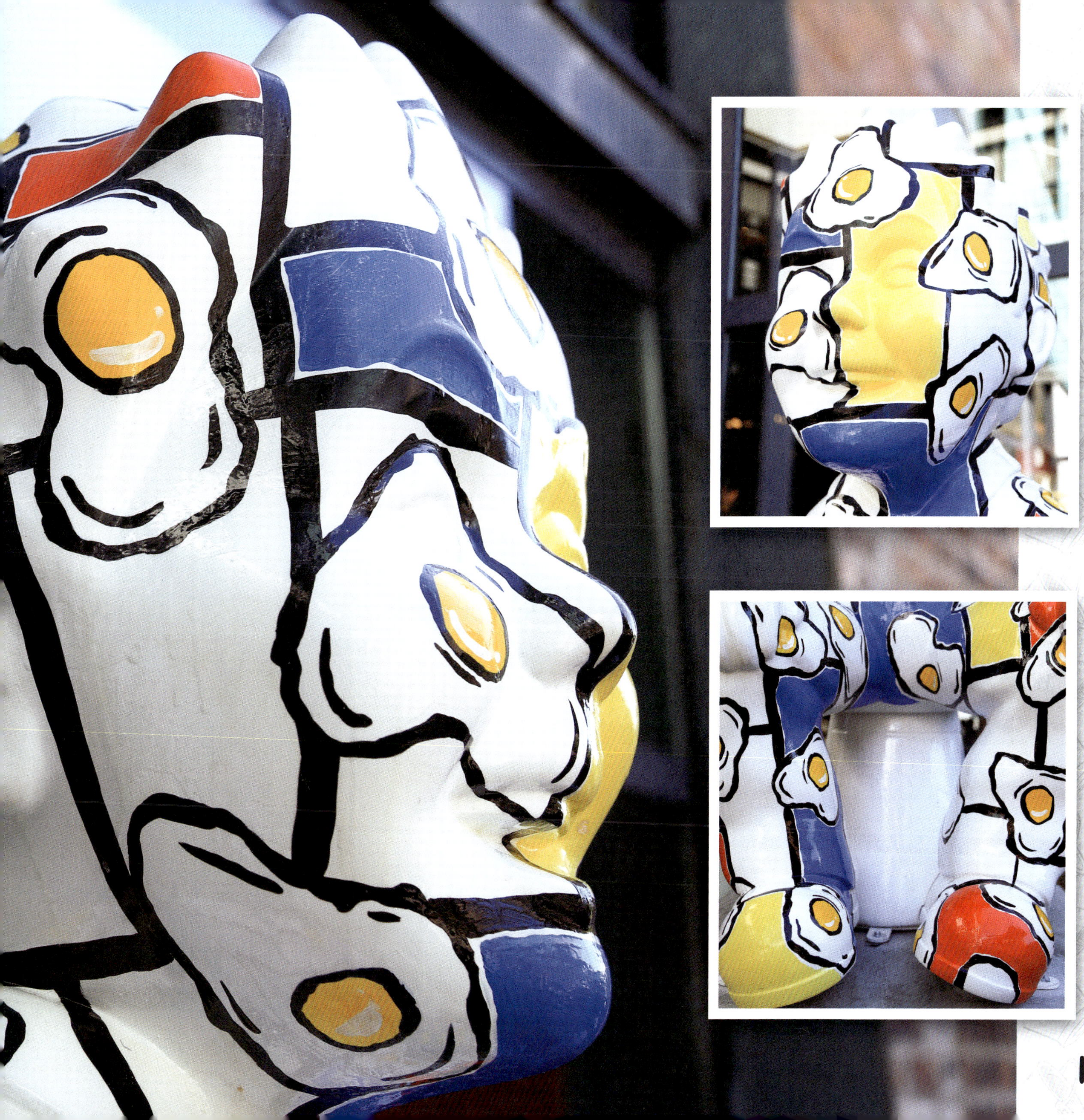

ASTRO WULLIE

Location on the Bucket Trail: Dundee Science Centre.

Designed by: Lesley D McKenzie.

About this sculpture:

Wullie watches, eyes awide,
as Tim prepares for his first space ride.

That's what I'm gonna be when I'm all grown up,

With my own space rocket I'll be an astronaut.

Until then Wullie you'll have to make dee,

With a fishbowl helmet and your pal Jeemy.

Lesley initially trained as a graphic artist before becoming a self-employed artist in 1996. She has been involved in several public art projects including Wild Dolphins in Aberdeen in 2014. She has won many awards and accolades for her artwork and exhibits her work in galleries throughout Scotland, including in her own gallery just outside Aberdeen.

Sponsor: Volpa.

Winning bid: £12,000.

Winning bidder: DC Thomson, The Sunday Post.

Where is he now? DC Thomson bought four sculptures; each visits the company's offices on rotation.

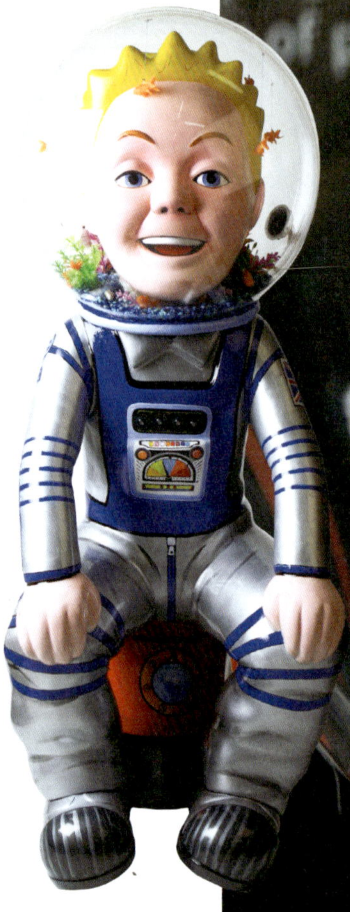

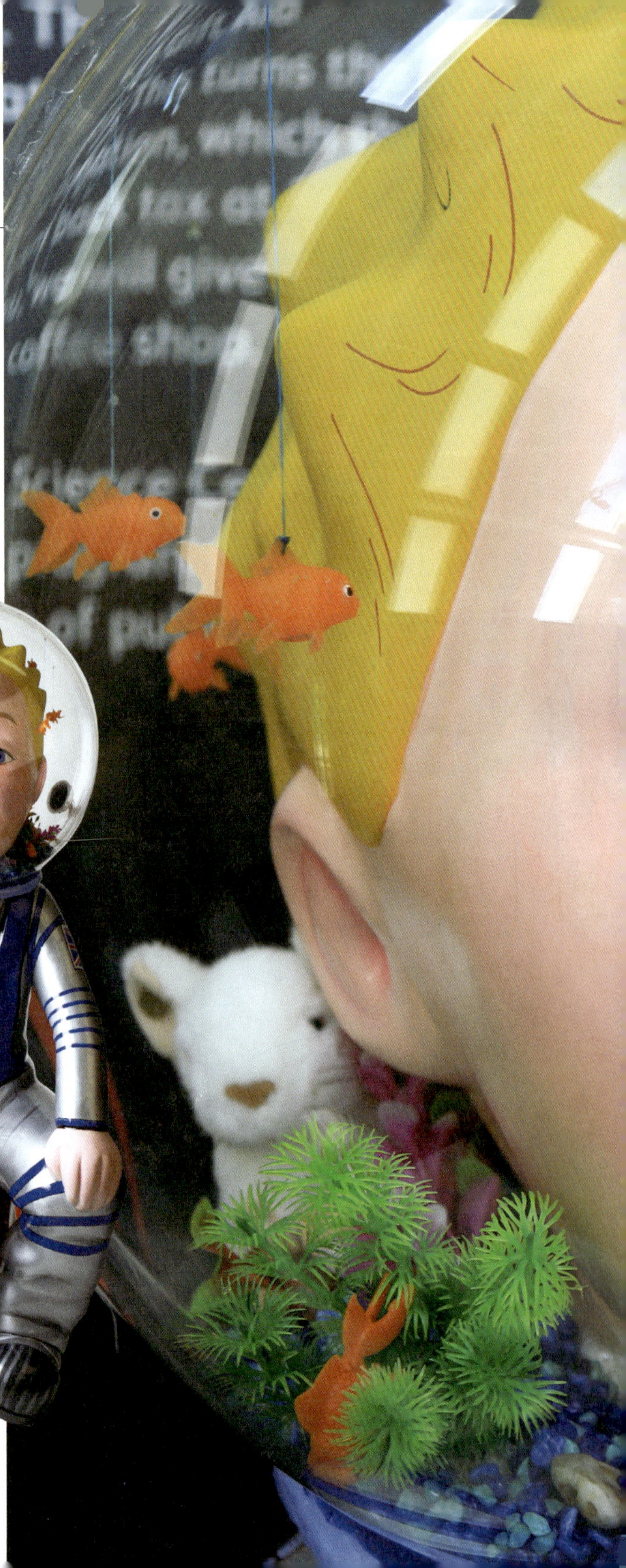

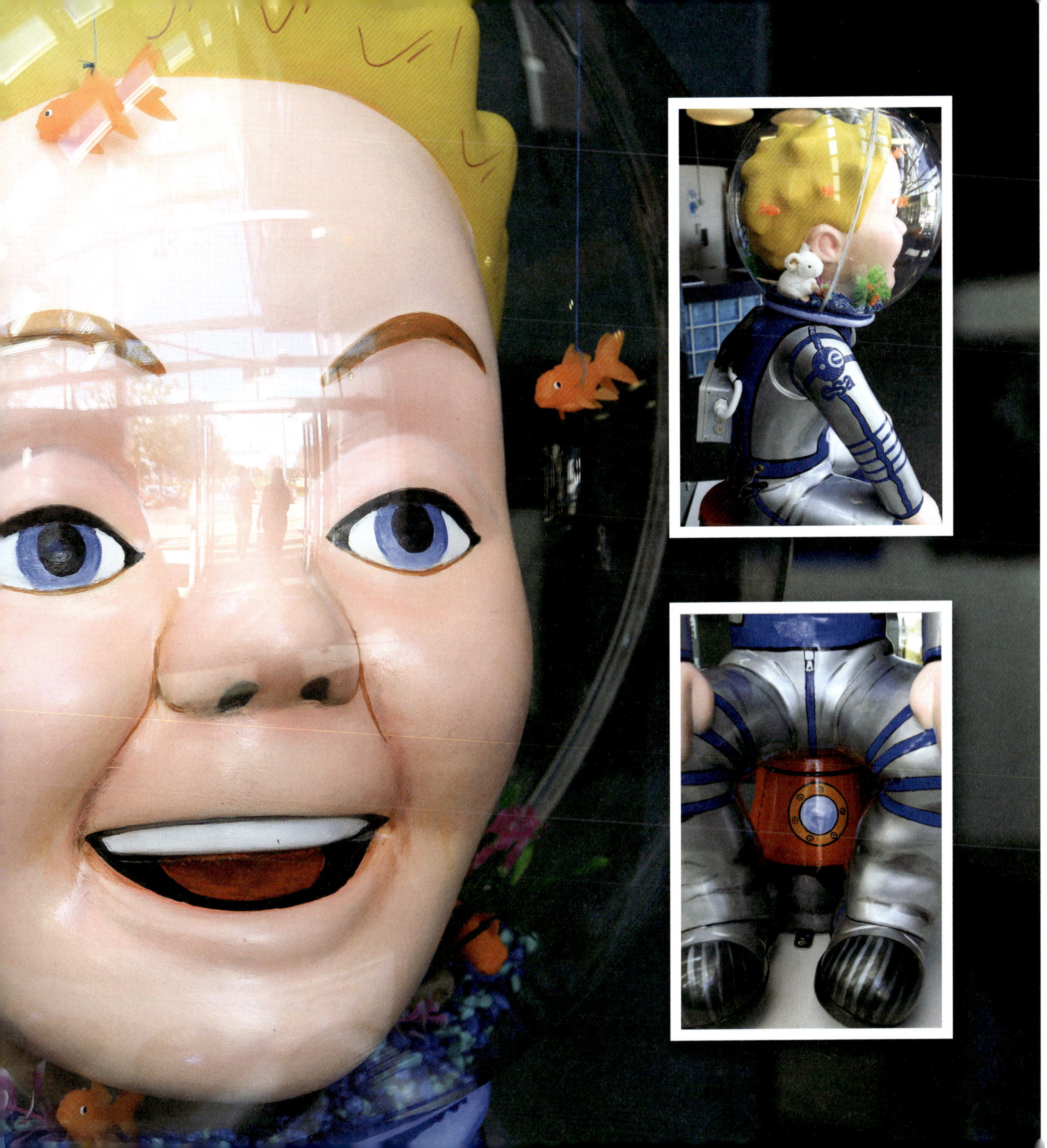
esa

THE SCULPTURES No.44

SILICON

Location on the Bucket Trail: Mills Observatory.

Designed by: David Marr.

About this sculpture: Silicon Wullie is Wullie's android double who is visiting from the future. His bucket is a battery pack that powers him up. He is inspired by cyberpunk, which imagines a future of advanced cybernetic technology, and by circuit boards, computers and science fiction films such as Robocop and The Terminator.

David studied at Forth Valley College, Gray's School of Art and Edinburgh College of Art. He currently works for the arts charity Art in Healthcare which aims to bring art and creativity to the patients, staff and visitors of Scotland's hospitals and other healthcare venues.

Sponsor: Nane but too guid no'tae include!

Winning bid: £10,000.

Winning bidder: Abertay University, Dundee.

Where is he now? Studying for his honorary degree at Abertay University!

Why was he bought? Abertay University Principal and Vice-Chancellor, Nigel Seaton, said: "We were delighted to be a part of the Oor Wullie Bucket Trail, which was a fantastic event for the Dundee community.
"Silicon Wullie now sits in pride of place in our foyer here at Abertay to welcome staff, students and guests, and even made it to City Square for our summer graduation ceremony."

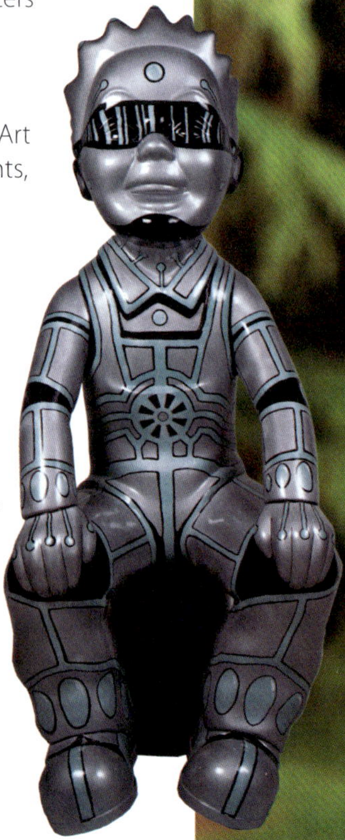

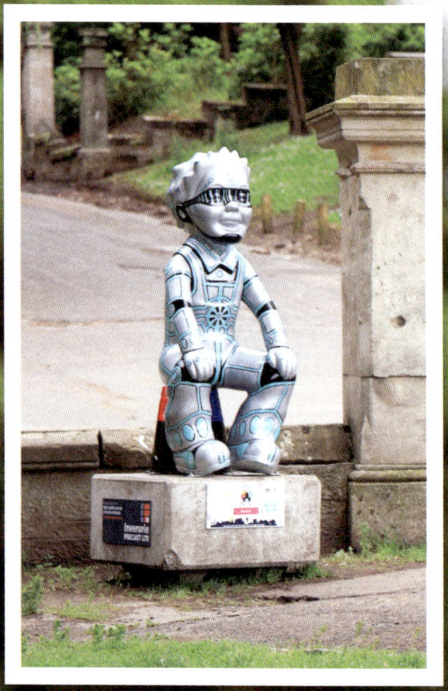

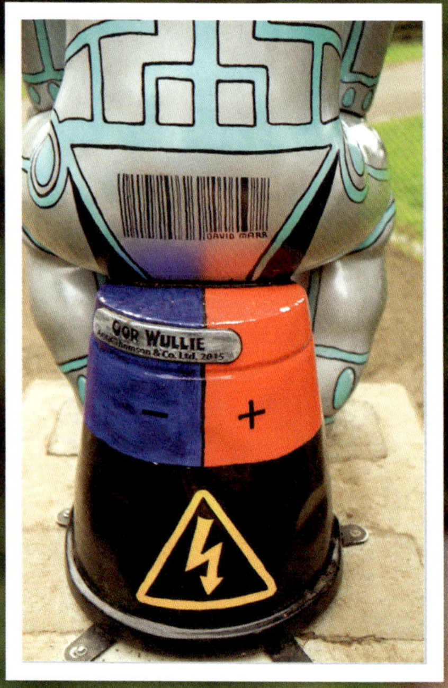

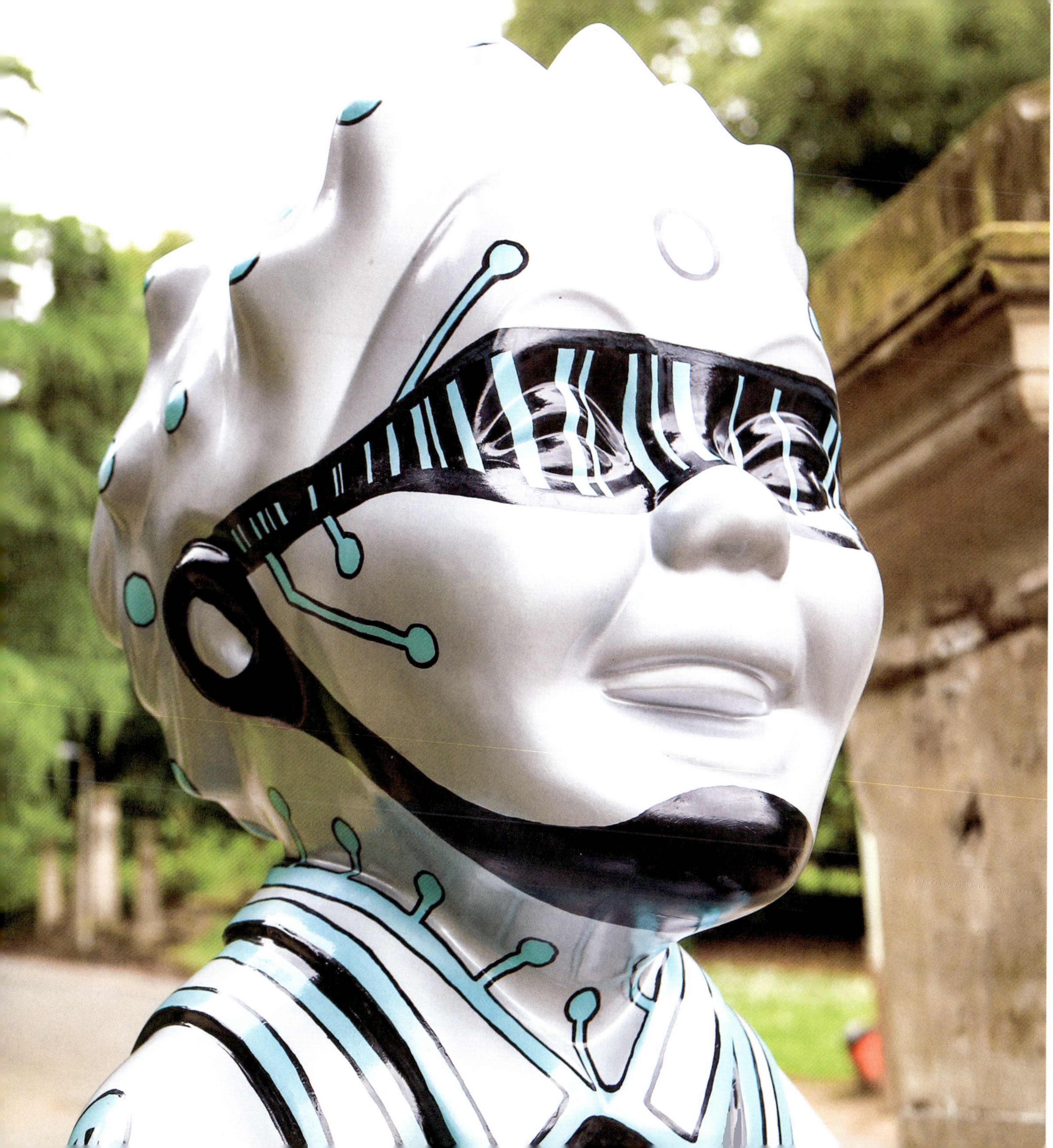

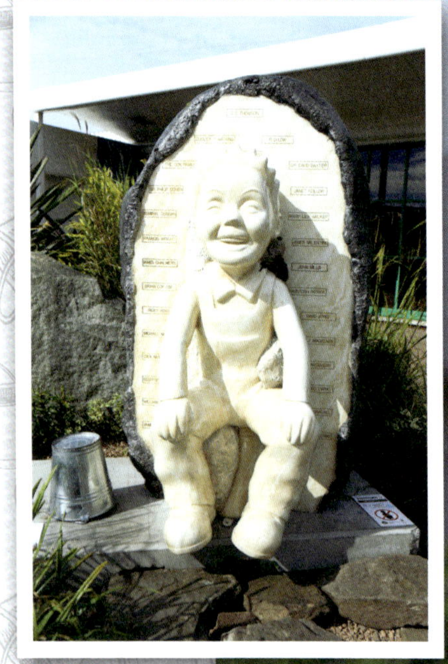

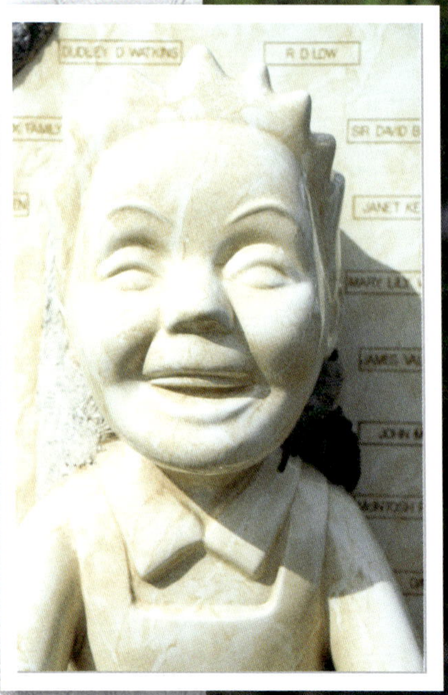
DUDLEY D WATKINS
R D LOW

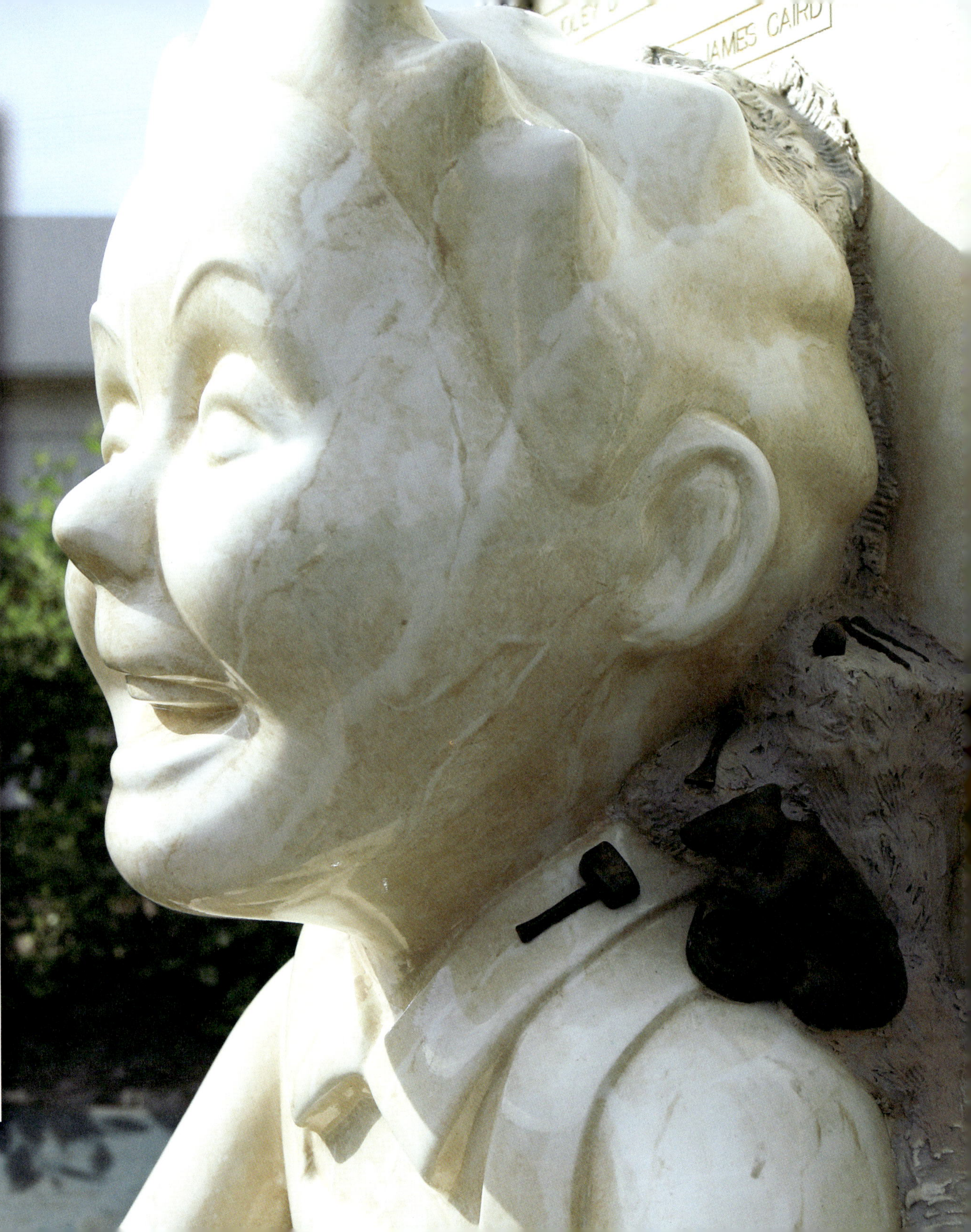
JAMES CAIRD

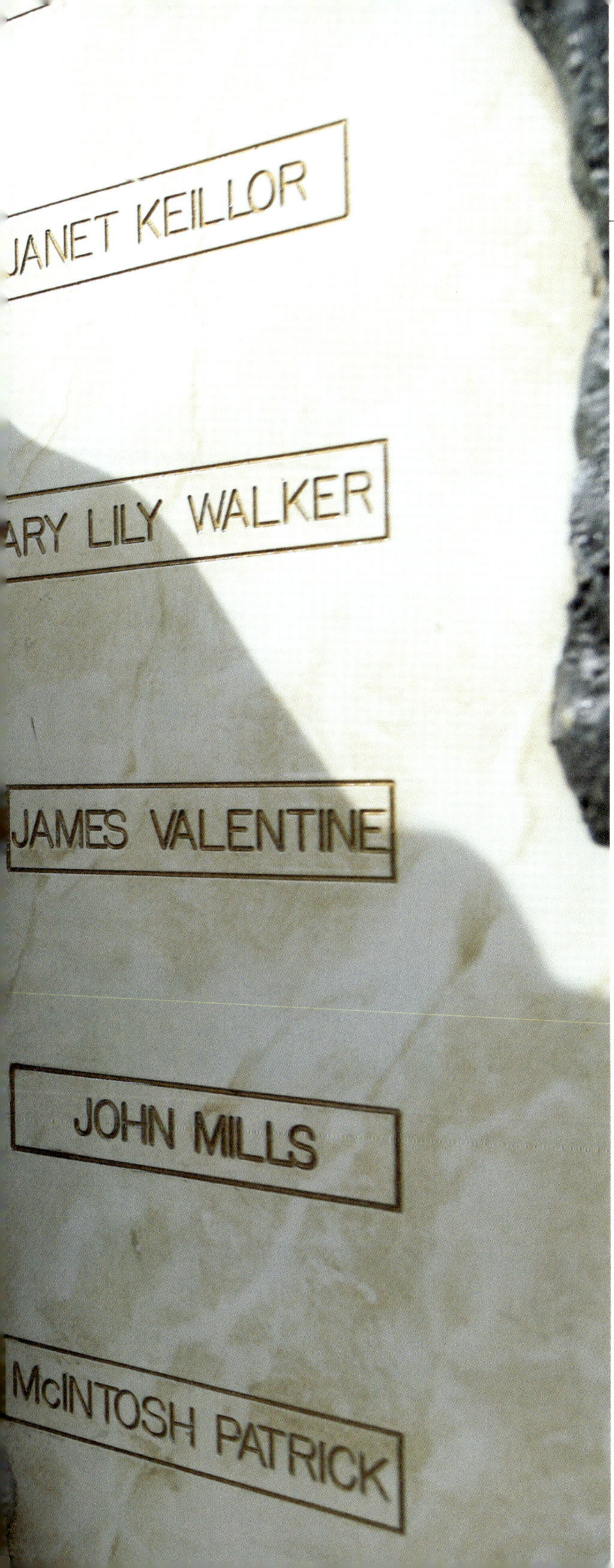

HEWN OOT THE ROCKS O' DUNDEE

Location on the Bucket Trail: Dundee Airport.

Designed by: Stewart Small and Mark Gilmour.

About this sculpture: Stewart and Mark's inspiration for this work is derived from a lifetime's friendship with Oor Wullie, and their esteem of his established place among the many stalwart historical and contemporary figures who they feel have contributed to the shaping of the place we fondly call Dundee.

Mark and Stewart are long-term friends and business associates. Both have roots entrenched in the arts. Mark is a graduate of Falmouth School of Art and Stewart is a fourth-generation painter to the great and the good of Dundee, and a graduate of 'The School of Life'.

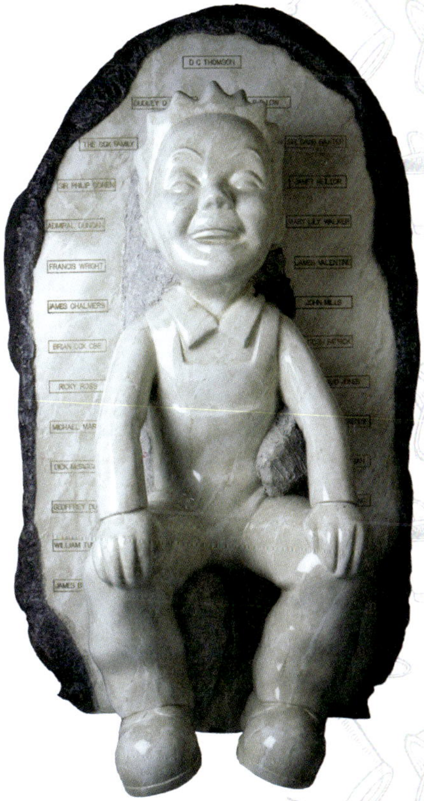

Sponsor: The Spray Factory.

Winning bid: £10,000.

Winning bidder: We dinae ken!

Where is he now? We dinae ken that either but he's mibbe making his own wee bit of history!

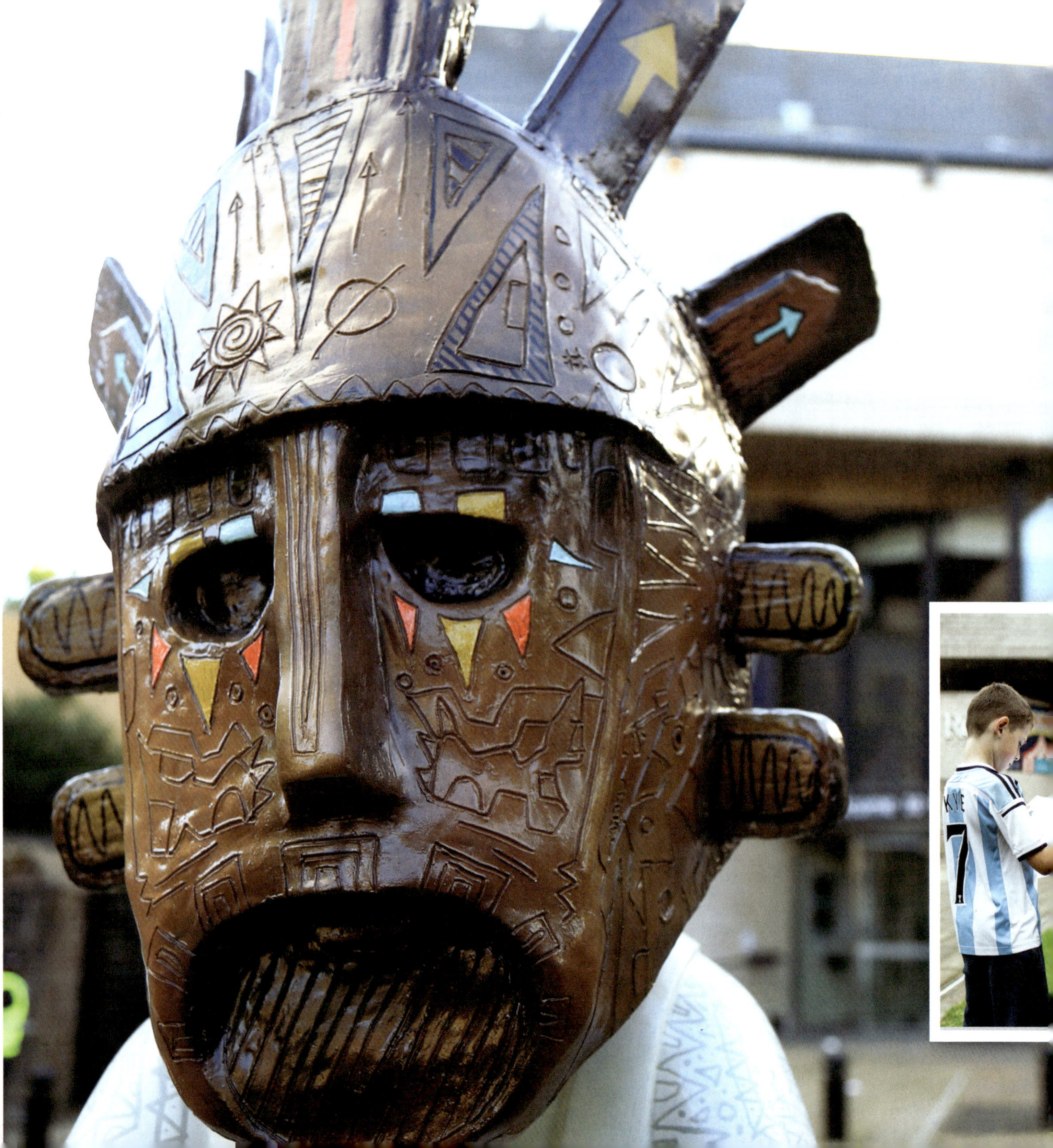

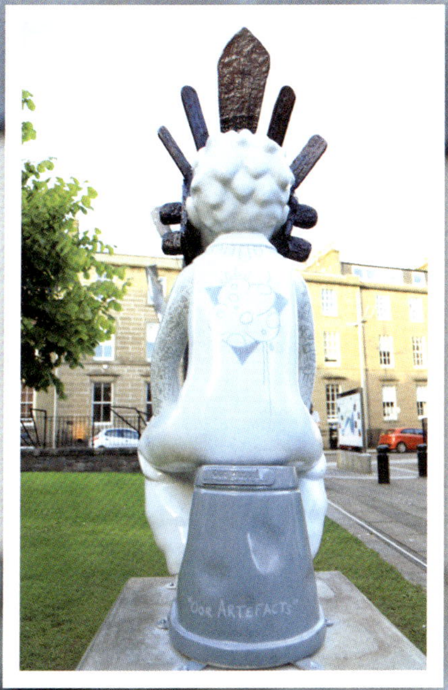

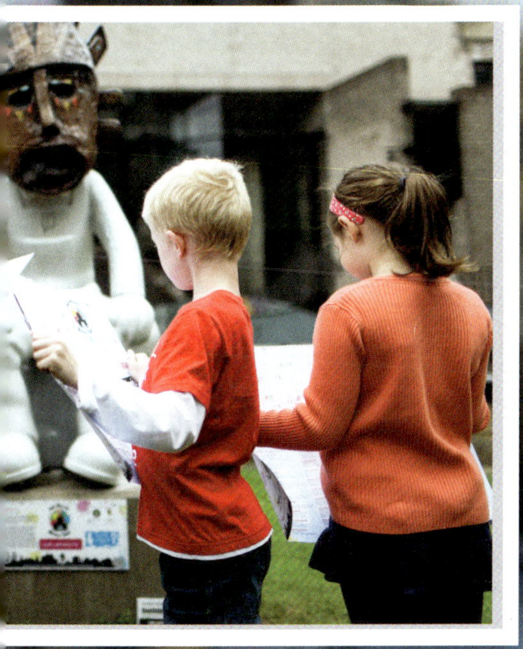

OOR ARTIFACTS

Location on the Bucket Trail: Tay Square, Dundee Rep Theatre.

Designed by: Andy MacVicar (Inflatable Monster)

About this sculpture: This Wullie is inspired by an imagined Oor Wullie comic strip in which he visits the McManus Art Gallery & Museum. On his visit, Wullie was impressed with the braw collection of weird and wonderful objects from across the globe that have somehow all ended up in Dundee. He especially liked the mba mask from Africa. It is believed that putting on the mask transforms the performer into a spirit, so Wullie thought he'd hae a go at that. Momentarily Wullie is exploring the spirit realm and will soon return the mask to the gallery!

Andy is a Scottish sculptor and graduated in fine art from Duncan of Jordanstone College of Art and Design. He is a traditionally trained bronze foundryman for a leading Scottish fine art foundry and his work has been exhibited internationally.

Sponsor: The Cooney Family.

Winning bid: £8,000.

Winning bidder: Leisure and Culture, Dundee.

Where is he now? Stepping into the past at the McManus Art Gallery & Museum in Dundee!

Why was he bought? Billy Gartley, head of cultural services at Leisure & Culture Dundee, said: "Oor Wullie is such an iconic character and really intertwines with Dundee's comic history so it's great to have him sitting alongside other items from the city's rich heritage. He's a great addition to what we have to offer and really popular with our visitors. We do keep a close eye on him though as we don't want him to get up to any more mischief while he is here!"

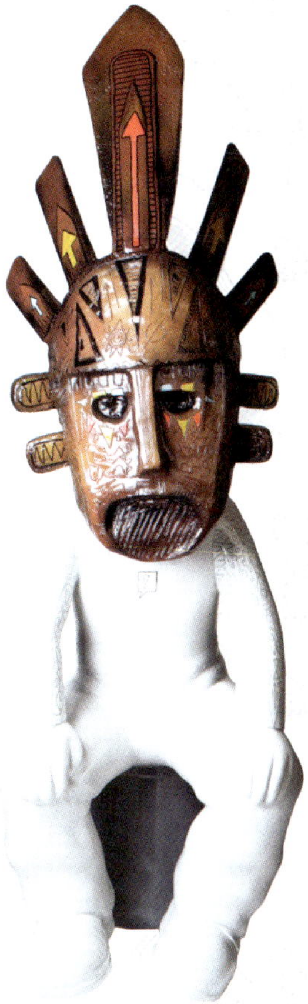

THE SCULPTURES No.47

JUTE, JAM & JOURNALISM

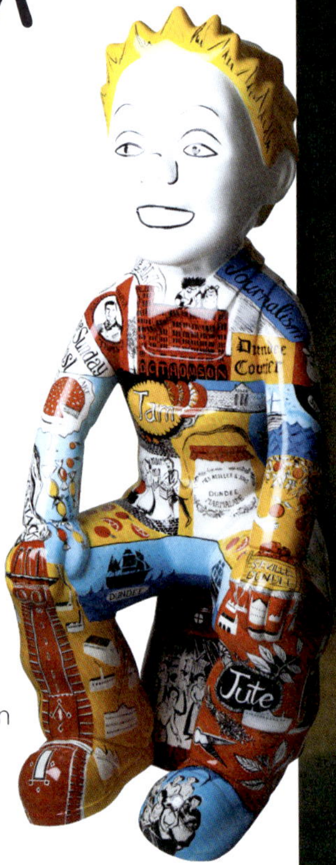

Location on the Bucket Trail: Verdant Works.

Designed by: Alice Newman.

About this sculpture: Alice's design illustrates Dundee's colourful history. The front celebrates the three industries which made it famous: jute, jam and journalism. The back tells the story of Dundee's shipbuilding industry and the proud workers of the nine trades of Dundee.

Alice is an illustrator and printmaker based in Edinburgh. Her work is bright and cheerful and she finds her inspiration from everyday places and her surroundings. She has her own business, Alice Newman Illustration and Printmaking, which sells a range of prints, cards and other paper products.

Sponsor: Apex Hotels.

Winning bid: £13,000.

Winning bidder: DC Thomson.

Where is he now? DC Thomson bought four sculptures; each visits the company's offices on rotation.

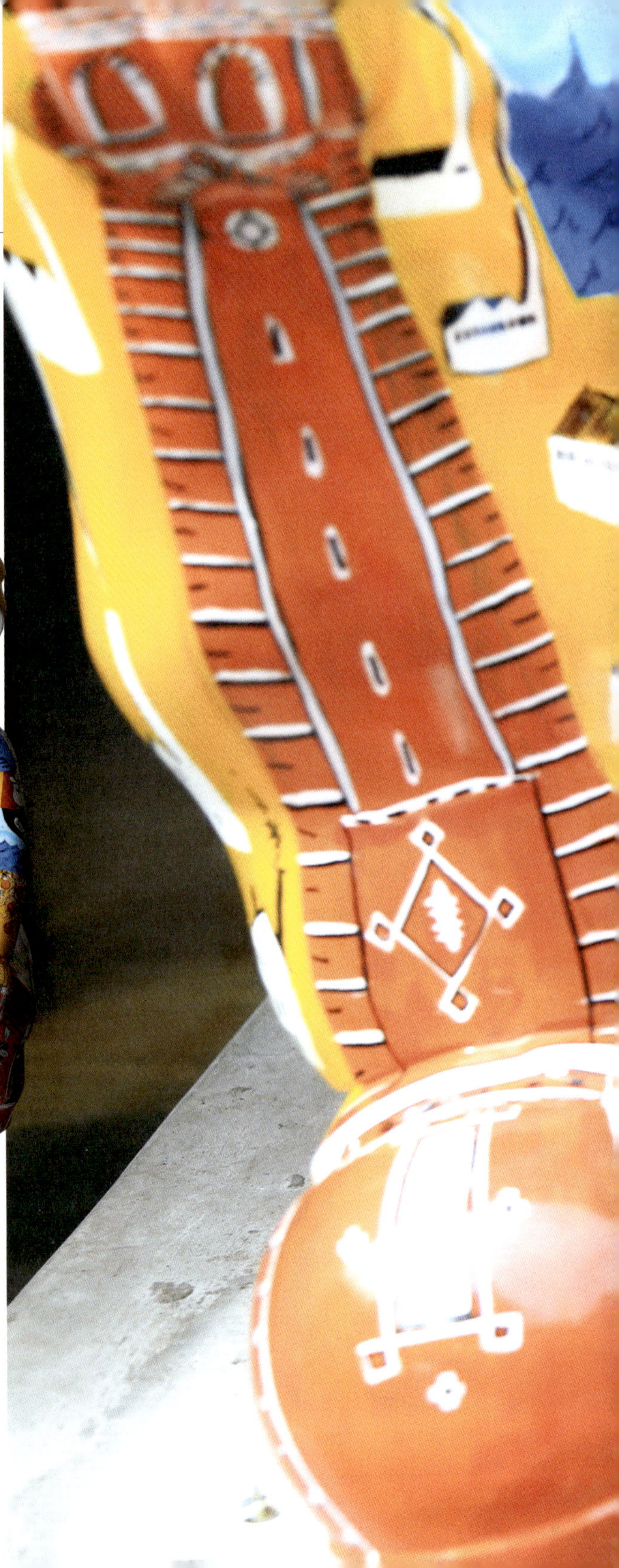

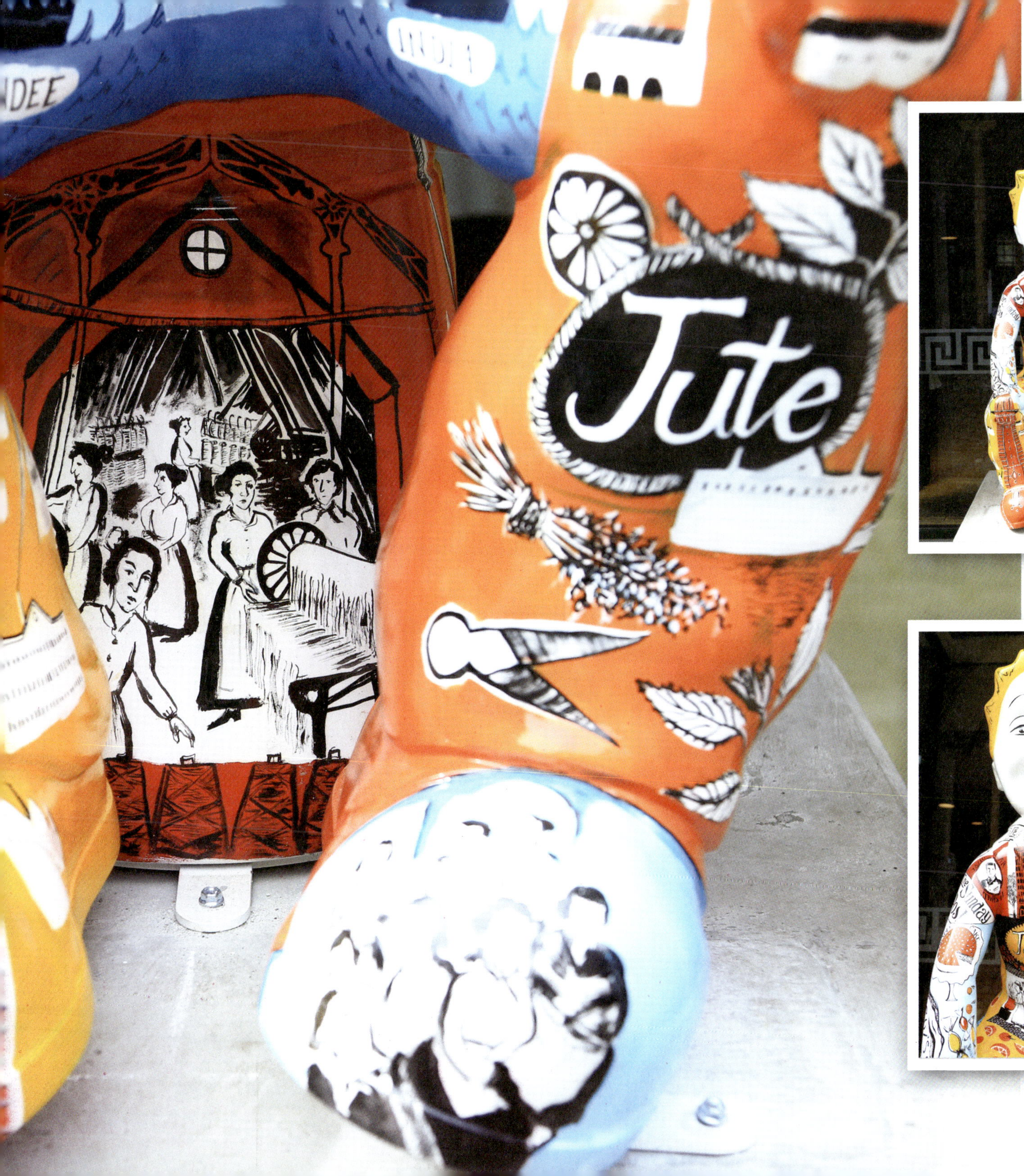
Jute

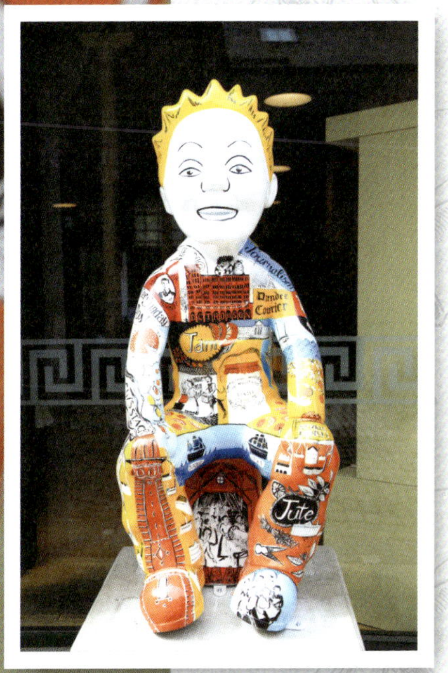

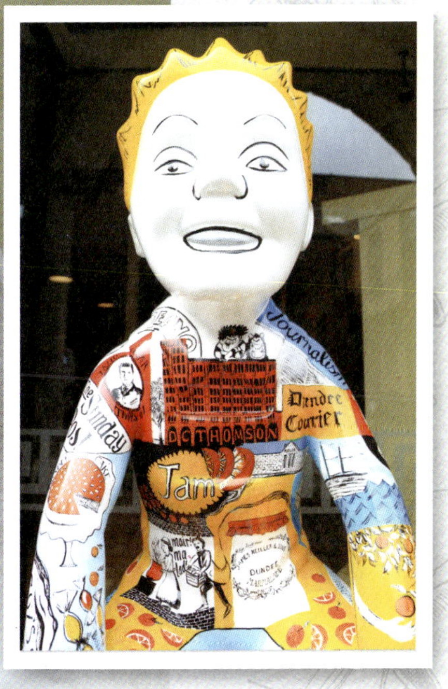
Dundee Courier
DC THOMSON

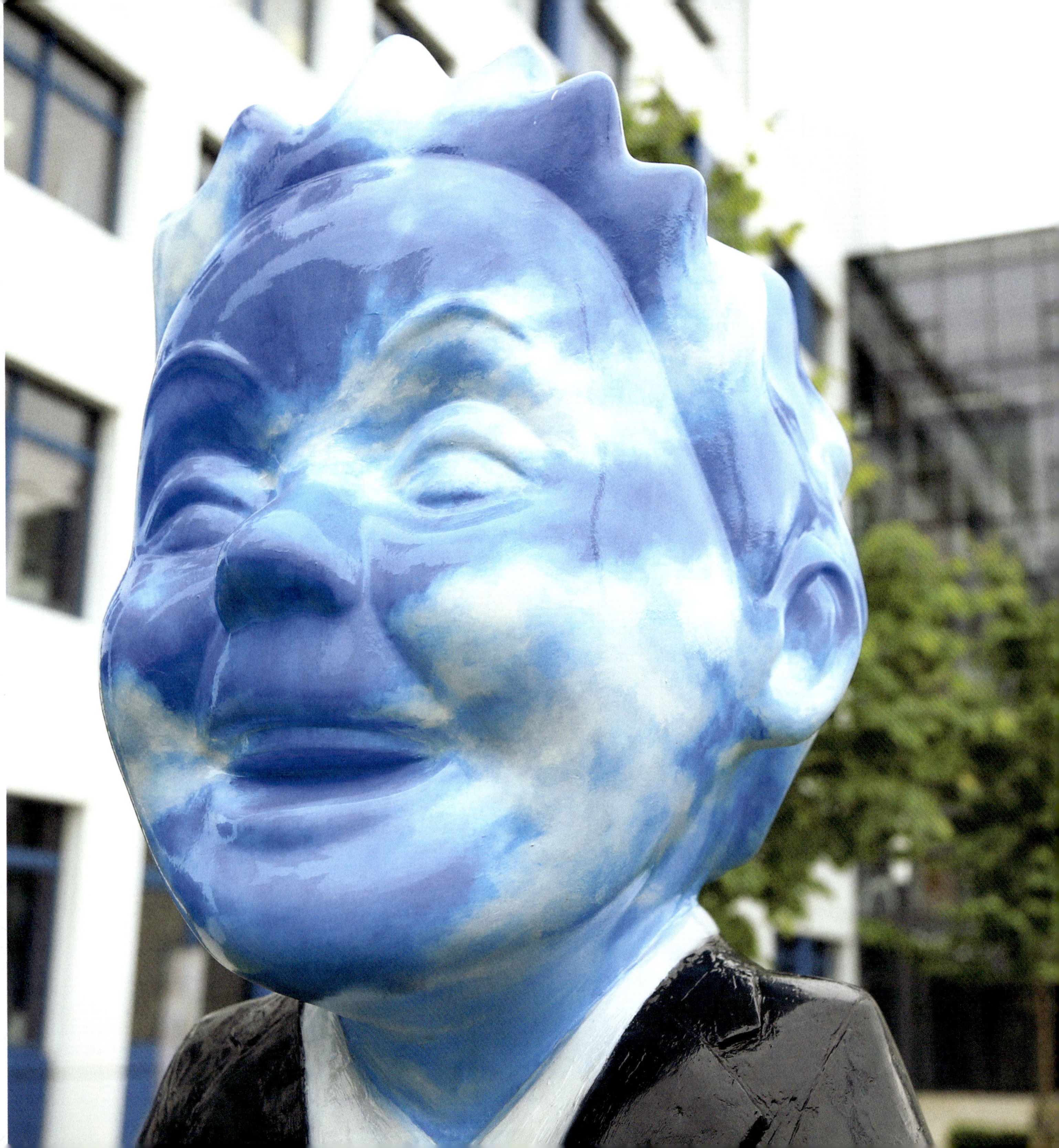

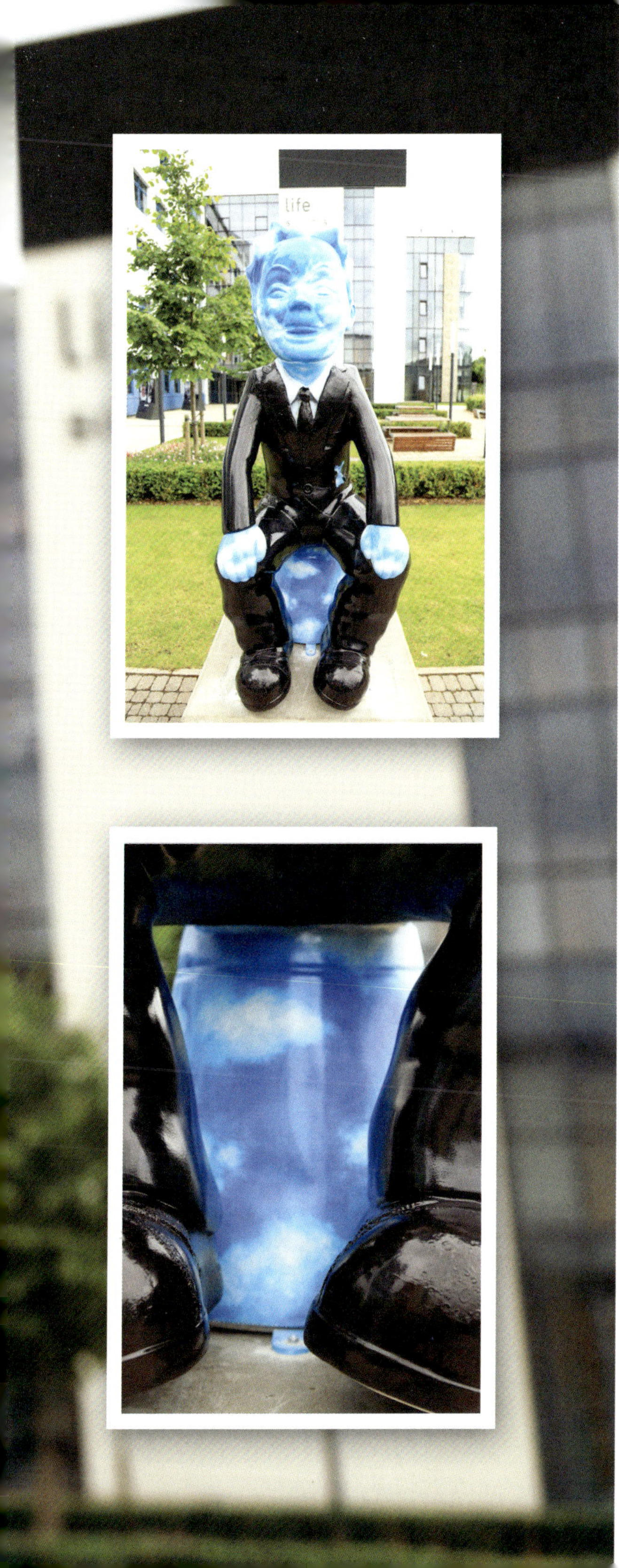

THE SCULPTURES No.48

THE DREAMER

Location on the Bucket Trail: Welcome Trust Complex.

Designed by: Mary Butterworth.

About this sculpture: Oor Wullie is a much-loved character from our childhood and evokes the spirit of youth. He loves life, fun, mischief and laughter. With his head in the clouds, The Dreamer represents everyone's inner Oor Wullie…the child with an open heart, dreams and schemes. The bucket of dreams is our own bucket list. These can often be forgotten when wearing the 'suit' of adult constraints and responsibilities. Abody has dreams…even a wee moose…

A full-time painter, Mary's subjects are contemporary spaces for reflection and exploration. In her work, she captures the dramatic qualities of light - rich in colour, depth and emotion. Her innovative use of colour is instantly recognisable and her work hangs in private collections worldwide.

Sponsor: John Clark Motor Group.

Winning bid: £11,000.

Winning bidder: We dinae ken!

Where is he now? We dinae ken that either but he's probably daydreaming and looking up at the clouds!

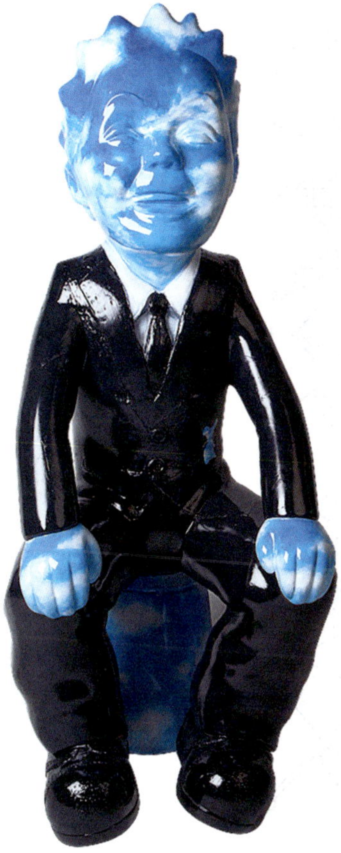

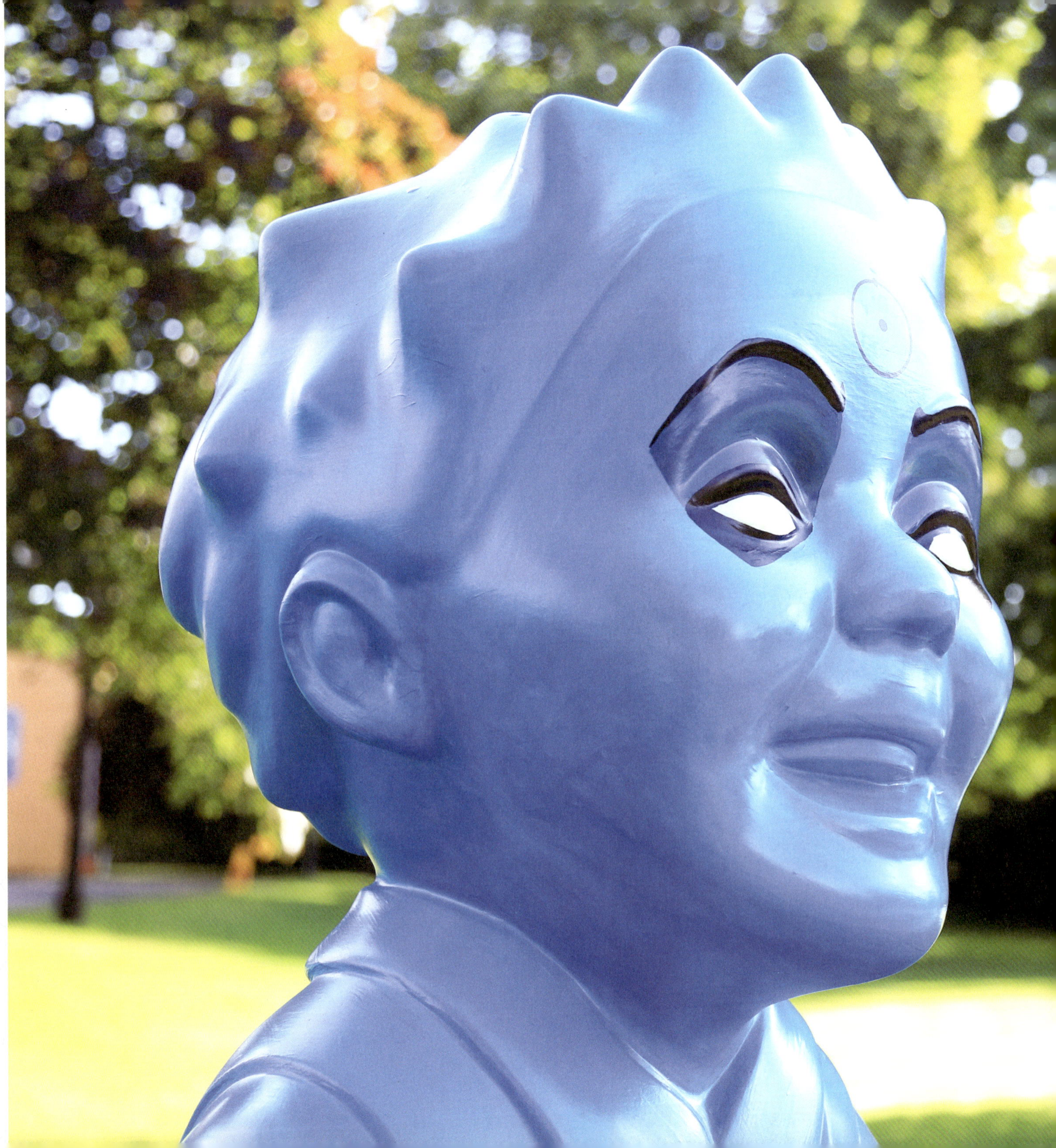

WHEN WULLIE MET DR MANHATTAN

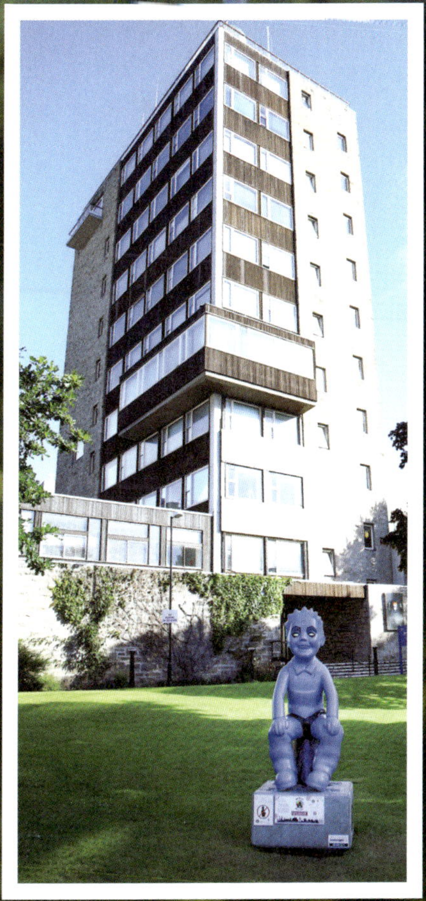

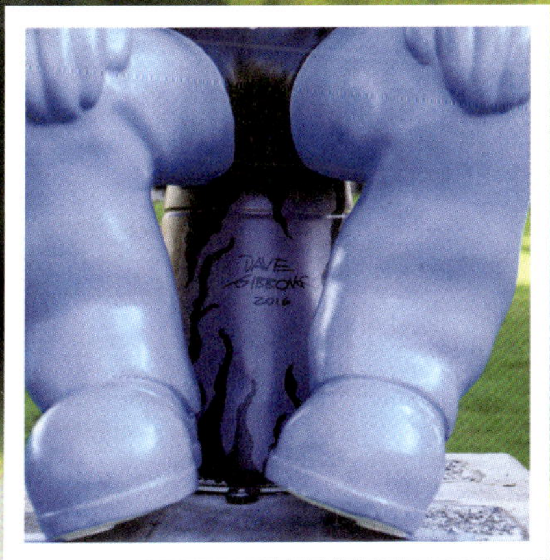

Location on the Bucket Trail: The University of Dundee, Tower Building.

Designed by: Sarah Coonan and Dave Gibbons.

About this sculpture: Sarah was commissioned to create a Watchmen's Dr Manhattan inspired Oor Wullie. The sculpture was designed by Watchmen creator Dave Gibbons, a well-known comic book artist and writer. Dave is best-known for the comics Watchmen and 2000 AD, and loved the sculpture so much that he signed it!

Sarah is a ceramicist based in Aberdeenshire. She is inspired by the fine, crisp detailing of Japanese woodprints and ceramics. She uses pen and ink to create her intricate designs.

Sponsor: The University of Dundee.

Winning bid: £9,500.

Winning bidder: Chris van der Kuyl, Dundee-based games entrepreneur.

Where is he now? Gifted to the University of Dundee and keeping all the students in line!

Why was he bought?
Chris van der Kuyl said: "I really wanted to see the Dr Manhattan Oor Wullie in the University of Dundee. When I realised they probably didn't have enough budget to buy it I was delighted to be able to gift it to them. It was a wonderful touch that the Principal then donated the money that they had raised to the student bureau fund."

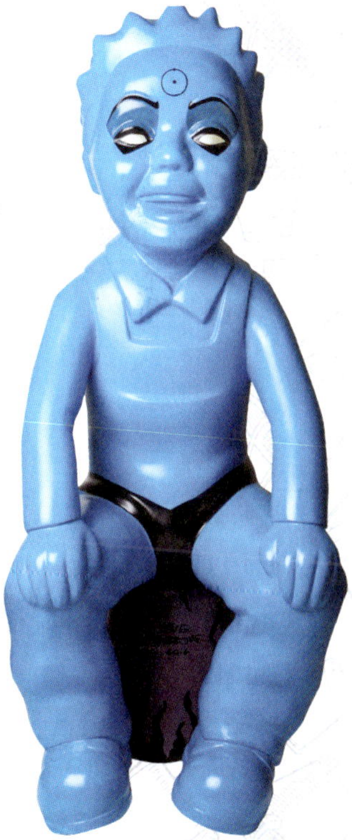

THE SCULPTURES No.50

LITTLE HANDS

Location on the Bucket Trail:
Baxter Park.

Designed by: Emma White and the children of Tayside Children's Hospital.

About this sculpture: The children at Tayside Children's Hospital worked enthusiastically over the course of a fun-filled morning to design Little Hands. They covered their hands in paint to create hand prints to stamp on their design. The children were encouraged to leave as many of their hand prints as possible on the sculpture to transform it into something beautiful. With its colourful and uplifting design, this sculpture provided an eye-catching work of art worthy of its place alongside the other sculptures.

Sponsor: The ARCHIE Foundation.

Winning bid: £11,000.

Winning bidder: The Speratus Group Ltd.

Where is he now? We dinae ken but we hope he's still spreading joy and happiness!

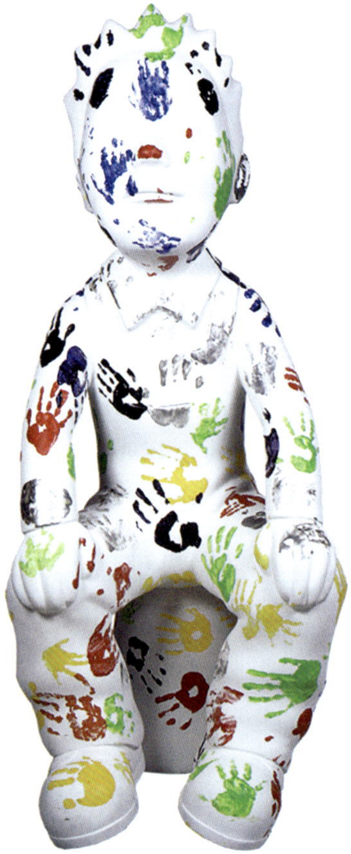

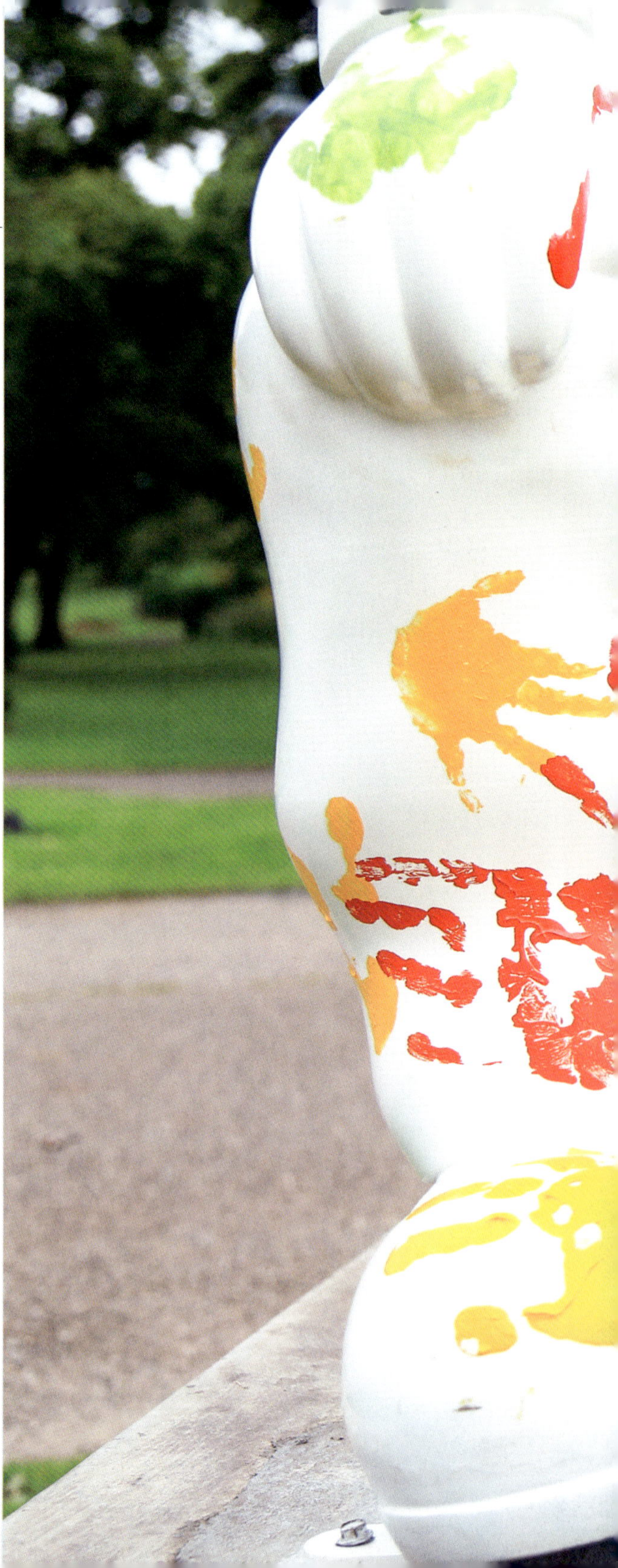

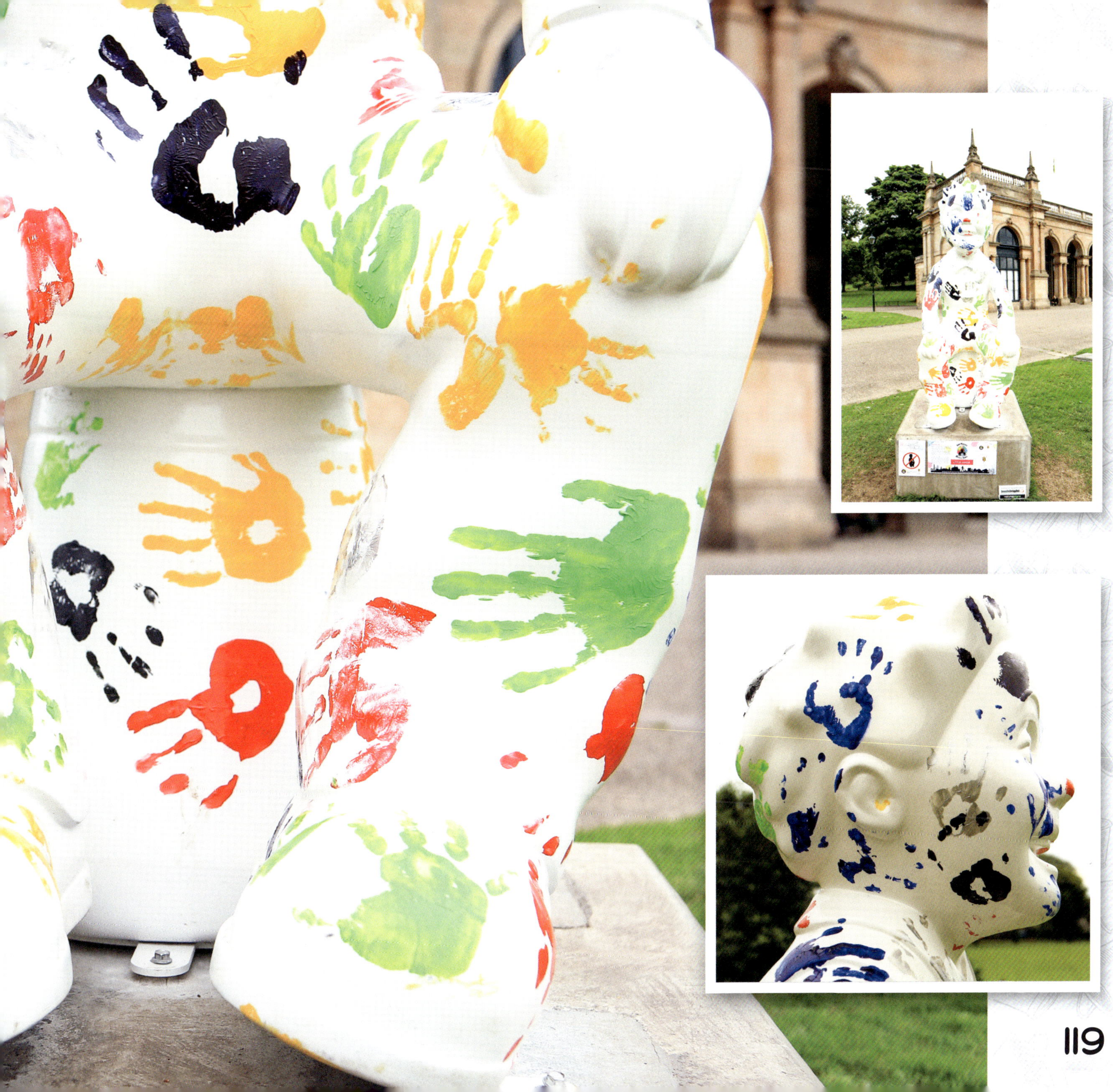

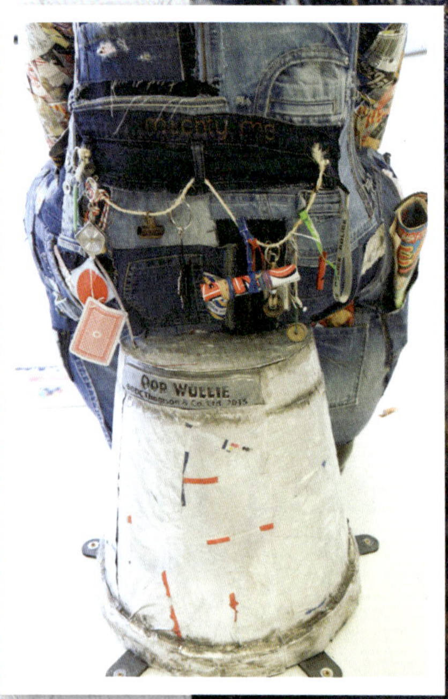
OOR WULLIE

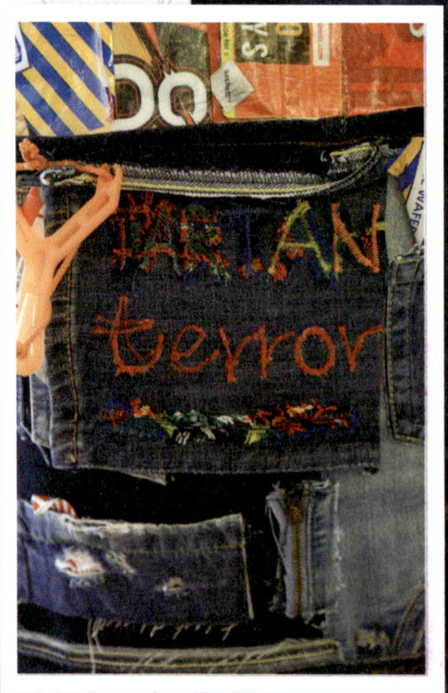
TARTAN
terror

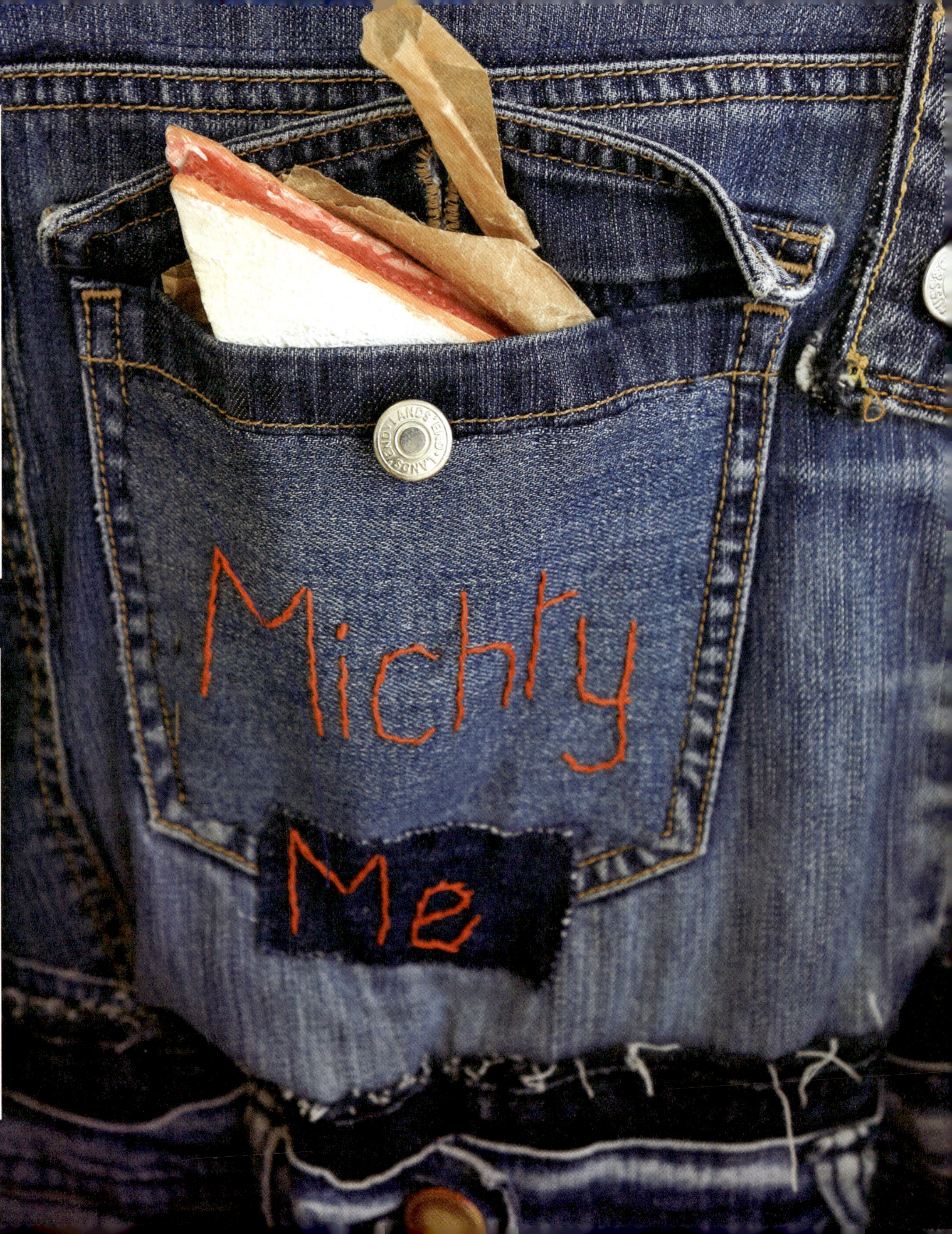
Michty
Me

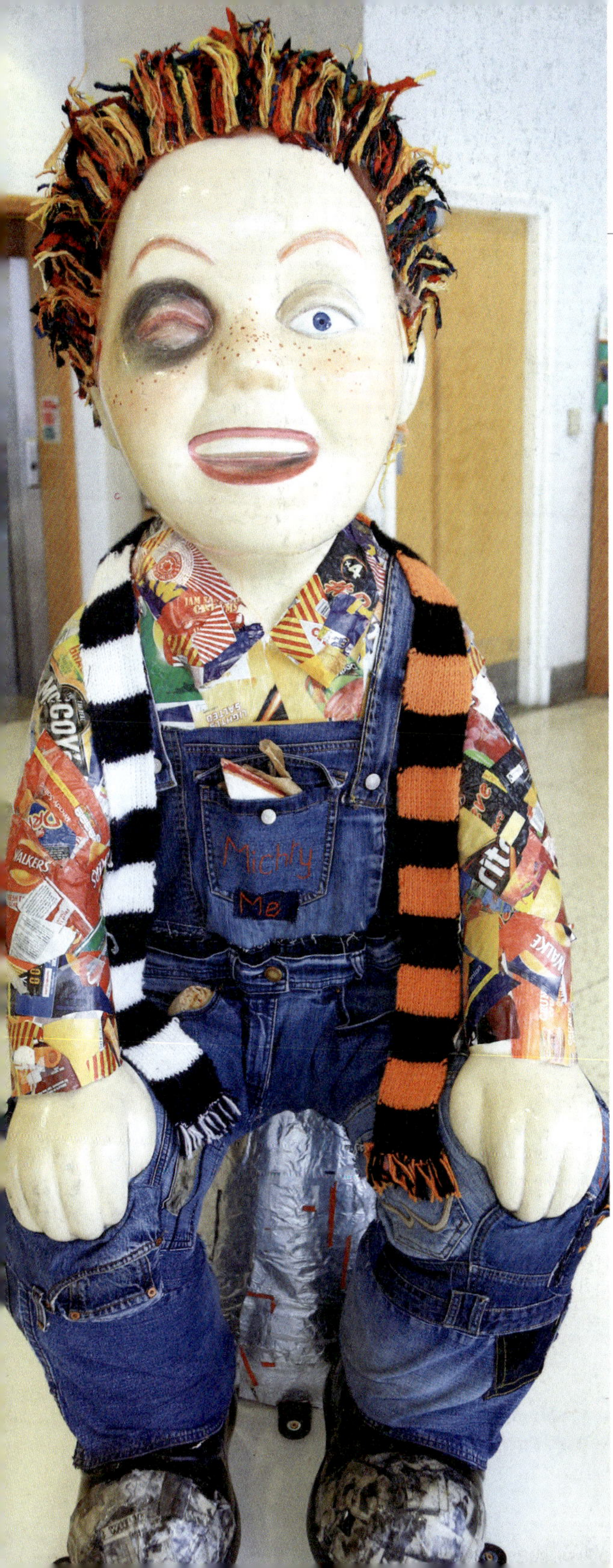

A POCKETFU' O'PIECES

Location on the Bucket Trail: Dundee Central Library.

Designed by: Kalamkari Textile Group.

About this sculpture: Dundee has a long-standing connection with textiles and the Kalamkari Textile Group take their name from an Indian printing process, paying tribute to Dundee's former jute trade with India. All nine members of the Kalamkari Textile Group work in stitched textiles for exhibitions and some also teach their skills to others.

For this sculpture, Wullie's dungarees are made from auld jeans (from Dundee). The dungarees feature plenty o' pooches for a'thin' abody wid need when oot and aboot which is just as weel as Wullie has plenty o'treasures ready tae swap for sweeties!

Sponsor: Nane but too guid no' tae include!

Winning bid: £9,000.

Winning bidder: The Sands Restaurant, Broughty Ferry.

Where is he now? Enjoying the view over the silvery Tay from the Sands Restaurant in Broughty Ferry!

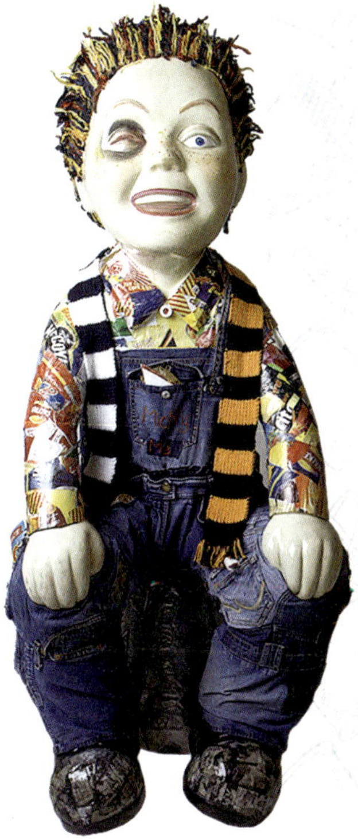

DISCO WULLIE

Location on the Bucket Trail: Oor Wullie's Bucket Trail Headquarters, Overgate Shopping Centre.

Designed by: Helen Stephenson.

About this sculpture: Decorated with hundreds of small mirror tiles, Disco Wullie stands out from the crowd and makes abody want to dance and smile!

Helen is a visual artist and works from her studio in Edinburgh where she designs and creates custom artwork and visual displays for retail windows, commercial interiors and event spaces.

Sponsor: T in the Park.

Winning bid: £12,000.

Winning bidder: Tony Cochrane, director, TGC Leisure Ltd.

Where is he now? Dancing the night away at Club Tropicana & Vogue in Dundee!

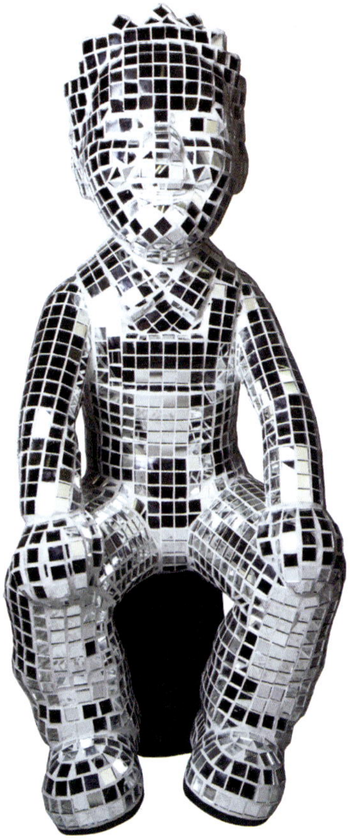

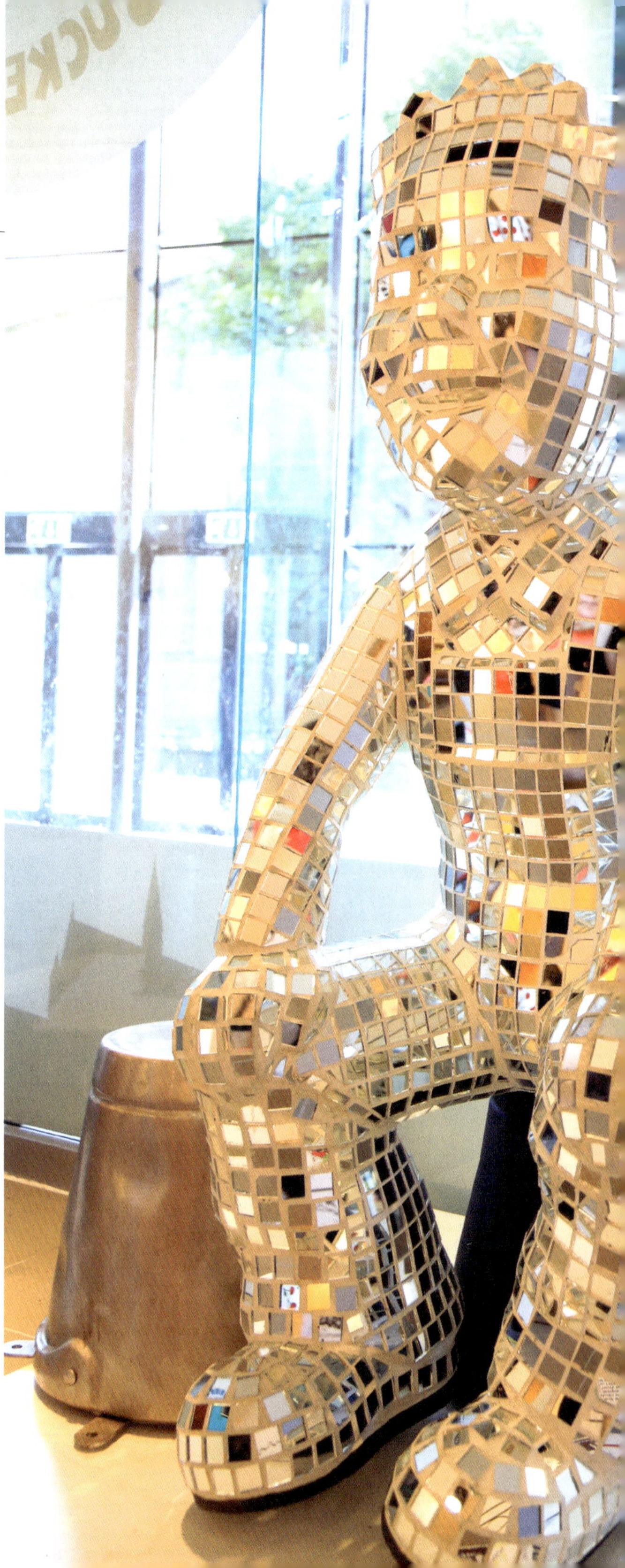

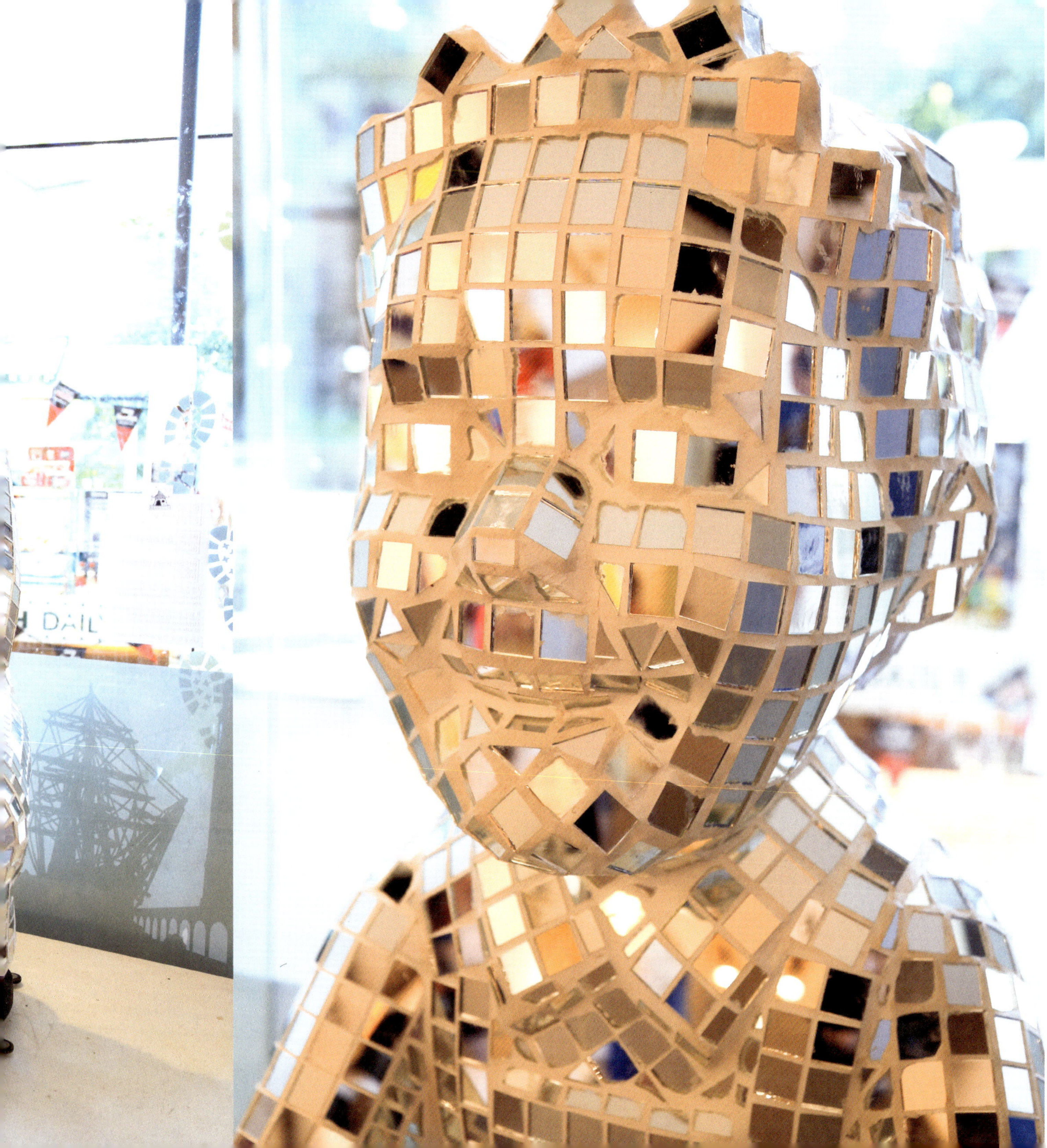

OOR DREAMCATCHER

Location on the Bucket Trail: Oor Wullie's Bucket Trail Headquarters, Overgate Shopping Centre.

Designed by: Suzanne Scott (WhimSicAL LusH).

About this sculpture: Oor Dreamcatcher is all about inspiring people to follow their dreams. It's about having a dream and chasing it...but then catching and following it too. With this sculpture, Suzanne encouraged children to join her on a dream-catching mission as they added in their dreams.

Suzanne is an artist and illustrator based in Dundee, working under the name WhiSicAL LusH. She loves going on inky adventures and adores the little things in life. Whether she's creating creatures or castles, houses or robots, or turning people's ideas into reality, there is always a story on her drawing board.

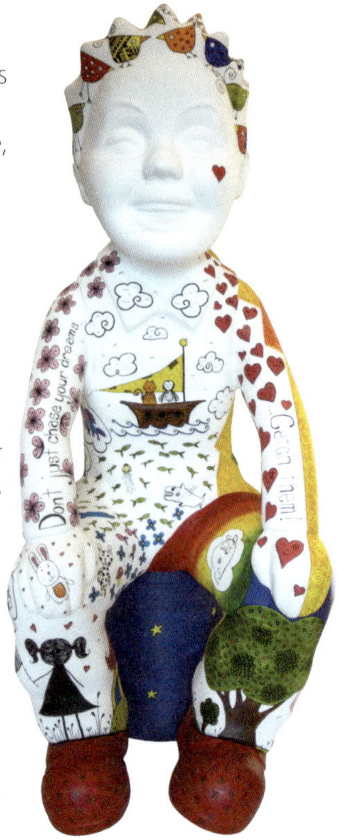

Sponsor: Nane but too guid no'tae include!

Winning bid: £12,000.

Winning bidder: NHS Tayside.

Where is he now? Causing mischief in Ward 30 at Ninewells Hospital, Dundee.

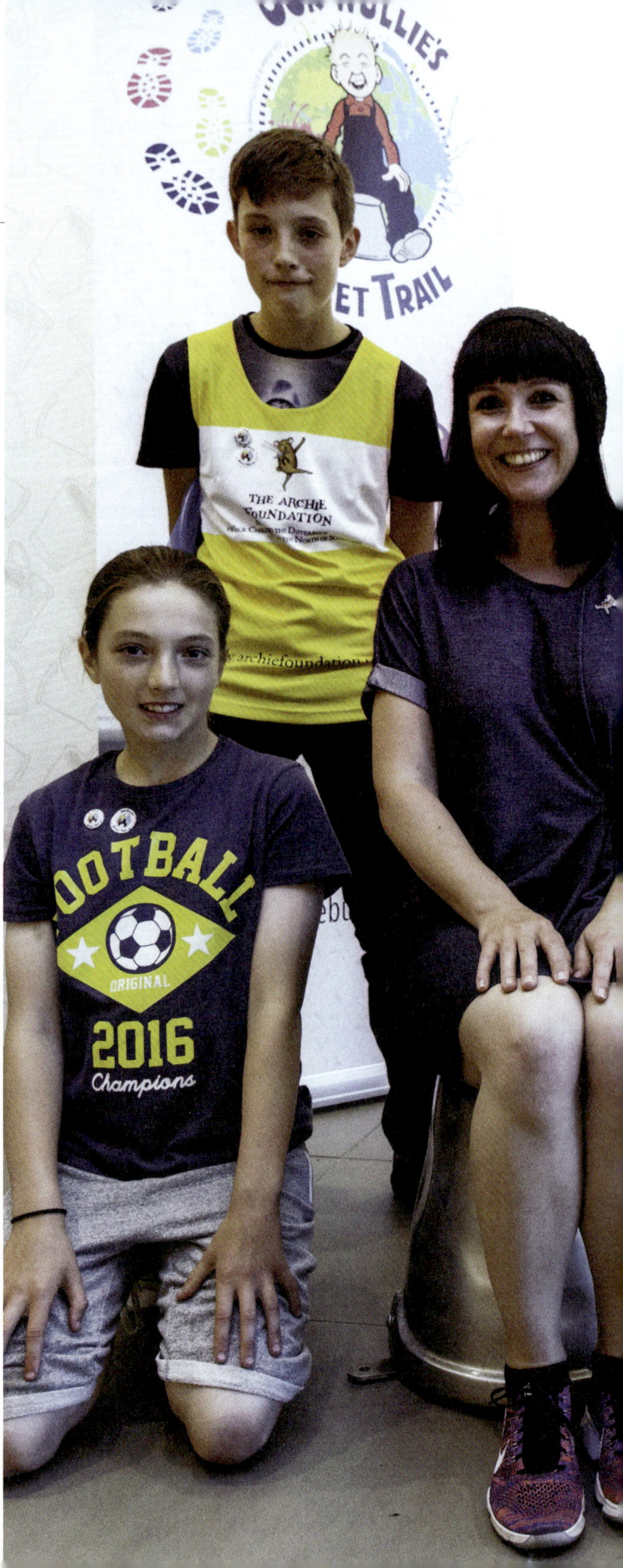

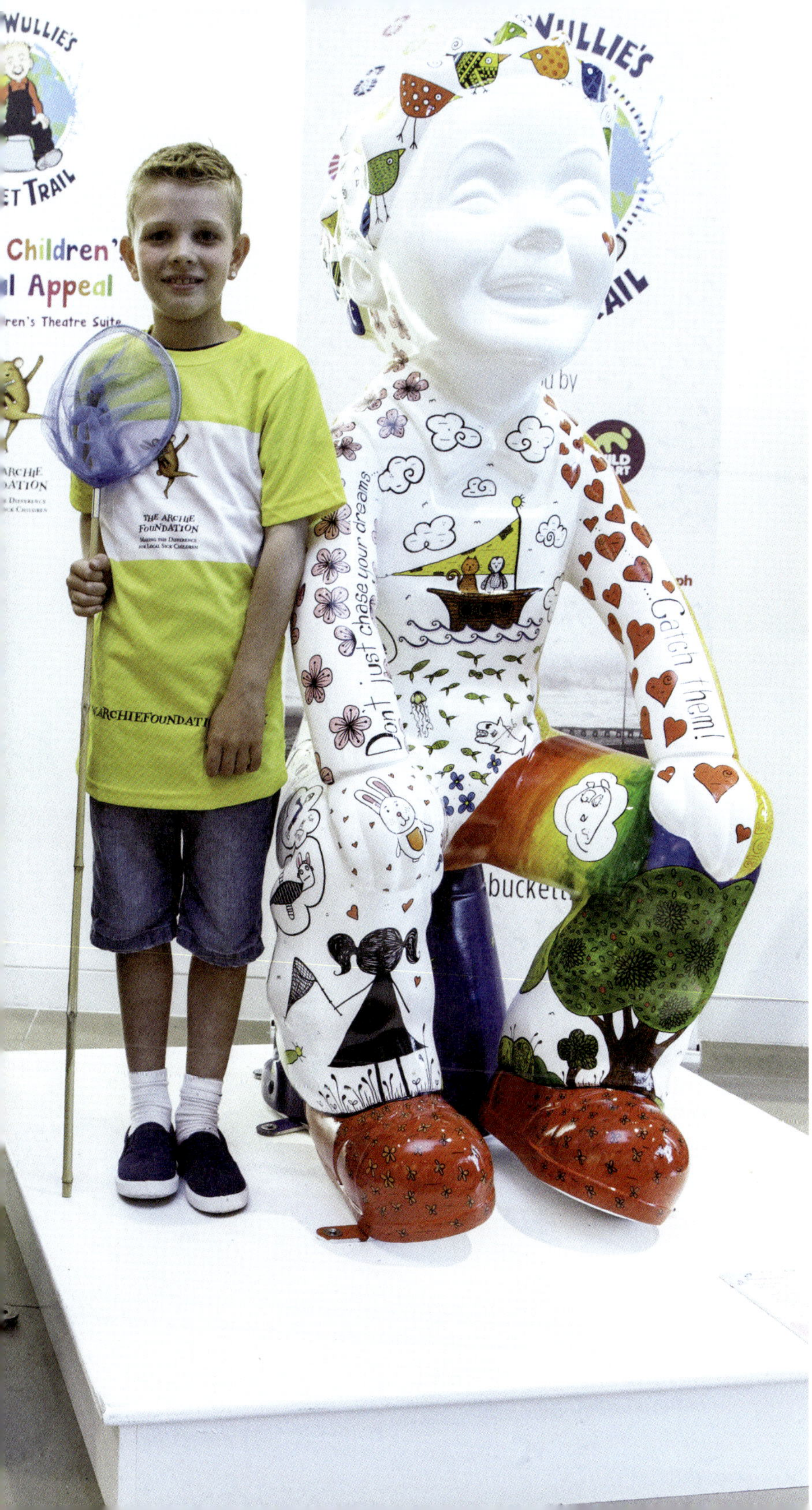

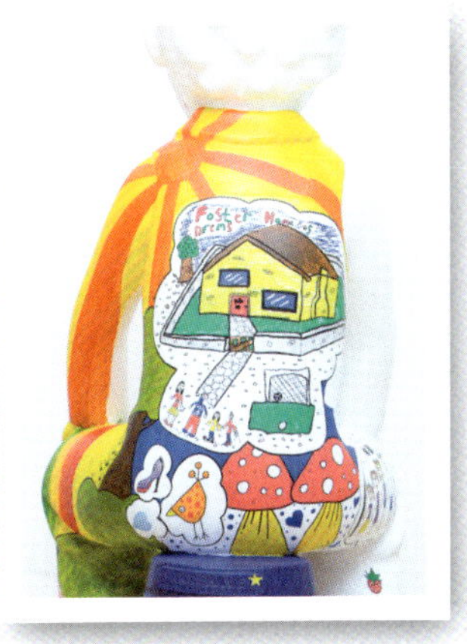

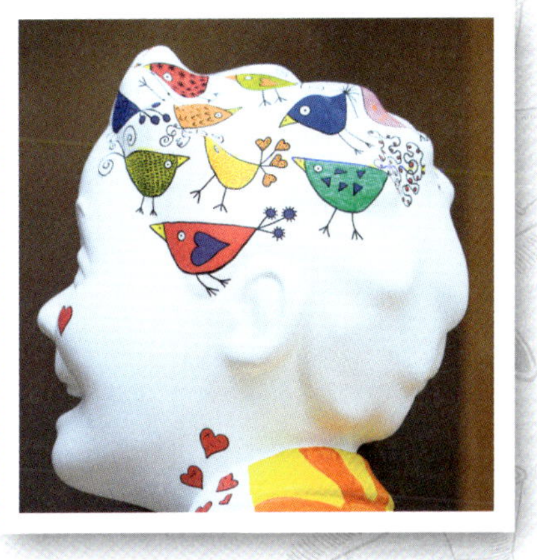

Why was he bought? Dr Simon Cawley launched a fundraising drive to have an Oor Wullie sculpture in the children's hospital: "The idea to fundraise to have an Oor Wullie at Ninewells was down to my young daughter's plea that she would really like to have one in our garden... and could I not get one for her?

"My work colleagues enthusiastically got behind the fundraising campaign initially but support very quickly started coming in from friends and family and staff working in other areas of NHS Tayside as well as from members of the public.

"Bidding on Dreamcatcher was slightly nerve-wracking but with the additional generous support from Gordon Deuchers, MD of GA Engineering, we were in a good position. I can't thank him enough for helping us achieve our goal. I was very relieved and delighted that the hammer finally fell on my winning bid - ensuring that Dreamcatcher would be coming to Ninewells.

"So, a massive thank you to everyone who donated, your support and generosity made it happen!"

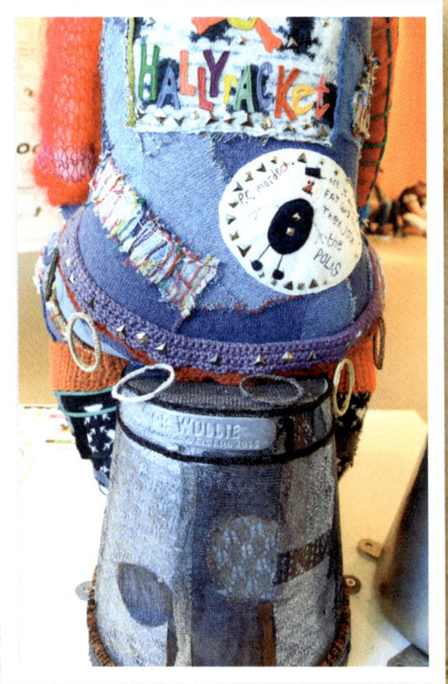
HALLYRACKET
the
POLIS

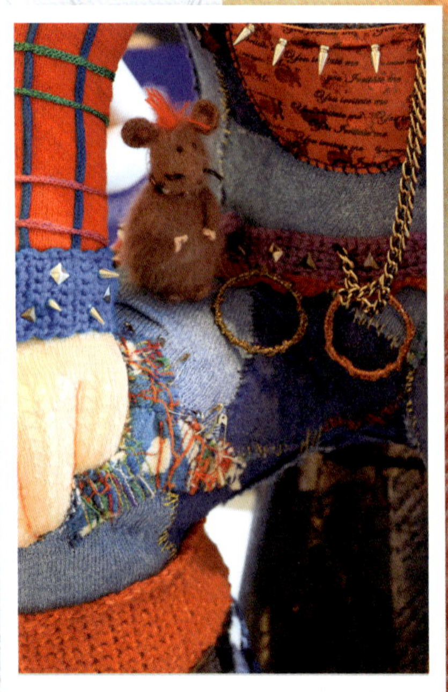

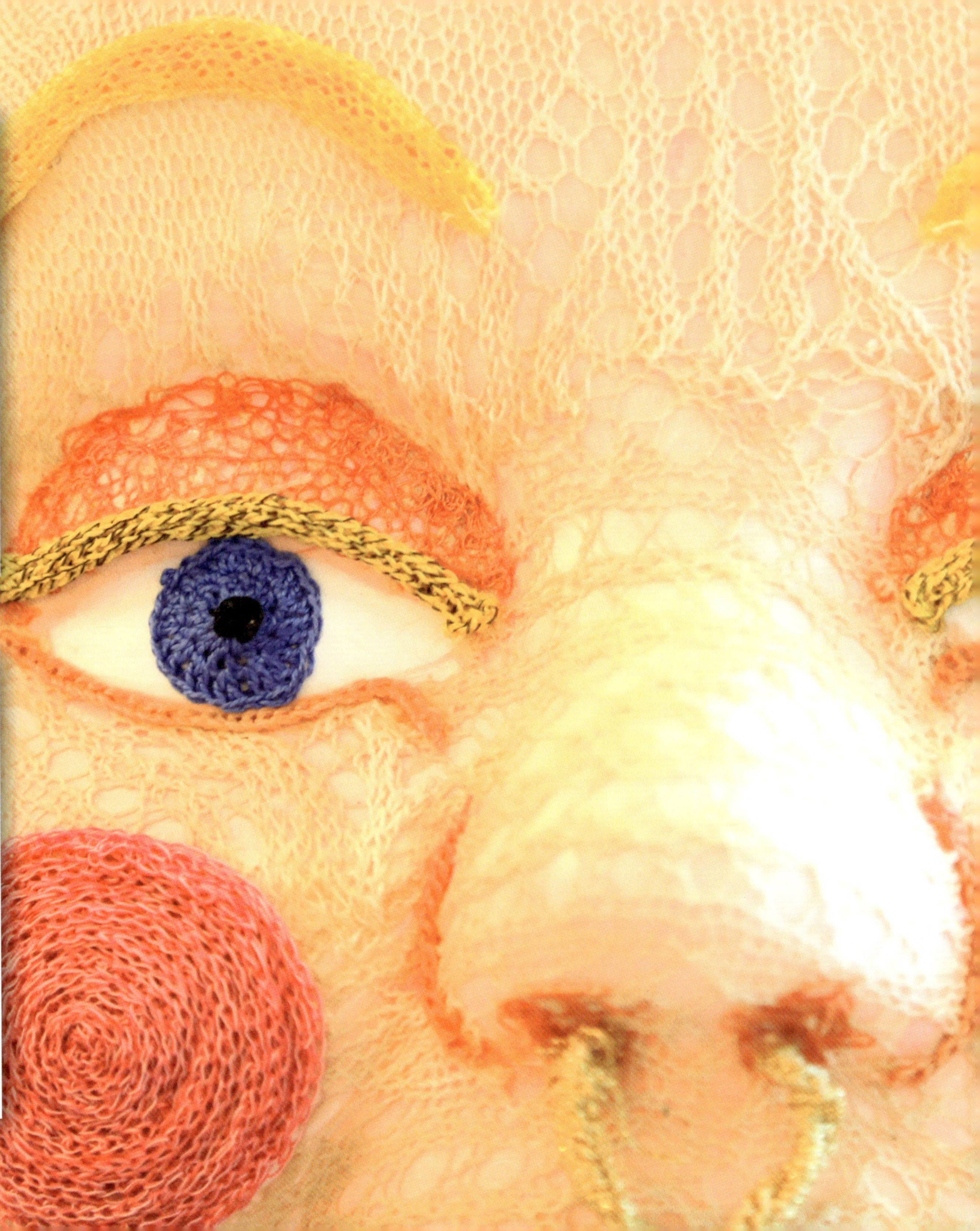

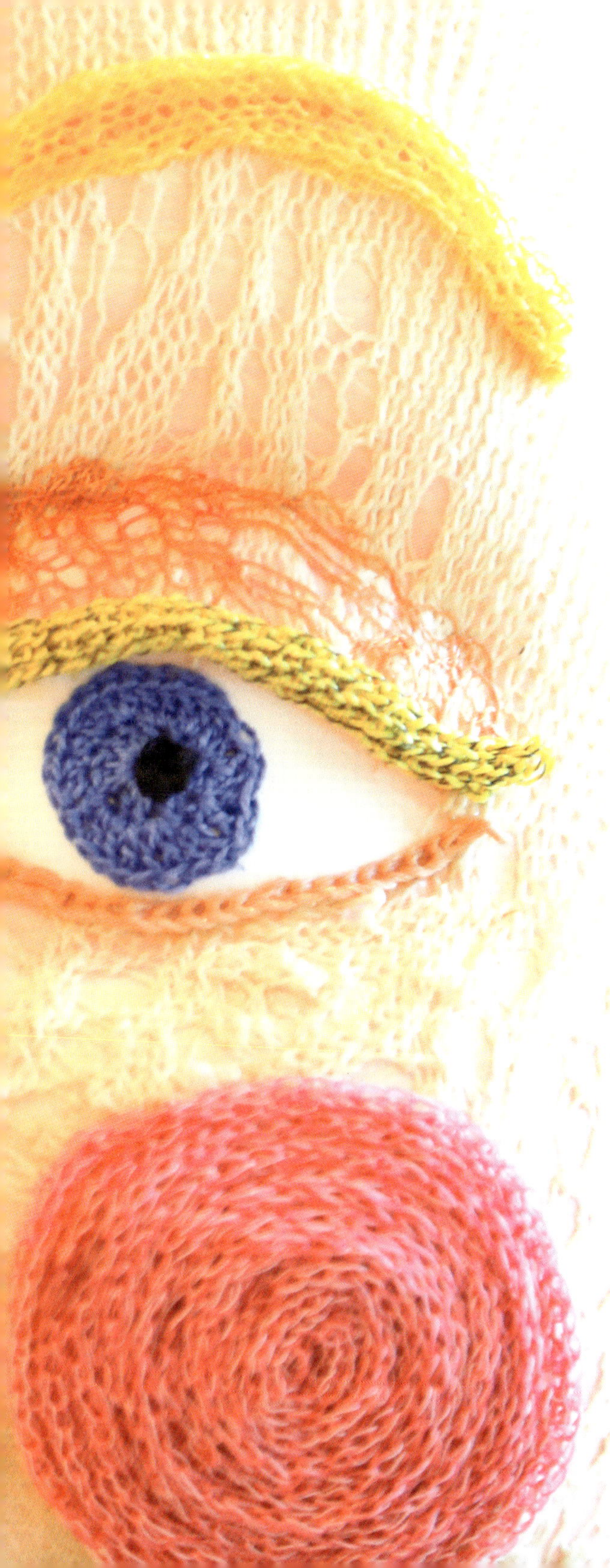

HALLYRACKET

Location on the Bucket Trail: Oor Wullie's Bucket Trail Headquarters, Overgate Shopping Centre.

Designed by: Jennifer McHardy (Nervous Stitch).

About this sculpture: Like most people, Jenny has grown up with Oor Wullie. As Jenny was born in the 1970's, she chose to dress Wullie up as a punk. The punk era was an exciting time for music, culture and fashion. Textiles is a very important part of Dundee's history and Jenny has used traditional and modern knit and textile techniques, combining these with specialist and everyday yarns, to showcase the diverse and exciting nature of knitted textiles.

A graduate of The Royal College of Art, Jenny is a knitwear designer who runs her own design business, Nervous Stitch. She also teaches at both school and university level. Jenny is interested in challenging the preconceptions people have about knitting by combining traditional craft techniques with specialist yarns and processes. She works on public and private commissions.

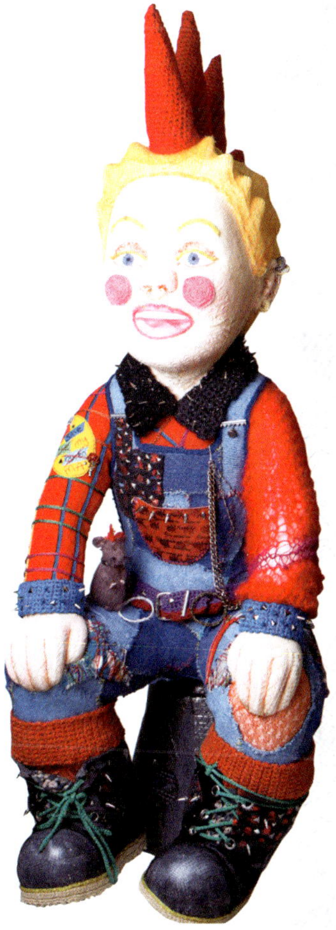

Sponsor: Spree Book.

Winning bid: £10,000.

Winning bidder: Gillian Kilfedder.

Where is he now? We dinae ken but we like to think he's still spreading joy and happiness!

TARTAN WULLIE

Location on the Bucket Trail: Dundee Railway Station.

Designed by: Sandra Kerr.

About this sculpture: Oor Wullie is something of an icon to Scottish people the world over, so it's only right that he has his own tartan. Wullie's tartan is a simple design that illustrates abody's love for the mischievous wee laddie frae Auchenshoogle. The red in the tartan represents the hackle of Uncle Wattie's regiment, while the grey symbolises his iconic bucket and Jeemy the moose, the yellow hints at his gold locks that never see a comb, and the black and white represents the newsprint of The Sunday Post in which Wullie and his pals have lived for over 80 years.

Sandra is a watercolour artist from Kirriemuir, Angus. She specialises in botanical and wildlife art and creates custom pet and people portraits in a variety of media.

Sponsor: ScotRail.

Winning bid: £13,000.

Winning bidder: Ninja Kiwi.

Where is he now? We dinae ken but he's mibbe playin' computer games like a ninja!

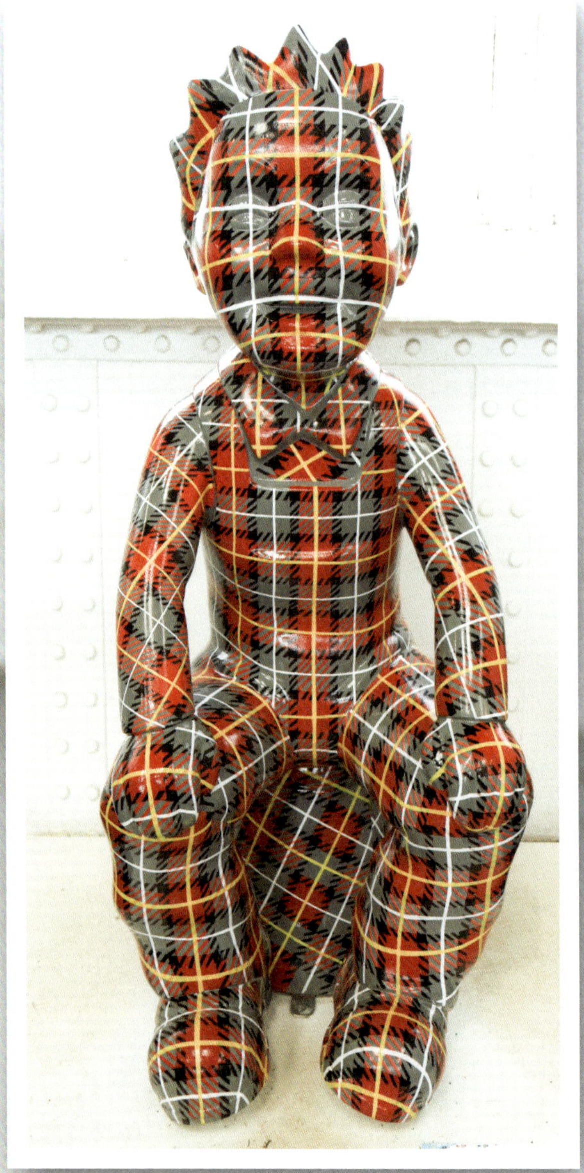

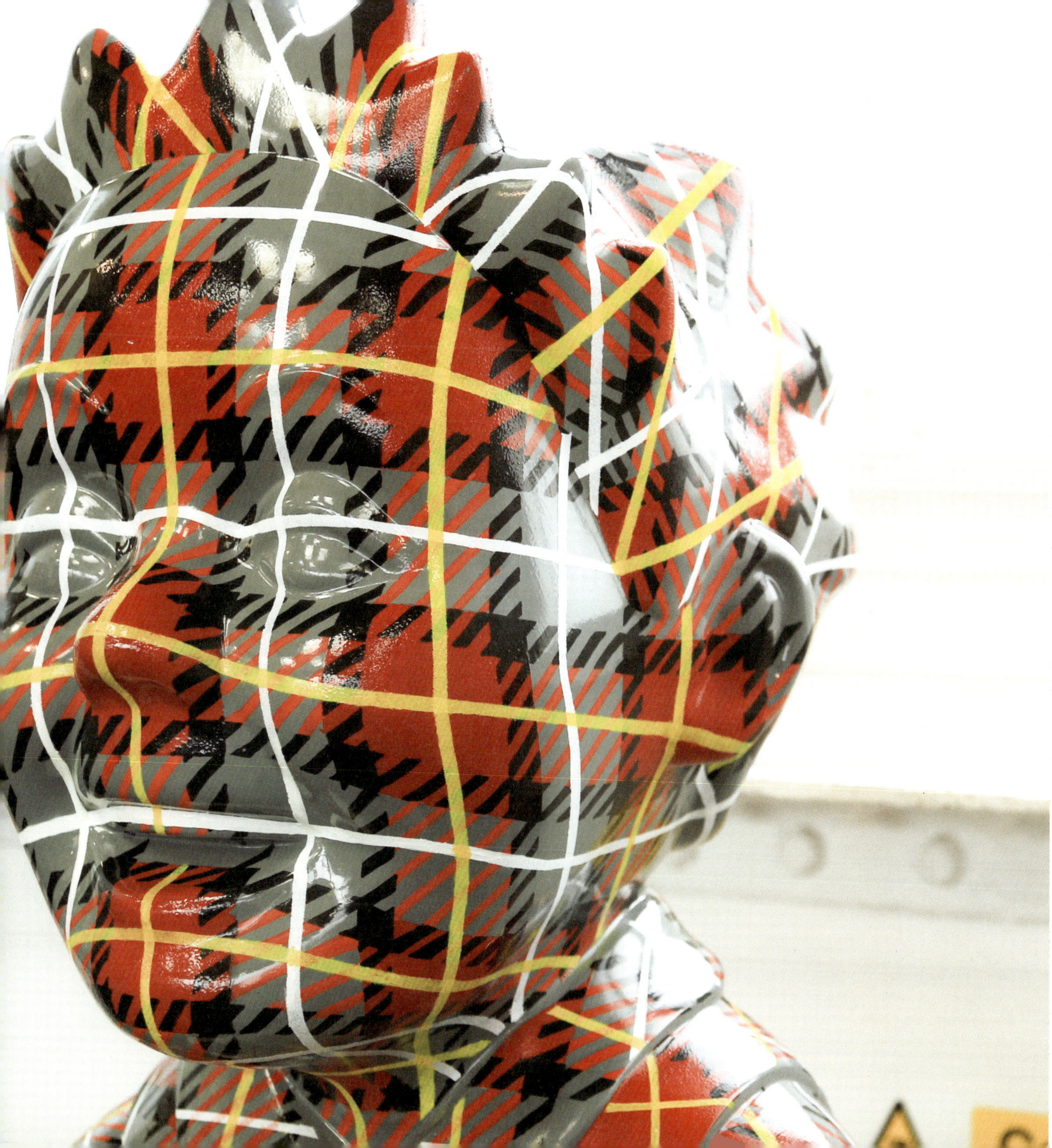

OOR PIRATE

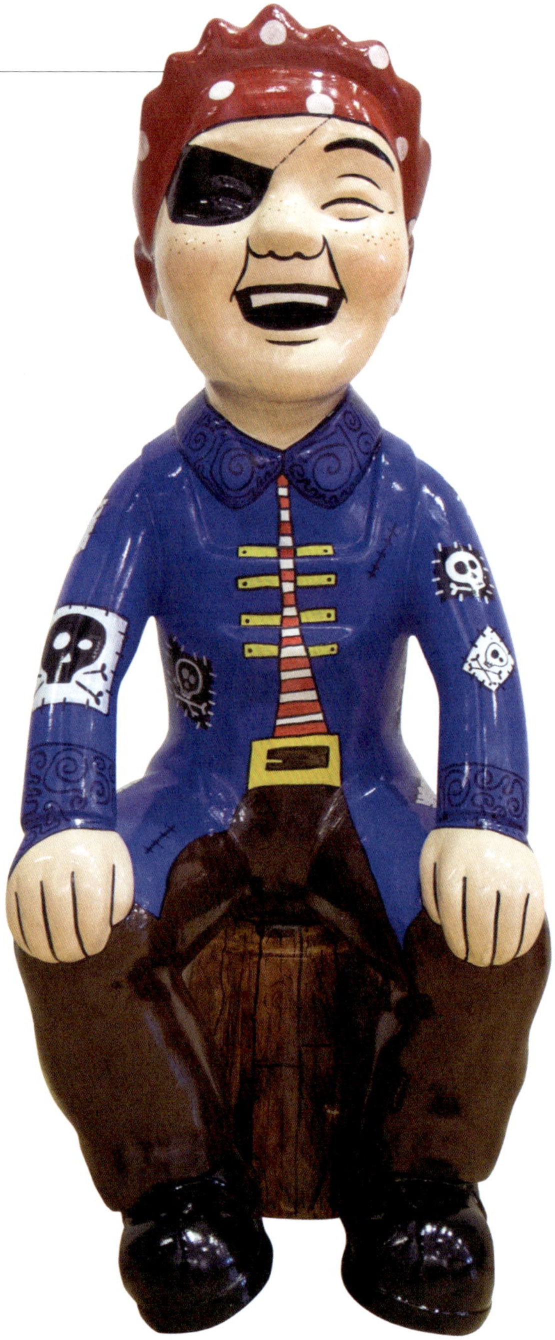

Location on the Bucket Trail: Oor Wullie's Bucket Trail Headquarters, Overgate Shopping Centre (when he wasn't out on adventures with Suzanne!).

Designed by: Suzanne Scott (WhimSicAL LusH).

About this sculpture: Yaar! Meet Oor Pirate! He wasn't part of the main Oor Wullie Bucket Trail but this cheeky wee guy loved drawing skulls and going on pirate adventures so he was often out visiting different locations.

He was created by Bucket Trail artist co-ordinator Suzanne, an artist and illustrator based in Dundee, working under the name WhimSicAL LusH. She loves going on inky adventures and adores the little things in life. Whether she is creating creatures or castles, houses or robots, or turning people's ideas into reality, there is always a story on her drawing board.

Sponsor: WhimSicAL LusH.

Winning bid: £12,000.

Winning bidder: Millie's Beach Huts and Gillies and Mackay Ltd.

Where is he now? Oor Pirate travels between Gillies and Mackay Ltd., the shed and summer home specialists in Errol, and Millie's Beach Huts. He also goes on day trips to the HM Frigate Unicorn when they host special pirate days. Arrrr!

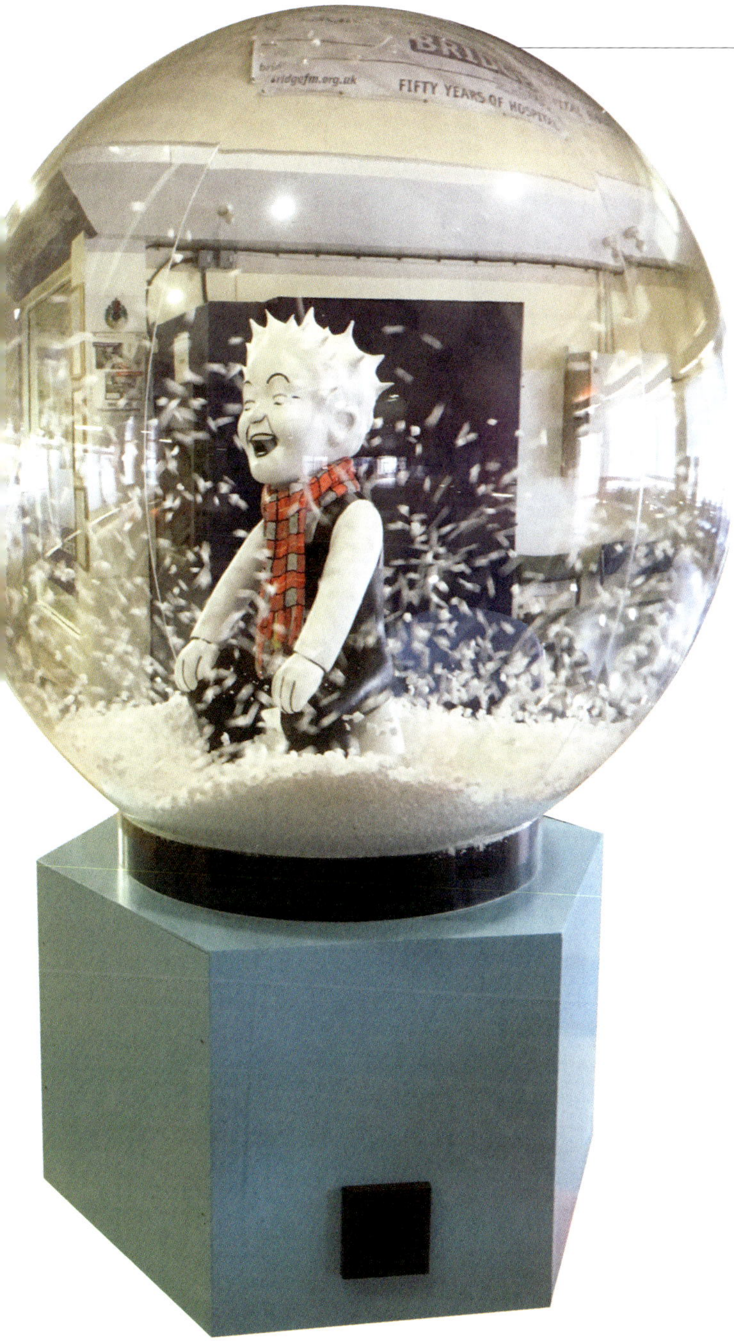

OOR WULLIE SNOWGLOBE

Location on the Bucket Trail: Ninewells Hospital.

Designed by: Debbie Lawson.

About this sculpture: Oor Wullie Snowglobe was inspired both by Debbie's lifelong love of the Oor Wullie comic strip and annuals, which often open with snowy scenes of Wullie on his bucket at Christmas, and by an interest in bringing sculptures to life using animation.

Debbie was born in Dundee and lives and works in London. She graduated in fine art from Central Saint Martins and in sculpture from the Royal College of Art. Her recent exhibitions include Magic Carpet at the Fergusson Gallery, Perth; Make Believe: Re-Imagining History and Landscape at Nottingham Castle Museum and Art Gallery; and Picaresque at Ha Gamle Prestegard, Norway. Her work is held in the collections of Charles Saatchi, Mario Testino, the House of Lords, Nottingham Castle Museum, the University of the Arts London and the University of Dundee. Debbie was the winner of the 2013 JD Fergusson Arts Award.

Sponsor: Nane but too guid no' tae include!

Winning bid: £20,000.

Winning bidder: Bruce Linton, James Keiller Estates.

Where is he now? Greeting guests at Westport Luxury Serviced Apartments in Dundee!

Sarah Linton-Rennie, owner of Westport Luxury Serviced Apartments said: "People are delighted to see it in a communal space, whether it is guests staying with us or passers-by. People love getting a selfie with Snowglobe Wullie."

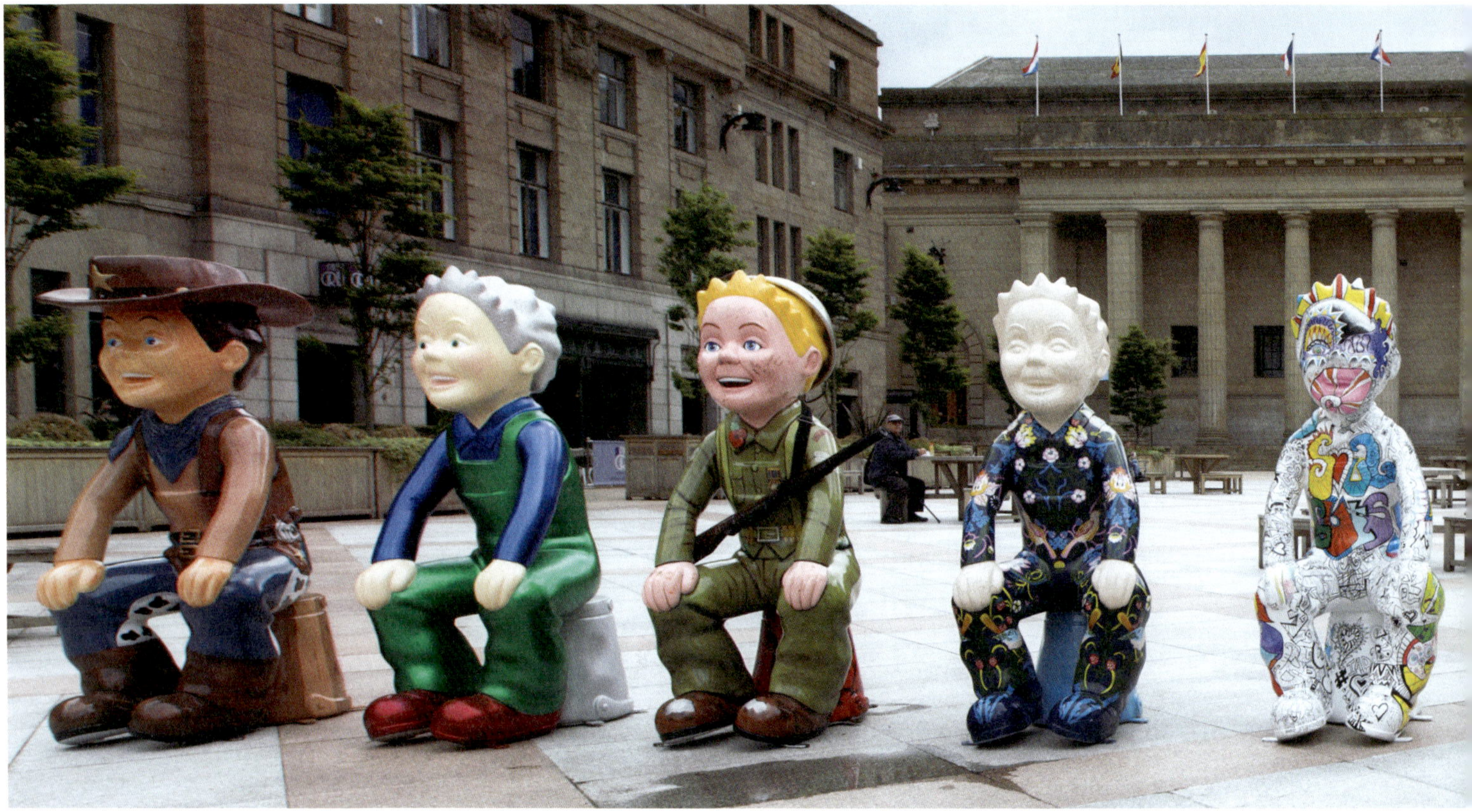

OOR WULLIE'S ON TOUR!

While Oor Wullie's Bucket Trail was underway across Dundee, 13 different Oor Wullies embarked on an eight-week national tour of Scotland. With the help of sponsors, the touring Wullies visited eight locations across the country, including Aberdeen, Edinburgh, Glasgow, Dundee, Stirling, Perth, Inverness and St Andrews. On their return, they were proudly placed on display in Dundee's City Square making it home in time for the farewell party and the grand auction.

Although the Oor Wullie Bucket Trail was a Dundee campaign, Oor Wullie himself is a national treasure so it was only right that he got out and about. The Tour took the appeal of the Bucket Trail to a wider audience around the country and helped more people enjoy the experience, even if they couldn't get to Dundee to take part in the full Trail.

Importantly, the Tour also helped increase awareness of the ARCHIE Foundation, encouraging more people to donate to the appeal for

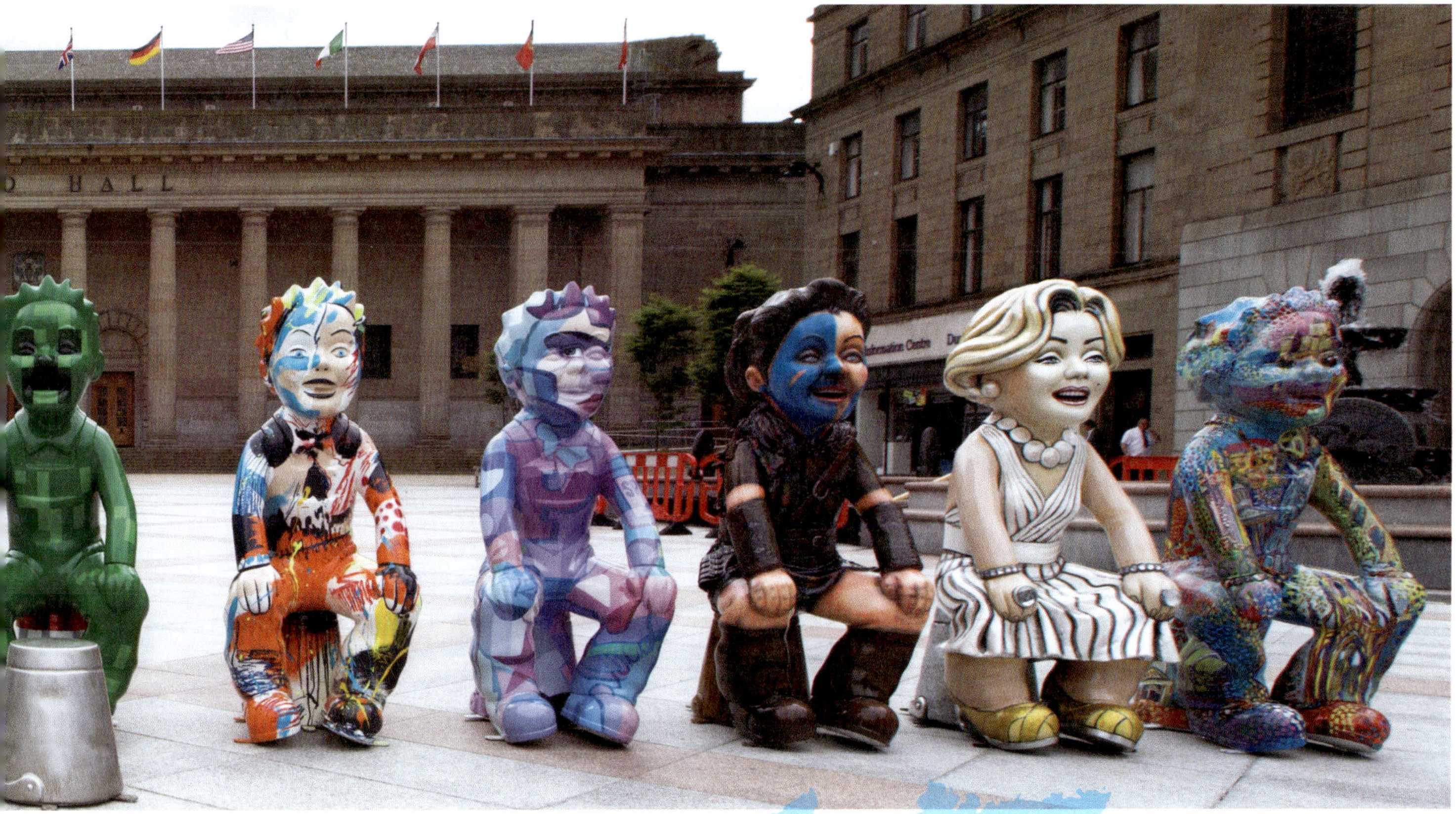

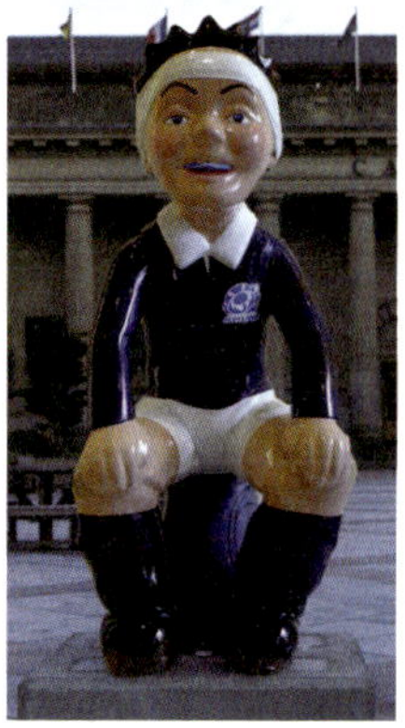

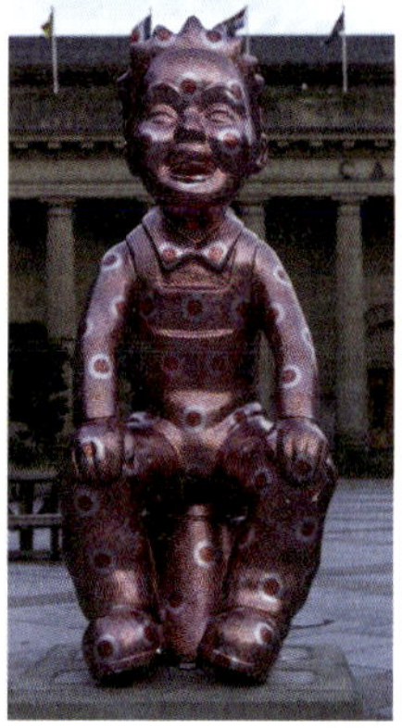

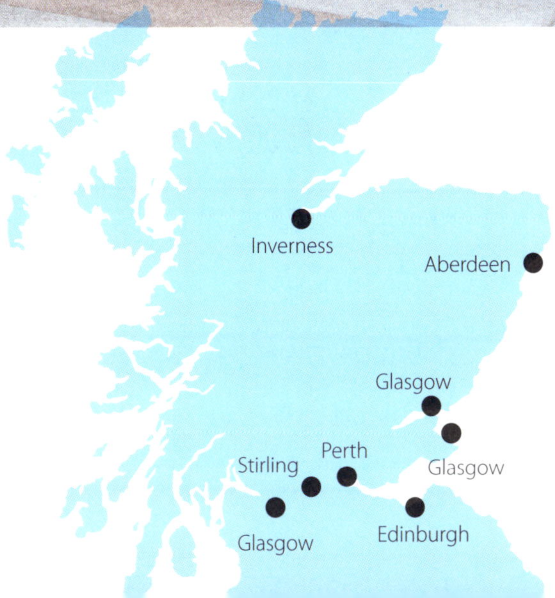

Tayside's Children's Hospital. Once people had a taste for the Trail, they often found themselves making the trip to bonnie Dundee to see all 55 sculptures, helping to bring more people to the city and boost the local economy.

Thanks go to Scotrail, Tunnock's, Arnold Clark, The Speratus Group Ltd., UNESCO, V&A, Signature Pub Group, Wild in Art, VisitScotland and The Sunday Post for making the Tour a reality.

WULLIE WALLACE

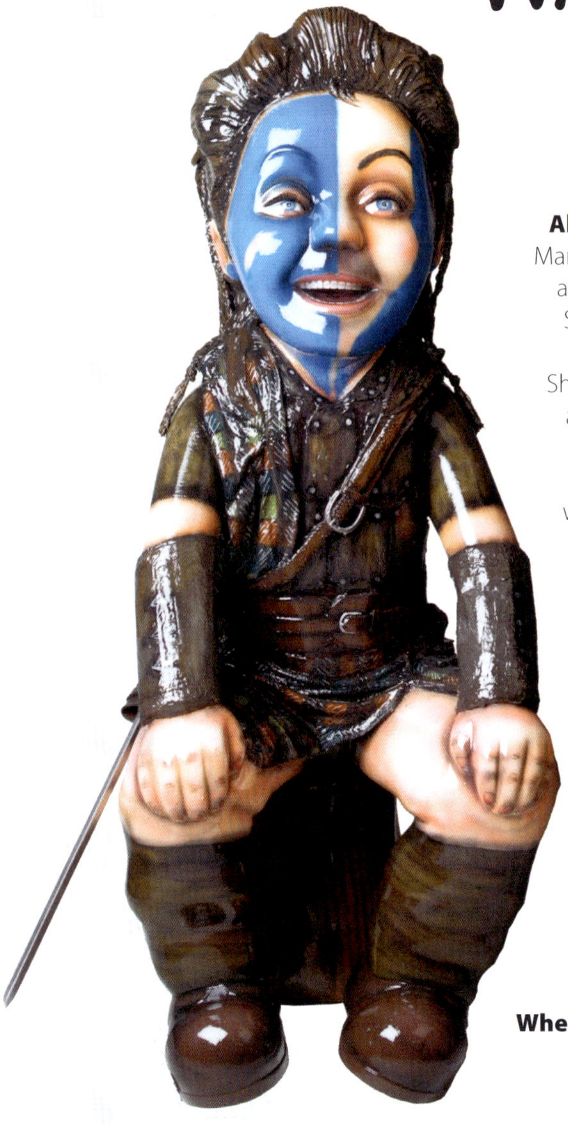

Designed by: Mandii Pope.

About this sculpture: Kiwi artist Mandii is fascinated with Oor Wullie and William Wallace and was sure Scotland and visitors alike would embrace this design. She has held exhibitions in Europe and the UK, including significant solo exhibitions in Cork Street, London and Dubai. Many of her works are in international private and commercial collections. Mandii has close links with several charities and often donates works to fundraise for various causes around the world.

Sponsor: DC Thomson, The Sunday Post.

Winning bid: £12,000.

Winning bidder: Signature Pub Group.

Where is he now? We dinae ken but he's probably fighting pretend battles with his pals!

GUILDED WULLIE

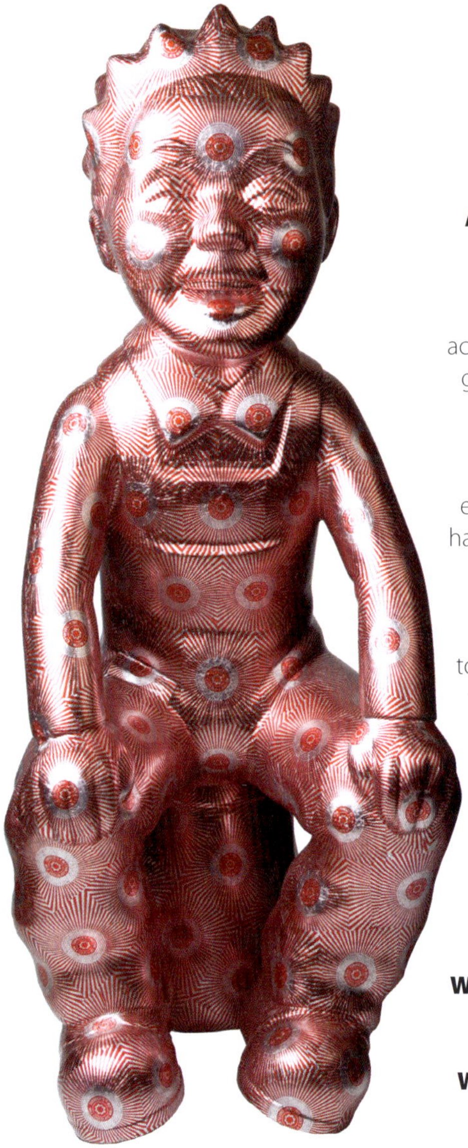

Designed by: Robert Mach.

About this sculpture: Robert Mach is always on the lookout for objects, sculptures and buildings that he can 'guild' in foil wrappings. He stumbled across one of the blank Oor Wullies and grabbed the opportunity to cover the sculpture in the iconic Tunnock's Teacakes foil wrappers! Although having worked and exhibited in a variety of media, Robert has increasingly focused on expanding his use of foil wrappings. He uses the brightly coloured wrappers from products such as Tunnock's Teacakes to 'guild' sculptures and to produce 3D work. His public works can be seen in Leven, in the collections of Sir Walter Scott in Edinburgh, and in Fife Health Board.

Sponsor: Tunnock's.

Winning bid: £11,000.

Winning bidder: Gillian Bayford, local business woman.

Where is he now? Spreading joy and happiness in Carnoustie!

WHERE'S WULLIE?

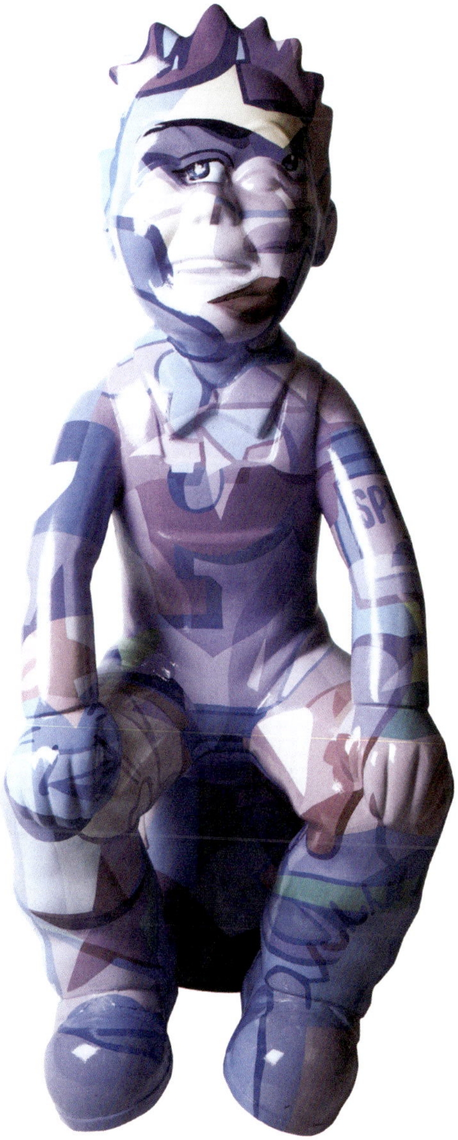

Designed by: Stuart McAlpine Miller.

About this sculpture: The artist added Wullie to certain areas on the sculpture and as it wasn't initially obvious where, it allowed the viewer to try to find Wullie. It's a playful take on 'Where's Wally?' The idea related to other cartoon heroes who find themselves in trouble and eventually resolve the main issue. The female image represents his mother's authority.

Stuart graduated in drawing and painting from Glasgow School of Art in 1990. He has enjoyed successful solo exhibitions with galleries such as Connaught Brown, London; Duncan Miller, London; Ruth O'Hara, New York, Catto Gallery, London; Rebecca Hossack Gallery, London and Kings Road Gallery, London, amongst others.

Sponsor: Signature Pub Group.

Winning bid: £13,000.

Winning bidder: Mark McAdam, Sky Sports TV reporter.

Where is he now? We dinae ken but we like to think he's still spreading joy and happiness!

WULLIE THE COWBOY

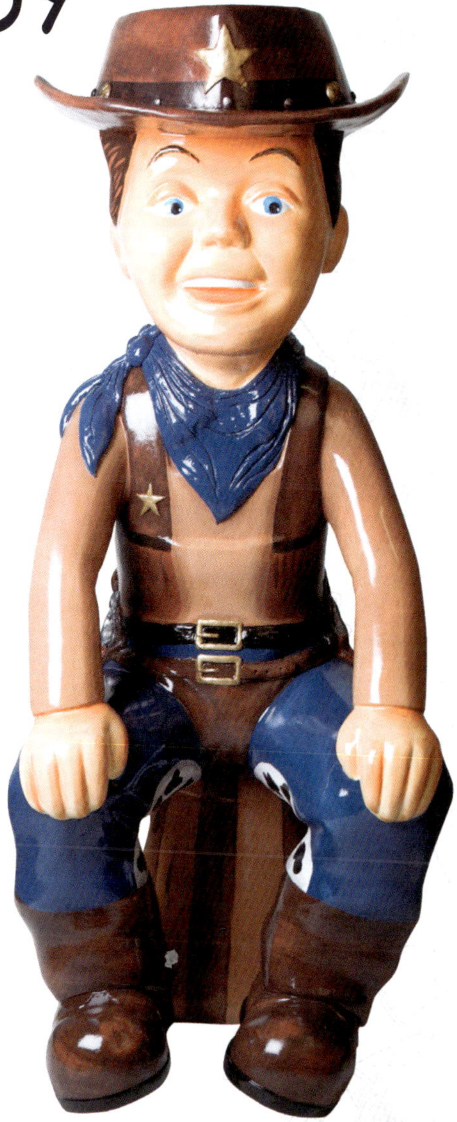

Designed by: Deven Bhurke.

About this sculpture: Wullie the Cowboy is a character who is chirpy and full of energy and is inspired by the cowboy tradition from north and south America.

Deven Bhurke is a Hampshire-based graphic designer and artist. His public art work involves abstracts, geometrical patterns and fun-loving characters. He was commissioned by GoGoRhinos in 2013, Bookbenches in London and Buses for Transport for London in 2014. In 2015, he was commissioned for several Wild in Art events.

Sponsor: Nane but too guid no'tae include!

Winning bid: £11,000.

Winning bidder: Jeanette Gibson.

Where is he now? Learning the tricks of the trade at the Scottish Antique & Arts Centre!

RUGBY WULLIE

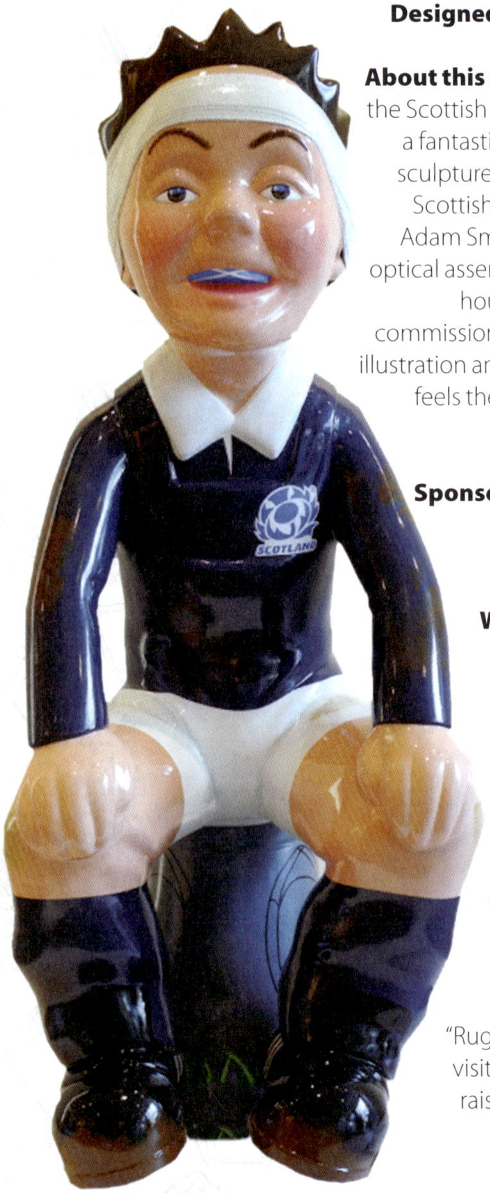

Designed by: Matthew Low and Neil Cooney.

About this sculpture: Rugby Wullie is based on the Scottish Rugby team. Artist Matthew Low did a fantastic job of getting Wullie match-fit! This sculpture was signed by members of the 2016 Scottish Rugby team. Matthew studied art at Adam Smith College. He currently works as an optical assembly technician but spends his spare hours working on personal projects and commissions. He is interested in urban art forms, illustration and pop-impressionism. He constantly feels the need to be creating something and always has paint on his clothes!

Sponsor: Nane but too guid no' tae include!

Winning bid: £14,000.

Winning bidder: Andy Lothian, CEO, Insights.

Where is he now? This Oor Wullie is usually based at Insights but he also gets oot an' aboot on lots o' trips!

Why was he bought? Andy Lothian, CEO, Insights, said: "The Oor Wullie Bucket Trail project is a shining example of how a community can make an impact when it comes together.

"Rugby Wullie now has a new career as he visits schools, sports clubs and dinners to raise more money. The legacy of the Oor Wullie Bucket Trail continues!"

SCOTSPIRIT WULLIE

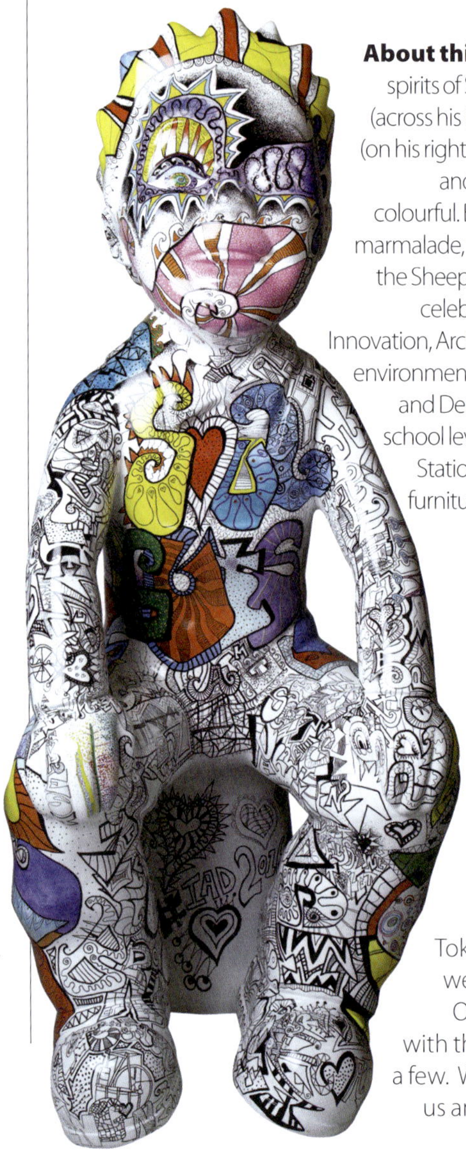

Designed by: Vanessa Gibson.

About this sculpture: Scotspirit Wullie features the seven spirits of Scotland including Soul (across his chest), Humour (across his bottom), Guts (across his stomach), Determination (on his right side), Fun (on his elbow), Spark (on his face / head), and Warmth (on his left side). The writing is bright and colourful. Black and white features include the Kelpies, a jar of marmalade, the Falkirk Wheel, the Riverside Museum and Dolly the Sheep. 25 more illustrations feature on this sculpture and celebrate Scotland's pioneering spirit in the 2016 Year of Innovation, Architecture and Design. Vanessa studied interior and environmental design at Duncan of Jordanstone College of Art and Design in Dundee. She teaches art and design at high school level and she also has a studio called Loved Up at Fire Station Creative in Dunfermline where she practices as a furniture artist. Most of her work features text, poems and song lyrics.

Sponsor: VisitScotland.

Winning bid: £11,000.

Winning bidder: Tokheim.

Where is he now? Lending the team a hand at Tokheim's Dundee Manufacturing Centre!

Why was he bought? Tokheim said: "Scotspirit is relevant to our company values: Tokheim drives continuous improvement, which we aim to do with Guts, Determination and Fun. Our engineering focus is represented on Wullie with the Falkirk Wheel and Dolly the Sheep, to name a few. We just knew he was the perfect Oor Wullie for us and he is very much part of the Tokheim family."

STRAWBERRY THIEF

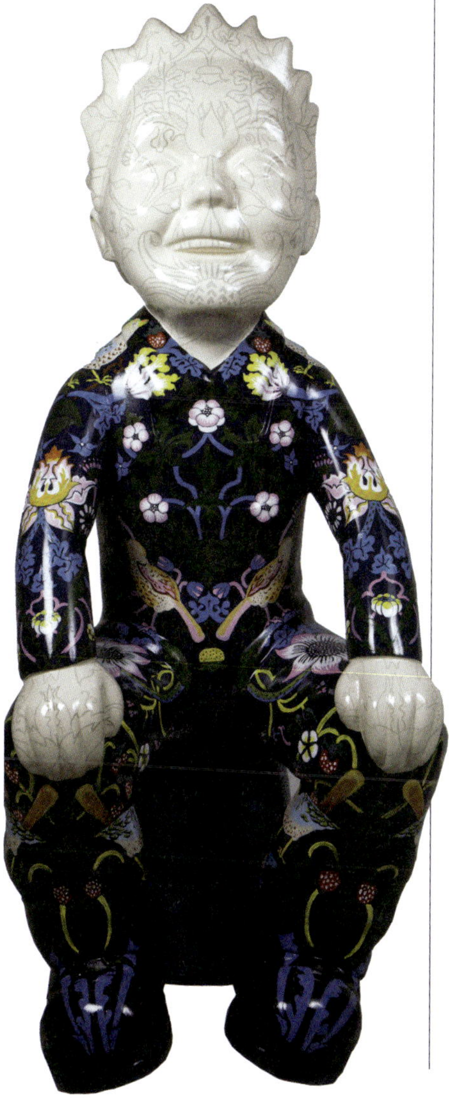

Designed by: Ellen Brown.

About this sculpture: Strawberry Thief was inspired by the work of William Morris and the iPad game Strawberry Thief, which Ellen Brown worked on with the V&A's first Game Designer in Residence, Sophia George, in 2014. This game also featured in V&A Dundee's first travelling exhibition in 2015.

Ellen Brown is a freelance computer games artist and graphic designer based in Edinburgh. She graduated in computer arts from Abertay University in 2015 and worked on the BAFTA-winning PlayStation 4 game, Everybody's Gone to the Rapture.

Sponsor: V&A Museum of Design Dundee.

Winning bid: £10,000.

Winning bidder: We dinae ken!

Where is he now? We dinae ken that either but he could be stealing strawberries!

BOOZY COW GRAFFITI

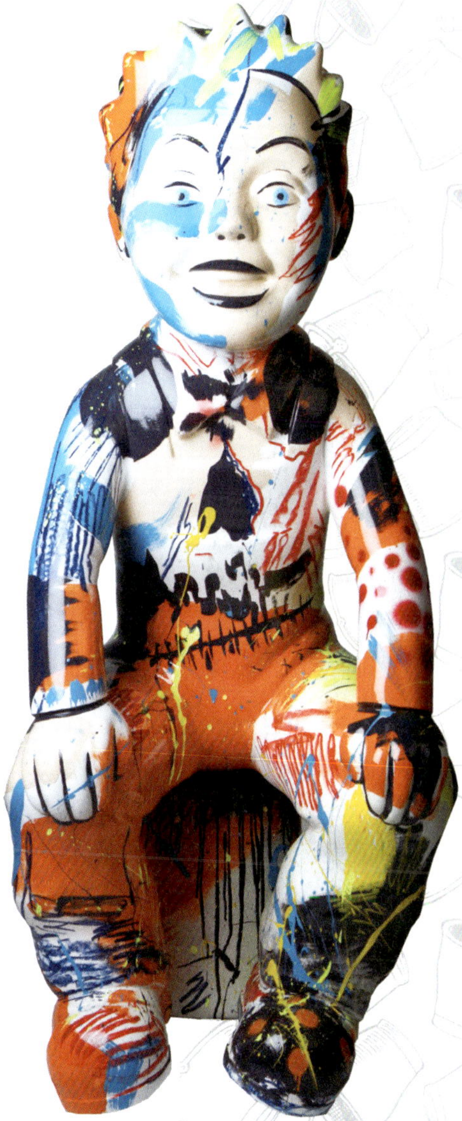

Designed by: Lynsey Henderson.

About this sculpture: Lynsey loves Oor Wullie's deep roots in Scottish culture: Wullie has stood the test of time and stayed true to his initial concept from when he was first published.

Her projects range from historical restorations on Scottish estates to label designs for whisky brands. She owns an award-winning art and design studio in Edinburgh and has exhibited at the Saatchi Gallery and Royal College in London. She is inspired by traditional craft techniques, colours and music and uses these as a starting point for all her creative ventures.

Sponsor: The Speratus Group Ltd.

Winning bid: £7,000.

Winning bidder: Garreth Wood, The Speratus Group Ltd.

Where is he now? Enjoying some tasty food at The Boozy Cow restaurant in Dundee!

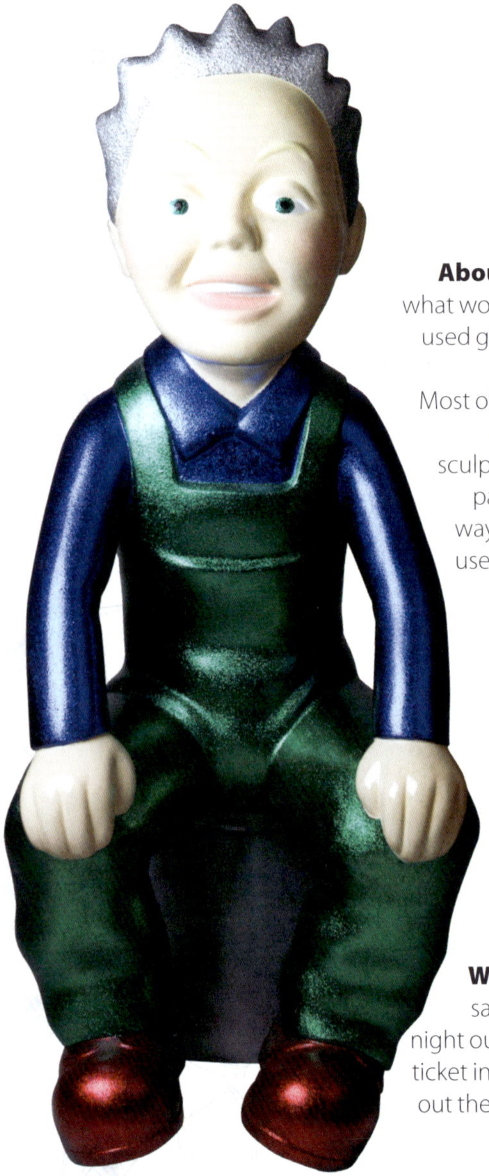

NIGHT ON THE TOON

Designed by: John Carr (Creative Rock).

About this sculpture: Normally Wullie is scruffy – so what would he look like if he was glammed up a bit? John used glitters and metallic flakes with a fibreglass resin to create a more polished look for Wullie. Most of John's work uses decorative concrete (faux rock) which creates the image of real stone and rock in sculptures, wall overlays, waterfalls and water features, paths and paving and in theme park work. In many ways, much of this work is public art as people get to use it or interact with it. John loves all kinds of artistic production in a variety of mediums.

Sponsor: Arnold Clark Car & Van Rental.

Winning bid: £10,000.

Winning bidder: The Fort Hotel.

Where is he now? Housed in the popular Fort Pub, this Oor Wullie is a firm favourite with the locals!

Why was he bought? John Black, owner, The Fort, said: "Night on the Toon was bought after a day and night out on the toon! I headed off to the auction with no ticket in hand but plenty of drink in body so budget went out the window and Wullie came home with me! A great cause and a great amount raised!"

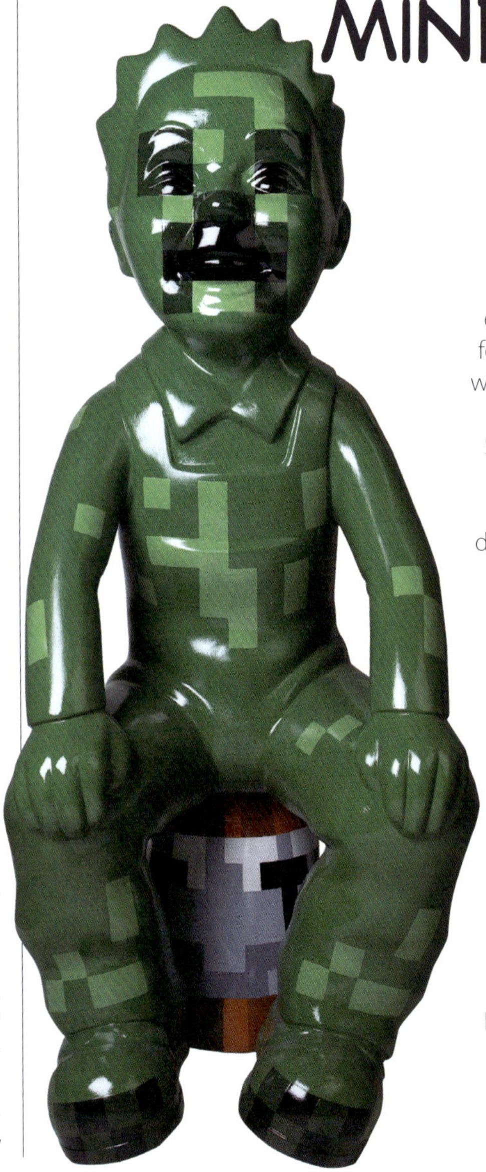

MINECRAFT

Designed by: 4J Studios.

About this sculpture: This Oor Wullie is based on the Creeper from Minecraft, an explosive character renowned for wrecking people's stuff, and was painted by Michael Hansen and Kate Wright, artists at 4J Studios Ltd. Based in Scotland with offices in east Linton and Dundee, 4J Studios is a game development studio. It is led by Chris van der Kuyl and Paddy Burns and developed the console edition of Mojang's Minecraft which won a BAFTA in 2015 for best family game.

Sponsor: Dundee United Nations Educational, Scientific and Cultural Organisation (UNESCO) City of Design.

Winning bid: £34,000.

Winning bidder: Gillian Bayford, local businesswoman.

Where is he now? Spreading joy and happiness in Carnoustie!

OOR WULLAMYN

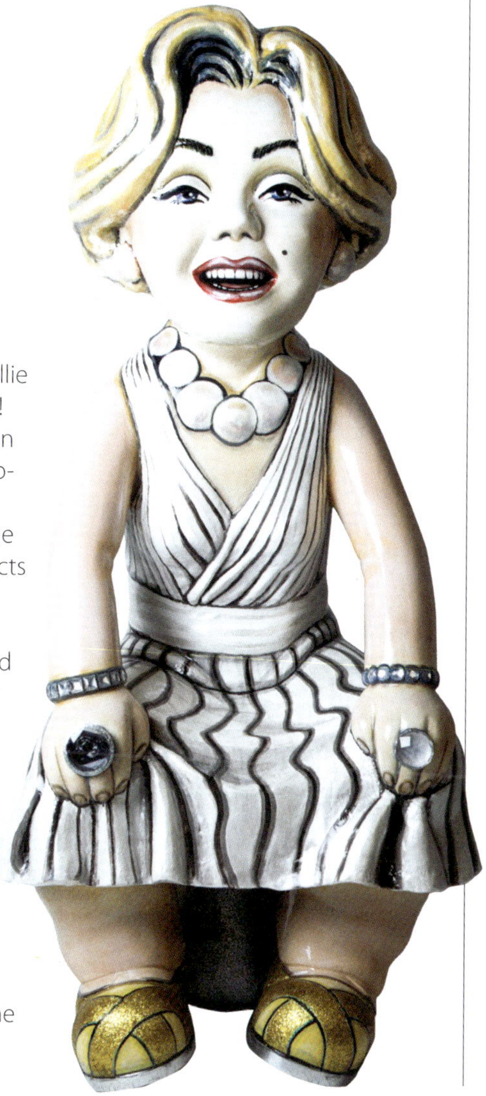

Designed by: Sally Adams.

About this sculpture : The design of one of Oor Wullie's Bucket Trail's most glamorous sculptures was inspired by Marilyn Monroe and treats Wullie to heels, diamonds and jewels!

Originally from south London and with a background in prop-making, Sally studied art in Taunton and then Norwich. She has accomplished many projects over the years and has some public works in and around Norfolk. Sally has been involved in previous Wild in Art events such as GoGoDragons.

Sponsor: Wild in Art.

Winning bid: £7,000.

Winning bidder: Gowrie Contracts, Ltd.

Where is he now? Doing a fine job as Gowrie Contracts' new community liaison officer!

SUDGER WULLIE

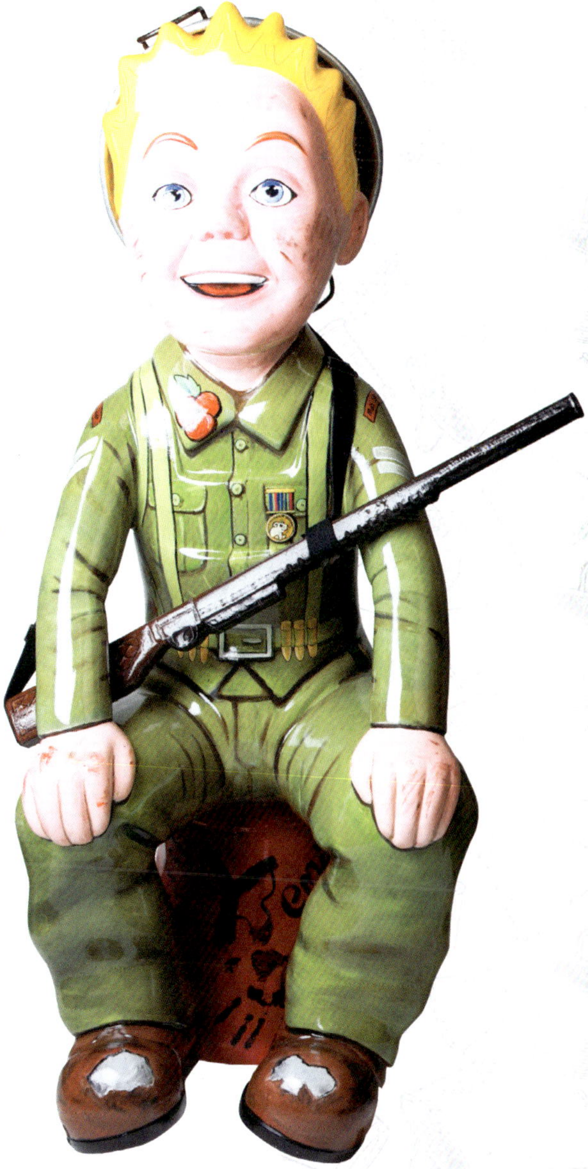

Designed by: Lesley D McKenzie.

About this sculpture: A tribute to soldiers present and past, Wullie's new rig-out is a bit of a blast. As a WWII sudger, there's nothing more he could need with his gun on his shooder and maw's colander on his heed!

Lesley initially trained as a graphic artist before becoming a self-employed artist in 1996. She has been involved in several public art projects including Wild Dolphins in Aberdeen in 2014. She has won many awards and accolades for her artwork and exhibits her work in galleries throughout Scotland including in her own gallery just outside Aberdeen.

Sponsor Nane but too guid no' tae include!

Winning bid: £9,500.

Winning bidder: We dinae ken!

Where is he now? We dinae ken that either but he's mibbe playin' at sudgers with his chums!

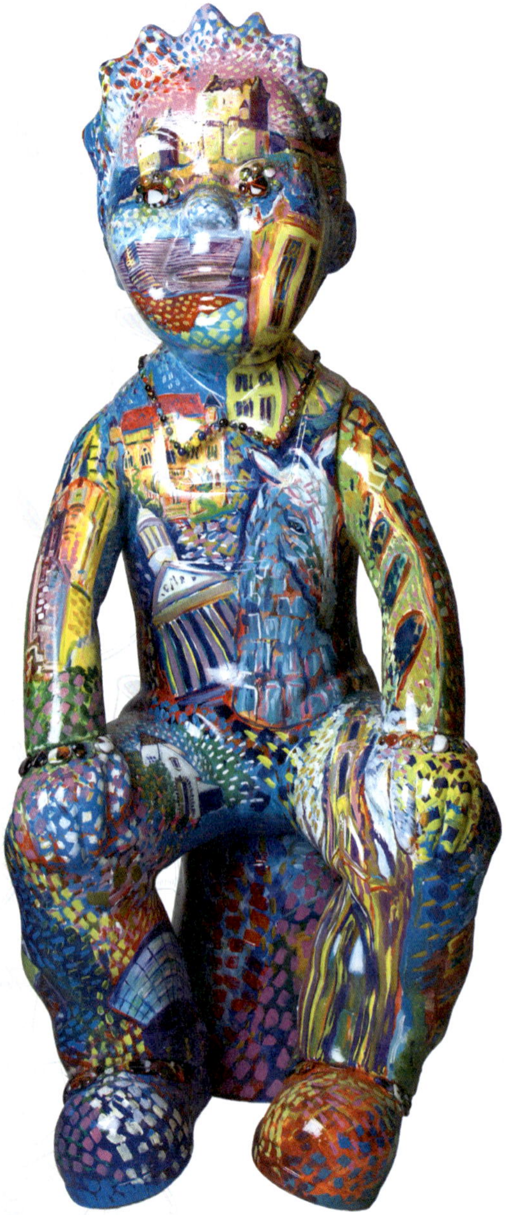

GG

Designed by: Shelagh Swanson.

About this sculpture: Shelagh's Oor Wullie is a celebration of Scotland's most iconic architecture and design in honour of Scotland's 2016 Year of Innovation, Architecture and Design. As a Gray's School of Art graduate, Shelagh creates work in both painting and glass. She recently relocated her studio to Footdee, Aberdeen and creates commissioned pieces which are inspired by her surroundings, all in her signature colourful style.

Sponsor Nane but too guid no' tae include!

Winning bid: £10,000.

Winning bidder: We dinae ken!

Where is he now? We dinae ken that either but we like to think he's still spreading joy and happiness!

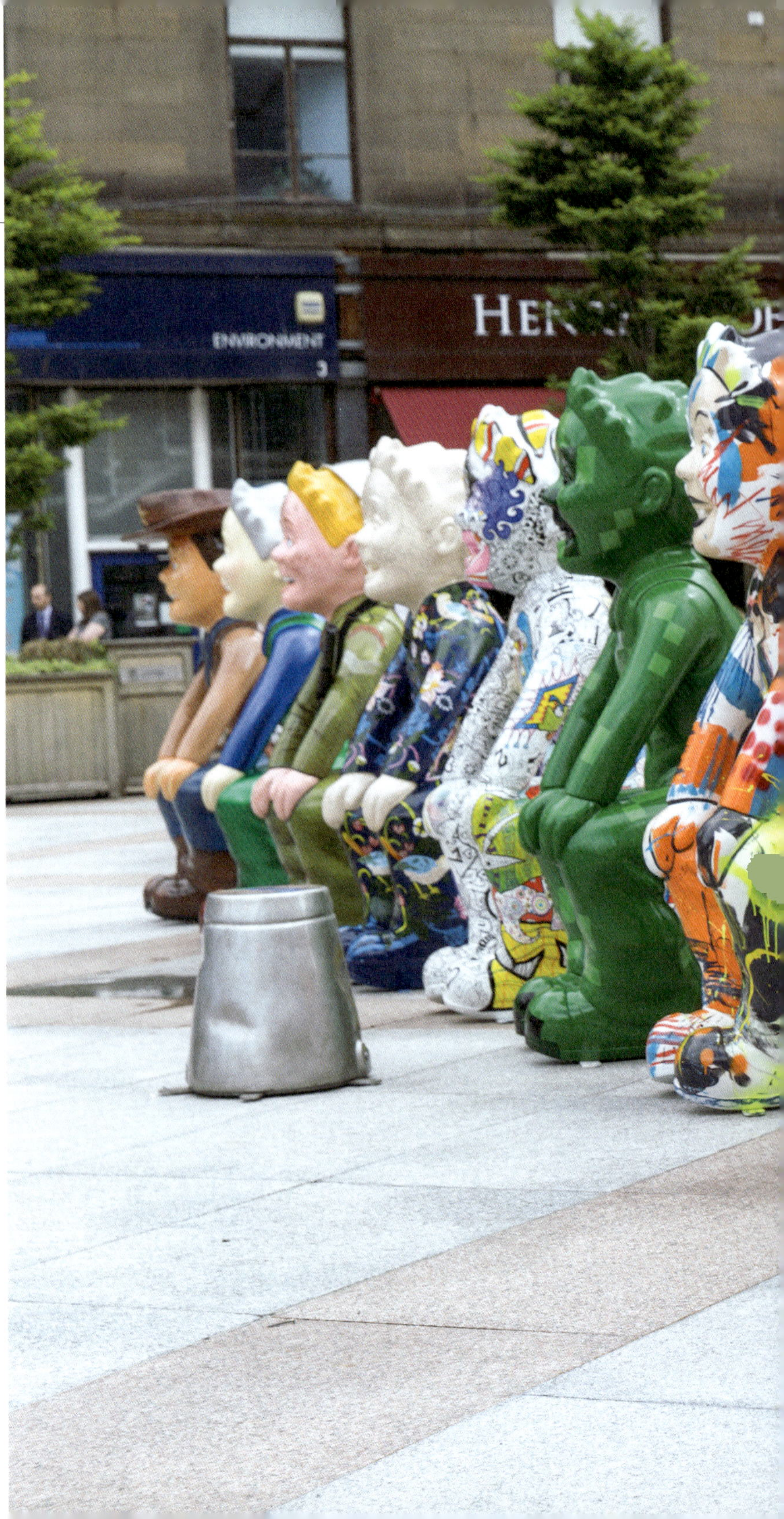

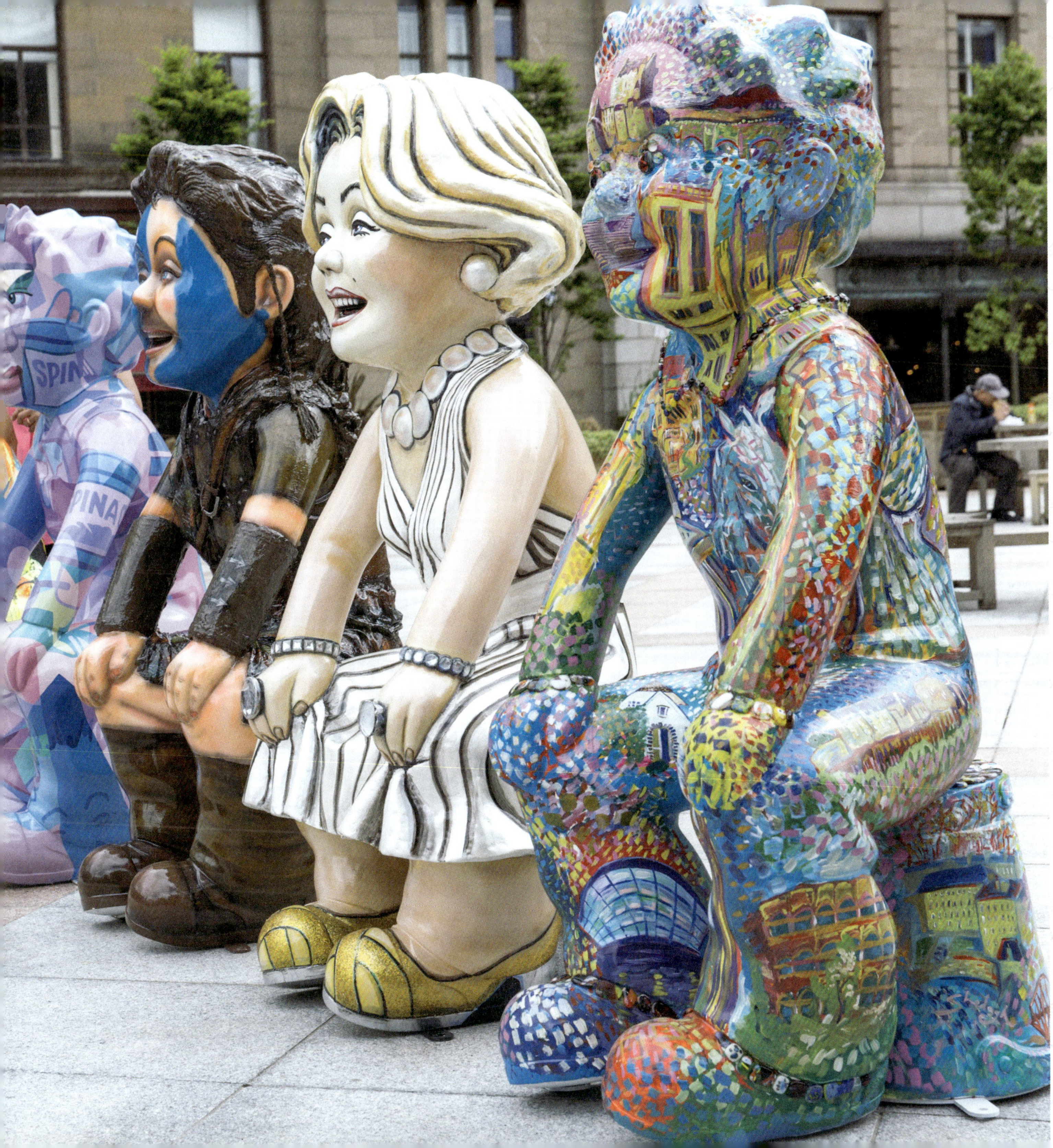

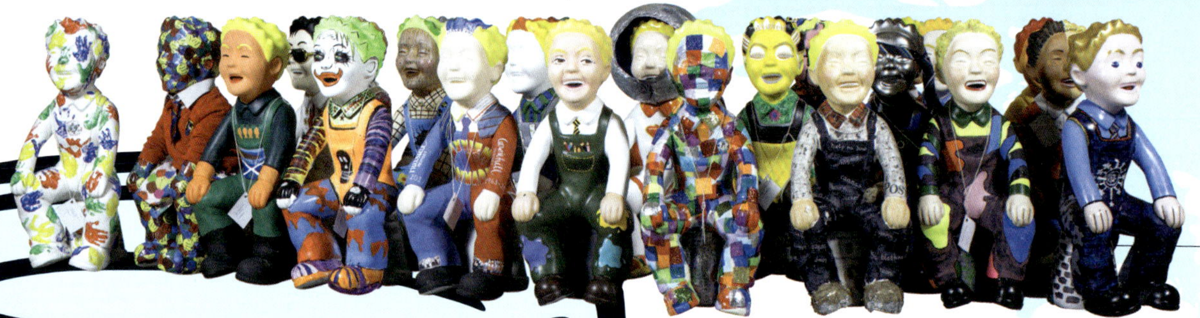

EDUCATION PROGRAMME

Craigowl Primary School	**Oor Jammie Gamer**
Kingspark School	**Oor Jokey**
St Andrews RC Primary School	**St Andrew the Fisherman**
Clepington Primary School	**Cleppies Creation**
Balgay Hill Nursery	**Patchwork Wullie**
Victoria Park Primary School	**I'm proud to be me**
Eastern Primary School	**Space Wullie**
Forthill Primary School	**Jute, Jam and Journalism**
The High School of Dundee	**Oor Wullie, Oor School**
Tayside Children's Hospital	**Oor ARCHIE**
Burnside Primary School, Carnoustie	**Oor Burnside Boy**
Carlogie Primary School, Carnoustie	**Oor Carlogie**
Grange Primary School, Monifieth	**Oor Grange**
Small World Nursery, Brechin	**Helping Hands**
Woodlands Primary School, Carnoustie	**Wullie loves Bees**
Frances Wright Pre-school Centre	**Silly Billy fae Bonnie Dundee**
Fintry Primary School	**Oor Fintry**
Happy Days Nursery	**Oor Wullie fae the Dighty**
Rowantree Primary School	**Oor Rowantree**
Baldragon Academy	**Wullie fae Baldragon**
Downfield Primary School	**The Whale of the Tay**
St Mary's Primary School	**Oor St Mary's Wullie**
Tayview Primary School	**Tayview Primary**
St Ninian's Primary School	**Where's Oor Wullie**
Dundee Comics Creative Space	**Oor Elvis**
Castlehill Primary School, Cupar, Fife	**Oor Wullie, Your Wullie, Abody's Wullie**
Cortachy Primary School, Cortachy, Kirriemuir	**Oor Cortachy**
St Clement's and Camperdown Primary Schools	**Gourdie Wullie**
Dundee and Angus ADHD Support Group	**The one and only ADHD Oor Wullie!**

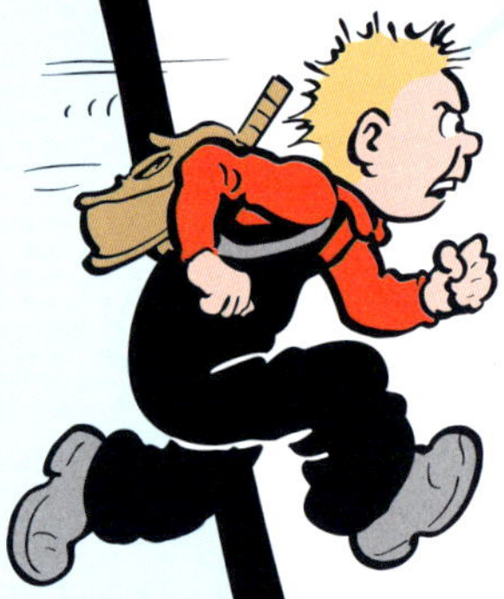

More than 1000 children from schools, nurseries and children's groups across Tayside took part in Oor Wullie's Bucket Trail Education programme which saw children design and decorate their very own wee Oor Wullie sculptures. This allowed children to experience and enjoy the magic of the visual arts while helping to fundraise for the ARCHIE Foundation's Tayside Children's Hospital appeal.

The Education Programme linked into the Scottish education curriculum, mixing creativity with learning about Scottish culture and iconic characters like Oor Wullie who is very well-known by children across Dundee. Oor Wullie's famous phrases were used to teach youngsters all about traditional Scots language in a fun and exciting way. Braw!

Children had a great time designing their own versions of the spikey-haired scallywag and were invited to colour-in a template that was handed out to schools in the Dundee area. The winning designs were then chosen by each school and the children painted the designs onto blank mini Oor Wullie sculptures.

29 of these sculptures formed the mini Bucket Trail around Dundee, which took place at the same time as the main Bucket Trail. The mini sculptures were displayed in local community libraries to showcase the creativity of the young people of Tayside, before being returned to the schools for them to keep.

FINAL APPEARANCES

CHEERIO WULLIE!

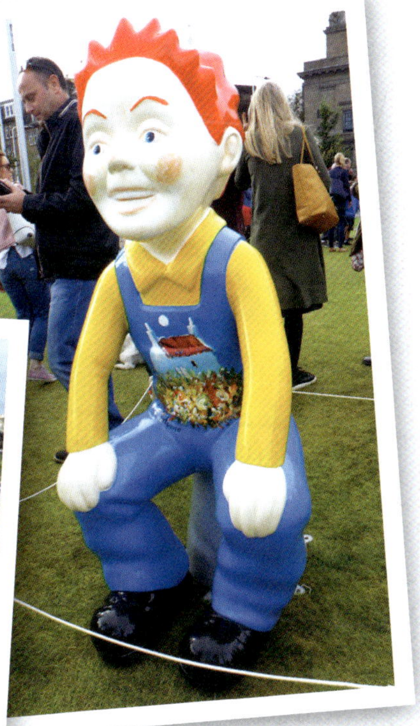

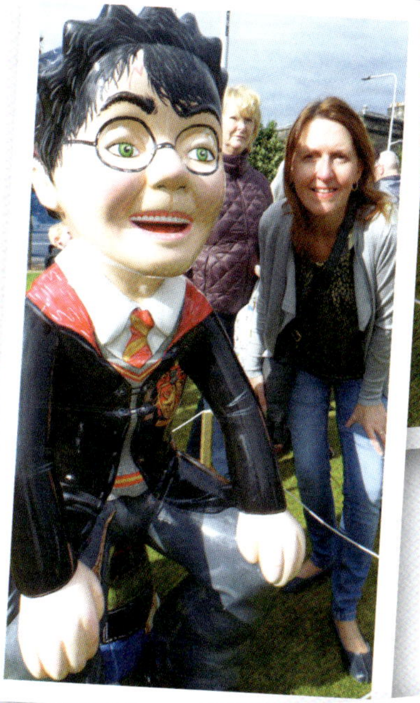

Oor Wullie's Bucket Trail enjoyed a right proper send-off with a special farewell party in September 2016. The event gave the public one last chance to see every single Oor Wullie sculpture in one place in Slessor Gardens in the heart of Dundee.

Over 20,000 people attended the three-day event to say goodbye to the sculptures and to enjoy having their photos taken once more with the cheeky scamps. The event was for lucky ticket holders only and all proceeds from the sale of the tickets went to the ARCHIE Foundation in aid of its Tayside Children's Hospital appeal for a new twin theatre children's surgical suite. An incredible 8,000 tickets were sold in the first 24 hours!

99 Oor Wullie sculptures were displayed, including all the sculptures from the Bucket Trail, the touring Wullies and even the miniature sculptures which were designed and painted by primary school pupils from across Dundee as part of Oor Wullie's Bucket Trail Education Programme.

The mini sculptures were returned to the schools after the event while the Bucket Trail and touring sculptures were taken to be polished up ready to be sold at the grand auction.

The atmosphere at the farewell event was wonderful as it allowed people to come together to celebrate the success of the Trail. The whole project really captured the public's imagination and celebrated art in such a fun and creative way that everyone was tickled pink to be part of a happy cheerio event.

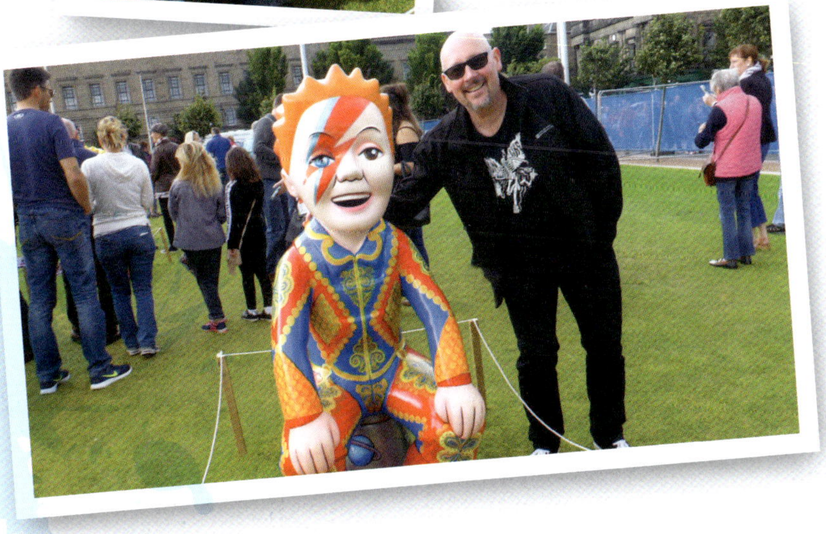

THE SCULPTURES GO UNDER THE HAMMER

OOR WULLIE'S BUCKET TRAIL CHARITY AUCTION

After a sizzling summer of Bucket Trail fun, and the laughter and joy of the farewell party, the time eventually came to auction off the Oor Wullie sculptures.

All proceeds were donated to the ARCHIE Foundation to support its appeal for a new twin theatre children's surgical suite at Tayside Children's Hospital, making a real difference to the lives of sick children and their families across the area.

The international auction was held on 13 September 2016 in Dundee's Rep Theatre where the hopeful bidders battled to take home a piece of history in the form of their very own Oor Wullie sculpture. The event was attended in person by bidders, businesses, supporters and spectators. More than several hundred online bidders registered from all over the UK and even some online bidders from the US and Australia joined in the fun. A remarkable 174,500 people watched the auction online – more than the population of Dundee itself!

70 individually designed Oor Wullie sculptures, including all the Oor Wullie Bucket Trail sculptures and the touring sculptures, were auctioned.

An astonishing £883,000 was raised for the Foundation's appeal, all thanks to the generosity of the bidders. The auction surpassed all expectations and there were gasps from the audience on the evening as the much-loved characters who captured the hearts and minds of so many people during the summer, went under the hammer.

The bidding wars for each sculpture were packed full of drama and excitement and the atmosphere was electric as the fundraising targets were smashed in no time. Winning bidders included businesses such as Insights, Birkhill Inn and Kerr's Dairy; business people; the Royal National Lifeboat Institution and generous fans. Two sculptures were even bought by a bidder from the US and some winning bidders chose to remain anonymous. The highest individual amount raised was set by Sir Ian Wood and his wife Lady Helen Wood, who bought Oor Original on behalf of their family for a spectacular £50,000.

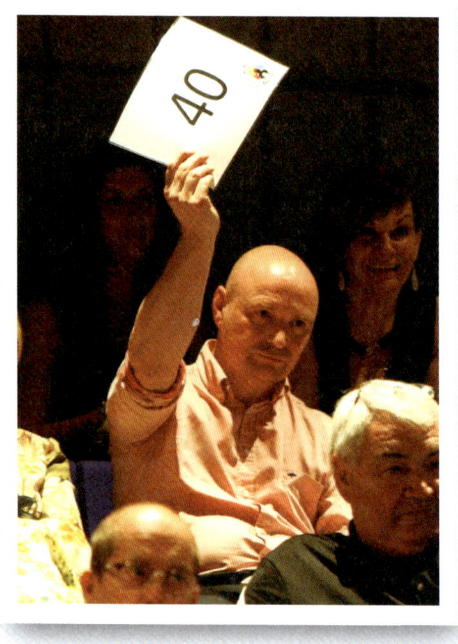

In true Oor Wullie's Bucket Trail spirit, the auctioneers Colin Slessor, Alan Hutcheon and Alan Donald from ANM Group gave their services free of charge for the evening and did a wonderful job of managing the auction.

It just goes to show the effect that Oor Wullie's Bucket Trail had on the public and how much Oor Wullie himself is adored, all to help the ARCHIE Foundation raise money for a very worthy cause.

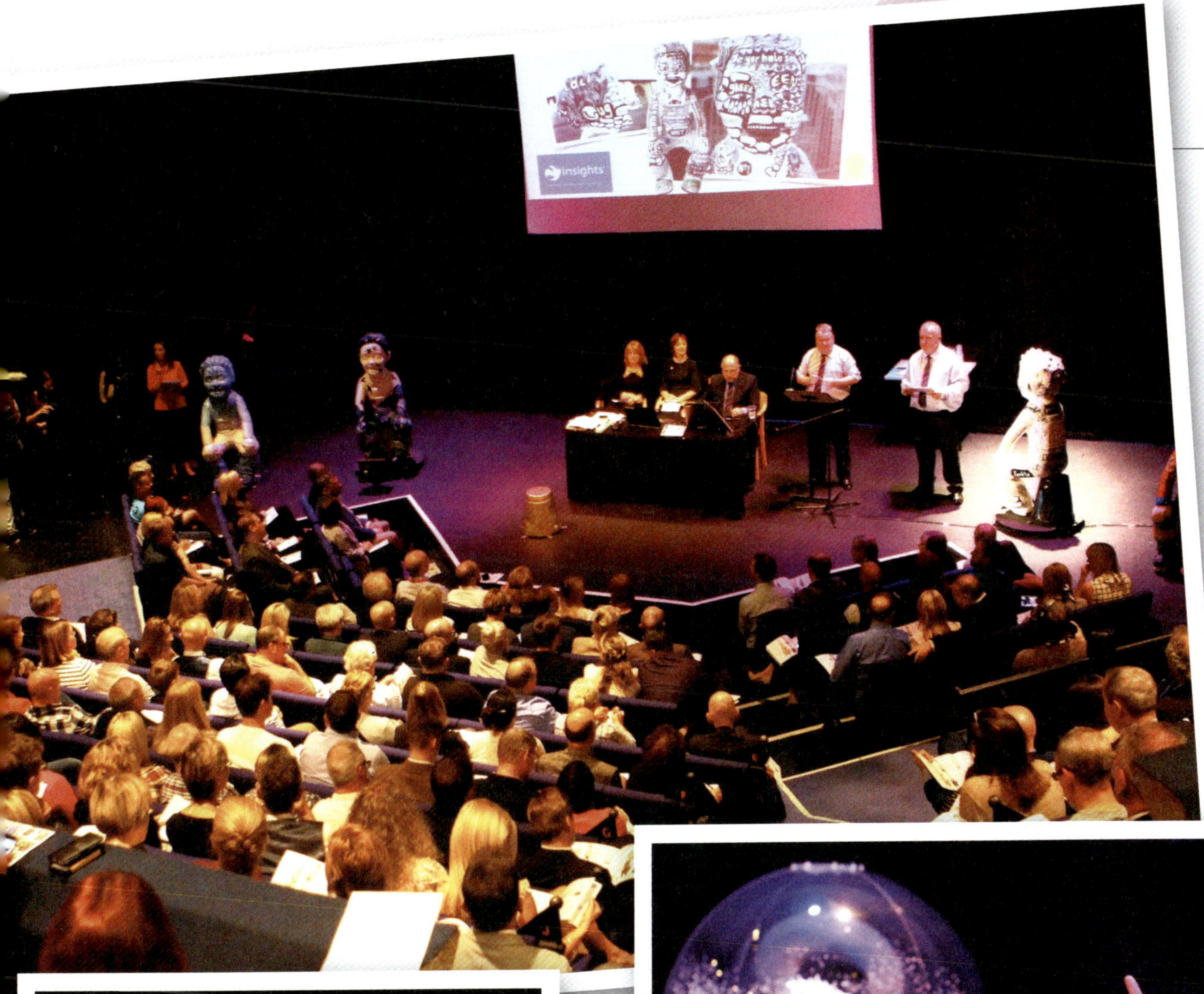

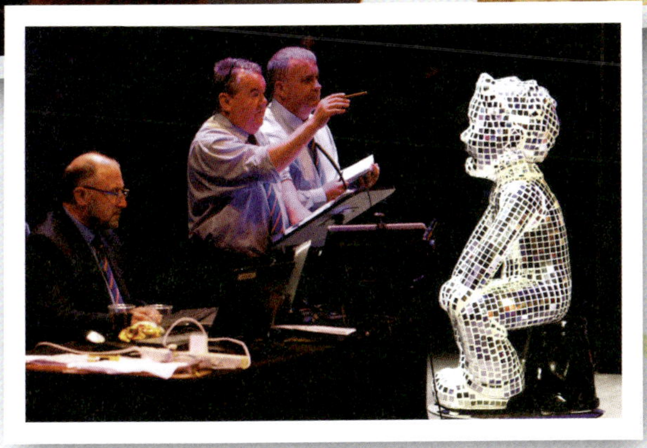

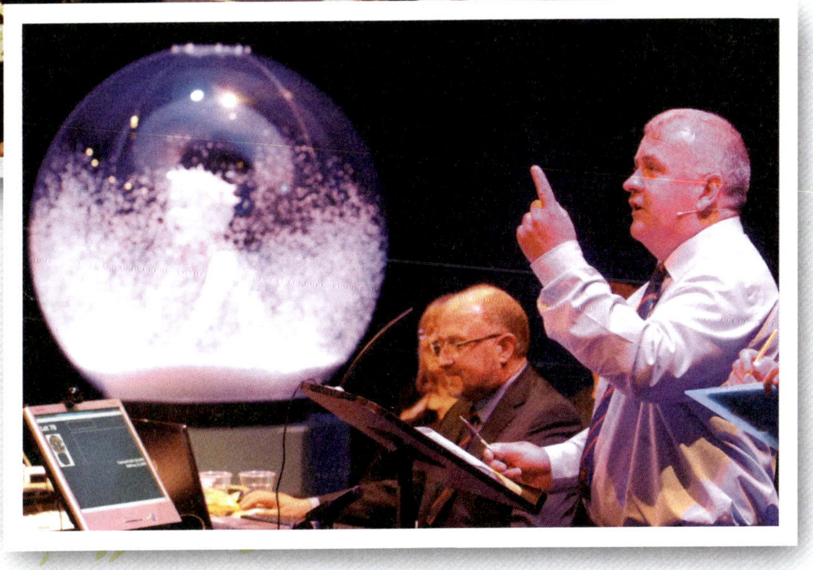

THANKS & ACKNOWLEDGEMENTS

Oor Wullie's Bucket Trail was made possible thanks to the support and collaboration of a whole host of individuals, businesses and organisations across Scotland. Thank you to all those who made the dream a reality, including the artists, sponsors, communities, schools, media partners, volunteers, photographers, the installations team and of course the ARCHIE Foundation's Oor Wullie's Bucket Trail team.

Here are your names on Oor Wullie's wall of fame!

The Bucket Trail Team:

Cassie Thompson
Caitlan Wolsey
Dave Tipping
Emma White
Hannah Clark
Neil Cooney
Suzanne Scott

Trail Partners:

The ARCHIE Foundation
DC Thomson
Wild in Art

With a special thanks to…

All the amazing sponsors
All the incredibly generous bidders and buyers
All the fantastic volunteers
Andy and Sue West and family
Angela Allan
Annemarie Gorrie
Apex City Quay Hotel & Spa
Arnold Clark
ARR Craib
Blue2
Buildright Interiors
Chris Scott
Colin Slessor, Alan Hutcheon and Alan Donald
Dundee City Council
Dundee Rep
Ellis Watson
George Reid
Grant Rodney and the team at Tayside Children's Hospital
Gus Rodney
Harry Lawson Transport
Iain Henderson and Stuart Jackson at Vivid Elements
Jarvie Plant Hire
Jason Park
Jim Pickett at Liftruks
John Clark Motor Group
John Hunter Barrie (JoHuBa)
Leisure and Culture Dundee
Linda Meiklejohn
Louis Richard George
Martin Lindsay
Michael Bott
Morris Heggie
Overgate and staff
Paula Bones
Peter Davidson
Peter Menzies
Primesigns Ltd.
Roberta West and Alan Robb
Scott Stephen
Stewart Small and the team at The Spray Factory
The Courier
The Evening Telegraph
STV
The Sunday Post
Tracey Falconer
Tradeprint
Viktoria Begg
Vision Sound and Light
Volpa
Volume Signs
Wellgate and staff.

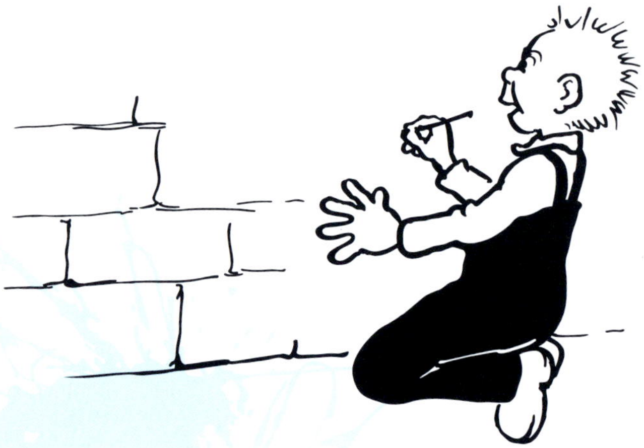

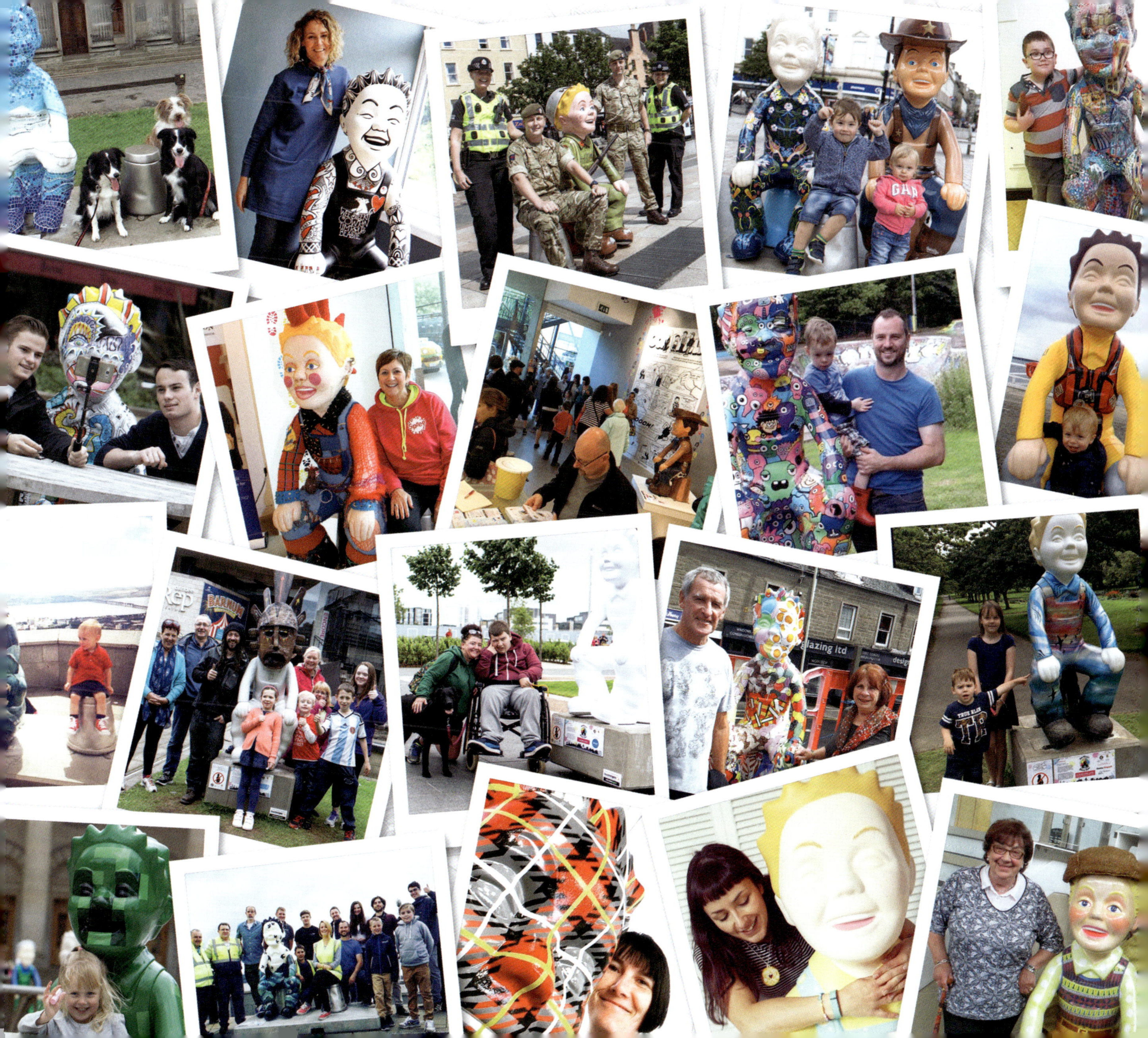
GAP
BARNUM

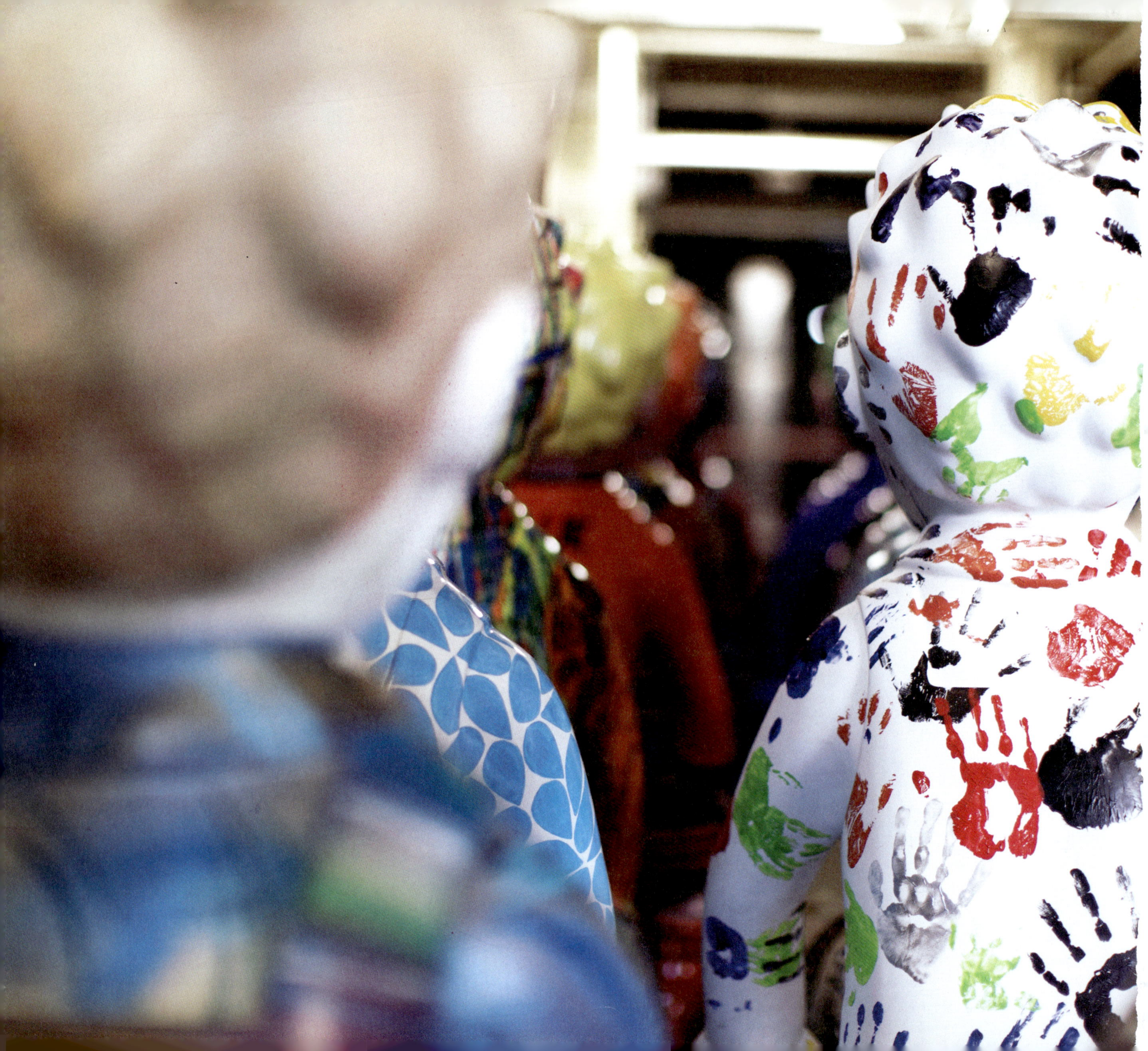